State-of-the-Art Mathematical Applications in Europe

State-of-the-Art Mathematical Applications in Europe

Editors

**Irina Cristea
Yuriy Rogovchenko
Gintautas Dzemyda
Patrick Siarry**

Basel • Beijing • Wuhan • Barcelona • Belgrade • Novi Sad • Cluj • Manchester

Editors

Irina Cristea
University of Nova Gorica
Nova Gorica
Slovenia

Yuriy Rogovchenko
University of Agder
Kristiansand
Norway

Gintautas Dzemyda
Vilnius University Institute of
Data Science and Digital
Technologies
Akademijos
Lithuania

Patrick Siarry
University Paris-Est Creteil
Creteil
France

Editorial Office
MDPI AG
Grosspeteranlage 5
4052 Basel, Switzerland

This is a reprint of articles from the Special Issue published online in the open access journal *Mathematics* (ISSN 2227-7390) (available at: https://mdpi.com/si/86350).

For citation purposes, cite each article independently as indicated on the article page online and as indicated below:

Lastname, A.A.; Lastname, B.B. Article Title. *Journal Name* **Year**, *Volume Number*, Page Range.

ISBN 978-3-7258-1779-5 (Hbk)
ISBN 978-3-7258-1780-1 (PDF)
doi.org/10.3390/books978-3-7258-1780-1

© 2024 by the authors. Articles in this book are Open Access and distributed under the Creative Commons Attribution (CC BY) license. The book as a whole is distributed by MDPI under the terms and conditions of the Creative Commons Attribution-NonCommercial-NoDerivs (CC BY-NC-ND) license.

Contents

About the Editors vii

Irina Cristea, Patrick Siarry, Gintautas Dzemyda and Yuriy Rogovchenko
Preface to the Special Issue "State-of-the-Art Mathematical Applications in Europe"
Reprinted from: *Mathematics* **2024**, *12*, 2161, doi:10.3390/math12142161 1

Mireya Cabezas-Olivenza, Ekaitz Zulueta, Ander Sánchez-Chica, Adrian Teso-Fz-Betoño and Unai Fernandez-Gamiz
Dynamical Analysis of a Navigation Algorithm
Reprinted from: *Mathematics* **2021**, *9*, 3139, doi:10.3390/math9233139 4

Xuan Hoang Khoa Le, Ioan Pop and Mikhail A. Sheremet
Thermogravitational Convective Flow and Energy Transport in an Electronic Cabinet with a Heat-Generating Element and Solid/Porous Finned Heat Sink
Reprinted from: *Mathematics* **2022**, *10*, 34, doi:10.3390/math10010034 24

Le Xuan Hoang Khoa, Ioan Pop and Mikhail A. Sheremet
Numerical Simulation of Solid and Porous Fins' Impact on Heat Transfer Performance in a Differentially Heated Chamber
Reprinted from: *Mathematics* **2022**, *10*, 263, doi:10.3390/math10020263 36

Burcu Nişancı Türkmen, Hashem Bordbar and Irina Cristea
Supplements Related to Normal π-Projective Hypermodules
Reprinted from: *Mathematics* **2022**, *10*, 1945, doi:10.3390/math10111945 50

Elías Berriochoa, Alicia Cachafeiro, Héctor García-Rábade and José Manuel García-Amor
A Note on Lagrange Interpolation of $|x|$ on the Chebyshev and Chebyshev–Lobatto Nodal Systems: The Even Cases
Reprinted from: *Mathematics* **2022**, *10*, 2558, doi:10.3390/math10152558 65

Ilia Beloglazov and Kirill Krylov
An Interval-Simplex Approach to Determine Technological Parameters from Experimental Data
Reprinted from: *Mathematics* **2022**, *10*, 2959, doi:10.3390/math10162959 79

Yılmaz Mehmet Demirci and Ergül Türkmen
WSA-Supplements and Proper Classes
Reprinted from: *Mathematics* **2022**, *10*, 2964, doi:10.3390/math10162964 91

Jahangir Alam, Ghulam Murtaza, Eugenia N. Petropoulou, Efstratios Em. Tzirtzilakis and Mohammad Ferdows
Applications of a Group Theoretical Method on Biomagnetic Fluid Flow and Heat Transfer for Different Shapes of Fe_3O_4 Magnetic Particles under the Influence of Thermal Radiation and a Magnetic Dipole over a Cylinder
Reprinted from: *Mathematics* **2022**, *10*, 3520, doi:10.3390/math10193520 103

Viviana Ventre and Roberta Martino
Quantification of Aversion to Uncertainty in Intertemporal Choice through Subjective Perception of Time
Reprinted from: *Mathematics* **2022**, *10*, 4315, doi:10.3390/math10224315 137

Cristina Flaut and Dana Piciu
Some Examples of BL-Algebras Using Commutative Rings
Reprinted from: *Mathematics* **2022**, *10*, 4739, doi:10.3390/math10244739 153

Salvatore Fragapane
Advances in Singular and Degenerate PDEs
Reprinted from: *Mathematics* **2022**, *10*, 4760, doi:10.3390/math10244760 . . . . **168**

Srdjan Kadić, Božidar V. Popović and Ali İ. Genç
Two Families of Continuous Probability Distributions Generated by the Discrete Lindley Distribution
Reprinted from: *Mathematics* **2023**, *11*, 290, doi:10.3390/math11020290 . . . . **184**

Luís P. Castro and Anabela S. Silva
On the Existence and Stability of Solutions for a Class of Fractional Riemann–Liouville Initial Value Problems
Reprinted from: *Mathematics* **2023**, *11*, 297, doi:10.3390/math11020297 . . . . **206**

About the Editors

Irina Cristea

Irina Cristea received her PhD degree in Mathematics from the University Ovidius of Constanta, Romania. She concluded her post-doc studies at University of Udine, Italy. She currently works as an associate professor at University of Nova Gorica, Slovenia, where she leads the Centre of Information Technologies and Applied Mathematics. Her research interests are related to the theory of hypercompositional algebra, having published more than 80 articles in journals indexed by Scopus or Web of Science and co-authored one book *"Fuzzy Algebraic Hyperstructures: An Introduction"*, published by Springer in 2015. Over the past 4 years, she has acted as Chief Editor of the *Italian Journal of Pure and Applied Mathematics*, Associate Editor of *Mathematics* (published by MDPI), *Heliyon Mathematics* (published by Cell press), and of other four international journals. Additionally, she has edited two other books published by MDPI.

Yuriy Rogovchenko

Yuriy Rogovchenko is a professor of mathematics at UiA. Prior to joining the Department of Mathematical Sciences at UiA in 2012, he held Professor positions in Sweden (Kalmar University and Umeå University) and North Cyprus (Eastern Mediterranean University). His research interests lie within qualitative theory of ordinary and functional differential equations, impulsive systems, mathematical modelling, and university mathematics education. Dr. Rogovchenko was a Regular Associate of the Abdus Salam International Centre for Theoretical Physics in Trieste, Italy, during 2004–2011 and was awarded research stay at the Mathematisches Forschungsinstitut Oberwolfach within the RiP2003: Research in Pairs program. Dr. Rogovchenko was awarded CNR research scholarships (1993, 1995) and CNR-NATO guest fellowship (1997). He was a recipient of the Sørlandet kompetansefonds research award in 2016. Dr. Rogovchenko has been on the editorial board of 11 international journals (Springer, Taylor & Francis, Hindawi, etc.), has contributed as the Lead Guest Editor to 2, and as a Guest Editor to 10 Special Issues. Dr. Rogovchenko has published over ninety research papers, two of which were ranked as highly cited by the ISI Web of Science (in 2014 and in 2018) and one as Hot Paper in a Field (2021). Dr. Rogovchenko has coordinated two educational projects, PLATINUM (Partnership for Learning and Teaching in University Mathematics, Erasmus+) and DeDiMaMo (Development of students' mathematical competencies through Digital Mathematical Modeling, Eurasia 2019). He was a partner in the educational project BoostEdU (Boosting Sustainable Digital Education for European Universities, Erasmus+) and in the research project CareWell (Cooperative Human Activity Recognition and Localization for Healthcare and Well-being) funded by the NFR, Norwegian Research Council.

Gintautas Dzemyda

Gintautas Dzemyda was born in Vilnius, Lithuania. In 1984, he received a doctoral degree in technical sciences (PhD), and in 1997 he received a degree of Doctor Habilius from Kaunas University of Technology. He is a full member of the Lithuanian Academy of Sciences (2011) and is Head of Division of Technical Sciences of the Academy. His current employment is at the Institute of Data Science and Digital Technologies of Vilnius University as a Professor and Head of Cognitive Computing Research Group. His main area of scientific interest is the development and application of data science methods and technologies, including artificial intelligence. His research includes the following main directions: reduction in data dimensionality and visualization; optimization theory and applications; visual multidimensional data analysis, artificial neural networks, multicriteria decision making, artificial intelligence, cognitive computing, image and signal analysis. He is Editor in Chief of the international journals *Informatica* and the *Baltic Journal of Modern Computing*.

Patrick Siarry

Patrick Siarry received a PhD degree from the University Paris 6, in 1986 and a Doctorate of Sciences (Habilitation) from the University Paris 11, in 1994. He was first involved in the development of analog and digital models of nuclear power plants at Electricité de France (E.D.F.). Since 1995, he has been a professor in automatics and informatics. His main research interests are computer-aided design of electronic circuits, and the applications of new stochastic global optimization heuristics to various engineering fields. He is also interested in the fitting of process models to experimental data, the learning of fuzzy rule bases, and of neural networks.

Editorial

Preface to the Special Issue "State-of-the-Art Mathematical Applications in Europe"

Irina Cristea [1,*], Patrick Siarry [2,*], Gintautas Dzemyda [3,*] and Yuriy Rogovchenko [4,*]

1. Centre for Information Technologies and Applied Mathematics, University of Nova Gorica, Vipavska Cesta 13, 5000 Nova Gorica, Slovenia
2. Images, Signals and Intelligent Systems Laboratory, University Paris-Est Creteil, 61 Avenue du General de Gaulle, 94010 Creteil, France
3. Vilnius University Institute of Data Science and Digital Technologies, Akademijos Str. 4, LT-08412 Vilnius, Lithuania
4. Department of Mathematical Sciences, University of Agder, P.O. Box 422, N-4604 Kristiansand, Norway
* Correspondence: irina.cristea@ung.si (I.C.); siarry@u-pec.fr (P.S.); gintautas.dzemyda@mif.vu.lt (G.D.); yuriy.rogovchenko@uia.no (Y.R.)

Citation: Cristea, I.; Siarry, P.; Dzemyda, G.; Rogovchenko, Y. Preface to the Special Issue "State-of-the-Art Mathematical Applications in Europe". *Mathematics* 2024, 12, 2161. https://doi.org/10.3390/math12142161

Received: 17 June 2024
Accepted: 20 June 2024
Published: 10 July 2024

Copyright: © 2024 by the authors. Licensee MDPI, Basel, Switzerland. This article is an open access article distributed under the terms and conditions of the Creative Commons Attribution (CC BY) license (https://creativecommons.org/licenses/by/4.0/).

This book collects under one cover twelve original research papers and one review paper submitted to the Special Issue "State-of-the-Art Mathematical Applications in Europe" and published in the MDPI journal *Mathematics* from December 2021 to January 2023. This Special Issue welcomed original research contributions from European researchers and their collaborators in all fields of mathematics on popular topics. The Editors received papers from Spain, Slovenia, Romania, Italy, Greece, Russia, Montenegro and Turkey. Most of the contributions were related to various fields in applied mathematics, and several papers addressed problems in pure mathematics, particularly algebra. We provide a brief overview of the papers included in this Special Issue, allowing readers to become acquainted with the submissions close to their research interests.

The first four articles published in this collection present different mathematical models to solve problems arising in mathematical physics. In particular, the first two deal with the study of heat transfer in engineering devices, the third study tackles bio-magnetic fluid dynamics and the fourth one concerns solid particle dissolution. Contribution 1 proposes a numerical solution to one problem related to heat transfer performance in an electronic cabinet with a heat-generating element placed in a solid/porous finned heat sink using a code in C++ programming language. In Contribution 2, a numerical analysis of the natural convective energy transport in a differentially heated chamber with isothermal vertical walls and a porous fin system has been performed. This study reveals the importance of the porous fins for energy removal from heated surfaces. An interesting mathematical method based on the application of two-parameter group theory is proposed in Contribution 3 for the study of blood flow with magnetic particles, combining ferrohydrodynamic and magnetohydrodynamic principles in a two-dimensional cylinder. The authors argue that this research could have applications in biomedical sciences, drug administration, cancer therapy and surgery. A new mathematical model describing transformations of chemical kinetics equations and the heterogeneous processes of solid particle dissolution is proposed in Contribution 4. Theoretical results are presented related to the process of coke calcination in a tabular rotary kiln.

Contribution 5 focuses on navigation algorithms for autonomous industrial vehicles. The authors implemented an algorithm for indoor navigation of automated guided vehicles, combining ideas from computer vision and neural networks to achieve collision-free navigation. The advantages of the proposed algorithm and its stability are discussed. The aim of Contribution 6 is to design an expectation maximization (EM) algorithm for estimating the parameters of some models by using maximum likelihood. To achieve this, two new general probability distribution families generated by the discrete Lindley distribution have been constructed. Contribution 7 develops a decision-making model that refers to the discrepancy between normative models and empirical evidence in the context of intertemporal choices. The experimental part illustrates the implementation of the proposed theoretical model.

Three articles in the collection are in the field of algebra. In Contribution 8, the authors describe the structure of BL-algebras, a special type of residuated lattice corresponding to Hajek's fuzzy logic, through the theory of commutative rings. These ideas form the basis of a recursive algorithm that generates all isomorphism classes of finite BL-algebras. In Contribution 9, the authors introduce the concept of weakly semi-artinian supplements (WSA supplements), investigate their properties, and apply WSA supplements for the characterization of weakly semi-artinian modules. Several homological properties of the proper class of short exact sequences determined by WSA-supplemented submodules are discussed. Contribution 10 presents new developments in hypercompositional algebra, in particular in the field of Krasner hypermodules. The authors provide equivalent characterizations of the supplemented Krasner hypermodules, connecting the supplements and the direct summands to the normal projectivity.

The behaviour of the Lagrange interpolation polynomials of the absolute value function is the topic of Contribution 11. The authors employ Chebyshev and Chebyshev–Lobatto nodal systems with an even number of points to demonstrate that the Gibbs–Wilbraham phenomena are significantly different in shape and amplitude. The last original article in this collection, Contribution 12, is in the field of nonlinear fractional differential equations. Conditions for the existence, uniqueness and stability of the solutions for a class of fractional Riemann–Liouville initial value problems are obtained. The theoretical results are supported by concrete examples.

This Special Issue concludes with Contribution 13, providing an overview of the topic of singular and degenerate partial differential equations. Most of the results recalled here were presented during the conference "Advances in Singular and Degenerate PDEs", dedicated to the research career of Prof. Maria Agostina Vivaldi. This issue discusses recent research problems on the topic and contains a very rich bibliography.

The papers in the Special Issue "State-of-the-Art Mathematical Applications in Europe" were published online after their acceptance. We are pleased to say that one year after their publication, each article in this Special Issue has been viewed more than one thousand times, which is evidence of both researchers' interest in Applied Mathematics and the importance of open access research. The Guest Editors would like to express their gratitude to all the authors for their valuable contributions to this Special Issue, as well as to the anonymous reviewers for their useful and professional comments that helped the authors substantially improve the final quality of the submitted manuscripts. We also acknowledge with pleasure the great cooperation of the publisher, the help from MDPI editors in the realization of this project, and the unfailing support from the Managing Editor of this Special Issue, Dr. Syna Mu.

Conflicts of Interest: The authors declare no conflicts of interest.

List of Contributions

1. Le, X.H.K.; Pop, I.; Sheremet, M.A. Thermogravitational Convective Flow and Energy Transport in an Electronic Cabinet with a Heat-Generating Element and Solid/Porous Finned Heat Sink. *Mathematics* **2022**, *10*, 34. https://doi.org/10.3390/math10010034.
2. Xuan Hoang Khoa, L.; Pop, I.; Sheremet, M.A. Numerical Simulation of Solid and Porous Fins' Impact on Heat Transfer Performance in a Differentially Heated Chamber. *Mathematics* **2022**, *10*, 263. https://doi.org/10.3390/math10020263.
3. Alam, J.; Murtaza, G.; Petropoulou, E.N.; Tzirtzilakis, E.E.; Ferdows, M. Applications of a Group Theoretical Method on Biomagnetic Fluid Flow and Heat Transfer for Different Shapes of Fe3O4 Magnetic Particles under the Influence of Thermal Radiation and a Magnetic Dipole over a Cylinder. *Mathematics* **2022**, *10*, 3520. https://doi.org/10.3390/math10193520.
4. Beloglazov, I.; Krylov, K. An Interval-Simplex Approach to Determine Technological Parameters from Experimental Data. *Mathematics* **2022**, *10*, 2959. https://doi.org/10.3390/math10162959.

5. Cabezas-Olivenza, M.; Zulueta, E.; Sánchez-Chica, A.; Teso-Fz-Betoño, A.; Fernandez-Gamiz, U. Dynamical Analysis of a Navigation Algorithm. *Mathematics* **2021**, *9*, 3139. https://doi.org/10.3390/math9233139.
6. Kadić, S.; Popović, B.V.; Genç, A.İ. Two Families of Continuous Probability Distributions Generated by the Discrete Lindley Distribution. *Mathematics* **2023**, *11*, 290. https://doi.org/10.3390/math11020290.
7. Ventre, V.; Martino, R. Quantification of Aversion to Uncertainty in Intertemporal Choice through Subjective Perception of Time. *Mathematics* **2022**, *10*, 4315. https://doi.org/10.3390/math10224315.
8. Flaut, C.; Piciu, D. Some Examples of BL-Algebras Using Commutative Rings. *Mathematics* **2022**, *10*, 4739. https://doi.org/10.3390/math10244739.
9. Demirci, Y.M.; Türkmen, E. WSA-Supplements and Proper Classes. *Mathematics* **2022**, *10*, 2964. https://doi.org/10.3390/math10162964.
10. Nişancı Türkmen, B.; Bordbar, H.; Cristea, I. Supplements Related to Normal π-Projective Hypermodules. *Mathematics* **2022**, *10*, 1945. https://doi.org/10.3390/math10111945.
11. Berriochoa, E.; Cachafeiro, A.; García-Rábade, H.; García-Amor, J.M. A Note on Lagrange Interpolation of $|x|$ on the Chebyshev and Chebyshev–Lobatto Nodal Systems: The Even Cases. *Mathematics* **2022**, *10*, 2558. https://doi.org/10.3390/math10152558.
12. Castro, L.P.; Silva, A.S. On the Existence and Stability of Solutions for a Class of Fractional Riemann–Liouville Initial Value Problems. *Mathematics* **2023**, *11*, 297. https://doi.org/10.3390/math11020297.
13. Fragapane, S. Advances in Singular and Degenerate PDEs. *Mathematics* **2022**, *10*, 4760. https://doi.org/10.3390/math10244760.

Disclaimer/Publisher's Note: The statements, opinions and data contained in all publications are solely those of the individual author(s) and contributor(s) and not of MDPI and/or the editor(s). MDPI and/or the editor(s) disclaim responsibility for any injury to people or property resulting from any ideas, methods, instructions or products referred to in the content.

Article

Dynamical Analysis of a Navigation Algorithm

Mireya Cabezas-Olivenza [1], Ekaitz Zulueta [1,*], Ander Sánchez-Chica [1], Adrian Teso-Fz-Betoño [1] and Unai Fernandez-Gamiz [2]

[1] System Engineering and Automation Control Department, University of the Basque Country (UPV/EHU), Nieves Cano, 12, 01006 Vitoria-Gasteiz, Spain; mireya.cabezas@ehu.eus (M.C.-O.); ander.sanchez@ehu.eus (A.S.-C.); ateso001@ehu.eus (A.T.-F.-B.)

[2] Department of Nuclear and Fluid Mechanics, University of the Basque Country (UPV/EHU), Nieves Cano, 12, 01006 Vitoria-Gasteiz, Spain; unai.fernandez@ehu.eus

* Correspondence: ekaitz.zulueta@ehu.eus

Citation: Cabezas-Olivenza, M.; Zulueta, E.; Sánchez-Chica, A.; Teso-Fz-Betoño, A.; Fernandez-Gamiz, U. Dynamical Analysis of a Navigation Algorithm. *Mathematics* **2021**, *9*, 3139. https://doi.org/10.3390/math9233139

Academic Editors: Irina Cristea, Yuriy Rogovchenko, Justo Puerto, Gintautas Dzemyda and Patrick Siarry

Received: 15 November 2021
Accepted: 4 December 2021
Published: 6 December 2021

Publisher's Note: MDPI stays neutral with regard to jurisdictional claims in published maps and institutional affiliations.

Copyright: © 2021 by the authors. Licensee MDPI, Basel, Switzerland. This article is an open access article distributed under the terms and conditions of the Creative Commons Attribution (CC BY) license (https://creativecommons.org/licenses/by/4.0/).

Abstract: There is presently a need for more robust navigation algorithms for autonomous industrial vehicles. These have reasonably guaranteed the adequate reliability of the navigation. In the current work, the stability of a modified algorithm for collision-free guiding of this type of vehicle is ensured. A lateral control and a longitudinal control are implemented. To demonstrate their viability, a stability analysis employing the Lyapunov method is carried out. In addition, this mathematical analysis enables the constants of the designed algorithm to be determined. In conjunction with the navigation algorithm, the present work satisfactorily solves the localization problem, also known as simultaneous localization and mapping (SLAM). Simultaneously, a convolutional neural network is managed, which is used to calculate the trajectory to be followed by the AGV, by implementing the artificial vision. The use of neural networks for image processing is considered to constitute the most robust and flexible method for realising a navigation algorithm. In this way, the autonomous vehicle is provided with considerable autonomy. It can be regarded that the designed algorithm is adequate, being able to trace any type of path.

Keywords: navigation; localization; SLAM; computer vision; neural network; semantic segmentation; Lyapunov; AGV; path planning; path following

1. Introduction

In industrial applications, the current demand is to have an intelligent navigation system for mobile robots. Those systems must include navigation and localization methods, both of which are implemented in automated guided vehicles (AGVs). Nevertheless, the study of those methods has usually been carried out in independent ways. The consideration of the study as separate techniques in not a disadvantage, but rather a division of problems. The unification of these systems is major research; however, while performing, the AGVs must integrate all of them. This paper is focused on giving more robustness to this type of autonomous vehicle. With that purpose, the following topics specify the analyses that have been performed for the various techniques that form the whole AGV system.

1.1. Localization

One of the indispensable systems of autonomous guided vehicles is the one that determines their positioning, defined by the vector $\vec{pose}$. With this information, it is possible to generate a map of the environment where the AGV is located and to determine where the vehicle is placed on the map. This is known as simultaneous localization and mapping (SLAM) and it is important to execute it in real-time.

A traditional approach to the actual problem is to use the wheel odometry as Kilic et al. [1] studied, combined with an inertial navigation system, where measurements are taken by an encoder. The present work rejects this method due to the slippage that the wheels suffer during the movement, being necessary data to be predicted. It also penalizes accuracy. According to Chen [2], it is recognized that these aspects can be clarified with a Kalman filter.

The Kalman filter can also be suitable for use in conjunction with matching techniques. According to the study carried out by Cho et al. [3], two matching methods can be employed in combination with that filter. Firstly, the geometric method, and secondly, a method based on the point-to-line matching of the iterative closest point (ICP) algorithm. In this way, the geometric method is applied to predict, and the ICP is used for correcting the estimated position. This requires prior information concerning the environment in which the AGV is located. The unique use of geometric methods is also possible, as Shamsfakhr et al. [4] demonstrate in their developed algorithm. Geometric pattern registration is performed based on the segmentation of the real laser range data and simulated laser data. Looking for the critical points of both and with the discrepancy between them, it is possible to achieve a robust and computationally efficient algorithm for determining the $\vec{pose}$ in real-time.

The iterative closest point (ICP) persist in being a recurrent approach to solving the localization problem. In addition, knowing that LiDAR sensors do not require external spatial infrastructure, they can be utilized for SLAM (see Naus et al. [5]). Employing architecture to reduce iterations (wP-ICP) coupled with LiDAR sensors, Wang et al. [6] achieve a reduction of computational effort. In this way, it can be better managed in real-time. It is equally possible to generate more 3D point sets by focusing on the geometry of the environment as Senin et al. [7] do, obtaining better results. Using different sensors such as INS and GPS coupled with LiDAR, Gao et al. [8] achieved localization in indoor and outdoor areas. However, it is impossible to distinguish areas with unevenness, solved with KITTI arrays as Kim et al. [9] summarized.

Avoiding the application of a GPS antenna, one approach to localize AGVs is to use trilateration, through a number of signals that can estimate their distance to the vehicle. For algorithms that need more speedup and high efficiency, Sadeghi Bigham et al. [10] prove that by focusing on orthogonal polygons the n/2 landmarks are sufficient to solve the localization problem. So that trilateration of an orthogonal n-gon can be performed. Further to the concept of using landmarks, it is possible to merge them with computer vision to be detected. As Yap et al. [11] explain, the distance between the landmarks and the AGV is estimated with an algorithm based on two landmarks according to the idea of the intersection of two circles.

The noise that can be generated by the sensing devices used must also be taken into account, so the choice of the sensors implemented in the AGV is crucially important. A cost-effective option represents the use of RGB sensors, which process images to extract features by finding similarities between frames (see Gao and Zhang [12]). Deriving the ICP algorithm with all necessary sensing elements and constructing random point maps, develops the algorithm for SLAM independent of sensor type as Clemens et al. [13] discussed. In this way, noise becomes a measure for determining uncertainty.

The use of an algorithm based on Bayesian filtering has also given good results in the localization of mobile robots, without the need for prior information about the environment as Gentner et al. [14] explained. In this way, it is possible to obtain the positioning of the AGV in the SLAM. Continuing with the use of filters, the particle filter has remained a recurring method when trying to solve the localization problem. With it, it is possible to estimate the state of an environment over time. The precision is related to the number of particles, but it should be noted that increasing the number of particles penalizes the computational cost (see Yang and Wu [15]).

For that reason, a method of optimizing the cells produced in the SLAM is necessary. Because of this optimization, Zhang et al. [16] demonstrated that there is a difficulty in distinguishing between areas with the same appearance. Therefore, the reference has to be taken as a global localization. However, at large distances, the accuracy decreases. Carrera Villacres et al. [17] described that focusing the problem on a deep learning model provides a satisfactory result, with the need to include new filters to reduce failures. In addition, combining the particle filter with a vector field histogram (VFH) provides a way to circumvent obstacles (see Wang [18]).

Integrated into a particle filter, Tao et al. [19] include a novel ratio frequency identification (RFID) based method. By combining the information from two RFID signals, this strategy is able to predict the $\vec{pose}$. In addition, in AGVs where magnetic field lines are involved, it is equally possible to use a for-field active RFID locating method, providing higher accuracy, more stable movements and a smaller fluctuating rate. (see Lu et al. [20]).

1.2. Path Following

Another faculty that AGVs must possess is the ability to navigate in diverse environments. This is based on immediate sensor readings, providing the mobile robot with the capacity to decide and circumvent obstacles. The dynamic properties of the vehicle must also be taken into account. The most commonly used method for trajectory tracking is the dynamic window approach (DWA). By hybridizing with a teaching-learning based technique, it is possible to achieve the endpoint to be reached by the AGV, as Kashyap et al. studied [21]. This additionally provides the ability to avoid obstacles without stopping. In succession, it is possible to combine it with a real-time motion planning method, giving the AGV the possibility to gain a high speed (see Brock and Khatib [22]).

By mixing Dijkstra's algorithm and the DWA, it is possible to attain the desired position with the information provided by a SLAM system, as Liu et al. [23] summarised. Another fusion option is discussed by Dobrevski et al. [24] in their work, where they manage a convolutional neural network to select the parameters of the DWA algorithm. This provides a combination between data-driven learning and the dynamic model of the mobile robot. It is substantial to take into account the dynamic properties due to the constraints imposed by the AGV itself on velocity and acceleration, as pointed out by Fox et al. [25].

As Wang et al. [26] studied, the problem can be divided into two layers. On one hand, decision-making is performed for the path, and on the other hand, trajectory tracking is carried out. In the second layer, it is possible to employ the virtual force field (VFF) to detect objects. Similarly, it is possible to combine it with a potential force field (PFF) to build a viable means of navigation (see Burgos et al. [27]). Another algorithm used to solve the path following is the vector field histogram (VFH), as done by Borenstein et al. [28], where they employ histogram grids as a model to generate a map of the environment. In this way, it is possible to obtain the AGV control commands. There is a modification of the latter method called the traversability field histogram (TFH), which is independent of the instantaneous vehicle speed, as Ye [29] noted. In this way, distant obstacles can be prevented from impairing optimal path following.

From another perspective, the use of a lateral control for path following resolution represents an interesting method, performing an identification of the closest point between the trajectory and the AGV. One of the algorithms that can conclude this is the Stanley. It performs a discrete prediction model of the subsequent states of the mobile robot. In the study by AbdElmoniem et al. [30] a combination with a LiDAR is used, creating a local path planner and being able to complete collision-free navigation.

1.3. Path Planning

Path planning is one of the most complex areas of mobile robotics, where it is necessary to calculate the trajectory to be followed by the AGV. In this case, the most conventional technique is Particle Swarm Optimization (PSO). By improving the inertia weights with a linear variation, the algorithm can be prevented from falling into a local minimum, achieving a higher convergence speed as Fei et al. [31] demonstrated. In this way, it is possible to obtain the optimal trajectory in any environment, with better path length than with the A* algorithm on 2D maps.

Authors such as Liu et al. [32] explained that the A* algorithm can be used as a map modelling method to procure path planning. In many cases, considering only the optimal distance to the destination point is not enough, so it is meaningful to evaluate also the shortest time to that point. The A* algorithm, depending on these attributes, can search for one or another trajectory as Cheng et al. [33] explained. Combining this algorithm with the Rapidly-Exploring Radom Tree (RRT) achieves good efficiency (see da Silva Costa et al. [34]). A modification of the RTT itself gets a new path planning diagram, in which the trajectory is found instantly, as the study of Wang et al. [35] develop. Another design represents the one by Wen and Rei [36], called Smoothly RRT, where the optimization strategy focuses on the maximum curve of the trajectory, achieving a higher exploration speed.

The Wavefront algorithm is equally implemented to calculate the path, employing it to obtain the closest front points. In this way, it is possible to select the optimal point based on the motion requirements. Therefore, the Wavefront algorithm can search for additional paths, if necessary, as Tang et al. [37] summarized. The generalized Wavefront algorithm is also discussed. Multiple sets of target points, multilevel grid costs and geometric expansions around obstacles are combined, and with this information, the path is optimized, recognizing a safe and smooth trajectory (see Sifan et al. [38]).

A less conventional, but also interesting technique to perform trajectory planning represents the use of neural networks. Using the Q-learning algorithm with reinforcement learning can support the features of the environment, as Sdwk et al. [39] do. Advancing neural network training provides an optimal path. In addition, with an incremental training method, where algorithms are first evaluated, a more pleasing ultimate design of the deep learning algorithm can be obtained (see Gao et al. [40]).

Operating the Resnet-50 network, a path planning algorithm based on deep reinforcement learning has been created. In this way, the parameters of the deep Q-network are trained, solving the path planning problem, as Zheng et al. [41] demonstrated. Another option is to implement a convolutional neural network (CNN) that segments an image to condition the navigation zone, proposed by Teso-Fz-Betoño et al. [42]. The study manages a residual neural network that participates in the learning of the Resnet-18 network. As follows, it is possible to perform semantic segmentation for AGV navigation by selecting the mask of the navigation area.

Focusing on computer vision, there are networks established specifically for path planning, such as PilotNet, which can detect lanes using cameras and apply vehicle following algorithms to gain the direction, as discussed by Olgun et al. [43]. This is merely effective for single-lane trajectories. LaneNet is, furthermore, a network that applies computer vision, detecting lane markings and lane locations, and being able to create maps and paths using semantic segmentation (see Azimi et al. [44]).

The fundamental objective of the present study is to ensure the stability of an indoor navigation algorithm in a 2D environment for the AGV shown in Figure 1. Based on Stanley's algorithm, a lateral control adapted to this autonomous vehicle is proposed. The algorithm calculates the velocity and rotation angle commands to perform the movement, applying different mathematical operations. In this manner, lateral control and longitudinal control should coexist.

Figure 1. The AGV for which the algorithm is proposed.

The main goal of the current work is to implement the algorithm in the AGV and be able to perform collision-free navigation. This issue is achieved by using computer vision and a neural network that segments the environment to generate a path.

2. Materials and Methods

This article presents an algorithm for indoor navigation of AGVs and the study of its stability. With the idea of the Stanley algorithm (see Hoffmann et al. [45]), this work proposes a modification because of the use of the AGV shown in Figure 1. This autonomous vehicle allows the adjustment of the angular and linear velocity criteria.

Accordingly, in this paper, the algorithm focuses on the lateral control of the AGV, acting mainly on the rotational speed θ (rad/s). It is necessary to observe that the alignment error φ (rad) remains the difference between the vehicle angle θ (rad) and the path curvature φ_{path} (rad). The positioning error noted as e (m), refers to the minimum distance between the autonomous vehicle and the closest point of the trajectory in reference to the vehicle as represented in Figure 2.

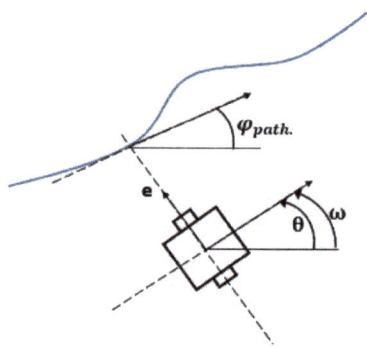

Figure 2. Schematic representation of the lateral control proposal.

The side wheels of the AGV used, rotate on the same axis, as represented in Figure 2. Note that ω should take into account both the positioning error noted as e and the alignment error noted as φ. The alignment error remains a revealed fact, so the positioning error is the variable, where two opposite cases are assumed. If e is remarkably large, it is of interest to situate the AGV perpendicular to the path, in order to get closer to it, so the value of φ is be $\frac{\pi}{2}$. In the case that e is significantly smaller, there is no alignment error, so it is of interest to keep both angles with the same value. The curve given by the values of φ is an Arctangent function, which also appears in Stanley's algorithm.

In this manner, it is proposed to implement Stanley's algorithm as shown in the following equations. Knowing that θ is derivable in time, the value that ω should have is proposed in Equation (1).

$$\frac{d\theta}{dt} = \omega = K_1(\varphi_{setpoint}(e)) - \left(\theta - \varphi_{path}\right) \quad (1)$$

The introduction of the parameter $\varphi_{setpoint}$ (rad) is necessary, to adapt the range of values of φ. Its value is defined in Equation (2):

$$\varphi_{setpoint}(e) = arctg(K_2 \cdot e) \quad (2)$$

In this way, it is proposed to have two functions depending on the constants K_1 (s^{-1}) and K_2 (1/m), which are to be determined. It can be appreciated that the constant K_1 is the one related to the alignment error φ and K_2 controls the value of the positioning error e.

Some other equations also need to be accounted for. $\dot{x}$ (m/s) and $\dot{y}$ (m/s) represent the linear velocities in the directions of the axes, as indicated in Equations (3) and (4).

$$\dot{x} = V \cos \theta \tag{3}$$

$$\dot{y} = V \sin \theta \tag{4}$$

As mentioned throughout this work, the objectives of the lateral control are that the positioning error tends to be 0 and that θ equals φ_{path}.

A study is required to demonstrate the proposed design is stable for all types of paths. For this purpose, the Lyapunov function will be used. Through the study, it is equally possible to dictate the value of the constants K_1 and K_2 in Equations (1) and (2). The Lyapunov energy equation noted as L (m^2) is proposed based on the previous equations in Equation (5).

$$\begin{cases} L = e^2 > 0 \\ \frac{dL}{dt} < 0 \end{cases} \tag{5}$$

For the first approach, the linear velocity V (m/s) is assumed to be constant.

The autonomous vehicle is placed with a random $\vec{pose} = [x, y, \theta]$ value, and the constants K_1 and K_2 are applied to the lateral control, analysing how the AGV behaves as a function of these coefficients. To simplify the analysis, a trajectory of the form $Ax + By + C = 0$ will be considered.

Distinction of the Positioning Error Sign

To implement the lateral control design, it is necessary to contemplate the sign of e because it is not taken into account in either of Equation (1) or Equation (2). It is necessary to differentiate on which side of the path the AGV is located because depending on this; it must be steered with a positive or negative sign.

Hence, to consider the sign, the positioning error e is to be taken as a vector $\vec{e}$. The vector $\vec{N}$ is the one that represents in which direction the AGV will follow the path. Finally, α is the angle formed between these two vectors, as illustrated in Figure 3.

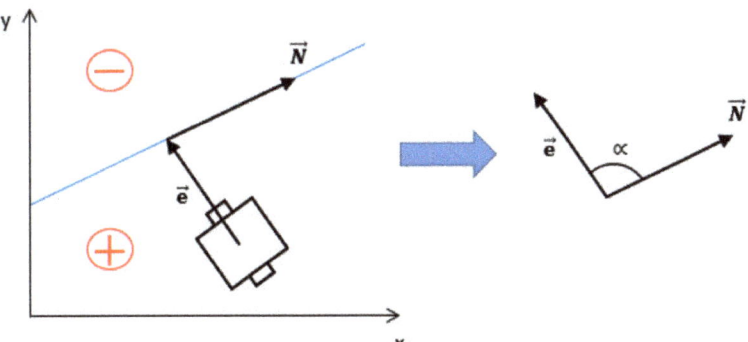

Figure 3. Positioning error vector and trajectory direction vector.

Figure 3 also shows in which region the positioning error is considered positive and in which negative. Due to that consideration, the direction of $\vec{e}$ is conditioned by that sign, representing the course the AGV needs to take to reduce the positioning error. Like so, if the AGV is on the right side of the path, the value of φ needs to be increased. If the AGV is on the left side, the value of the alignment error has to be reduced, supporting negative values. To resolve it, the vector product of $\vec{e}$ and $\vec{N}$ must be performed.

If $\left|\vec{N}\right|$ and $\left|\vec{e}\right|$ take the value 1, an analysis can be performed as a function of α. In case α is positive, the positioning error has to be positive as well. In the opposite case, that is when α is negative, the positioning error has to bear a negative sign. Knowing the path is defined, it is possible to acquire the values of the points $P1(x, y)$ and $P2(x, y)$.

$P1$ refers to the point on the path most adjacent to the AGV. The position of the autonomous vehicle is noted as $p(x, y)$. In the case of $P2$, it refers to the nearest next point from the AGV after $P1$. Thus, the values of the vectors $\vec{e}$ and $\vec{N}$ can be determined as presented in Equations (6) and (7).

$$\vec{N} = \frac{\vec{P2} - \vec{P1}}{\|\vec{P2} - \vec{P1}\|} \tag{6}$$

$$\vec{e} = \vec{P1} - \vec{p} \tag{7}$$

With this knowledge, in the line of code that calculates the positioning error, it is necessary to apply the approximation of Equation (8) to consider the sign of e.

$$e \sin \alpha = T = N(1)e(2) - N(2)e(1) \tag{8}$$

Considering the path form and the previous equations, the positioning error is defined in Equation (9).

$$e = \frac{|Ax + By + C|}{\sqrt{A^2 + B^2}} = (sign(e))distmin.\left(\vec{p}, path\right) \tag{9}$$

3. Proposal Explanation

A combination of neural networks and hardware devices, such as the AGV itself, is employed. Regarding the hardware, the use of a Beckhoff PLC (C6925) and its automation software allows the drivers to be managed on a real-time industrial platform. This platform is highly robust and widely used therein type of industrial applications. In addition, the employment of Matlab R2019b provides the advantage of utilizing a platform that allows very rapid development of control engineering algorithms. From a sensor point of view, and in the present case, the use of a vision-based navigation system that recognises lanes, the advantage resides in the fact that it is a very rapid way of implementing path-following systems.

3.1. Necessary Data Acquisition

To obtain the trajectory, the example of the study by Teso-Fz-Betoño et al. [42] is followed. A convolutional neural network (CNN) is managed to perform semantic segmentation of an image. It is classified into several masks, generating a vector of the interest points from the mask corresponding to the navigation area. This vector with the position of the path in pixels x and y represents the information provided to the navigation algorithm. The scenario comprises a room with a yellow line representing the trajectory. The neural network has to detect this line, which will be followed by the AGV. This is concluded by employing a camera. The processing of the image is represented in Figure 4.

Figure 4a shows the image captured by the AGV, with the yellow line to be followed. After obtaining the image, the convolutional neural network performs semantic segmentation, obtaining two independent masks. The shaded mask constitutes the part that is not of interest to the autonomous vehicle, so the shinier one attends the important one, as illustrated in Figure 4b. In addition, the image is cropped at the lower part to remove the portion of the AGV that is captured by the camera.

From the clearest mask, the midpoints represented by red crosses are gained, as shown in Figure 4c. Thus, the trajectory to be followed by the AGV is obtained. Conclusively, the points approached with the semantic segmentation are connected to forge the path as represented in light blue in Figure 4d. Due to the pronounced curves generated in this path, an interpolation is performed to acquire a smoother trajectory, coloured with dark blue. The AGV follows that final trajectory.

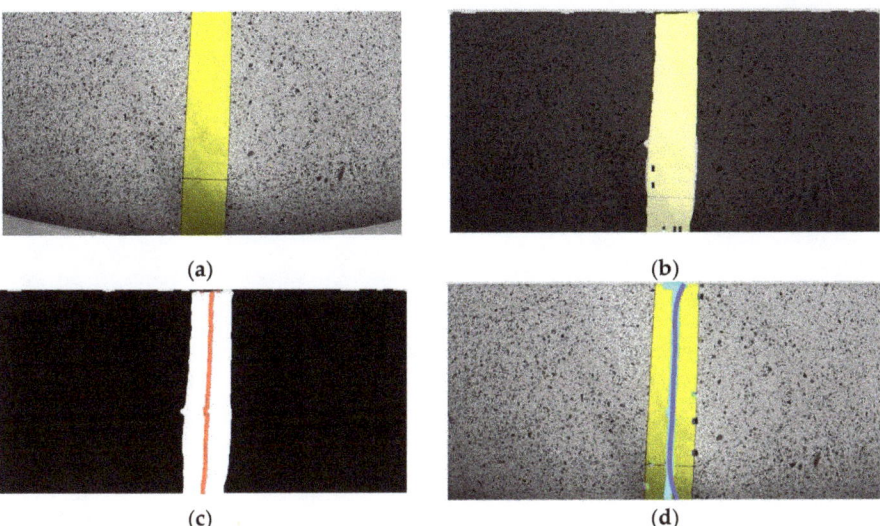

Figure 4. Process of obtaining trajectory: (**a**) Image that AGV takes of the path; (**b**) Semantic segmentation of the path; (**c**) Medium point of the navigable mask; (**d**) Obtained path.

With the image taken of the path, the AGV can acquire the information of the positioning error and the angle of the trajectory as graphed in Figure 5. Note that the measurement is produced considering the location of the AGV as the position of the camera. The camera is placed at the leading centre of the autonomous vehicle.

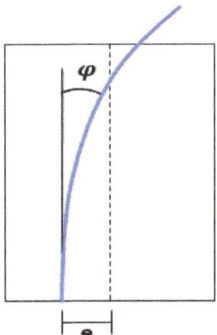

Figure 5. Localization data for the AGV from image.

This approach provides all the data necessary for the navigation resolution.

3.2. Concurrency in the Approach

The designed algorithm has fast dynamics. This implies that regardless of the initial position of the AGV as a function of e, it is necessary to obtain an $\theta_{optimun}$ (rad) for the autonomous vehicle. This value is not the same as θ, and this is where K_1 comes in. $\theta_{optimun}$ refers to the sum between φ_{path} and $\varphi_{setpoint}(e)$. Accordingly, because of the fast dynamic, the AGV orients itself on the way of the trajectory rapidly, being able to consider that the path has no inclination. This is depicted in Figure 6. In the case of the positioning error, it is not possible to make an approximation, and the path will be considered to be angled. In conclusion, it can be declared that the time constants of the orientation loop are smaller than those of the displacement. Ergo, two situations are envisaged as represented in Figure 6a,b.

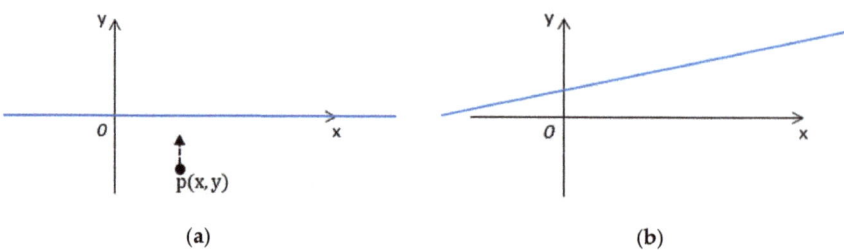

Figure 6. Path approach: (**a**) Situation where φ_{path} is zero; (**b**) Situation where φ_{path} is not zero.

With this approach, it is possible to analyse the stability of the system and to get the K_1 and K_2 values.

4. Value of K_1

4.1. System Stability Study

Lyapunov stability analysis is performed as mentioned above. Conventional techniques, for instance "frecuency" methods, are generally carried out on cases where the dynamical model of the system is linear. In the present study, the dynamical model is non-linear and the use of Lyapunov provides a generalist manner of assuring the stability of a dynamical system.

The first scenario is where can be assumed that the angle of the trajectory is zero, as illustrated in Figure 6a. Considering that assumption, the terms A and C of the path equation disappear, the path being By = 0. Hence, the study is simplified.

The initial consideration is when the AGV is away from the trajectory, so the positioning error value is obtained directly as indicated in Equation (10).

$$e = -y \tag{10}$$

The objective is to guarantee that the system is stable, being L consistently positive. Therefore, considering the previous equation, it can be formulated in Equation (11).

$$L = e^2 = y^2 \tag{11}$$

As the value of y is squared, it is confirmed that L is always positive, so the difficulty now lies in the second expression of Equation (5). In this manner, the derivate must be considered taking into account the Equation (12).

$$\frac{dL}{dt} = 2 \cdot e \cdot \dot{e} = 2 \cdot y \cdot \dot{y} \tag{12}$$

Additionally, Equation (1) can be restated considering φ_{path} = 0, as shown in Equation (13).

$$\dot{\theta} = K_1\left(\varphi_{setpoint}(e) - \theta\right) \tag{13}$$

As mentioned, assuming that the dynamic of Equation (13) is extremely fast, it is possible to obtain the value of the angle θ, because of the rapid tendency of the AGV will have, positioning with the orientation of Figure 6a. Then θ is defined in Equation (14).

$$\theta = \varphi_{setpoint}(e) = arctg(K_2 \cdot e) \tag{14}$$

Equation (4) can directly be raised anew, bearing in mind Equations (10) and (14).

$$\dot{y} = V\sin(-arctg(K_2 \cdot y)) = -V\sin(arctg(K_2 \cdot y)) \tag{15}$$

To obtain the value of $\dot{L}$, the Equation (12) can be complemented with that seen in Equation (15).

$$\dot{L} = 2y(-V\sin(arctg(K_2 \cdot y))) \tag{16}$$

By the way, Equation (2) is designed knowing that K_2 will always be positive, so the following remarks can be made.

$$sign(arctg(K_2 \cdot y)) = sign(y) \tag{17}$$

$$sign(\sin(arctg(K_2 \cdot y))) = sign(arctg(K_2 \cdot y)) \tag{18}$$

This leads to the following conclusion.

$$sign(y) = sign(\sin(arctg(K_2 \cdot y))) \tag{19}$$

With this information, analysing Equation (19) and knowing the positioning error is negative as stated in Equation (10), it can be guaranteed that the Lyapunov function is fulfilled.

4.2. Procurement of Value of K_1

For the system to be stable when the AGV is distant from the trajectory, it has been assumed that the dynamics are so fast. Accordingly, the AGV is oriented perpendicular to the path. In addition, it will approach rapidly, producing a minor positioning error, which is considered to be zero. Carrying on with that consideration, therein case, only the angle of the AGV can be taken into account, reformulating Equation (13).

$$\dot{\theta} = K_1(0 - \theta) = -K_1\theta \tag{20}$$

In this situation, it is necessary to study again the stability of the system. Recalling the Lyapunov system of Equations (11) and (12), it will not be a problem to confirm that L is by squaring. The problem is again in the derivative of the energy. The study examines the case where the AGV is under the trajectory, so it is recognized that in that area θ will allow positive values. So, if e is null, it is also comprehensible that θ tends to be equal to φ_{path}. Therefore, one can formulate the integral of Equation (20), which remains a linear system.

$$\theta = \frac{\pi}{2}exp^{-K_1 \cdot \tau} \tag{21}$$

Equation (12) requires the value of y and $\dot{y}$, which can be obtained from Equation (4) by substituting Equation (21).

$$\dot{y} = V\sin\left(\frac{\pi}{2}exp^{-K_1\tau}\right) \tag{22}$$

$$y = V\int_0^t \sin\left(\frac{\pi}{2}exp^{-K_1\tau}\right)d\tau + y(0) \tag{23}$$

From Equation (22) it can be deduced that the value is always negative because the function sin is always between 0 and π. In the case of Equation (23), the initial condition is also always negative, so it is necessary to ensure that the integral never obtains a value greater than $y(0)$, to confirm the stability. So it is necessary to guarantee that the positioning error never changes sing, whereby the value of K_1 can be known. In Equations (24) and (25) the integral is noted as I.

$$y = VI(K_1, t) + y(0) < 0 \tag{24}$$

$$VI(K_1, t) < -y(0) \tag{25}$$

Thus, the linear velocity and K_1 are related. Analysing Equations (23) and (25), the following conclusions can be drawn. If the value of K_1 is very aggressive, the exponential tends to 0 quickly obtaining a sinusoidal function with value 0 and making the expression vanish very briefly. This makes it independent of the value V that is set. On the contrary, if K_1 is small, the velocity is limited. Otherwise, an undesired oscillation system would appear.

This system is implemented in Matlab Ver. R2019b (The Matworks Inc., Madrid, Spain), obtaining the plots revealed in Figure 7. In Figure 7a the values of V = 100 m/s and K_1 = 1 s^{-1} are set for plotting. It can be visualized how the value of the integral (red line) takes time to fade out, in the order of seconds. In this case, the value of y admits an extremely significant positive value which does not ensure stability as it cannot be guaranteed to be lower than y(0). In the plot of Figure 7b, V = 10 m/s and K_1 = 1000 s^{-1} are set. The value of the integral disappears instantly, ensuring the stability of the system and regardless of the velocity value set.

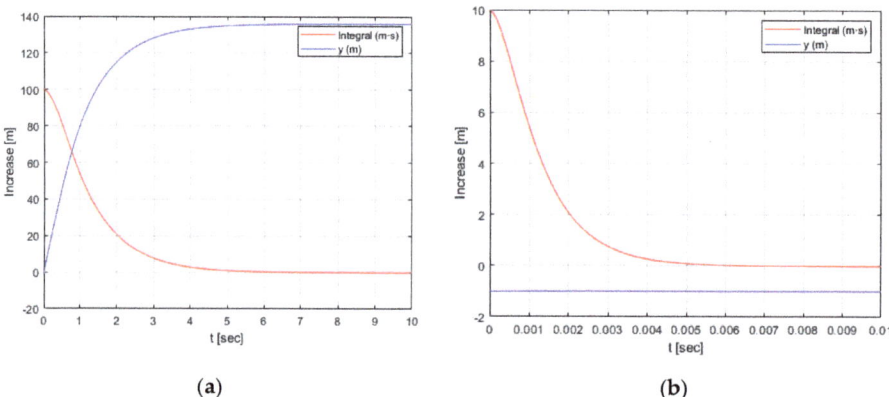

Figure 7. Results of simulation: (**a**) Plot when V is high and K_1 low; (**b**) Plot when V is low and K_1 high.

With this analysis, the need for longitudinal control is acknowledged to ensure that the system is always stable. As 10 m/s is a reasonable speed value for the AGV used, the value of K_1 is set to 1000 s^{-1}. This value refers to the gain of the alignment error control loop.

5. Value of K_2

5.1. System Stability Study

As previously indicated in the stability analysis of the K_1 value, once again a non-linear system is observed, so Lyapunov is employed in order to ensure stability.

The second scenario to be investigated is when the angle of the trajectory needs to be taken into account, as shown in Figure 6b. As already known, the system has highly fast dynamics so Equation (1) is adapted because the AGV assumes the desired direction very quickly. As K_1 is already defined, it can be ignored.

$$\dot{\theta} = \varphi_{setpoint}(e) + \varphi_{path}(e) \tag{26}$$

Therein situation, φ_{path} must also attend a function that depends on the positioning error, due to the position (x, y) of the AGV. Depending on this, the most adjacent point of the path will vary. In this case, the positioning error is calculated as in Equations (27) and (28).

$$(x_{near}, y_{near}) = Argmin\left(\|(x,y) - (x_{path}, y_{path})\|\right) \tag{27}$$

$$\varphi_{path}(e) = \varphi_{path}(x_{near}, y_{near}) \tag{28}$$

Resolving this analytically can be complex. Remembering the Lyapunov system of Equation (5), the e can be defined as in Equation (9). However, this time it is necessary to calculate the parameters A, B and C, considering the position of the AGV because the sign of e depends on that.

$$\{(A, B, C) = f\left((x_{near}, y_{near}), \vec{p}\right) \tag{29}$$

Due to the added difficulty, the systems must be expounded in a discrete form. An optimization algorithm is proposed in which e is calculated for every point in a bounded area. With this information and fixing θ, K_2 is varied, allowing its value to be dictated. The following system is considered at instant t.

$$\theta(x, y, K_2) = f(e, K_2) + \varphi_{path}(e) \tag{30}$$

$$e(x(t), y(t)) = e(t) \tag{31}$$

Knowing that e and θ depend on the position of the AGV and K_2, it is possible to determine some expression at $t + dt$, taking into account Equations (3) and (4).

$$x(t + dt) = x + V \cos \theta \tag{32}$$

$$y(t + dt) = y + V \sin \theta \tag{33}$$

$$e(x(t + dt), y(t + dt)) = e(t + dt) \tag{34}$$

$$\Delta e = e(t + dt) - e(t) \tag{35}$$

Equation (35) has to be negative to ensure stability. The problem is discontinuities can be generated. This issue occurs when the closest point of the path at t is not the same at $t + dt$ or does not continue in the corresponding direction. Instead of considering the whole e (from AGV to the path), it is analysed in sections, guaranteeing that Equation (35) is negative. Hence, the value of Δe is to be taken in absolute values to demonstrate the system is stable. A simulation is performed on all $\vec{p}$ of a bounded area to visualize this phenomenon. It is affected by a sinusoidal trajectory as it is more in line with reality (curves and straight lines).

Figure 8a shows that the Lyapunov energy function is consistently positive over the whole space. L represents a (m^2) value. The derivative of L in Figure 8b is negative throughout the space considered, coinciding with the value of the variation of the positioning error. Therefore, the stability of the system is confirmed.

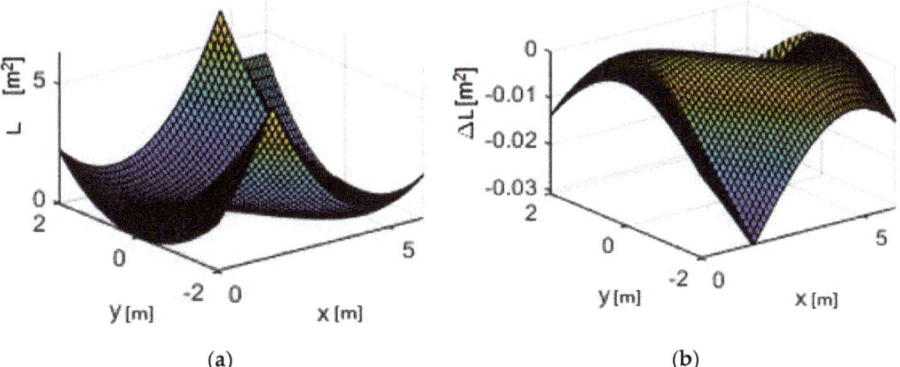

Figure 8. Results of the simulation: (**a**) The values of L in all the space; (**b**) The values of ΔL in all the space.

5.2. Optimization of Value of K_2

Once it is comprehended that the system is stable, a code has been generated that tests all the values of K_2 in a range for the whole amount $\vec{p}$. By setting a value of K_2 it is possible to visualize the evolution of Δe, and the optimal value can be acquired. In Equations (36) and (37), a cost function is proposed that depends on the mean square error, denoted as J.

$$\| e \| = \sqrt{(x - x_{near})^2 + (y - y_{near})^2} \tag{36}$$

$$J = \frac{1}{t}\left(\int_0^t \| e(K_2, \vec{p}, path) \| \, dt\right) = \frac{1}{N} \sum_{k=0}^{k=N} e^2(k) \tag{37}$$

This provides the average of J, as a function of the initial position of the AGV.

$$E_{\vec{p}}\left(K_2, \vec{p}, path\right) = \overline{J}\left(K_2, \vec{p}, path\right) \tag{38}$$

The path persists in attending to a non-variable parameter, just like $\vec{p}$, so to vary J the entirely dependent value is K_2, formulated in Equation (39).

$$K_2 = Argmin\left(\overline{J}\right) \tag{39}$$

The optimization strategy in this test is to perform an exhaustive analysis of all possible combinations of the space in order to get the most optimal result. This approach is simulated, resulting in the K_2 values presented in Figure 9.

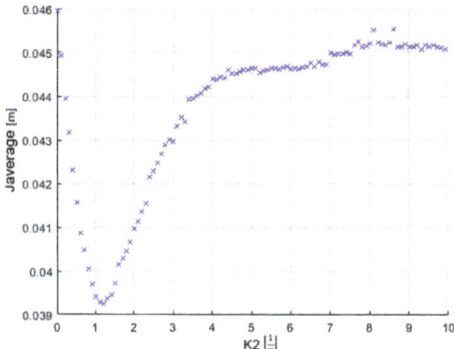

Figure 9. The optimal value of K_2.

This figure also shows that there is an optimal value that minimizes J. Note that K_2 attends the parameter that acts on the rate of evolution of the $\varphi_{setpoint}$. Accordingly, this value is set as $K_2 = 1.21$ (1/m).

6. Longitudinal Control Algorithm

As already noted, the trajectory represents an acknowledged fact, so it is possible to identify the state of a point at $t + 1$. It is equally recognized that there are curves in the path so each point must provide a tangential acceleration, denoted as a_T (m/s^2) and a normal acceleration, denoted as a_N (m/s^2). The latter can be defined as in Equation (40), from which ρ (m) can be known.

$$a_N = \frac{V^2}{\rho} = \omega^2 \rho = V\omega \tag{40}$$

In the same way, it is decided that a_N needs to be under maximum speeding up, called a_{Nmax} (m/s²), as in Equation (41).

$$\| a_N \| \leq a_{Nmax} \tag{41}$$

Due to Equation (41), it is possible to achieve the linear velocity from Equation (40).

$$V = \frac{a_N}{\omega} \tag{42}$$

Keep in mind that the angular velocity is given by K_1 and K_2, so a maximum velocity can be fixed as well, as in Equation (43).

$$V_{max}' = \frac{a_{Nmax}}{\omega} \tag{43}$$

Therefore, by taking Equation (43) it is possible to enhance the value of the linear velocity of the AGV, allowing it to be determined by the positioning error.

$$V = \min\left(\frac{a_{Nmax}}{\omega}, V_{max} = f(e)\right) \tag{44}$$

Equation (44) contemplates the velocity policy designed in a previous section. Depending on e the AGV adjusts the speed, but it will also be subject to the curvature of the trajectory. It is substantial to know the angle that the path will occupy at the continuous instant, being able to predict the V at $t + 1$. In that manner, the AGV will have knowledge of if it is close to a curve, allowing it to reduce the velocity. Therefore, with this idea of prediction, the vectors that compose the acceleration are proposed, perceiving the relation of Equation (45), where a represents the acceleration (m/s²).

$$a^2 = a_N^2 + a_T^2 \rightarrow a_T = \sqrt{a^2 - a_N^2} \tag{45}$$

With this information, it is possible to propose the velocity at $t + 1$ for the AGV.

$$V(t+1) = V(t) + \Delta t \cdot a_T \tag{46}$$

In Equation (46) it is viable to substitute a_T, as seen in Equation (40).

$$V(t+1) = V(t) + \Delta t \sqrt{a^2 - V(t)^2 \omega(t)^2} \tag{47}$$

Knowing all the variables of Equation (47), it is possible to obtain the value of the maximum speed at $t + 1$, denoted as V_{max}''. Taking into account Equation (44), Equation (48) is defined.

$$V(t+1) = \min(V_{max}'', V_{max}' = f(e)) \tag{48}$$

To such a degree, if the AGV maintains a significantly high angular velocity, the linear speed is reduced. The parameter V_{max}' is provided by the AGV, representing the maximum nominal velocity.

$$V(t+1) = f(e, \omega(t), V(t), a) \tag{49}$$

Ultimately, e is contemplated, attaching importance to the trajectory execution speed.

7. Results

Beforehand, the algorithm is proved in simulation, analysing the compliance drop the various objectives. As designed, the lateral control and the longitudinal control work together to allow proper trajectory tracking. In the simulations, it is observed that regardless of the values of the $\vec{pose}$, the autonomous vehicle redirects and reaches the path. As the AGV approaches, it adjusts itself to be able to develop over the trajectory and not overshoot it, obtaining correct trajectory tracking.

At the beginning of the simulation, the algorithm can determine the closest position of the trajectory based on the AGV. Therefore, the first objective is to attain that point. In this situation, the value of the positioning error is considerable. Regardless of the initial θ, the AGV is required to take an angle of $\frac{\pi}{2}$ (rad) to correct the value of e and reach the trajectory quickly. When the AGV assumes $\theta = \frac{\pi}{2}$ rad, the forward motion begins. With the decrease in the positioning error, the value of the vehicle angle starts adapting, adjusting to fit the trajectory angle and generating a curve. The linear velocity also starts increasing. As the AGV approaches the path, the closest point is necessarily unmaintained.

While the positioning error decreases, the alignment error has to do so as well. Because of that, and as the closest point is changing, the value of φ is adapting.

When the AGV is on a straight trajectory, both error values are approximately null, making accurate tracking of the trajectory achievable. In this case, the speed of the movement is limited by the V_{nom} of the AGV. In the case of a curve in the path, it can be observed that the autonomous vehicle reduces its speed to prevent deviating from the predetermined path. Simultaneously, it is making a constant redirection to adhere to the reduced value of alignment error.

In this way, it is proved that the designed algorithm produces a satisfactory result due to the good following of any type of trajectory as can be seen in Figure 10. It exhibits diverse types of paths and $\overrightarrow{pose}$s of the AGV. The red line represents the established trajectory. The black crosses are the nearest point calculated by the algorithm. The coloured line represents the route followed by the AGV. It can be perceived that irrespective of the positioning error, the navigation algorithm performs well in all cases. In Figure 10a,b, the established path is sinusoidal where it can be seen how the AGV can reach the trajectory and adapt to it in both cases. In Figure 10c,d a purely linear trajectory is considered where the AGV also tracks the path well. At long last, a fully curved trajectory is presented in Figure 10e,f. Once more, the following is performed accurately.

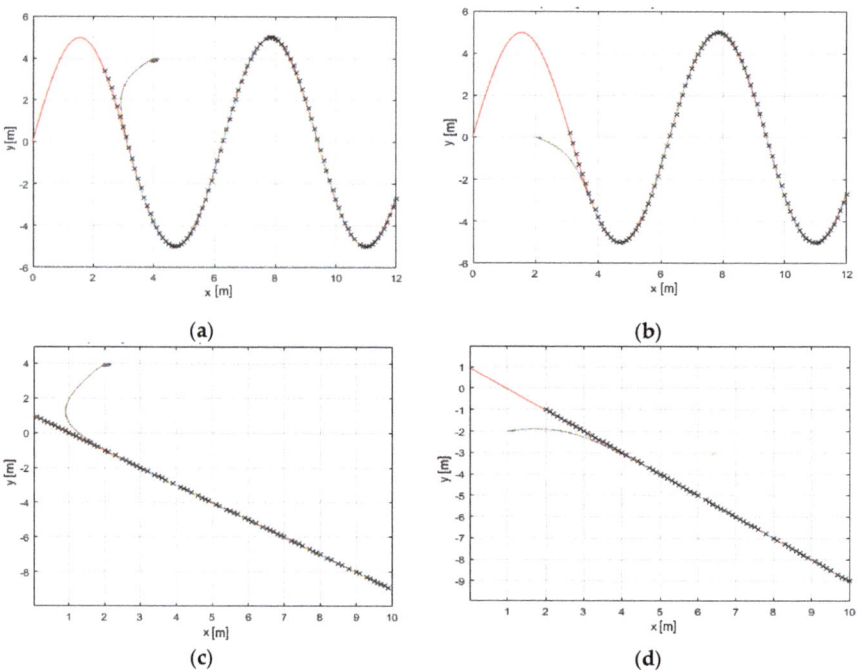

Figure 10. *Cont.*

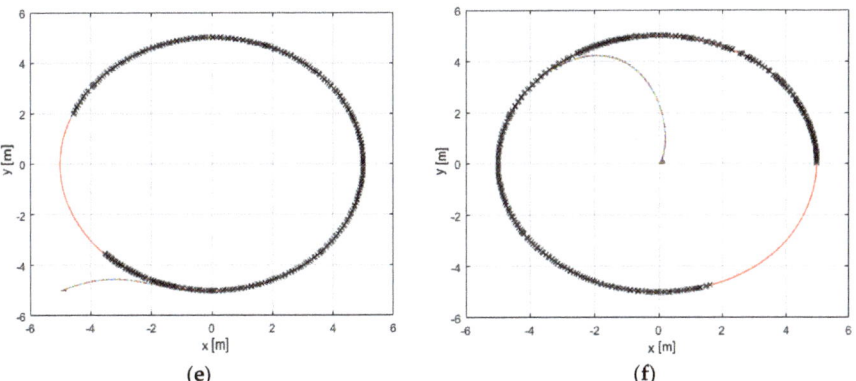

Figure 10. Different path simulation: (**a**) Sinusoidal with AGV at the right side; (**b**) Sinusoidal with AGV at the left side; (**c**) Linear with AGV at the right side; (**d**) Linear with AGV at the left side; (**e**) Circular with AGV outside; (**f**) Circular with AGV inside.

Additionally, it can be marked from all the graphs in Figure 10 that the tracking of the trajectory is correct independently of the positioning of the AGV and therefore, of the sign of e.

It is equally necessary to test whether the algorithm as a whole is suitable for the real AGV. To perform this, two instances are created in MATLAB. One of them processes the image, and the other one executes the navigation algorithm. These are communicated by ROS nodes, to give concurrency to the execution. The movement of the AGV is achieved with a PLC. It is observed that the AGV can follow the whole route correctly.

In the interest of clarifying the execution times of the algorithm, it should be marked that the processor employed is Intel® Core™ i9-9880H CPU @ 2.30 GHz 3.30 GHz. The RAM memory of the computer on which the algorithm is executed is 16 GB and it has an NVIDIA Quadro T1000 graphics card.

Under these conditions, the neural network execution time is 144ms. This time is incorporated into the total period of the ROS publishing node, which is the one that manages the images and takes 186 ms to send the trajectory data vector, measured as an average of 1550 executions.

Regarding the subscriber node, that is the one that executes the control and sends the commands to the PLC, it takes 136 ms on average in 5510 iterations.

8. Discussion

In considering the advantages of this study, comparisons with other techniques commonly used in the control of AGVs are mentioned.

On the one hand, one of the most frequently used sensor techniques in this type of vehicles is LiDAR. These devices are highly effective when it comes to localizing ad receiving data related to the environment in which the AGV is located. In studies such as the one performed by Quan and Chen [46], these devices are employed in conjunction with the odometry of the wheels in order to localize an autonomous guided vehicle. Despite their extensive use, these sensors do not provide the necessary robustness for this type of systems. In the present paper, this robustness is consistently achieved.

On the other hand, in the industrial field, it has been frequent to employ philo-guided vehicles (see Chet et al. [47]). These vehicles use electromagnetism to perform navigation, providing the necessary robustness and accuracy. However, it is not a flexible solution. The AGV and navigation system presented in this work have the benefit of achieving minimum cost when implementing a fixed trajectory. By the use of tape of a determined color, any type of path can be established without the need for expensive and specific infrastructure.

Furthermore, with the re-training of the neural network the path can be adapted to any color or operating area.

To conclude, it is possible to get the positioning error committed with this navigation algorithm in a specific trajectory, as graphited in Figure 11. The figure, therefore, shows that in curved areas, like in the beginning and the end iterations, the positioning error increases, because of the location of the wheels and the camera in the AGV itself. However, in the central iterations, it can be appreciated that in straight areas the positioning error is close to zero.

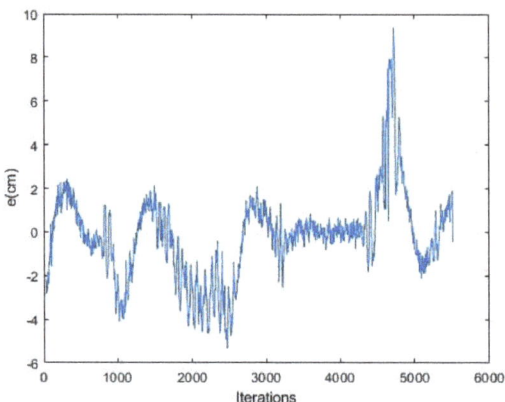

Figure 11. Positioning error values in a specific trajectory.

As demonstrated by Hoffmann et al. [45] in the Stanley algorithm, a typical RMS cross-track error of less than 0.1 m is obtained. In the case of this modification of the algorithm, the RMS of the positioning error is around 0.02 m.

9. Conclusions

The present work focuses on the search for solutions for the navigation and localization of an AGV, because of the need to discover robust techniques, achieving greater precision and reliability.

Fundamentally, it is demonstrated that the proposed algorithm modification is stable. As mentioned in the previous section, the advantages over conventional techniques can be recognized. This algorithm is remarkably simple, requiring no previous training to perform properly. When changing path, no retraining is necessary, it merely requires the colour of the trajectory to match.

In terms of navigation, starting from a base such as the Stanley algorithm and presenting it another perspective comprehends its complexity. In addition, demonstrating stability and ensuring the given solution is adequate is uneasy. For this, other alternatives have to be tested until a solution is obtained that proves its robustness. Therein way, the values of the constants can be demonstrated and a sense for them, as well. This issue has been one of the most arduous tasks of this work.

The main objective set in this work represents the stability analysis of the modification of a navigation algorithm capable of performing lateral control and longitudinal control. This has been achieved, obtaining satisfactory results. As mentioned, the difficulty was in the stability analysis, but due to the results, its proper performance has been demonstrated.

Continuing with localization, instead of designing a new algorithm, some data derived from the other algorithms are employed. In this case, the necessary parameters can be obtained from the navigation and path planning codes, without using sensors.

Sensors remain the conventional method for calculating the trajectory. In this work, it is completed with artificial vision and a neural network, a less common method but with remarkably pleasing results as well. The latter algorithm was considered with Hough transforms, for example, but concluded that the use of a neural network was more appropriate. Nevertheless, in some areas, further study is required to achieve more accuracy. These areas are related to light shimmers generated in the image that create indistinctness.

Furthermore, it has been possible to decouple the problem of data acquisition from the problem of navigation. Consequently, until a new image is received, predictions are used.

Overall, the work accomplishes the objective of ensuring stability of an algorithm for the free navigation of an industrial autonomous vehicle.

As a prolongation of this research, attempts will be made to enhance the architecture of the convolutional neural network with the aim of achieving higher speed rates.

For future work, the execution of the algorithm in real-time but with more excessive speed may reveal a lack in the concurrency of the ROS nodes. An analysis of resource consumption can in addition be effected.

On the other hand, numerous tests can be done with the neural network, changing the configuration or performing different learning, to improve the accuracy of the navigable path. This can give an idea of the characteristics that the CNN may need for this application.

An explicability analysis using the LIME technique can clarify whether the semantic segmentation errors are related to the similarities between the images. In all images, the trajectory is mostly linear and close to the centre of the image. This analysis provides insight into what the neural network relies on to classify the parts of the image. It will also be interesting to investigate the interpretation of deep learning.

In addition, if the semantic segmentation has mask discontinuities to compute the trajectory, it is necessary to consider alternatives in the algorithm to finalize the navigation.

As for the algorithm used, it is necessary to incorporate the case where there is no trajectory and how to stop the AGV's movement. In the simulation, the AGV attains the final of the trajectory and turns π (rad), following the path in reverse. In the real AGV, when it does not visualize any more trajectory, it starts to turn on its own to detect the yellow line again. Therefore, there exists an understandable need for a stopping policy that contemplates different situations.

Author Contributions: Conceptualization, M.C.-O. and E.Z.; methodology, M.C.-O.; software, M.C.-O. and E.Z.; validation, E.Z. and U.F.-G.; formal analysis, E.Z. and A.T.-F.-B.; investigation, M.C.-O. and A.S.-C.; resources, U.F.-G.; writing—original draft preparation, M.C.-O. and E.Z.; writing—review and editing, U.F.-G.; All authors have read and agreed to the published version of the manuscript.

Funding: The current study has been sponsored by the Government of the Basque Country-ELKARTEK21/10 KK-2021/00014 ("Estudio de nuevas técnicas de inteligencia artificial basadas en Deep Learning dirigidas a la optimización de procesos industriales") research program.

Institutional Review Board Statement: Not applicable.

Informed Consent Statement: Not applicable.

Data Availability Statement: The data presented in this study are available on request from the corresponding author.

Acknowledgments: The authors are grateful for the support provided by UPV/EHU.

Conflicts of Interest: The authors declare no conflict of interest.

References

1. Kilic, C.; Ohi, N.; Gu, Y.; Gross, J. Slip-Based Autonomous ZUPT through Gaussian Process to Improve Planetary Rover Localization. *IEEE Robot. Autom. Lett.* **2021**, *6*, 4782–4789. [CrossRef] [PubMed]
2. Chen, S.Y. Kalman filter for robot vision: A survey. *IEEE Trans. Ind. Electron.* **2012**, *59*, 4409–4420. [CrossRef]
3. Cho, H.; Kim, E.K.; Kim, S. Indoor SLAM application using geometric and ICP matching methods based on line features. *Rob. Auton. Syst.* **2018**, *100*, 206–224. [CrossRef]
4. Shamsfakhr, F.; Sadeghi Bigham, B. GSR: Geometrical scan registration algorithm for robust and fast robot pose estimation. *Assem. Autom.* **2020**, *40*, 801–817. [CrossRef]

5. Naus, K.; Marchel, Ł. Use of a weighted ICP algorithm to precisely determine USV movement parameters. *Appl. Sci.* **2019**, *9*, 3530. [CrossRef]
6. Wang, Y.T.; Peng, C.C.; Ravankar, A.A.; Ravankar, A. A single LiDAR-based feature fusion indoor localization algorithm. *Sensors* **2018**, *18*, 1294. [CrossRef]
7. Senin, N.; Colosimo, B.M.; Pacella, M. Point set augmentation through fitting for enhanced ICP registration of point clouds in multisensor coordinate metrology. *Robot. Comput. Integr. Manuf.* **2013**, *29*, 39–52. [CrossRef]
8. Gao, Y.; Liu, S.; Atia, M.M.; Noureldin, A. INS/GPS/LiDAR integrated navigation system for urban and indoor environments using hybrid scan matching algorithm. *Sensors* **2015**, *15*, 23286–23302. [CrossRef]
9. Kim, H.; Song, S.; Myung, H. GP-ICP: Ground Plane ICP for Mobile Robots. *IEEE Access* **2019**, *7*, 76599–76610. [CrossRef]
10. Sadeghi Bigham, B.; Dolatikalan, S.; Khastan, A. Minimum landmarks for robot localization in orthogonal environments. *Evol. Intell.* **2021**, *1*, 1–4. [CrossRef]
11. Yap, Y.Y.; Khoo, B.E. Landmark-based Automated Guided Vehicle Localization Algorithm for Warehouse Application. *Pervasive Health Pervasive Comput. Technol. Healthc.* **2019**, 47–54. [CrossRef]
12. Gao, X.; Zhang, T. Robust RGB-D simultaneous localization and mapping using planar point features. *Rob. Auton. Syst.* **2015**, *72*, 1–14. [CrossRef]
13. Clemens, J.; Kluth, T.; Reineking, T. β-SLAM: Simultaneous localization and grid mapping with beta distributions. *Inf. Fusion* **2019**, *52*, 62–75. [CrossRef]
14. Gentner, C.; Jost, T.; Wang, W.; Zhang, S.; Dammann, A.; Fiebig, U.C. Multipath Assisted Positioning with Simultaneous Localization and Mapping. *IEEE Trans. Wirel. Commun.* **2016**, *15*, 6104–6117. [CrossRef]
15. Yang, P.; Wu, W. Efficient particle filter localization algorithm in dense passive RFID tag environment. *IEEE Trans. Ind. Electron.* **2014**, *61*, 5641–5651. [CrossRef]
16. Zhang, Q.B.; Wang, P.; Chen, Z.H. An improved particle filter for mobile robot localization based on particle swarm optimization. *Expert Syst. Appl.* **2019**, *135*, 181–193. [CrossRef]
17. Carrera Villacres, J.L.; Zhao, Z.; Braun, T.; Li, Z. A Particle Filter-Based Reinforcement Learning Approach for Reliable Wireless Indoor Positioning. *IEEE J. Sel. Areas Commun.* **2019**, *37*, 2457–2473. [CrossRef]
18. Wang, L. Automatic control of mobile robot based on autonomous navigation algorithm. *Artif. Life Robot.* **2019**, *24*, 494–498. [CrossRef]
19. Tao, B.; Wu, H.; Gong, Z.; Yin, Z.; Ding, H. An RFID-Based Mobile Robot Localization Method Combining Phase Difference and Readability. *IEEE Trans. Autom. Sci. Eng.* **2021**, *18*, 1406–1416. [CrossRef]
20. Lu, S.; Xu, C.; Zhong, R.Y. An Active RFID Tag-Enabled Locating Approach with Multipath Effect Elimination in AGV. *IEEE Trans. Autom. Sci. Eng.* **2016**, *13*, 1333–1342. [CrossRef]
21. Kashyap, A.K.; Parhi, D.R.; Muni, M.K.; Pandey, K.K. A hybrid technique for path planning of humanoid robot NAO in static and dynamic terrains. *Appl. Soft Comput. J.* **2020**, *96*, 106581. [CrossRef]
22. Brock, O.; Khatib, O. High-speed navigation using the global dynamic window approach. In Proceedings of the 1999 IEEE International Conference on Robotics and Automation (Cat. No.99CH36288C), Detroit, MI, USA, 10–15 May 1999; Volume 1, pp. 341–346. [CrossRef]
23. Liu, L.S.; Lin, J.F.; Yao, J.X.; He, D.W.; Zheng, J.S.; Huang, J.; Shi, P. Path Planning for Smart Car Based on Dijkstra Algorithm and Dynamic Window Approach. *Wirel. Commun. Mob. Comput.* **2021**, *2021*, 8881684. [CrossRef]
24. Dobrevski, M.; Skocaj, D. Adaptive dynamic window approach for local navigation. In Proceedings of the 2020 IEEE/RSJ International Conference on Intelligent Robots and Systems (IROS), Las Vegas, NV, USA, 24 October–24 January 2021; pp. 6930–6936. [CrossRef]
25. Fox, D.; Burgard, W.; Thrun, S. The dynamic window approach to collision avoidance. *IEEE Robot. Autom. Mag.* **1997**, *4*, 23–33. [CrossRef]
26. Wang, T.; Yan, X.; Wang, Y.; Wu, Q. A distributed model predictive control using virtual field force for multi-ship collision avoidance under COLREGs. In Proceedings of the 2017 4th International Conference on Transportation Information and Safety (ICTIS), Banff, AB, Canada, 8–10 August 2017; pp. 296–305. [CrossRef]
27. Burgos, E.; Bhandari, S. Potential flow field navigation with virtual force field for UAS collision avoidance. In Proceedings of the 2016 International Conference on Unmanned Aircraft Systems ICUAS 2016, Arlington, VA, USA, 7–10 June 2016; pp. 505–513. [CrossRef]
28. Borenstein, J.; Koren, Y. The Vector Field Histogram—Fast obstacle avoidance for mobile robots. *IEEE J. Robot. Autom.* **1991**, *7*, 278–288. [CrossRef]
29. Ye, C. Navigating a mobile robot by a traversability field histogram. *IEEE Trans. Syst. Man, Cybern. Part B Cybern.* **2007**, *37*, 361–372. [CrossRef]
30. AbdElmoniem, A.; Osama, A.; Abdelaziz, M.; Maged, S.A. A path-tracking algorithm using predictive Stanley lateral controller. *Int. J. Adv. Robot. Syst.* **2020**, *17*, 1–11. [CrossRef]
31. Fei, W.; Ziwei, W.; Meijin, L. Robot Path Planning Based on Improved Particle Swarm Optimization. In Proceedings of the 2021 IEEE 2nd International Conference on Big Data, Artificial Intelligence and Internet of Things Engineering ICBAIE 2021, Nanchang, China, 26–28 March 2021; Volume 21, pp. 887–891. [CrossRef]

32. Liu, Z.; Liu, H.; Lu, Z.; Zeng, Q. A Dynamic Fusion Pathfinding Algorithm Using Delaunay Triangulation and Improved A-Star for Mobile Robots. *IEEE Access* **2021**, *9*, 20602–20621. [CrossRef]
33. Cheng, L.; Liu, C.; Yan, B. Improved hierarchical A-star algorithm for optimal parking path planning of the large parking lot. In Proceedings of the ICIA 2014—IEEE International Conference on Information and Automation, Hailar, China, 28–30 July 2014; pp. 695–698. [CrossRef]
34. da Silva Costa, L.; Tonidandel, F. DVG+A* and RRT Path-Planners: A Comparison in a Highly Dynamic Environment. *J. Intell. Robot. Syst.* **2021**, *101*, 1–20. [CrossRef]
35. Wang, J.; Li, B.; Meng, M.Q.H. Kinematic Constrained Bi-directional RRT with Efficient Branch Pruning for robot path planning. *Expert Syst. Appl.* **2021**, *170*, 114541. [CrossRef]
36. Wei, K.; Ren, B. A method on dynamic path planning for robotic manipulator autonomous obstacle avoidance based on an improved RRT algorithm. *Sensors* **2018**, *18*, 571. [CrossRef]
37. Tang, C.; Sun, R.; Yu, S.; Chen, L.; Zheng, J. Autonomous Indoor Mobile Robot Exploration Based on Wavefront Algorithm. *Lect. Notes Comput. Sci.* **2019**, *11744*, 338–348.
38. Wu, S.; Du, Y.; Zhang, Y. Mobile Robot Path Planning Based on a Generalized Wavefront Algorithm. *Math. Probl. Eng.* **2020**, *2020*, 6798798. [CrossRef]
39. Sdwk, U.; Edvhg, S.; Ohduqlqj, R.Q.; Dqj, L.; Lqj, L.X.; Hiilflhqf, F.; Wkh, R.I.; Dojrulwkp, S.; Ri, J.; Vlqfh, U.; et al. Mobile robot path planning based on Q-learnig algorithm*. In Proceedings of the 2019 WRC Symposium on Advanced Robotics and Automation (WRC SARA), Beijing, China, 21–22 August 2019; pp. 160–165.
40. Gao, J.; Ye, W.; Guo, J.; Li, Z. Deep reinforcement learning for indoor mobile robot path planning. *Sensors* **2020**, *20*, 5493. [CrossRef]
41. Zheng, K.; Gao, J.; Shen, L. UCAV Path Planning Algorithm Based on Deep Reinforcement Learning. *Lect. Notes Comput. Sci.* **2019**, *11902*, 702–714.
42. Teso-Fz-Betoño, D.; Zulueta, E.; Sánchez-Chica, A.; Fernandez-Gamiz, U.; Saenz-Aguirre, A. Semantic segmentation to develop an indoor navigation system for an autonomous mobile robot. *Mathematics* **2020**, *8*, 855. [CrossRef]
43. Olgun, M.C.; Baytar, Z.; Akpolat, K.M.; Koray Sahingoz, O. Autonomous vehicle control for lane and vehicle tracking by using deep learning via vision. In Proceedings of the 2018 6th International Conference on Control Engineering and Information Technology, CEIT 2018, Istanbul, Turkey, 25–27 October 2018; pp. 25–27. [CrossRef]
44. Azimi, S.M.; Fischer, P.; Korner, M.; Reinartz, P. Aerial LaneNet: Lane-Marking Semantic Segmentation in Aerial Imagery Using Wavelet-Enhanced Cost-Sensitive Symmetric Fully Convolutional Neural Networks. *IEEE Trans. Geosci. Remote Sens.* **2019**, *57*, 2920–2938. [CrossRef]
45. Hoffmann, G.M.; Tomlin, C.J.; Montemerlo, M.; Thrun, S. Autonomous automobile trajectory tracking for off-road driving: Controller design, experimental validation and racing. In Proceedings of the 2007 American Control Conference, New York, NY, USA, 9–13 July 2007; pp. 2296–2301. [CrossRef]
46. Quan, S.; Chen, J. AGV localization based on odometry and LiDAR. In Proceedings of the 2019 2nd World Conference on Mechanical Engineering and Intelligent Manufacturing (WCMEIM), Shanghai, China, 22–24 November 2019; pp. 483–486. [CrossRef]
47. Chen, X.; Lin, W.; Liu, J.; Guan, L.; Zheng, Y.; Gao, F. Electromagnetic Guided Factory Intelligent AGV. In Proceedings of the 2016 3rd International Conference on Mechatronics and Information Technology, Shenzhen, China, 9–10 April 2016; pp. 1–6. [CrossRef]

Article

Thermogravitational Convective Flow and Energy Transport in an Electronic Cabinet with a Heat-Generating Element and Solid/Porous Finned Heat Sink

Xuan Hoang Khoa Le [1], Ioan Pop [2] and Mikhail A. Sheremet [1,3,*]

[1] Butakov Research Center, National Research Tomsk Polytechnic University, 634050 Tomsk, Russia; lexuanhoangkhoa@gmail.com
[2] Department of Mathematics, Babeș-Bolyai University, 400084 Cluj-Napoca, Romania; popm.ioan@yahoo.co.uk
[3] Laboratory on Convective Heat and Mass Transfer, Tomsk State University, 634045 Tomsk, Russia
* Correspondence: sheremet@math.tsu.ru

Abstract: Heat transfer enhancement poses a significant challenge for engineers in various practical fields, including energy-efficient buildings, energy systems, and aviation technologies. The present research deals with the energy transport strengthening using the viscous fluid and solid/porous fins. Numerical simulation of natural convective energy transport of viscous fluid in a cooling cavity with a heat-generating element placed in a finned heat sink was performed. The heat-generating element is characterized by constant volumetric heat generation. The Darcy–Brinkman approach was employed for mathematical description of transport processes within the porous fins. The governing equations formulated using the non-primitive variables were solved by the finite difference method of the second-order accuracy. The influence of the fins material, number, and height on the flow structure and heat transfer was also studied. It was found that the mentioned parameters can be considered as control characteristics for heat transfer and fluid flow for the cooling system.

Keywords: natural convection; solid/porous fins; heat sink; local heat-generating element; numerical technique

Citation: Le, X.H.K.; Pop, I.; Sheremet, M.A. Thermogravitational Convective Flow and Energy Transport in an Electronic Cabinet with a Heat-Generating Element and Solid/Porous Finned Heat Sink. *Mathematics* **2022**, *10*, 34. https://doi.org/10.3390/math10010034

Academic Editors: Irina Cristea, Yuriy Rogovchenko, Justo Puerto, Gintautas Dzemyda and Patrick Siarry

Received: 3 December 2021
Accepted: 20 December 2021
Published: 23 December 2021

Publisher's Note: MDPI stays neutral with regard to jurisdictional claims in published maps and institutional affiliations.

Copyright: © 2021 by the authors. Licensee MDPI, Basel, Switzerland. This article is an open access article distributed under the terms and conditions of the Creative Commons Attribution (CC BY) license (https://creativecommons.org/licenses/by/4.0/).

1. Introduction

Many different engineering fields demand the heat transfer enhancement that can be achieved using the extended heat transfer surfaces. Such an approach helps to develop energy-efficient buildings, modern energy and electronic systems, aviation technologies, and others. Nowadays, extended heat transfer surfaces are widely used in different engineering applications [1–5]. There are some published researches on convective heat transport augmentation in chambers with a fins system [3–12]. Thus, Hatami [6] has studied thermal convection in a rectangular cabinet with two isothermal fins placed on the lower adiabatic surface under an influence of cold upper border. By using Pak and Cho relation for nanosuspension viscosity and Maxwell–Garnett relation for heat conductivity, the formulated partial differential equations could be worked out with the FlexPDE commercial code. It has been found that an increase in the fins' height results in a higher mean Nusselt number. Siavashi et al. [7] computationally scrutinized free convection in a differentially warmed square chamber filled with copper–water nanoliquid, and placed porous fins on the left vertical hot border. By employing the Corcione's correlations for nanosuspension viscosity and thermal conductivity with the two-phase nanofluid model, the governing partial differential equations could be worked out by the finite volume technique. It has been revealed that, for high Darcy numbers, energy transport strength can be increased with fins number and fins length, while for low Darcy numbers, one can find the opposite effect. Hejri and Malekshah [8] have scrutinized computationally natural convective energy transport and entropy production in a rectangular cabinet saturated with CuO–water nanoliquid under an influence of isothermally heated fins and isothermally cooled vertical and upper cavity walls. The used a single-phase nanofluid model with the Koo–Kleinstreuer–Li approach for nanofluid thermal conductivity, and numerically worked out the viscosity. Authors have found that a reduction in the aspect ratio of fins characterizes the heat transfer strength diminution. Massoudi et al. [9] examined computationally MHD natural convection of MWCNT–H_2O nanosuspension in an inclined T-shaped enclosure with isothermal trapezoidal fins mounted on the lower border. Numerical analysis was conducted by employing the single-phase nanosuspension approach with the Brinkman model to work out viscosity, and the Xue approach was conducted to work out thermal conductivity on the basis of the COMSOL Multiphysics commercial software. Authors have ascertained an increase in the mean Nusselt number with fins height. Furthermore, the fins location and shape, in combination with the chamber inclination, have an essential influence on the heat transport rate. Astanina et al. [10] have computationally investigated free convective energy transference in a porous chamber saturated with variable viscosity liquid under an impact of heat-producing source and finned heat sink. Using the created computational code, analysis has shown that the fins number plays an essential role in energy removal from the heated element for the passive cooling systems.

Natural convection with the second thermodynamic law for alumina–water nanoliquid in a differentially warmed chamber with isothermally heated fins of various shapes mounted on left vertical hot wall under the influence of uniform Lorentz force has been investigated by Yan et al. [11]. By employing single-phase nanosuspension approach with the Koo–Kleinstreuer model for nanofluid heat conductivity and viscosity, the governing equations could be worked out using the finite volume method. Authors have found that the energy transport can be intensified by attaching the inclined fins. Gireesha et al. [12] have numerically analyzed an influence of the hybrid nanofluid on liquid motion and energy transfer over a porous fin moving with constant velocity. The single-phase nanofluid model with Brinkman and Maxwell relations for viscosity and heat conductivity, in combination with one-dimensional approximation, has been solved using the Runge–Kutta–Fehlberg technique for ordinary differential equations. It has been found that hybrid nanofluid helps to intensify the energy transport. Buonomo et al. [5] have generalized the previous research to the local thermal non-equilibrium model for the porous fin in the case of natural convection and heat radiation. The defined ordinary differential relations were worked out using the Adomian decomposition method. Authors have revealed that low Rayleigh numbers and intensive external cooling reflect a possibility to use the local thermal equilibrium approach. Some interesting results can also be found in [13–18].

This brief review illustrates the actuality of the considered topic, but there are no papers that analyze the influence of porous–solid fins on heat-generating element within the highly heat-conducting heat sink in a closed cooling chamber. Therefore, the aim of the research is a computational simulation of heat transfer performance in a closed cooling cabinet saturated with viscous fluid under an impact of porous/solid fins on the heat-generating element within the heat sink.

2. Mathematical Simulation

Herein, we analyze the viscous, laminar, incompressible, and conjugate convective energy transfer and liquid circulation in a closed hermetic electronic cabinet with a thermally producing source placed inside a finned heat sink. The cooling system is shown in Figure 1, where the liquid (water) is circulated within the chamber. To have the impact of buoyancy, the cabinet requires to be regarded in vertical location, since the analysis is of natural convection. Let $\bar{x}$ and $\bar{y}$ be the coordinate axes in horizontal and vertical directions, respectively, with $\bar{u}$ and $\bar{v}$ denoting the corresponding velocity components. Let the temperature of vertical and upper horizontal walls be denoted by T_c. The density changes are modeled using the Boussinesq approach [3,4,10]. The local heater is a heat-conducting solid element with a constant volumetric heat generation Q. The temperature of the solid structure equals the temperature of the liquid phase for the porous fins, and the local thermal equilibrium approach is employed. The transport processes in porous fins are modeled on the basis of the Brinkman–extended Darcy approximation.

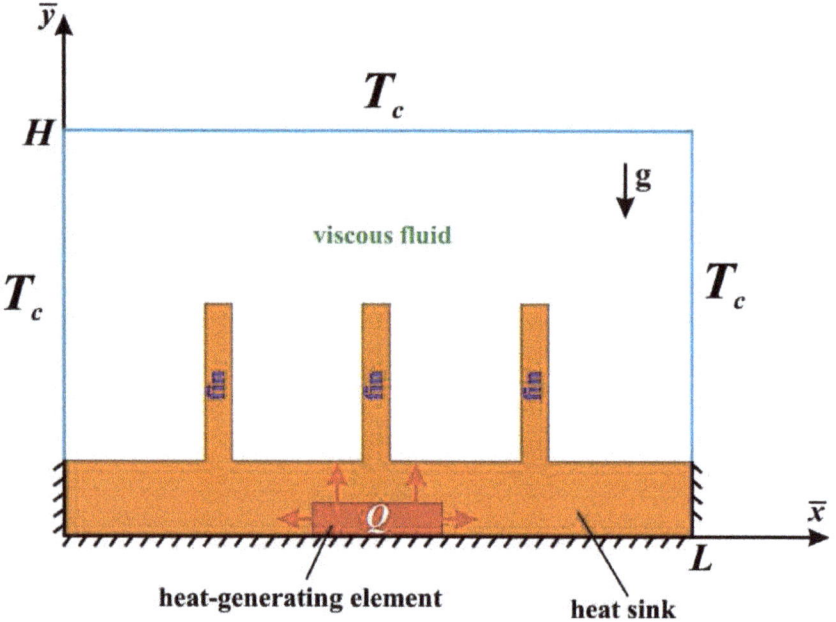

Figure 1. Sketch of the problem with coordinates.

The governing equations representing the liquid circulation and energy transport are as follows [3,4,10].

- For the viscous fluid

$$\frac{\partial \bar{u}}{\partial \bar{x}} + \frac{\partial \bar{v}}{\partial \bar{y}} = 0 \tag{1}$$

$$\rho \left(\frac{\partial \bar{u}}{\partial t} + \bar{u} \frac{\partial \bar{u}}{\partial \bar{x}} + \bar{v} \frac{\partial \bar{u}}{\partial \bar{y}} \right) = -\frac{\partial p}{\partial \bar{x}} + \mu \left(\frac{\partial^2 \bar{u}}{\partial \bar{x}^2} + \frac{\partial^2 \bar{u}}{\partial \bar{y}^2} \right) \tag{2}$$

$$\rho \left(\frac{\partial \bar{v}}{\partial t} + \bar{u} \frac{\partial \bar{v}}{\partial \bar{x}} + \bar{v} \frac{\partial \bar{v}}{\partial \bar{y}} \right) = -\frac{\partial p}{\partial \bar{y}} + \mu \left(\frac{\partial^2 \bar{v}}{\partial \bar{x}^2} + \frac{\partial^2 \bar{v}}{\partial \bar{y}^2} \right) + \rho g \beta (T - T_c) \tag{3}$$

$$\frac{\partial T}{\partial t} + \bar{u} \frac{\partial T}{\partial \bar{x}} + \bar{v} \frac{\partial T}{\partial \bar{y}} = \frac{k_f}{(\rho c)_f} \left(\frac{\partial^2 T}{\partial \bar{x}^2} + \frac{\partial^2 T}{\partial \bar{y}^2} \right) \tag{4}$$

- For the solid fins and solid heat sink

$$(\rho c)_s \frac{\partial T}{\partial t} = k_s \left(\frac{\partial^2 T}{\partial \bar{x}^2} + \frac{\partial^2 T}{\partial \bar{y}^2} \right) \tag{5}$$

- For the heat-generating element

$$(\rho c)_{hs} \frac{\partial T}{\partial t} = k_{hs} \left(\frac{\partial^2 T}{\partial \bar{x}^2} + \frac{\partial^2 T}{\partial \bar{y}^2} \right) + Q \tag{6}$$

- For the porous fins

$$\frac{\partial \bar{u}}{\partial \bar{x}} + \frac{\partial \bar{v}}{\partial \bar{y}} = 0 \qquad (7)$$

$$\rho\left(\frac{1}{\varepsilon}\frac{\partial \bar{u}}{\partial t} + \frac{\bar{u}}{\varepsilon^2}\frac{\partial \bar{u}}{\partial \bar{x}} + \frac{\bar{v}}{\varepsilon^2}\frac{\partial \bar{u}}{\partial \bar{y}}\right) = -\frac{\partial p}{\partial \bar{x}} + \frac{\mu}{\varepsilon}\left(\frac{\partial^2 \bar{u}}{\partial \bar{x}^2} + \frac{\partial^2 \bar{u}}{\partial \bar{y}^2}\right) - \frac{\mu}{K}\bar{u} \qquad (8)$$

$$\rho\left(\frac{1}{\varepsilon}\frac{\partial \bar{v}}{\partial t} + \frac{\bar{u}}{\varepsilon^2}\frac{\partial \bar{v}}{\partial \bar{x}} + \frac{\bar{v}}{\varepsilon^2}\frac{\partial \bar{v}}{\partial \bar{y}}\right) = -\frac{\partial p}{\partial \bar{y}} + \frac{\mu}{\varepsilon}\left(\frac{\partial^2 \bar{v}}{\partial \bar{x}^2} + \frac{\partial^2 \bar{v}}{\partial \bar{y}^2}\right) - \frac{\mu}{K}\bar{v} + \rho g \beta (T - T_c) \qquad (9)$$

$$\eta\frac{\partial T}{\partial t} + \bar{u}\frac{\partial T}{\partial \bar{x}} + \bar{v}\frac{\partial T}{\partial \bar{y}} = \frac{k_{pm}}{(\rho c)_f}\left(\frac{\partial^2 T}{\partial \bar{x}^2} + \frac{\partial^2 T}{\partial \bar{y}^2}\right) \qquad (10)$$

where $\eta = \varepsilon + (1-\varepsilon)\frac{(\rho c)_{spm}}{(\rho c)_f}$ is the overall heat capacity ratio and $k_{pm} = \varepsilon k_f + (1-\varepsilon)k_{spm}$ is the thermal conductivity of porous medium.

Including the stream function $\left(\bar{u} = \frac{\partial \bar{\psi}}{\partial \bar{y}}, \bar{v} = -\frac{\partial \bar{\psi}}{\partial \bar{x}}\right)$, vorticity $\left(\bar{\omega} = \frac{\partial \bar{v}}{\partial \bar{x}} - \frac{\partial \bar{u}}{\partial \bar{y}}\right)$, and non-dimensional parameters:

$$\begin{aligned} x = \bar{x}/H, \; y = \bar{y}/H, \; \tau = t\sqrt{g\beta\Delta T/H}, \; \theta = (T - T_c)/\Delta T, \\ u = \bar{u}/\sqrt{g\beta\Delta TH}, \; v = \bar{v}/\sqrt{g\beta\Delta TH}, \; \psi = \bar{\psi}/\sqrt{g\beta\Delta TH^3}, \; \omega = \bar{\omega}\sqrt{H/g\beta\Delta T} \end{aligned} \qquad (11)$$

The control non-dimensional equations are as follows [3,4,10].

- For the viscous fluid

$$\frac{\partial^2 \psi}{\partial x^2} + \frac{\partial^2 \psi}{\partial y^2} = -\omega \qquad (12)$$

$$\frac{\partial \omega}{\partial \tau} + \frac{\partial \psi}{\partial y}\frac{\partial \omega}{\partial x} - \frac{\partial \psi}{\partial x}\frac{\partial \omega}{\partial y} = \sqrt{\frac{Pr}{Ra}}\left(\frac{\partial^2 \omega}{\partial x^2} + \frac{\partial^2 \omega}{\partial y^2}\right) + \frac{\partial \theta}{\partial x} \qquad (13)$$

$$\frac{\partial \theta}{\partial \tau} + u\frac{\partial \theta}{\partial x} + v\frac{\partial \theta}{\partial y} = \frac{1}{\sqrt{Ra \cdot Pr}}\left(\frac{\partial^2 \theta}{\partial x^2} + \frac{\partial^2 \theta}{\partial y^2}\right) \qquad (14)$$

- For the solid fins and solid heat sink

$$\frac{\partial \theta}{\partial \tau} = \frac{\alpha_s/\alpha_f}{\sqrt{Ra \cdot Pr}}\left(\frac{\partial^2 \theta}{\partial x^2} + \frac{\partial^2 \theta}{\partial y^2}\right) \qquad (15)$$

- For the heat-generating element

$$\frac{\partial \theta}{\partial \tau} = \frac{\alpha_{hs}/\alpha_f}{\sqrt{Ra \cdot Pr}}\left(\frac{\partial^2 \theta}{\partial x^2} + \frac{\partial^2 \theta}{\partial y^2} + 1\right) \qquad (16)$$

- For the porous fins

$$\frac{\partial^2 \psi}{\partial x^2} + \frac{\partial^2 \psi}{\partial y^2} = -\omega \qquad (17)$$

$$\varepsilon\frac{\partial \omega}{\partial \tau} + \frac{\partial \psi}{\partial y}\frac{\partial \omega}{\partial x} - \frac{\partial \psi}{\partial x}\frac{\partial \omega}{\partial y} = \varepsilon\sqrt{\frac{Pr}{Ra}}\left(\frac{\partial^2 \omega}{\partial x^2} + \frac{\partial^2 \omega}{\partial y^2} - \varepsilon\frac{\omega}{Da}\right) + \varepsilon^2\frac{\partial \theta}{\partial x} \qquad (18)$$

$$\frac{\partial \theta}{\partial \tau} + u\frac{\partial \theta}{\partial x} + v\frac{\partial \theta}{\partial y} = \frac{k_{pm}/k_f}{\sqrt{Ra \cdot Pr}}\left(\frac{\partial^2 \theta}{\partial x^2} + \frac{\partial^2 \theta}{\partial y^2}\right) \qquad (19)$$

The employed additional conditions are

$\tau = 0:$ $\quad\quad\quad \psi(x,y,0) = 0, \omega(x,y,0) = 0, \theta(x,y,0) = 0$
$\tau > 0:$

$\frac{\partial \theta}{\partial x} = 0$ at $x = 0$, $x = L/H$ and $0 \leq y \leq h/H$

$\frac{\partial \theta}{\partial y} = 0$ at $y = 0$, $0 \leq x \leq L/H$

$\psi = 0, \omega = -\frac{\partial^2 \psi}{\partial x^2}, \theta = 0$ at $x = 0$, $x = L/H$ and $h/H \leq y \leq 1$

$\psi = 0, \omega = -\frac{\partial^2 \psi}{\partial y^2}, \theta = 0$ at $y = 1$ and $0 \leq x \leq L/H$

$$\begin{cases} \theta_{hs} = \theta_s \\ \frac{k_{hs}}{k_s}\frac{\partial \theta_{hs}}{\partial n} = \frac{\partial \theta_s}{\partial n} \end{cases} \text{at heater surface} \quad (20)$$

$\psi = 0, \omega = -\frac{\partial^2 \psi}{\partial n^2},$ $\begin{cases} \theta_f = \theta_s \\ \frac{\partial \theta_f}{\partial n} = \frac{\lambda_s}{\lambda_f}\frac{\partial \theta_s}{\partial n} \end{cases}$ at finned heat sink surface

$\begin{cases} \theta_f = \theta_{pm}, \\ \frac{\partial \theta_f}{\partial n} = \frac{k_{pm}}{k_f}\frac{\partial \theta_{pm}}{\partial n}, \end{cases}$ $\begin{cases} \psi_f = \psi_{pm}, \\ \frac{\partial \psi_f}{\partial n} = \frac{\partial \psi_{pm}}{\partial n}, \end{cases}$ $\begin{cases} \omega_f = \omega_{pm}, \\ \frac{\partial \omega_f}{\partial n} = \frac{\partial \omega_{pm}}{\partial n} \end{cases}$ at porous fins/fluid interface

$\psi = 0, \omega = -\frac{\partial^2 \psi}{\partial y^2},$ $\begin{cases} \theta_s = \theta_{pm}, \\ \frac{\partial \theta_s}{\partial n} = \frac{k_{pm}}{k_s}\frac{\partial \theta_{pm}}{\partial n} \end{cases}$ at porous fins/solid heat sink interface

Here, $Ra = \rho_f g \beta \Delta T H^3 / (\alpha_f \mu)$ is the Rayleigh number, $Pr = \mu/(\rho_f \alpha_f)$ is the Prandtl number, and $Da = K/H^2$ is the Darcy number.

3. Solution Technique

The formulated partial differential Equations (12)–(19) with additional conditions (20) have been worked out by the finite difference technique of the second-order accuracy using the uniform mesh [3,4,10]. For the discretization of the convective and diffusive members, we applied the finite differences of the second-order accuracy. The energy and vorticity equations were worked out using the Samarskii locally one-dimensional technique. The approximated relations were resolved by the Thomas method. Equations (12) and (17) were approximated employing the five-point differences. Obtained relations were carried out by the successive over relaxation technique. The described numerical procedure was included in the in-house computational code developed using C++ programming language. The created computational code was verified comprehensively using numerical data of other authors and mesh sensitivity analysis. It should be noted that the developed code can solve the conjugate natural convection problems for different fins numbers, fins materials, and geometry in laminar regimes of fluid flow and heat transfer.

The developed numerical algorithm was then verified for different grids at $Ra = 10^5$ and $Pr = 6.82$. Figure 2 demonstrates an influence of the grid characteristics on the mean Nusselt number at the heat sink surface.

Considering this impact of the mesh characteristics, the uniform mesh of 200×100 elements were chosen for further analysis.

Validation of the created computational program was performed for different model problems. The first problem [19] is the conjugate thermal convection in a closed cabinet with a thermally conducting wall of finite thickness. Dependences of the mean Nusselt number on the Rayleigh number, heat conductivity ratio, and solid wall thickness in comparison with numerical data [19] are shown in Figure 3.

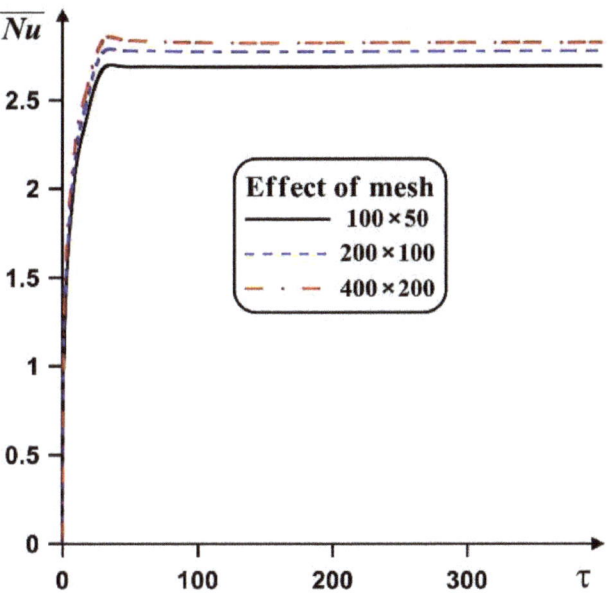

Figure 2. Time dependences of mean Nusselt number with grid parameters for $Pr = 6.82$ ans $Ra = 10^5$.

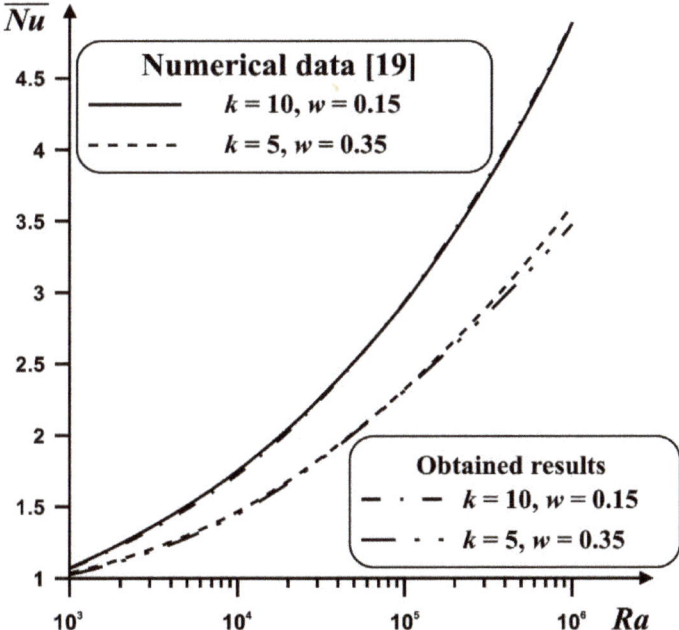

Figure 3. Dependences of the mean Nusselt number on Ra, heat conductivity ratio, and solid wall thickness in comparison with the numerical data [19].

In the case of porous medium, the validation was performed for the problem of natural convection of viscous liquid in a differentially heated cabinet which was partially saturated with porous material. Figure 4 demonstrates a good agreement between the obtained results and computational data [20] for streamlines and isotherms at $Da = 10^{-5}$ and $Ra = 10^6$.

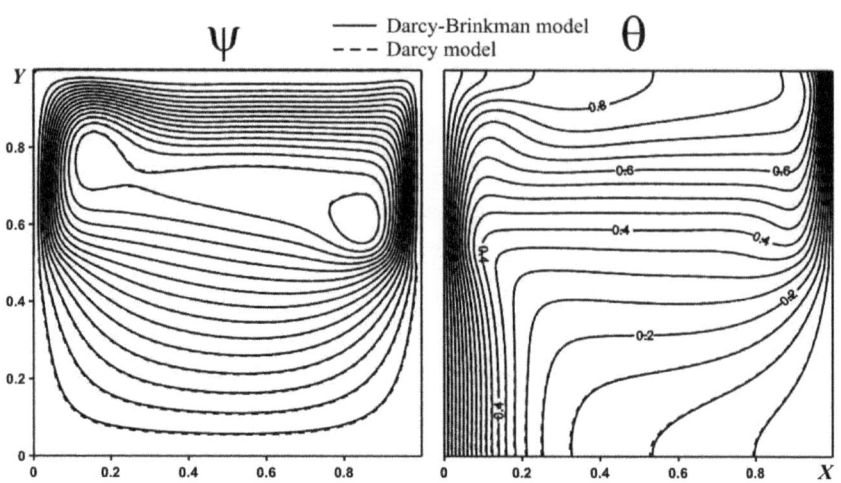

Figure 4. Streamlines ψ and isotherms θ at $Da = 10^{-5}$ and $Ra = 10^6$: these obtained results have a good agreement with data from [20] (see Figure 2c in [20]).

This performed validation demonstrates that the developed numerical code helps to correctly solve the conjugate convective heat transfer problems for clear and porous media. Therefore, this code was employed for calculations of convective–conductive energy transfer in a closed electronic cabinet, as presented in Figure 1.

4. Results and Discussion

Numerical solution of the considered problem was obtained for $Ra = 10^5$, $Pr = 6.82$, $Da = 10^{-5}$, and $\varepsilon = 0.8$, as well as for a different fins number, fins material, and fins height. It should be noted that the porosity of a porous medium is defined as the fraction of the total volume of the medium that is occupied by void space [21]. It is well known that, for natural media, the porosity does not normally exceed 0.6. In the present study, the porous material is a man-made material lsuch as metallic foam, where porosity can approach the value 1. The main focus is on the influence of the solid and porous fins on flow structure and energy transport within the closed cabinet.

Authors should highlight that all results were obtained using the developed computational code. This code is a home-made program using non-primitive variables, such as stream function and vorticity (see Equations (12)–(19)). An application of such variables helps to reduce the number of equations as well as the computational time. Moreover, in the present research, the conjugated natural convection problem was solved with boundary conditions of a forth kind by illustrating an equality of temperatures and heat fluxes at interfaces. From the mathematical point of view, an approximation of governing equations and boundary conditions for space coordinates was performed using the second order of accuracy.

Figure 5 shows the streamlines and isotherms within the closed chamber with solid fins. Solid fins are natural obstacles to the liquid flow, which can be confirmed by the formation of reverse flows near the surfaces of these fins. The development of thermal plumes above the fins occurs due to the high thermal conductivity of the material of these solid fins. Material of the solid fins and heat sink is copper. The presence of a solid fin directly above the local heater reflects the ability to form a thermal plume and, as it might seem, to dissipate energy more intensively. If the fins are located at the periphery relative to the energy source, a downward flow with a cold two-dimensional plume from the upper cooling wall is formed in the central part, which also initiates cooling of the energy source. Furthermore, an inclusion of solid fins characterizes a complication of flow structures, namely, a transition between one, two, and three fins reflects a transition between two, four, and eight vortices. The considered constant value of the volumetric heat generation flux in a heater means that a thermal plume cannot be formed in a viscous fluid over the heater and that the descending flow from the upper cooled wall cannot interact (Figure 5b). In the case of three fins, the flow structure is too complex with four major eddies and four secondary eddies of less scale, but the symmetry of the flow structure characterizes a formation of steady mode. Moreover, one can find an interesting interaction between the central thermal plume and two side thermal plumes in the case of two and three fins. The presence of central descending flow illustrates an attraction between the two-side thermal plumes (Figure 5b), while the presence of the central ascending flow illustrates a repulsion between the two-side thermal plumes (Figure 5c).

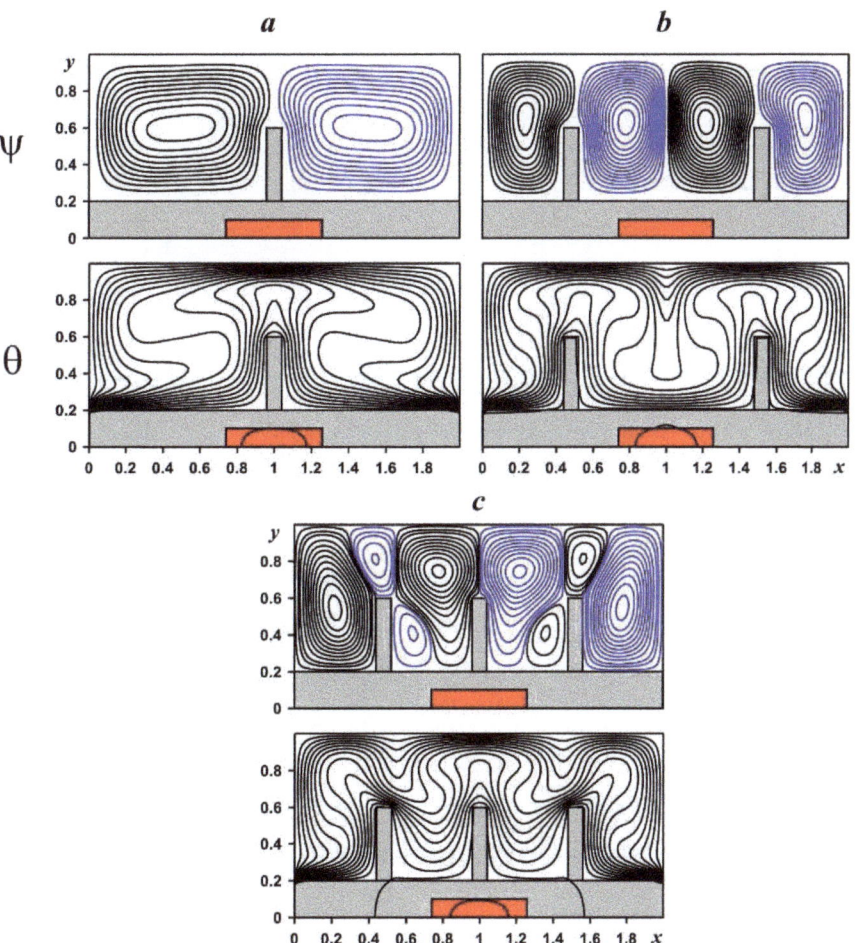

Figure 5. Streamlines and isotherms in a cavity with solid fins: one fin—(**a**), two fins—(**b**), three fins—(**c**).

An introduction of porous fins characterizes a formation of a flow structure with less resistance from these fins. It should be noted that material of porous fins is the copper foam with $Da = 10^{-5}$ and $\varepsilon = 0.8$. It should be noted that fins can be considered as thermal bridges for the formation of thermal plumes, but these bridges are permeable and such a structure helps to intensify the energy removal because the surface of such a porous fin is greater than the surface of a solid fin. As previously mentioned above, for the solid fins, an addition of fins leads to a formation of additional eddies in the closed cabinet (see Figures 5a,b and 6a,b). However, in the case of three porous fins, the hydrodynamic situation is changed, namely, a permeability of porous fins results in a combination of side vortices due to a combination of thermal plumes over these fins. As a result, a formation of only the thermal plume over the central part can reduce the energy removal from the heater in comparison with the two fins. Still, the flow structures for one and two fins in the case of solid and porous material are similar.

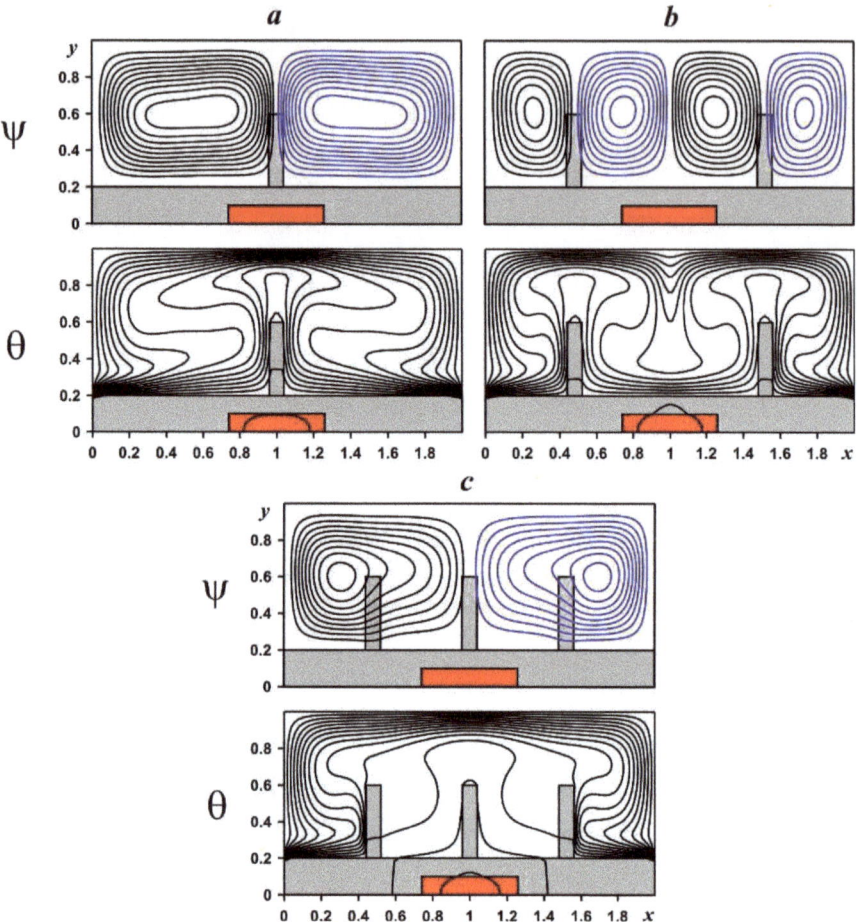

Figure 6. Streamlines and isotherms in a cavity with porous fins at $Da = 10^{-5}$ and $\varepsilon = 0.8$: one fin—(**a**), two fins—(**b**), three fins—(**c**).

Figure 7 demonstrates the time dependences of the mean heater temperature on fins number and height for solid and porous materials. As expected, the addition of fins helps to reduce the heater temperature, but an increase in the fins number has a non-monotonic influence on the heater temperature. At the same time, an increase in the fins height for the solid material results in a reduced heater temperature, while for porous material, one can reveal a temperature diminution for one and two fins. However, for three fins, the behavior is opposite. It should be noted that more intensive cooling of the heater is for two fins when central descending cooling flow interacts with the bottom solid plate. By comparing solid and porous fins, it is possible to conclude that porous permeable obstacles help to strongly decrease the heater temperature, but the influence of the fins number and fins height is non-monotonic.

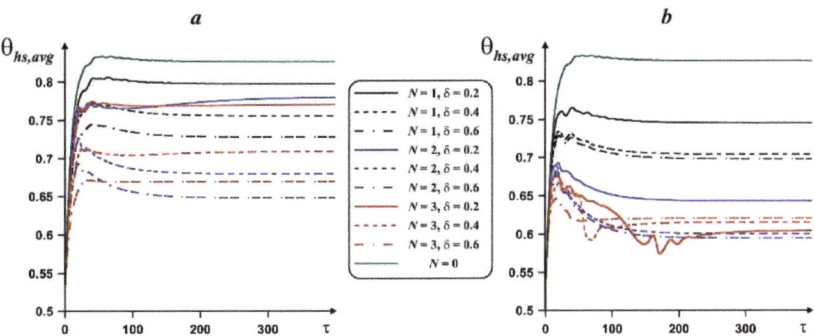

Figure 7. Dependences of average heater temperature on time, fins number and fins height at $Ra = 10^5$: solid fins—(**a**); porous fins at Da = 10^{-5}, $\varepsilon = 0.8$—(**b**).

5. Conclusions

This research considers the natural convection circulation and energy transfer of viscous fluid in a closed electronic cabinet with heat-producing source and finned heat sink. Numerical analysis was conducted by employing the created computational software. The developed in-house computational code using C++ programming language was verified comprehensively on the basis of the mesh sensitivity analysis and numerical data of other authors. It should be noted that usage of non-primitive variables helps to reduce essential computational time and obtain the correct physical results. The influence of fins number, fins height, and fins material on the circulation structure and energy transport was studied. Taking into account the performed detailed analysis, the obtained outcomes are as follows:

- An addition of fins changes the motion structure and energy transfer. In the case of solid material of fins, a growth of the fins number results to a complication of flow structure, while for the porous foam flow nature can be simplified due to the permeability of the fins;
- A growth of the fins height illustrates more essential average heater temperature reduction for the solid fins, while in the case of porous fins, such influence can be reversed;
- An increase in the fins number characterizes a non-monotonic influence on the mean heater temperature. Namely, more essential cooling of the heater occurs in the case of two fins.

Author Contributions: Conceptualization, I.P. and M.A.S.; methodology, M.A.S.; formal analysis, X.H.K.L. and M.A.S.; investigation, X.H.K.L. and M.A.S.; writing—original draft preparation, X.H.K.L., I.P. and M.A.S.; writing—review and editing, X.H.K.L., I.P. and M.A.S.; supervision, M.A.S. All authors have read and agreed to the published version of the manuscript.

Funding: The work was supported by the Grants Council (under the President of the Russian Federation), Grant No. MD-5799.2021.4.

Institutional Review Board Statement: Not applicable.

Informed Consent Statement: Not applicable.

Data Availability Statement: All data are presented in this article.

Conflicts of Interest: The authors declare no conflict of interest.

Nomenclature

c	heat capacity
Da	Darcy number
g	acceleration due to gravity

h	height of the bottom solid plate
H	electronic cabinet height
k	thermal conductivity
K	porous medium permeability
L	electronic cabinet length
N	fins number
Nu	Nusselt number
p	pressure
Pr	Prandtl number
Q	volumetric heat generation density
Ra	Rayleigh number
t	time
T	temperature
T_c	cooled wall temperature
$\bar{u}, \bar{v}$	velocity components
u, v	non-dimensional velocity components
$\bar{x}, \bar{y}$	Cartesian coordinates
x, y	non-dimensional Cartesian coordinates

Greek symbols

α	thermal diffusivity
β	thermal expansion parameter
δ	non-dimensional fins height
ε	porous medium porosity
θ	non-dimensional temperature
μ	dynamic viscosity
ρ	density
τ	non-dimensional time
$\bar{\psi}$	stream function
ψ	non-dimensional stream function
$\bar{\omega}$	vorticity
ω	non-dimensional vorticity

Subscripts

f	fluid
hs	heat source
pm	porous medium
s	solid
spm	solid matrix of porous medium

References

1. Nguyen, D.H.; Ahn, H.S. A comprehensive review on micro/nanoscale surface modification techniques for heat transfer enhancement in heat exchanger. *Int. J. Heat Mass Transf.* **2021**, *178*, 121601. [CrossRef]
2. Mousa, M.H.; Miljkovic, N.; Nawaz, K. Review of heat transfer enhancement techniques for single phase flows. *Renew. Sustain. Energy Rev.* **2021**, *137*, 110566. [CrossRef]
3. Bondareva, N.S.; Sheremet, M.A. Conjugate heat transfer in the PCM-based heat storage system with finned copper profile: Application in electronics cooling. *Int. J. Heat Mass Transf.* **2018**, *124*, 1275–1284. [CrossRef]
4. Asl, K.A.; Hossainpour, S.; Rashidi, M.M.; Sheremet, M.A.; Yang, Z. Comprehensive investigation of solid and porous fins influence on natural convection in an inclined rectangular enclosure. *Int. J. Heat Mass Transf.* **2019**, *133*, 729–744.
5. Buonomo, B.; Cascetta, F.; Manca, O.; Sheremet, M. Heat transfer analysis of rectangular porous fins in local thermal non-equilibrium model. *Appl. Therm. Eng.* **2021**, *195*, 117237. [CrossRef]
6. Hatami, M. Numerical study of nanofluids natural convection in a rectangular cavity including heated fins. *J. Mol. Liq.* **2017**, *233*, 1–8. [CrossRef]
7. Siavashi, M.; Yousofvand, R.; Rezanejad, S. Nanofluid and porous fins effect on natural convection and entropy generation of flow inside a cavity. *Adv. Powder Technol.* **2018**, *29*, 142–156. [CrossRef]
8. Hejri, S.; Malekshah, E.H. Cooling of an electronic processor based on numerical analysis on natural convection and entropy production over a dissipating fin equipped with copper oxide/water nanofluid with Koo-Kleinstreuer-Li model. *Therm. Sci. Eng. Prog.* **2021**, *23*, 100916. [CrossRef]

9. Massoudi, M.D.; Hamida, M.B.B.; Almeshaal, M.A.; Hajlaoui, K. The influence of multiple fins arrangement cases on heat sink efficiency of MHD MWCNT-water nanofluid within tilted T-shaped cavity packed with trapezoidal fins considering thermal emission impact. *Int. Commun. Heat Mass Transf.* **2021**, *126*, 105468. [CrossRef]
10. Astanina, M.S.; Rashidi, M.M.; Sheremet, M.A.; Lorenzini, G. Cooling system with porous finned heat sink for heat-generating element. *Transp. Porous Media* **2020**, *133*, 459–478. [CrossRef]
11. Yan, S.R.; Pordanjani, A.H.; Aghakhani, S.; Goldanlou, A.S.; Afrand, M. Managment of natural convection of nanofluids inside a square enclosure by different nano powder shapes in presence of Fins with different shapes and magnetic field effect. *Adv. Powder Technol.* **2020**, *31*, 2759–2777. [CrossRef]
12. Gireesha, B.J.; Sowmya, G.; Khan, M.I.; Oztop, H.F. Flow of hybrid nanofluid across a permeable longitudinal moving fin along with thermal radiation and natural convection. *Comput. Methods Programs Biomed.* **2020**, *185*, 105166. [CrossRef] [PubMed]
13. Esfe, M.H.; Barzegarian, R.; Bahiraei, M. A 3D numerical study on natural convection flow of nanofluid inside a cubical cavity equipped with porous fins using two-phase mixture model. *Adv. Powder Technol.* **2020**, *31*, 2480–2492. [CrossRef]
14. Kumar, D.S.; Jayavel, S. Optimization of porous fin location and investigation of porosity and permeability effects on hydro-thermal behavior of rectangular microchannel heat sink. *Int. Commun. Heat Mass Transf.* **2021**, *129*, 105737. [CrossRef]
15. Ahmad, I.; Ilyas, H.; Raja, M.A.Z.; Khan, Z.; Shoaib, M. Stochastic numerical computing with Levenberg-Marquardt backpropagation for performance analysis of heat Sink of functionally graded material of the porous fin. *Surf. Interfaces* **2021**, *26*, 101403. [CrossRef]
16. Tu, J.; Qi, C.; Tang, Z.; Tian, Z.; Chen, L. Experimental study on the influence of bionic channel structure and nanofluids on power generation characteristics of waste heat utilisation equipment. *Appl. Therm. Eng.* **2022**, *202*, 117893. [CrossRef]
17. Tu, J.; Qi, C.; Li, K.; Tang, Z. Numerical analysis of flow and heat characteristic around micro-ribbed tube in heat exchanger system. *Powder Technol.* **2022**, *395*, 562–583. [CrossRef]
18. Tang, J.; Qi, C.; Ding, Z.; Afrand, M.; Yan, Y. Thermo-hydraulic performance of nanofluids in a bionic heat sink. *Int. Commun. Heat Mass Transf.* **2021**, *127*, 105492. [CrossRef]
19. Yedder, R.B.; Bilgen, E. Laminar natural convection in inclined enclosures bounded by a solid wall. *Heat Mass Transf.* **1997**, *32*, 455–462. [CrossRef]
20. Singh, A.K.; Thorpe, G.R. Natural convection in a confined fluid overlying a porous layer—A comparison study of different models. *Indian J. Pure Appl. Math.* **1995**, *26*, 81–95.
21. Nield, D.A.; Bejan, A. *Convection in Porous Media*; Springer: New York, NY, USA, 2006.

Article

Numerical Simulation of Solid and Porous Fins' Impact on Heat Transfer Performance in a Differentially Heated Chamber

Le Xuan Hoang Khoa [1], Ioan Pop [2] and Mikhail A. Sheremet [1,3,*]

[1] Butakov Research Center, National Research Tomsk Polytechnic University, 634050 Tomsk, Russia; lexuanhoangkhoa@gmail.com
[2] Department of Mathematics, Babeş-Bolyai University, 400084 Cluj-Napoca, Romania; popm.ioan@yahoo.co.uk
[3] Laboratory on Convective Heat and Mass Transfer, Tomsk State University, 634045 Tomsk, Russia
* Correspondence: sheremet@math.tsu.ru

Abstract: The development of different industrial fields, including mechanical and power engineering and electronics, demands the augmentation of heat transfer in engineering devices. Such enhancement can be achieved by adding extended heat transfer surfaces to the heated walls or heat-generating elements. This investigation is devoted to the numerical analysis of natural convective energy transport in a differentially heated chamber with isothermal vertical walls and a fin system mounted on the heated wall. The developed in-house computational code has been comprehensively validated. The Forchheimer–Brinkman extended Darcy model has been employed for the numerical simulation of transport phenomena in a porous material. The partial differential equations written, employing non-primitive variables, have been worked out by the finite difference technique. Analysis has been performed for solid and porous fins with various fin materials, amounts and heights. It has been revealed that porous fins provide a very good technique for the intensification of energy removal from heated surfaces.

Keywords: natural convection; solid and porous fins; differentially heated cavity; numerical technique

1. Introduction

Energy transport enhancement can be achieved using different passive techniques, including modern heat transfer liquids (non-Newtonian fluids, nanofluids) or extended heat transfer surfaces [1–3]. It should be noted that passive energy transport enhancement techniques are more attractive for engineers and scientists due to low financial expense, low noise and the natural conditions involved in such a system. Nowadays, there are several published papers on the application of extended heat transfer surfaces in engineering devices, including modes of natural, forced or mixed convection [4–15].

In the case of forced and mixed convective energy transport, solid and porous fins are widely used in different channels and tubes [4–10]. Thus, Gong et al. [4] have calculated convective energy transport in a channel with solid and metallic porous fins on the basis of the boundary-value problem for the partial differential equations. Numerical analysis has been conducted by employing the primitive variables and finite volume technique. Authors have revealed that porous fins for the considered problem are not effective due to their low effective thermal conductivity. Kumar and Jayavel [5] have numerically analyzed the influence of porous fins in a rectangular microchannel on heat transference augmentation compared to solid fins. Using primitive variables combined with Navier–Stokes equations for the viscous fluid and the Forchheimer–Brinkman extended Darcy approach for the porous fins, the developed equations have been solved by using commercial CFD software. Obtained outcomes have demonstrated that the introduction of porous fins allows for a reduction in the channel pressure drop. High fin porosity characterizes a low energy transport rate, while an increase in the porous fin permeability diminishes the average heat transfer coefficient. Computational analysis of an air-turbulent convective heat transport

in a system with porous pin fin heat sinks has been performed by Ranjbar et al. [6], using commercial CFD software. The authors revealed that the arrangement and permeability of pin fins have a huge influence on energy transport effectiveness. Vatanparast et al. [7] have scrutinized numerically forced convection in a partially heated horizontal channel with staggered semi-porous fins. Using the primitive variables and finite volume technique, the authors have analyzed the impact of the Reynolds and Darcy numbers, as well as fin sizes and the thermal conductivity ratio on flow structures, entropy generation and the heat transfer regime. It has been ascertained that entropy generation can be increased with the effective fins' thermal conductivity. Kansara et al. [8] have investigated computationally and experimentally forced convection in a channel mounted with fins or porous metal foam for the effectiveness of flat-plate solar collection. Computational research has been conducted employing commercial CFD software, while experiments have been conducted for two collectors, namely, an empty channel and finned channel. Authors have shown that the addition of porous material allows for intensification of the energy transport compared to empty and finned collectors. An analysis of the influence of pin fins on flow and energy transport parameters between two- and three-layer porous laminates has been performed experimentally and numerically using commercial software by Zhang et al. [9]. Authors have found that the shape of the pin fins has an essential influence on system effectiveness. Yerramalle et al. [10] have calculated the mixed convection in a horizontal channel with a porous fin over a heated part of the bottom wall. Analysis of the transport processes in a porous material has been performed employing the local thermal non-equilibrium model. Using commercial software, it has been demonstrated that a rise in the porosity, effective thermal conductivity and Reynolds number results in more essential heat removal from the heater.

According to the above literature review, fin shape, arrangement and material have a significant influence on heat transfer performance in various channels. It is interesting to note that in the case of forced or mixed convection in channels, porous fins can be effective [9,10], or not [4,5]. At the same time, researchers have mainly relied on commercial software for numerical analysis of the solid/porous fins' efficacy.

In the case of the natural convection phenomenon analysis of solid/porous fins' influence on energy transport, performance is not so widespread [11–15]. Thus, Alshuraiaan and Khanafer [11] have examined the influence of a single porous fin mounted on the left vertical heated wall or the bottom horizontal adiabatic wall. Analysis has been conducted numerically using Navier–Stokes equations for clear parts and the Forchheimer–Brinkman extended Darcy model for porous fins with the local thermal equilibrium approach. Using a finite element technique, the authors have found that the use of horizontal porous fins mounted on the vertical heated wall is more effective, and an average Nusselt number depends on the effective thermal conductivity. Martin et al. [12] have analyzed the numerically natural convection of copper/water nanosuspension in a porous medium under the influence of solid fins. Using primitive variables and a finite volume algorithm, the authors have ascertained that porous material saturated with nanosuspension allows for an improvement of the cooling effect. Keramat et al. [13] have scrutinized free convection in a differentially heated enclosure with a solid base and porous fins using commercial software. The Forchheimer–Brinkman extended Darcy approach has been employed for porous fins. The authors have found that a high energy transport rate is achieved for the porous finned cavity at high Rayleigh numbers, while solid fins degrade the energy transport efficacy. Asl et al. [14] have numerically studied the impact of solid and porous fins on heat transfer performance in an inclined, tall cavity. Using primitive variables and the Brinkman-extended Darcy approach for the porous fins, governing equations have been formulated and solved by the finite volume method. It has been concluded that porous fins are more effective, and an increase in the Darcy number augments the energy transport. Some interesting and useful data can also be found in [15–18].

The above review of an application of solid/porous fins in closed chambers with heated surfaces illustrates the efficacy of porous fins. Unfortunately, there is little information about the influence of a porous fin located at the heated wall, or the length of this fin on energy transference enhancement. Moreover, analysis is often performed using commercial software and sometimes in-house computational codes with primitive variables. Therefore, the aim of the present research is a computational analysis of energy transfer performance in a differentially heated chamber with solid and porous horizontal fins, taking into account the fins' number, length, location and material. Analysis has been conducted on the basis of a developed in-house computational technique using non-primitive variables.

2. Mathematical Modeling

The investigation of free convection of a viscous fluid in a square differentially heated chamber with solid or porous fins mounted on the heated vertical wall has been performed numerically. The considered vertically oriented system is presented in Figure 1, where air ($Pr = 0.71$) is circulated within the chamber. Here, $\bar{x}$ and $\bar{y}$ are the dimensional Cartesian coordinates, while the left vertical border is heated and the right one is cooled to maintain constant temperatures T_h and T_c, respectively. The density variation is described by the Boussinesq approximation [19,20]. Moreover, the temperature of the porous solid matrix is equal to the liquid temperature, and as a result, the local thermal equilibrium model is applied. The transport phenomena within the porous material are simulated using the Forchheimer–Brinkman extended Darcy model. It is assumed that viscous dissipation and pressure work are negligible.

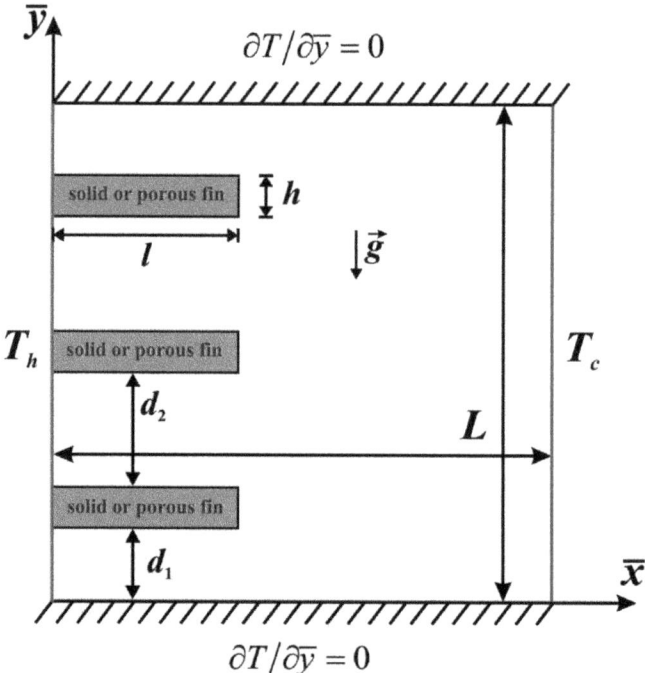

Figure 1. Coordinate system and thermal boundary conditions.

The governing equations in dimensional variables (denoted by an "overbar") are as follows [19,20]:

- For the viscous fluid:

$$\frac{\partial \bar{u}}{\partial \bar{x}} + \frac{\partial \bar{v}}{\partial \bar{y}} = 0, \tag{1}$$

$$\rho\left(\frac{\partial \bar{u}}{\partial t}+\bar{u}\frac{\partial \bar{u}}{\partial \bar{x}}+\bar{v}\frac{\partial \bar{u}}{\partial \bar{y}}\right)=-\frac{\partial p}{\partial \bar{x}}+\mu\left(\frac{\partial^2 \bar{u}}{\partial \bar{x}^2}+\frac{\partial^2 \bar{u}}{\partial \bar{y}^2}\right), \quad (2)$$

$$\rho\left(\frac{\partial \bar{v}}{\partial t}+\bar{u}\frac{\partial \bar{v}}{\partial \bar{x}}+\bar{v}\frac{\partial \bar{v}}{\partial \bar{y}}\right)=-\frac{\partial p}{\partial \bar{y}}+\mu\left(\frac{\partial^2 \bar{v}}{\partial \bar{x}^2}+\frac{\partial^2 \bar{v}}{\partial \bar{y}^2}\right)+\rho g \beta(T-T_c), \quad (3)$$

$$\frac{\partial T}{\partial t}+\bar{u}\frac{\partial T}{\partial \bar{x}}+\bar{v}\frac{\partial T}{\partial \bar{y}}=\frac{k_f}{(\rho c)_f}\left(\frac{\partial^2 T}{\partial \bar{x}^2}+\frac{\partial^2 T}{\partial \bar{y}^2}\right); \quad (4)$$

- For the solid fins:

$$(\rho c)_s \frac{\partial T}{\partial t}=k_s\left(\frac{\partial^2 T}{\partial \bar{x}^2}+\frac{\partial^2 T}{\partial \bar{y}^2}\right); \quad (5)$$

- For the porous fins:

$$\frac{\partial \bar{u}}{\partial \bar{x}}+\frac{\partial \bar{v}}{\partial \bar{y}}=0, \quad (6)$$

$$\rho\left(\frac{1}{\varepsilon}\frac{\partial \bar{u}}{\partial t}+\frac{\bar{u}}{\varepsilon^2}\frac{\partial \bar{u}}{\partial \bar{x}}+\frac{\bar{v}}{\varepsilon^2}\frac{\partial \bar{u}}{\partial \bar{y}}\right)=-\frac{\partial \bar{p}}{\partial \bar{x}}+\frac{\mu}{\varepsilon}\left(\frac{\partial^2 \bar{u}}{\partial \bar{x}^2}+\frac{\partial^2 \bar{u}}{\partial \bar{y}^2}\right)-\frac{\mu}{K}\bar{u}-\frac{c_F \rho}{\varepsilon^{3/2}\sqrt{K}}\bar{u}\sqrt{\bar{u}^2+\bar{v}^2}, \quad (7)$$

$$\rho\left(\frac{1}{\varepsilon}\frac{\partial \bar{v}}{\partial t}+\frac{\bar{u}}{\varepsilon^2}\frac{\partial \bar{v}}{\partial \bar{x}}+\frac{\bar{v}}{\varepsilon^2}\frac{\partial \bar{v}}{\partial \bar{y}}\right)=-\frac{\partial \bar{p}}{\partial \bar{y}}+\frac{\mu}{\varepsilon}\left(\frac{\partial^2 \bar{v}}{\partial \bar{x}^2}+\frac{\partial^2 \bar{v}}{\partial \bar{y}^2}\right)-\frac{\mu}{K}\bar{v}-\frac{c_F \rho}{\varepsilon^{3/2}\sqrt{K}}\bar{v}\sqrt{\bar{u}^2+\bar{v}^2}+ \\ +\rho g \beta(T-T_c), \quad (8)$$

$$\eta\frac{\partial T}{\partial t}+\bar{u}\frac{\partial T}{\partial \bar{x}}+\bar{v}\frac{\partial T}{\partial \bar{y}}=\frac{k_{pm}}{(\rho c)_f}\left(\frac{\partial^2 T}{\partial \bar{x}^2}+\frac{\partial^2 T}{\partial \bar{y}^2}\right), \quad (9)$$

where $\eta=\varepsilon+(1-\varepsilon)\frac{(\rho c)_{spm}}{(\rho c)_f}$ is the overall heat capacity ratio and $k_{pm}=\varepsilon k_f+(1-\varepsilon)k_{spm}$ is the effective thermal conductivity of porous material.

Introducing stream function $\left(\bar{u}=\frac{\partial \bar{\psi}}{\partial \bar{y}}, \bar{v}=-\frac{\partial \bar{\psi}}{\partial \bar{x}}\right)$, vorticity $\left(\bar{\omega}=\frac{\partial \bar{v}}{\partial \bar{x}}-\frac{\partial \bar{u}}{\partial \bar{y}}\right)$ and non-dimensional variables

$$x=\bar{x}/L,\ y=\bar{y}/L,\ \tau=t\sqrt{g\beta(T_h-T_c)/L},\ \theta=(T-T_c)/(T_h-T_c),\ u=\bar{u}/\sqrt{g\beta(T_h-T_c)L}, \\ v=\bar{v}/\sqrt{g\beta(T_h-T_c)L},\ \psi=\bar{\psi}/\sqrt{g\beta(T_h-T_c)L^3},\ \omega=\bar{\omega}\sqrt{L/g\beta(T_h-T_c)}, \quad (10)$$

the governing equations in dimensionless form become:
- For the air cavity:

$$\frac{\partial^2 \psi}{\partial x^2}+\frac{\partial^2 \psi}{\partial y^2}=-\omega, \quad (11)$$

$$\frac{\partial \omega}{\partial \tau}+u\frac{\partial \omega}{\partial x}+v\frac{\partial \omega}{\partial y}=\sqrt{\frac{Pr}{Ra}}\left(\frac{\partial^2 \omega}{\partial x^2}+\frac{\partial^2 \omega}{\partial y^2}\right)+\frac{\partial \theta}{\partial x}, \quad (12)$$

$$\frac{\partial \theta}{\partial \tau}+u\frac{\partial \theta}{\partial x}+v\frac{\partial \theta}{\partial y}=\frac{1}{\sqrt{Ra\cdot Pr}}\left(\frac{\partial^2 \theta}{\partial x^2}+\frac{\partial^2 \theta}{\partial y^2}\right); \quad (13)$$

- For the solid fins:

$$\frac{\partial \theta}{\partial \tau}=\frac{\alpha_s/\alpha_f}{\sqrt{Ra\cdot Pr}}\left(\frac{\partial^2 \theta}{\partial x^2}+\frac{\partial^2 \theta}{\partial y^2}\right); \quad (14)$$

- For the porous fins:

$$\frac{\partial^2 \psi}{\partial x^2}+\frac{\partial^2 \psi}{\partial y^2}=-\omega, \quad (15)$$

$$\varepsilon\frac{\partial \omega}{\partial \tau}+u\frac{\partial \omega}{\partial x}+v\frac{\partial \omega}{\partial y}=\varepsilon\sqrt{\frac{Pr}{Ra}}\left(\frac{\partial^2 \omega}{\partial x^2}+\frac{\partial^2 \omega}{\partial y^2}-\frac{\varepsilon}{Da}\omega\right)-c_F\sqrt{\frac{\varepsilon}{Da}}\omega\sqrt{u^2+v^2}- \\ -\frac{c_F}{\sqrt{u^2+v^2}}\sqrt{\frac{\varepsilon}{Da}}\left\{v^2\frac{\partial v}{\partial x}-u^2\frac{\partial u}{\partial y}+2uv\frac{\partial u}{\partial x}\right\}+\varepsilon^2\frac{\partial \theta}{\partial x}, \quad (16)$$

$$\eta\frac{\partial\theta}{\partial\tau}+u\frac{\partial\theta}{\partial x}+v\frac{\partial\theta}{\partial y}=\frac{k_{pm}/k_f}{\sqrt{Ra\cdot Pr}}\left(\frac{\partial^2\theta}{\partial x^2}+\frac{\partial^2\theta}{\partial y^2}\right). \tag{17}$$

The applied initial and boundary conditions are:

$$\tau=0: \quad \psi=0, \omega=0, \theta=0.5;$$
$$\tau>0:$$

$$\psi=0, \frac{\partial\psi}{\partial x}=0, \theta=1 \text{ at } x=0, 0\leq y\leq 1,$$
$$\psi=0, \frac{\partial\psi}{\partial x}=0, \theta=0 \text{ at } x=1, 0\leq y\leq 1,$$
$$\psi=0, \frac{\partial\psi}{\partial y}=0, \frac{\partial\theta}{\partial y}=0 \text{ at } y=0 \text{ and } y=1, 0\leq x\leq 1,$$

$$\left|\begin{array}{l}\psi=0,\\ \frac{\partial\psi}{\partial n}=0,\end{array}\right. \begin{cases}\theta_f=\theta_s\\ \frac{\partial\theta_f}{\partial n}=\frac{k_s}{k_f}\frac{\partial\theta_s}{\partial n}\end{cases} \text{at solid fins surface} \tag{18}$$

$$\begin{cases}\theta_f=\theta_{pm},\\ \frac{\partial\theta_f}{\partial n}=\frac{k_{pm}}{k_f}\frac{\partial\theta_{pm}}{\partial n},\end{cases}\begin{cases}\psi_f=\psi_{pm},\\ \frac{\partial\psi_f}{\partial n}=\frac{\partial\psi_{pm}}{\partial n},\end{cases}\begin{cases}\omega_f=\omega_{pm},\\ \frac{\partial\omega_f}{\partial n}=\frac{\partial\omega_{pm}}{\partial n}\end{cases}\text{at porous fins/fluid interface.}$$

Here, $Ra=\rho_f g\beta(T_h-T_c)L^3/\left(\alpha_f\mu\right)$ is the Rayleigh number, $Pr=\mu/\left(\rho_f\alpha_f\right)$ is the Prandtl number, $Da=K/L^2$ is the Darcy number and $c_F=\frac{1.75}{\sqrt{150}}$ is the Forchheimer parameter.

3. Numerical Technique

The boundary-value problem under consideration and described by Equations (11)–(18) was solved by the finite difference method [19–21]. Difference schemes of second-order accuracy were used for diffusive and convective terms, while a first-order scheme was applied for the time derivatives. The used difference scheme for the clear fluid can be found in [20]. In the case of porous fins, the analysis of the vorticity Equation (16) was conducted using the Samarskii locally one-dimensional difference scheme involving two time levels as follows:

$$\varepsilon\frac{\omega_{i,j}^{k+1/2}-\omega_{i,j}^k}{\Delta\tau}+u_{i,j}^{k+1}\frac{\omega_{i+1,j}^{k+1/2}-\omega_{i-1,j}^{k+1/2}}{2h_x}-\left|u_{i,j}^{k+1}\right|\frac{\omega_{i+1,j}^{k+1/2}-2\omega_{i,j}^{k+1/2}+\omega_{i-1,j}^{k+1/2}}{2h_x}=$$
$$=\varepsilon\sqrt{\frac{Pr}{Ra}}\left(1+\left|u_{i,j}^{k+1}\right|\sqrt{\frac{Ra}{Pr}}\frac{h_x}{2\varepsilon}\right)^{-1}\frac{\omega_{i+1,j}^{k+1/2}-2\omega_{i,j}^{k+1/2}+\omega_{i-1,j}^{k+1/2}}{h_x^2}-$$
$$-\left(\frac{\varepsilon^2}{Da}\sqrt{\frac{Pr}{Ra}}+c_F\sqrt{\frac{\varepsilon}{Da}}\sqrt{\left(u_{i,j}^{k+1}\right)^2+\left(v_{i,j}^{k+1}\right)^2}\right)\omega_{i,j}^{k+1/2}+\varepsilon^2\frac{\theta_{i+1,j}^k-\theta_{i-1,j}^k}{2h_x}, \tag{19}$$

$$\varepsilon\frac{\omega_{i,j}^{k+1}-\omega_{i,j}^{k+1/2}}{\Delta\tau}+v_{i,j}^{k+1}\frac{\omega_{i,j+1}^{k+1}-\omega_{i,j-1}^{k+1}}{2h_y}-\left|v_{i,j}^{k+1}\right|\frac{\omega_{i,j+1}^{k+1}-2\omega_{i,j}^{k+1}+\omega_{i,j-1}^{k+1}}{2h_y}=$$
$$=\varepsilon\sqrt{\frac{Pr}{Ra}}\left(1+\left|v_{i,j}^{k+1}\right|\sqrt{\frac{Ra}{Pr}}\frac{h_y}{2\varepsilon}\right)^{-1}\frac{\omega_{i,j+1}^{k+1}-2\omega_{i,j}^{k+1}+\omega_{i,j-1}^{k+1}}{h_y^2}-\frac{c_F}{\sqrt{\left(u_{i,j}^{k+1}\right)^2+\left(v_{i,j}^{k+1}\right)^2+\kappa}}\sqrt{\frac{\varepsilon}{Da}}\times \tag{20}$$
$$\times\left\{\left(v_{i,j}^{k+1}\right)^2\frac{v_{i+1,j}^{k+1}-v_{i-1,j}^{k+1}}{2h_x}-\left(u_{i,j}^{k+1}\right)^2\frac{u_{i,j+1}^{k+1}-u_{i,j-1}^{k+1}}{2h_y}+2u_{i,j}^{k+1}v_{i,j}^{k+1}\frac{u_{i+1,j}^{k+1}-u_{i-1,j}^{k+1}}{2h_x}\right\}.$$

Here, i and j are the mesh nodes along the x and y coordinates, k is the time level number, $\Delta\tau$ is the time step, h_x and h_y are the mesh steps along the x and y coordinates and κ is a regularization parameter [22].

In the case of energy Equation (17) within the porous fins, the used difference scheme is similar to the previous one. Namely, the Samarskii locally one-dimensional difference algorithm involving two time levels is employed as follows:

$$\eta\frac{\theta_{i,j}^{k+1/2}-\theta_{i,j}^k}{\Delta\tau}+u_{i,j}^{k+1}\frac{\theta_{i+1,j}^{k+1/2}-\theta_{i-1,j}^{k+1/2}}{2h_x}-\left|u_{i,j}^{k+1}\right|\frac{\theta_{i+1,j}^{k+1/2}-2\theta_{i,j}^{k+1/2}+\theta_{i-1,j}^{k+1/2}}{2h_x}=$$
$$=\frac{k_{pm}/k_f}{\sqrt{Ra\cdot Pr}}\left(1+\left|u_{i,j}^{k+1}\right|\frac{h_x\sqrt{Ra\cdot Pr}}{2k_{pm}/k_f}\right)^{-1}\frac{\theta_{i+1,j}^{k+1/2}-2\theta_{i,j}^{k+1/2}+\theta_{i-1,j}^{k+1/2}}{h_x^2}, \tag{21}$$

$$\eta \frac{\theta_{i,j}^{k+1} - \theta_{i,j}^{k+1/2}}{\Delta \tau} + v_{i,j}^{k+1} \frac{\theta_{i,j+1}^{k+1} - \theta_{i,j-1}^{k+1}}{2h_y} - \left| v_{i,j}^{k+1} \right| \frac{\theta_{i,j+1}^{k+1} - 2\theta_{i,j}^{k+1} + \theta_{i,j-1}^{k+1}}{2h_y} =$$
$$= \frac{k_{pm}/k_f}{\sqrt{Ra \cdot Pr}} \left(1 + \left| v_{i,j}^{k+1} \right| \frac{h_y \sqrt{Ra \cdot Pr}}{2k_{pm}/k_f} \right)^{-1} \frac{\theta_{i,j+1}^{k+1} - 2\theta_{i,j}^{k+1} + \theta_{i,j-1}^{k+1}}{h_y^2}. \tag{22}$$

The difference scheme for the stream function within the porous medium is the same as in a clear fluid. Therefore, this scheme can be found in [20].

The vorticity at the borders was defined using the Pearson formula. The written difference schemes for vorticity and temperature (see Equations (19)–(22)) were solved using the Thomas algorithm.

It should be noted that the considered problem (see Equations (11)–(17)) was solved as a conjugate problem. In the case of solid fins, Equations (11) and (12) were solved within the air cavity. Energy Equation (13) and heat conduction Equation (14) were solved within the air cavity and solid fins, respectively. The solution was performed sequentially, taking into account the coordinates' directions and at the solid–fluid interface, the thermal boundary conditions of the fourth kind $\left(\theta_f = \theta_s, \frac{\partial \theta_f}{\partial n} = \frac{k_s}{k_f} \frac{\partial \theta_s}{\partial n} \right)$ were used. In the case of porous fins, all equations, including Poisson equations for the stream function (Equations (11) and (15)), vorticity equations (Equations (12) and (16)), and energy equations (Equations (13) and (17)) were solved within the air cavity and porous fins. The solution was performed sequentially, and at the porous–fluid interface, the boundary conditions of the fourth kind were used for all variables

$$\begin{cases} \theta_f = \theta_{pm}, \\ \frac{\partial \theta_f}{\partial n} = \frac{k_{pm}}{k_f} \frac{\partial \theta_{pm}}{\partial n}; \end{cases} \begin{cases} \psi_f = \psi_{pm}, \\ \frac{\partial \psi_f}{\partial n} = \frac{\partial \psi_{pm}}{\partial n}; \end{cases} \begin{cases} \omega_f = \omega_{pm}, \\ \frac{\partial \omega_f}{\partial n} = \frac{\partial \omega_{pm}}{\partial n}. \end{cases}$$

The solution of the coupled set of discretized equations at each time step begins by first solving the Poisson equation for the stream function. Thereafter, the vorticity transport equation and the energy equation can be solved.

The developed in-house computational code was comprehensively validated by employing the computational and experimental outcomes of other researchers. The verification is widely presented in [19–21].

The developed computational algorithm was verified for various meshes in the case of one porous copper fin placed in the center of the left vertical border at $Ra = 10^5$, $Pr = 0.71$, $Da = 10^{-2}$ and $\varepsilon = 0.9$. Figure 2 demonstrates the influence of the mesh characteristics on the mean Nusselt number and fluid flow rate. Comparing values of the average Nusselt number and fluid flow rate at steady state for different mesh parameters, we have $\overline{Nu}|_{50 \times 50} = 7.16$, $\overline{Nu}|_{100 \times 100} = 7.22$, $\overline{Nu}|_{200 \times 200} = 7.25$ and $|\psi|_{max}|_{50 \times 50} = 0.051$, $|\psi|_{max}|_{100 \times 100} = 0.0517$, $|\psi|_{max}|_{200 \times 200} = 0.0516$. Taking into account small differences between the considered meshes for $\overline{Nu}$ and $|\psi|_{max}$, e.g., $\frac{\overline{Nu}|_{200 \times 200} - \overline{Nu}|_{100 \times 100}}{\overline{Nu}|_{200 \times 200}} \cdot 100\% = 0.4\%$ and $\frac{|\psi|_{max}|_{100 \times 100} - |\psi|_{max}|_{200 \times 200}}{|\psi|_{max}|_{200 \times 200}} \cdot 100\% = 0.2\%$, and time consuming calculations for the mesh of 200 × 200 elements, the uniform mesh of 100 × 100 elements was chosen for the numerical simulation of the fins' influence on heat transfer performance due to good accuracy and resolution.

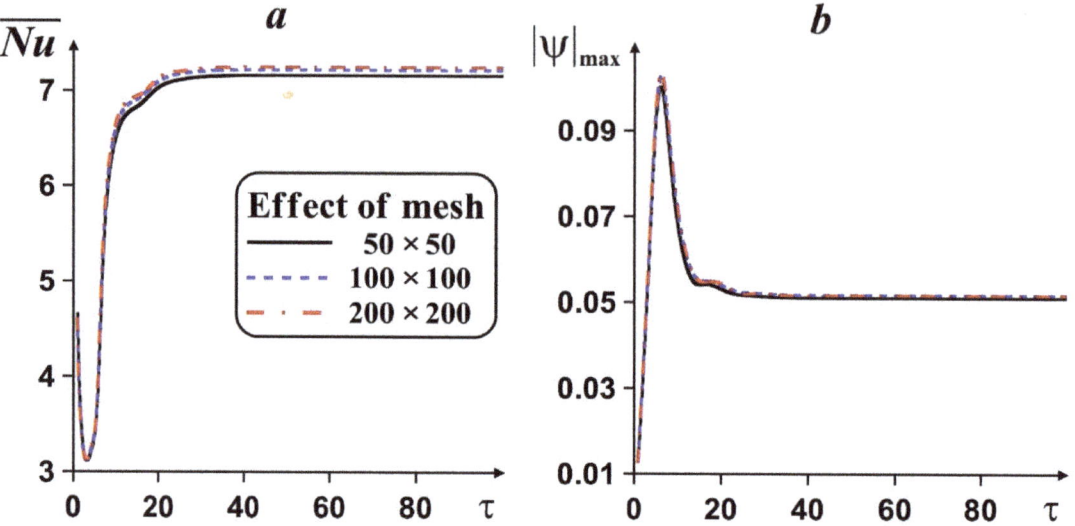

Figure 2. Evolution in time of mean Nusselt number (**a**) and fluid flow rate (**b**) with mesh parameters for $Ra = 10^5$, $Pr = 0.71$, $Da = 10^{-2}$ and $\varepsilon = 0.9$.

4. Results and Discussion

Numerical analysis was performed for $Ra = 10^5$, $Pr = 0.71$, solid and porous fins, $Da = 10^{-4}$–10^{-2}, $\varepsilon = 0.9$, $h/L = 0.1$, different numbers of fins (N), locations of fins (described by $\delta_1 = d_1/L$, the non-dimensional distance between the bottom wall and bottom border of the nearest fin, and $\delta_2 = d_2/L$, the non-dimensional distance between the upper border of one fin and the bottom border of the nearest fin) and lengths of fins (described by $\gamma = l/L$, the non-dimensional length of the fin). The material of solid fins is copper, while the material of porous fins is copper foam. The present investigation was devoted to the analysis of the impact of solid and porous fins and their characteristics on flow behavior and heat transfer in the chamber.

Figure 3 demonstrates streamlines and isotherms in a chamber without fins and with solid copper fins for $Ra = 10^5$, $Pr = 0.71$. In the case of a differentially heated clear cavity without fins (Figure 3a), one can find the formation of a typical flow structure that is known as "cat's eyes" [23]. For this regime, an ascending flow is formed near the heated wall, and a descending flow can be found near the cooled border, while two oppositely rotating eddies are formed in the center of the cavity. At the same time, the temperature field illustrates the formation of two thermal boundary layers near two vertical walls with a stratified core in the central part, where heating occurs from the upper part to the bottom one. The addition of one solid fin (Figure 3b) acts as a natural obstacle that deforms the flow and leads to the formation of a single convective cell in the central part of the right half of the cavity. Such a flow structure is defined by significant heating of the upper part, not only from the left isothermal wall, but also from the solid fin of high thermal conductivity. Therefore, isotherms are not presented within this solid element. The further addition of solid fins to the cavity results in a different deformation of flow structure and more essential heating of the left half of the chamber. As a result, the fluid volume decreases with the inclusion of solid fins. It is worth noting that a huge temperature difference can be found on the vertical end of the bottom fin, where a high density of isotherms is monitored.

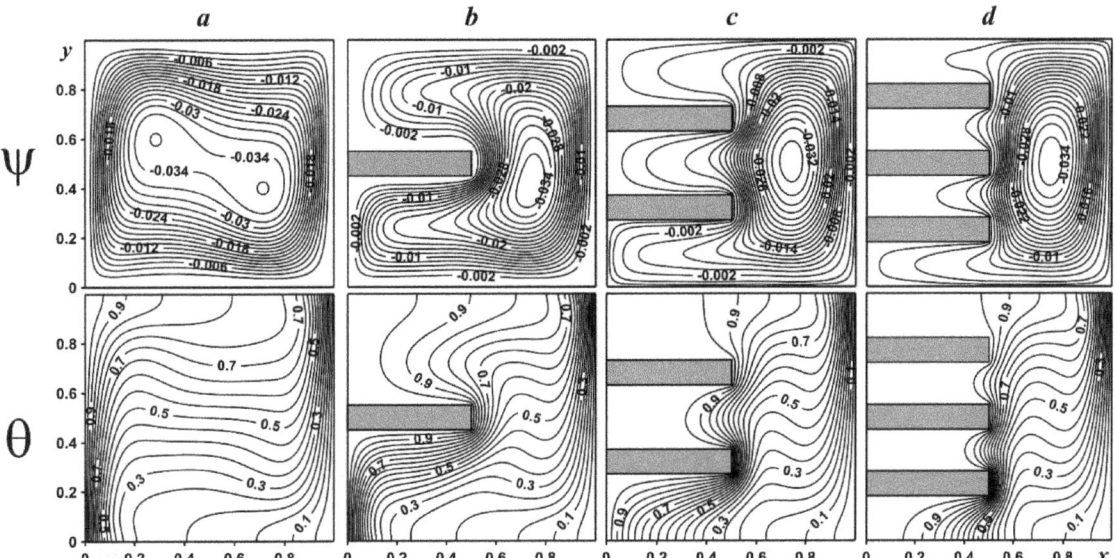

Figure 3. Streamlines and isotherms in a cavity with solid fins: without fins (**a**); one fin (**b**); two fins (**c**); three fins (**d**).

Figures 4 and 5 demonstrate isolines of stream function and temperature within the enclosure with several porous fins for $Da = 10^{-4}$ in Figure 4 and for $Da = 10^{-2}$ in Figure 5. Porous fins are made of metallic copper foam with $\varepsilon = 0.9$. The addition of porous, permeable fins reduces flow resistance from this obstacle and also increases the heat transfer surface. Therefore, air can circulate not only within the chamber, but also within the porous material, and air flow strength, in this case, is greater than for solid fins (Figure 3). Moreover, the addition of porous fins allows for the intensification of the heat removal from the vertical heated surface, whilst air going through these fins moves heat away, and as a result, the upper part of the cavity is heated significantly. As it can be seen, the same effect could be obtained by using a single porous fin placed in the bottom part of the chamber.

An increment in the porous fin permeability (see Figure 5) results in the strengthening of the convective flow and heat transport within the cabinet. More essential heating of the chamber can be found for $Da = 10^{-2}$ comparing Figures 4 and 5 due to more intensive air circulation.

Figure 6 shows the time evolution of the average Nusselt number on the right vertical wall and air flow strength within the chamber with either solid or porous fins and without fins. It is interesting to note that the addition of solid or porous fins intensifies the heat removal, namely, the average Nusselt number increases. In the case of solid fins, this heat transfer enhancement is not so significant. Moreover, the addition of solid fins has a non-monotonic influence on the average Nusselt number, which illustrates an essential influence of the fins' location on the heated vertical border. Whilst the use of porous fins achieves an increase in the average Nusselt number (for about 73%), solid fins lead to an increase of only 5%.

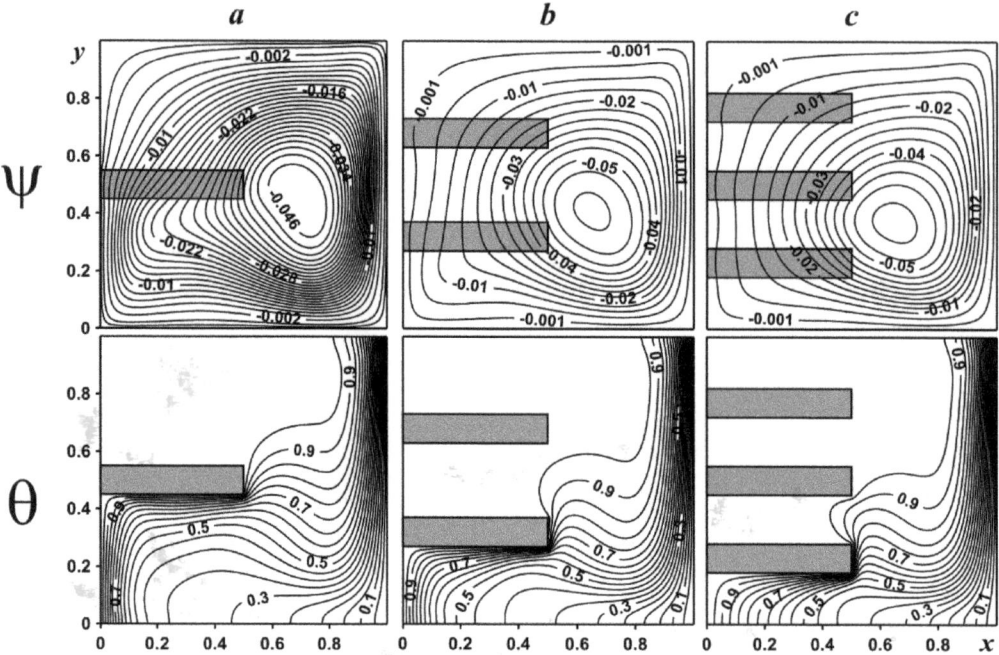

Figure 4. Streamlines and isotherms in a cavity with porous copper fins at $Da = 10^{-4}$: one fin (**a**); two fins (**b**); three fins (**c**).

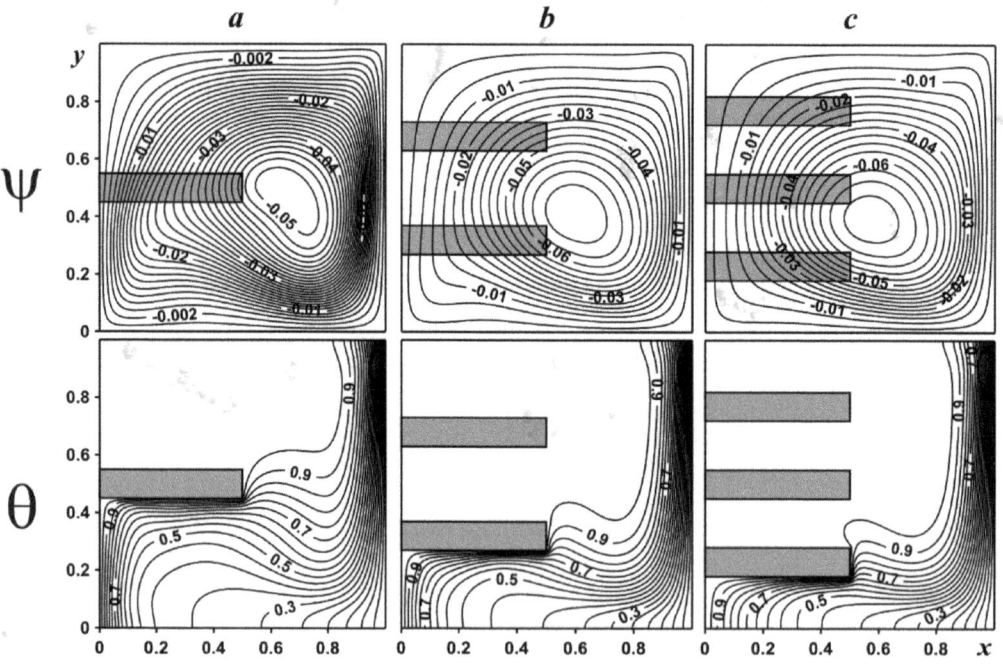

Figure 5. Streamlines and isotherms in a cavity with porous copper fins at $Da = 10^{-2}$: one fin (**a**); two fins (**b**); three fins (**c**).

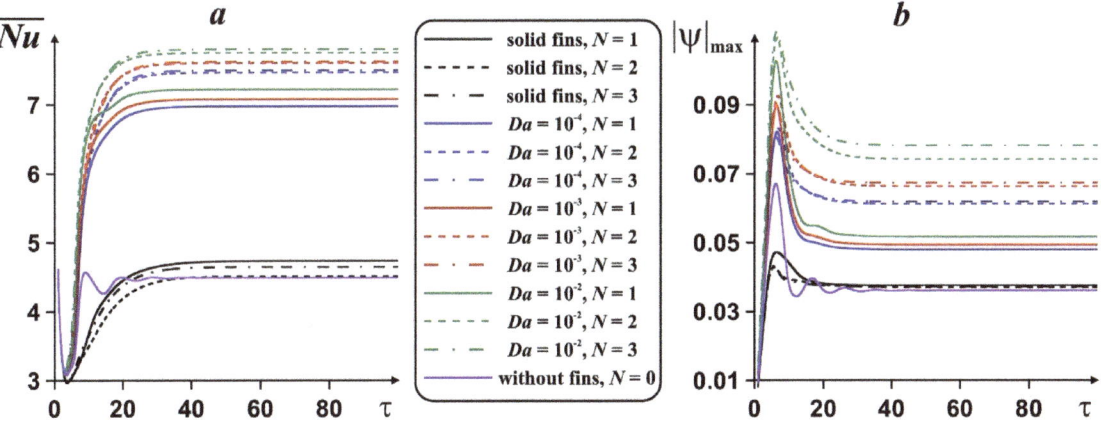

Figure 6. Time evolution of average Nusselt number (**a**) and fluid flow rate (**b**) on number of fins, material of fins and Darcy number for porous fins.

An increase in the number of porous fins leads to an increase in the mean Nusselt number compared to the use of a single fin. The effect of using two fins in the increase in $\overline{Nu}$ instead of one is much more intensive than that of using $N = 3$ instead of $N = 2$. An increase in the Darcy number results in enhancement of the energy transport rate. At the same time, the addition of solid fins causes a weak increment of air flow rate, while in the case of porous fins, one can find convective flow intensification that increases with the increase in Da and N.

Taking into account a possible essential intensification of energy removal from the heated surface using porous fins, a more detailed analysis was performed for one and two porous fins with respect to the location and length of the fins. Figure 7 demonstrates the influence of one porous fin position and length on the average Nusselt number and air flow rate. In general, an increase in the porous fin length results in an intensification of convective heat transfer; however, between $\gamma = 0.5$ and $\gamma = 0.7$, some non-monotonic influence is observed. At the same time, for $\gamma (= l/L) > 0.5$ (see Figure 1), an increase in δ_1 results in the minimization of the average Nusselt number, while in this case, maximum $\overline{Nu}$ can be found for the lower value of δ_1, i.e., $\delta_1 = 0.1$. Non-monotonic influence of δ_1 is observed for $\gamma < 0.5$. In particular, an increase in γ from 0.1 to 0.5 illustrates a decrease in the y-coordinate of the fin's location where the average Nusselt number has the maximum value. Namely, for $\gamma = 0.1$ maximum $\overline{Nu}$ can be found for $\delta_1 = 0.3$, for $\gamma = 0.3$ maximum $\overline{Nu}$ is achieved for $\delta_1 = 0.3$ and for $\gamma = 0.5$ maximum $\overline{Nu}$ is achieved for $\delta_1 = 0.2$. As a result, more intensive heat removal from the vertical heated wall can be achieved by using a single long porous fin placed in the bottom part of this wall. The behavior of the air flow intensity with the mentioned parameters is shown in Figure 7b, where for $\gamma > 0.3$, the increase in δ_1 results in a minimization of flow rate, whilst for $\gamma = 0.1$ and $\gamma = 0.3$ maximum $|\psi|_{max}$ can be found for $\delta_1 = 0.2$. At the same time, an increase in γ from 0.1 to 0.5 leads to a rise of $|\psi|_{max}$, while an increase in γ from 0.5 to 0.9 leads to a reduction in $|\psi|_{max}$.

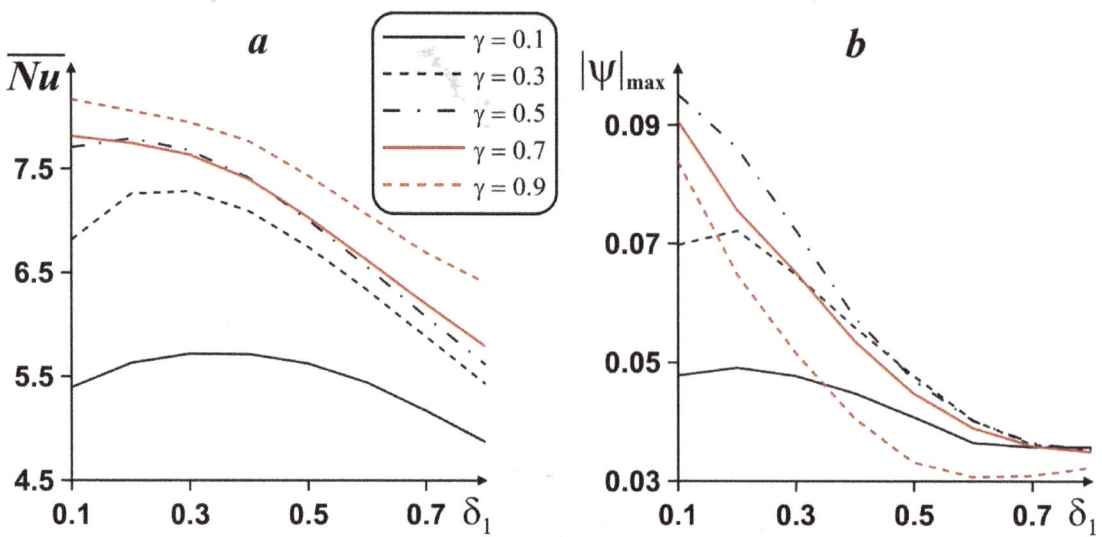

Figure 7. Dependence of mean Nusselt number (**a**) and fluid flow rate (**b**) for one porous fin on distance from the bottom wall to the fin and length of the fin, for $Da = 10^{-2}$.

Table 1 demonstrates the influence of the location and length of two porous fins on the average Nusselt number. As it has been mentioned in the case of one porous fin, the increase in the fin length leads to an increase in $\overline{Nu}$. For two fins with equal length ($\gamma = 0.1$), maximum $\overline{Nu}$ can be achieved for $\delta_1 = \delta_2 = 0.2$, while for $\gamma = 0.3$ and $\gamma = 0.5$, maximum $\overline{Nu}$ is achieved for $\delta_1 = \delta_2 = 0.1$. Such behavior has also been mentioned for one fin; namely, the increase in fin length leads to a reduction in the y-coordinate at the position where $\overline{Nu}$ becomes maximum. At the same time, the use of two porous fins allows for the enhancement of heat removal by about 10%.

Table 1. Average Nusselt number at vertical wall in the case of two porous fins for distance between fins, distance from the bottom wall to the first fin and length of fins when $Da = 0.01$.

		$\delta_1 = 0.1$	$\delta_1 = 0.2$	$\delta_1 = 0.3$	$\delta_1 = 0.4$	$\delta_1 = 0.5$	$\delta_1 = 0.6$
$\gamma = 0.1$	$\delta_2 = 0.1$	6.118	6.214	6.163	6.011	5.783	5.503
	$\delta_2 = 0.2$	6.204	6.243	6.137	5.944	5.713	–
	$\delta_2 = 0.3$	6.176	6.163	6.021	5.837	–	–
	$\delta_2 = 0.4$	6.054	6.007	5.878	–	–	–
	$\delta_2 = 0.5$	5.861	5.829	–	–	–	–
	$\delta_2 = 0.6$	5.646	–	–	–	–	–
$\gamma = 0.3$	$\delta_2 = 0.1$	7.677	7.628	7.451	7.16	6.78	6.348
	$\delta_2 = 0.2$	7.644	7.596	7.432	7.146	6.767	–
	$\delta_2 = 0.3$	7.557	7.55	7.395	7.118	–	–
	$\delta_2 = 0.4$	7.467	7.485	7.341	–	–	–
	$\delta_2 = 0.5$	7.353	7.388	–	–	–	–
	$\delta_2 = 0.6$	7.17	–	–	–	–	–
$\gamma = 0.5$	$\delta_2 = 0.1$	7.871	7.798	7.688	7.427	7.025	6.572
	$\delta_2 = 0.2$	7.828	7.787	7.699	7.436	7.03	–
	$\delta_2 = 0.3$	7.789	7.802	7.711	7.436	–	–
	$\delta_2 = 0.4$	7.778	7.829	7.71	–	–	–
	$\delta_2 = 0.5$	7.796	7.837	–	–	–	–
	$\delta_2 = 0.6$	7.807	–	–	–	–	–

5. Conclusions

Analysis of natural convection in a differentially heated chamber with solid or porous fins has been performed numerically using an in-house computational code developed with C++ programming language. The impact of fins with respect to their structure (solid or porous), number, length and location on the flow field and heat transport has been scrutinized. According to the obtained results, one can highlight that:

- Porous fins are more effective for heat removal compared to solid fins. The addition of solid fins can raise the average Nusselt number by about 5%, while the corresponding increase for porous fins is about 73%;
- An increase in the Darcy number and number of porous fins leads to an increase in the heat transfer rate;
- An increase in fins' length leads to a diminution of the y-coordinate for fins' position with maximum $\overline{Nu}$;
- The addition of two porous fins enhances heat transfer by about 10%.

Author Contributions: Conceptualization, I.P. and M.A.S.; methodology, M.A.S.; formal analysis, L.X.H.K. and M.A.S.; investigation, L.X.H.K. and M.A.S.; writing—original draft preparation, L.X.H.K., I.P. and M.A.S.; writing—review and editing, L.X.H.K., I.P. and M.A.S.; supervision, M.A.S. All authors have read and agreed to the published version of the manuscript.

Funding: The work was supported by the Grants Council (under the President of the Russian Federation), Grant No. MD-5799.2021.4.

Institutional Review Board Statement: Not applicable.

Informed Consent Statement: Not applicable.

Data Availability Statement: All data are presented in this article.

Conflicts of Interest: The authors declare no conflict of interest.

Abbreviation

Nomenclature

C	heat capacity
d_1	distance between the bottom wall and nearest fin
d_2	distance between first and second fins
Da	Darcy number
g	acceleration due to gravity
H	thickness of the fin
k	thermal conductivity
K	porous medium permeability
l	length of the fins
L	cavity size
N	number of fins
Nu	Nusselt number
p	pressure
Pr	Prandtl number
Ra	Rayleigh number
t	time
T	temperature
T_c	cooled wall temperature
T_h	heated wall temperature
$\overline{u}, \overline{v}$	velocity components
u, v	non-dimensional velocity components
$\overline{x}, \overline{y}$	Cartesian coordinates
x, y	non-dimensional Cartesian coordinates

Greek Symbols

α	thermal diffusivity
β	thermal expansion parameter
δ_1	non-dimensional distance between the bottom wall and nearest fin
δ_2	non-dimensional distance between first and second fins
ε	porous medium porosity
θ	non-dimensional temperature
μ	dynamic viscosity
ρ	density
τ	non-dimensional time
$\bar{\psi}$	stream function
ψ	non-dimensional stream function
$\bar{\omega}$	vorticity
ω	non-dimensional vorticity

Subscripts

f	fluid
hs	heat source
pm	porous medium
s	solid
spm	solid matrix of the porous medium

References

1. Sadeghianjahromi, A.; Wang, C.-C. Heat transfer enhancement in fin-and-tube heat exchangers—A review on different mechanisms. *Renew. Sustain. Energy Rev.* **2021**, *137*, 110470. [CrossRef]
2. Husain, S.; Khan, S.A. A review on heat transfer enhancement techniques during natural convection in vertical annular geometry. *Clean. Eng. Technol.* **2021**, *5*, 100333. [CrossRef]
3. Pandya, N.S.; Shah, H.; Molana, M.; Tiwari, A.K. Heat transfer enhancement with nanofluids in plate heat exchangers: A comprehensive review. *Eur. J. Mech. B Fluids* **2020**, *81*, 173–190. [CrossRef]
4. Gong, L.; Li, Y.; Bai, Z.; Xu, M. Thermal performance of micro-channel heat sink with metallic porous/solid compound fin design. *Appl. Therm. Eng.* **2018**, *137*, 288–295. [CrossRef]
5. Kumar, D.S.; Jayavel, S. Optimization of porous fin location and investigation of porosity and permeability effects on hydrothermal behavior of rectangular microchannel heat sink. *Int. Commun. Heat Mass Transf.* **2021**, *129*, 105737. [CrossRef]
6. Ranjbar, A.M.; Pouransari, Z.; Siavashi, M. Improved design of heat sink including porous pin fins with different arrangements: A numerical turbulent flow and heat transfer study. *Appl. Therm. Eng.* **2021**, *198*, 117519. [CrossRef]
7. Vatanparast, M.A.; Hossainpour, S.; Keyhani-Asl, A.; Forouzi, S. Numerical investigation of total entropy generation in a rectangular channel with staggered semi-porous fins. *Int. Commun. Heat Mass Transf.* **2020**, *111*, 104446. [CrossRef]
8. Kansara, R.; Patha, M.; Patel, V.K. Performance assessment of flat-plate solar collector with internal fins and porous media through an integrated approach of CFD and experimentation. *Int. J. Therm. Sci.* **2021**, *165*, 106932. [CrossRef]
9. Zhang, J.; Han, H.Z.; Li, Z.R.; Zhong, H.G. Effect of pin-fin forms on flow and cooling characteristics of three-layer porous laminate. *Appl. Therm. Eng.* **2021**, *194*, 117084. [CrossRef]
10. Yerramalle, V.; Premachandran, B.; Talukdar, P. Mixed convection from a heat source in a channel with a porous insert: A numerical analysis based on local thermal non-equilibrium model. *Therm. Sci. Eng. Prog.* **2021**, *25*, 101010. [CrossRef]
11. Alshuraiaan, B.; Khanafer, K. The effect of the position of the heated thin porous fin on the laminar natural convection heat transfer in a differentially heated cavity. *Int. Commun. Heat Mass Transf.* **2016**, *78*, 190–199. [CrossRef]
12. Martin, E.; Sastre, F.; Velazquez, A.; Bairi, A. Heat transfer enhancement around a finned vertical antenna by means of porous media saturated with Water-Copper nanofluid. *Case Stud. Therm. Eng.* **2021**, *28*, 101555. [CrossRef]
13. Keramat, F.; Azari, A.; Rahideh, H.; Abbasi, M. A CFD parametric analysis of natural convection in an H-shaped cavity with two-sided inclined porous fins. *J. Taiwan Inst. Chem. Eng.* **2020**, *114*, 142–152. [CrossRef]
14. Asl, K.A.; Hossainpour, S.; Rashidi, M.M.; Sheremet, M.A.; Yang, Z. Comprehensive investigation of solid and porous fins influence on natural convection in an inclined rectangular enclosure. *Int. J. Heat Mass Transf.* **2019**, *133*, 729–744.
15. Aly, A.M.; Mohamed, E.M.; Alsedais, N. The magnetic field on a nanofluid flow within a finned cavity containing solid particles. *Case Stud. Therm. Eng.* **2021**, *25*, 100945. [CrossRef]
16. Tu, J.; Qi, C.; Tang, Z.; Tian, Z.; Chen, L. Experimental study on the influence of bionic channel structure and nanofluids on power generation characteristics of waste heat utilisation equipment. *Appl. Therm. Eng.* **2022**, *202*, 117893. [CrossRef]
17. Tu, J.; Qi, C.; Li, K.; Tang, Z. Numerical analysis of flow and heat characteristic around micro-ribbed tube in heat exchanger system. *Powder Technol.* **2022**, *395*, 562–583. [CrossRef]
18. Tang, J.; Qi, C.; Ding, Z.; Afrand, M.; Yan, Y. Thermo-hydraulic performance of nanofluids in a bionic heat sink. *Int. Commun. Heat Mass Transf.* **2021**, *127*, 105492. [CrossRef]

19. Astanina, M.S.; Rashidi, M.M.; Sheremet, M.A.; Lorenzini, G. Cooling system with porous finned heat sink for heat-generating element. *Transp. Porous Media* **2020**, *133*, 459–478. [CrossRef]
20. Sheremet, M.A.; Rashidi, M.M. Thermal convection of nano-liquid in an electronic cabinet with finned heat sink and heat generating element. *Alex. Eng. J.* **2021**, *60*, 2769–2778. [CrossRef]
21. Sheremet, M.A.; Trifonova, T.A. Unsteady conjugate natural convection in a vertical cylinder partially filled with a porous medium. *Numer. Heat Transf. A* **2013**, *64*, 994–1015. [CrossRef]
22. Loenko, D.S.; Sheremet, M.A. Regularization models for natural convection of a pseudoplastic liquid in a closed differentially heated cavity. *Bull. Perm Univ. Phys.* **2021**, *3*, 13–22. [CrossRef]
23. Vahl Davis, G. Natural convection of air in a square cavity: A bench mark numerical solution. *Int. J. Numer. Methods Fluids* **1983**, *3*, 249–264. [CrossRef]

Article

Supplements Related to Normal π-Projective Hypermodules

Burcu Nişancı Türkmen [1], Hashem Bordbar [2] and Irina Cristea [2,*]

[1] Department of Mathematics, Faculty of Art and Science, Amasya University, Ipekköy, Amasya 05100, Turkey; burcu.turkmen@amasya.edu.tr
[2] Centre for Information Technologies and Applied Mathematics, University of Nova Gorica, 5000 Nova Gorica, Slovenia; hashem.bordbar@ung.si
* Correspondence: irina.cristea@ung.si or irinacri@yahoo.co.uk; Tel.: +386-0533-15-395

Abstract: In this study, the role of supplements in Krasner hypermodules is examined and related to normal π-projectivity. We prove that the class of supplemented Krasner hypermodules is closed under finite sums and under quotients. Moreover, we give characterizations of finitely generated supplemented and amply supplemented Krasner hypermodules. In the second part of the paper we relate the normal projectivity to direct summands and supplements in Krasner hypermodules.

Keywords: direct summand; normal π-projective hypermodule; supplement subhypermodule; small subhypermodule

MSC: 20N20; 16D80

Citation: Nişancı Türkmen, B.; Bordbar, H.; Cristea, I. Supplements Related to Normal π-Projective Hypermodules. *Mathematics* **2022**, *10*, 1945. https://doi.org/10.3390/math10111945

Academic Editor: Takayuki Hibi

Received: 17 May 2022
Accepted: 4 June 2022
Published: 6 June 2022

Publisher's Note: MDPI stays neutral with regard to jurisdictional claims in published maps and institutional affiliations.

Copyright: © 2022 by the authors. Licensee MDPI, Basel, Switzerland. This article is an open access article distributed under the terms and conditions of the Creative Commons Attribution (CC BY) license (https://creativecommons.org/licenses/by/4.0/).

1. Introduction

Hypercompositional algebra, a new branch of abstract algebra, started its development in 1934, when F. Marty introduced the concept of hypergroup as a natural generalization of the concept of group. The law of synthesis of two elements was extended, in the sense that the operation (defined on a group) was substituted with a multivalued operation (called hyperoperation), i.e., the result of the hyperoperation being a subset of the underlying set. As a consequence, new algebraic hypercompositional structures are defined and the properties of the classical structures are conserved, or not, for similar hyperstructures. This is also the case of the modules, extended to hypermodules, introduced firstly by Krasner [1], and known today as Krasner hypermodules. Their additive part is a canonical hypergroup. The fundamental aspects of the theory of hypermodules are very well covered, for example, by the studies of Massouros [2], Nakassis [3], Anvariyeh [4,5], Ameri and Shojaei [6], and Bordbar and Cristea [7–9].

Recently, the concept of smallness in module theory has been transported and investigated by Moniri et al. [10] in the class of hypermodules. Similarities and differences of this concept in both theories have been clearly highlighted and supported by several examples. As it was defined in [11] and then recalled in [12] already in the 1960s, a left R-submodule N of an R-module M, where R is an arbitrary unitary associative ring, is *small* if $N + K = M$, for any R-submodule K of M, implies $K = M$, and it is denoted by $N \ll M$ [13]. An R-module M is called a *hollow* if every proper R-submodule of M is small in M. In a similar way, we may define these two concepts in hypermodule theory, but we must pay attention, as it is explained in [10], to their meaning in a Krasner hypermodule (where the additive part is a canonical hypergroup) and in a general hypermodule having the additive part an arbitrary hypergroup (that can be also non-commutative). In addition, an R-hypermodule M, with the property that the intersection of its two R-subhypermodules is again an R-subhypermodule, is called *supplemented* if for each proper R-subhypermodule N of M there exists a proper R-subhypermodule K of M such that $K + N = M = N + K$ and $N \cap K \ll K$. In a Krasner hypermodule, the intersection of two subhypermodules is always a subhypermodule, while in a general hypermodule this property may not hold for arbitrary subhypermodules, only for closed subhypermodules [10].

In this paper, we aim to obtain more properties of supplements in Krasner R-hypermodules and understand their role related to projective hypermodules, in particular with normal π-projective hypermodules. After a brief introduction on hypermodules, homomorphisms, and supplements in hypermodules, in Section 3, we provide new properties of supplemented Krasner R-hypermodules. We prove that any quotient hypermodule of a supplemented hypermodule is again supplemented (see Theorem 1), and, similarly, the sum of two supplemented hypermodules is supplemented, too (see Theorem 2). In addition, we will provide also a new characterization of the finitely generated supplemented hypermodules (see Theorem 4) and finitely generated amply supplemented hypermodules (Theorems 5 and 6). In Section 4 we define the normal π-projective R-hypermodule and present several properties related to direct summands and supplements. The main results are represented by Proposition 2 and Corollary 2. The concept of normal projectivity has been recently introduced by Ameri and Shojaei [6], using different kinds of epimorphisms defined in the Krasner hypermodule category. Then, Bordbar and Cristea [14] provided their characterization by mean of chains of hypermodules. This study is a step forward in the theory of projective Krasner hypermodules.

2. Preliminaries and Notation

In this section, we briefly recall the main concepts and results related to Krasner hypermodules that we will use throughout this paper. For a better understanding of the topic, we start with some fundamental definitions in hypercompositional algebra presented in several books [15,16] and overview articles [3,17,18]. We refer the reader also to the first chapters of the book [13], containing an up-to-date account on lifting modules that generalize the projective supplemented modules, and to the book [19] for an introduction to module theory.

Hypermodules. Let H be a nonempty set and $\mathcal{P}^*(H)$ be the set of all nonempty subsets of H. The couple $(H, \circ)$ is a *hypergroupoid*, where the hyperoperation on H is a function $\circ : H \times H \longrightarrow \mathcal{P}^*(H)$. For any nonempty subsets X and Y of H, one defines $X \circ Y = \cup_{x \in X, y \in Y} x \circ y$. We simply write $a \circ X$ and $X \circ a$ instead of $\{a\} \circ X$ and $X \circ \{a\}$, respectively, for any $a \in H$ and any nonempty subset X of H. A hypergroupoid $(H, \circ)$ is called a *semihypergroup* if the hyperoperation $\circ$ is associative, i.e., for every $a, b, c \in H$, we have $a \circ (b \circ c) = (a \circ b) \circ c$. A hypergroupoid $(H, \circ)$ is called a *quasihypergroup* if the reproduction law holds, i.e., for every $x \in H$, $x \circ H = H = H \circ x$. If the hypergroupoid $(H, \circ)$ is a semihypergroup and quasihypergroup, then it is called a *hypergroup*. A nonempty subset S of a hypergroup $(H, \circ)$ is called a *subhypergroup* of H if, for every $a \in S$, $a \circ S = S = S \circ a$. A *canonical hypergroup* is a hypergroup $(H, \circ)$ satisfying the following conditions: (i) it is commutative, i.e., for every $a, b \in H$, $a \circ b = b \circ a$; (ii) there exists $e \in H$ such that $\{a\} = (a \circ e) \cap (e \circ a)$ for every $a \in H$ (such an element e is called an *identity* of the hypergroup); (iii) for every $a \in H$ there exists a unique $a^{-1} \in H$ such that $e \in a \circ a^{-1}$ (the element a' is called the *inverse* of a); (iv) for every $a, b, c \in H$, if $c \in a \circ b$, then $a \in c \circ b^{-1}$ and $b \in a^{-1} \circ c$.

An algebraic system $(R, +, \cdot)$ is called a *Krasner hyperring* if

1. $(R, +)$ is a canonical hypergroup;
2. $(R, \cdot)$ is a semigroup having zero as a bilaterally absorbing element, i.e., $a \cdot 0 = 0 = 0 \cdot a$ for any $a \in R$;
3. The multiplication distributes over the addition on both sides, i.e., for any $a, b, c \in R$, $a \cdot (b + c) = a \cdot b + a \cdot c$ and $(b + c) \cdot a = b \cdot a + c \cdot a$;

while $(R, +, \cdot)$ is called a *general hyperring* (or simply, a hyperring) if

1. $(R, +)$ is a canonical hypergroup with the scalar identity 0_R;
2. $(R, \cdot)$ is a semihypergroup;

3. The multiplication distributes over the addition on both sides.

A hyperring R is called *commutative* if it is commutative with respect to the multiplication. If $a \in a \cdot 1_R \cap 1_R \cdot a$ for every $a \in R$, then the element 1_R is called a *unit element* of the hyperring R.

Now, let R be a hyperring with the identity element 1_R. A *left R-hypermodule* is defined as an algebraic system $(M, +, \circ)$, where the hypergroup $(M, +)$ is endowed with an external multivalued operation $\circ$, i.e., $\circ : R \times M \longrightarrow \mathcal{P}^*(M)$ such that, for every $x, y \in R$ and $a, b \in M$, the following statements hold:

1. $x \circ (a + b) = x \circ a + x \circ b$;
2. $(x + y) \circ a = x \circ a + y \circ a$;
3. $(x \cdot y) \circ a = x \circ (y \circ a)$;
4. $a \in 1_R \circ a$.

Similarly, the concept of *right R-hypermodule* is defined and we say that $(M, +, \circ)$ is an R-hypermodule if it is a left and right one. Some authors call this hypercompositional structure a general hypermodule. A nonempty subset N of an R-hypermodule M is called a *subhypermodule* of M if N is an R-hypermodule under the same hyperoperations of M, and we denote this as $N \leq M$. In other words, N is a subhypermodule of M if and only if $x \circ a \subseteq N$ and $a - b \in N$ for every $x \in R$ and $a, b \in N$ [20]. A hypermodule M having the additive part of a canonical hypergroup is called a *canonical R-hypermodule* if it is a hypermodule over a Krasner hyperring $(R, +, \cdot)$.

If we consider a Krasner hyperring R, then we may endow a canonical hypergroup $(M, +)$ with an external operation $\cdot : R \times M \longrightarrow M$ defined as $(r, m) \longmapsto r \cdot m \in M$. If, for every $x, y \in R$ and $a, b \in M$, the following statements hold:

1. $x \cdot (a + b) = x \cdot a + x \cdot b$;
2. $(x + y) \cdot a = x \cdot a + y \cdot a$;
3. $(x \cdot y) \cdot a = x \cdot (y \cdot a)$;
4. $a = 1_R \cdot a$;
5. $x \cdot 0_M = 0_R$;

then M is called a *Krasner left R-hypermodule*. Similarly, a right Krasner R-hypermodule is defined and it is called a Krasner R-hypermodule (or simply a Krasner hypermodule) if it is both left and right.

Let $\{N_i\}_{i \in I}$ be a family of subhypermodules of an R-hypermodule M. The set $\sum_{i \in I} N_i = \cup \{\sum_{i \in I} a_i \mid a_i \in N_i \text{ for every } i \in I \text{ such that } \exists n \in \mathbb{N} : a_i = 0, \text{ for all but finitely many } i \geq n\}$ is a subhypermodule of M. A nonempty subset J of a commutative hyperring R is called a *hyperideal*, if $x - y \subseteq J$ and $a \cdot x \subseteq J$ for every $a \in R$ and $x, y \in J$. Recall that every hyperideal J of a hyperring R is a subhypermodule of the R-hypermodule R.

Let M be a left Krasner hypermodule over a Krasner hyperring R and K be a subhypermodule of M. Consider the set $\frac{M}{K} = \{a + K \mid a \in M\}$. Then, $\frac{M}{K}$ is a left Krasner hypermodule over R under the hyperoperation defined as $+ : \frac{M}{K} \times \frac{M}{K} \longrightarrow \mathcal{P}^*(\frac{M}{K})$ and the external operation $\odot : R \times \frac{M}{K} \longrightarrow \frac{M}{K}$ defined as $(a + K) + (a' + K) = \{b + K \mid b \in a + a'\}$ and $x \odot (a + K) = \{b + K \mid b \in x \cdot a\}$ for every $a, a', b \in M$ and $x \in R$. The Krasner hypermodule $\frac{M}{K}$ is called the *quotient hypermodule* of the hypermodule M. Note that $a + K = K$ if and only if $a \in K$.

A nonzero Krasner R-hypermodule M is called *simple* [20] if the only subhypermodules of M are $\{0_M\}$ and M itself. We denote by $S(M)$ the set of all simple subhypermodules of the Krasner R-hypermodule M.

The following technical result will be often used in the next sections.

Lemma 1 ((Modularity law) [21]). *Suppose that M is a Krasner R-hypermodule and A, B, and C are subhypermodules of M such that $B \leq A$. Then, $A \cap (B + C) = B + (A \cap C)$.*

Small subhypermodules. A subhypermodule N of a left Krasner R-hypermodule M is called a *small subhypermodule* of M and denoted by $N \ll M$, if $N + L \neq M$ for every proper subhypermodule L of M. We refer the reader to [21] for basic properties related to small subhypermodules. We recall here some basic properties of small subhypermodules that will be used throughout the paper.

Lemma 2 ([21]). *Let M be a hypermodule and $X \leq Y$ be subhypermodules of M. Then*
(1) $Y \ll M$ *if and only if* $X \ll M$ *and* $\frac{Y}{X} \ll \frac{M}{X}$.
(2) *Any finite sum of small subhypermodules of M is again small in M.*
(3) *If Y is a direct summand of M and $X \ll M$, then $X \ll Y$.*

A left Krasner R-hypermodule M is called a *hollow* [10] if every proper subhypermodule of M is small in M. Similarly to module theory, a left Krasner R-hypermodule is a hollow if and only if the sum of any of its proper subhypermodules is a proper subhypermodule. Moreover, M is called *local* if it has a proper subhypermodule that contains all proper subhypermodules of M.

Let M be a left Krasner R-hypermodule. We will denote by $Rad(M)$ the sum of all small subhypermodules of M, that is, $Rad(M) = \sum_{L \ll M} L$. If M has no small subhypermodules of M, then we set $Rad(M) = M$. Notice that $Rad(M)$ is always a subhypermodule of the left Krasner R-hypermodule M and M is local if and only if M is hollow and $Rad(M) \neq M$ [10].

Homomorphisms. Let M and M' be two left Krasner R-hypermodules. A function $f : M \longrightarrow M'$ is called a *homomorphism* if for every $a, b \in M$ and $r \in R$, it holds $f(a + b) \subseteq f(a) + f(b)$ and $f(r \circ a) = r \circ f(a)$, while it is called a *strong homomorphism* if $f(a + b) = f(a) + f(b)$ and $f(r \circ a) = r \circ f(a)$. For any subhypermodule N of a left Krasner R-hypermodule M, the image $f(N)$ is a subhypermodule of M' and the kernel $ker(f) = \{ a \in M \mid f(a) = 0_{M'} \}$ is a subhypermodule of M. If $f : M \longrightarrow M'$ is a strong epimorphism, i.e., a strong surjective homomorphism, and $ker(f) \ll M$, then f is called a *small strong epimorphism*. A subhypermodule U of a Krasner R-hypermodule M is called *fully invariant* in M if $\alpha(U)$ is a subhypermodule of U, for every strong endomorphism $\alpha : M \longrightarrow M$.

Supplements. Two subhypermodules N and N' of a left Krasner R-hypermodule M are called *independent* if $N \cap N' = \{0_M\}$, and in this case, their sum $N + N'$ is denoted by $N \oplus N'$ and called *direct sum*. Moreover, a subhypermodule N of M is called a *direct summand* of M if $M = N \oplus K$ for some subhypermodule K of M [21]. A left Krasner R-hypermodule M is called *semisimple*, if its subhypermodules are direct summands in M [20]. As a generalization of semisimple hypermodules, in [10], the class of supplemented hypermodules was introduced. Let M be a left Krasner R-hypermodule and U, V be subhypermodules of M. V is called a *supplement* of U in M if it is a minimal element in the set $\{ L \leq M \mid L + U = M \}$. Then M is called *supplemented* if every subhypermodule of M has a supplement in M [10]. Thus, it is clear that V is a supplement of U in M if and only if $V + U = M$ and $U \cap V \ll V$, i.e., the canonical map $V \longrightarrow \frac{M}{U}$ is a small strong epimorphism. Moreover, U has *amply supplements* in M if, whenever $U + V = M$, V contains a supplement V' of U in M. The left Krasner R-hypermodule M is called *amply supplemented* if every subhypermodule has amply supplements in M. These definitions have been initially introduced in [10] for general hypermodules, and several examples have been illustrated there.

It is clear that semisimple modules and hollow modules are examples of amply supplemented Krasner R- hypermodules. Moreover, a supplemented Krasner R-hypermodule M with zero $Rad(M)$ is semisimple. Thus, we can write the following implications between the three classes of Krasner R-hypermodules:

semisimple hypermodules$\Longrightarrow$ amply supplemented hypermodules$\Longrightarrow$ supplemented hypermodules.

3. Some Results of (Amply) Supplemented Hypermodules

Throughout this paper, we work with left Krasner R-hypermodules, that we briefly call hypermodules.

In this section, some basic properties of (amply) supplemented hypermodules are presented. For a better understanding of the concept, we will start with one example of amply supplemented hypermodule.

Example 1 ([10]). *Take the set $R = \{0,1,2,3\}$ equipped with the hyperoperation $+$ and operation $\cdot$ defined as follows:*

+	0	1	2	3
0	0	1	2	3
1	1	0,1	3	2,3
2	2	3	0	1
3	3	2,3	1	0,1

$$\text{and } r \cdot s = \begin{cases} 2, & \text{if } r,s \in \{2,3\} \\ 0, & \text{otherwise.} \end{cases}$$

Then R is a Krasner hyperring and $M = R$ is a left Krasner R-hypermodule with the proper subhypermodules $\{0\}$, $K = \{0,1\}$, and $L = \{0,2\}$. Since $L + K = M$, it follows that $\{0\}$ is the only small subhypermodule of M. In addition, all subhypermodules are direct summands of M and thus M is amply supplemented.

Recall here a result on the smallness property in quotient hypermodules.

Proposition 1 ([10]). *Let M be a hypermodule and $U \subset L$ be subhypermodules of M. Then $\frac{L}{U}$ is a small subhypermodule of $\frac{M}{U}$ if and only if for all subhypermodules K of M the equality $L + K = M$ implies $U + K = M$.*

In the following auxiliary result, we will present some properties of the supplements of a hypermodule and of the set $Rad(M) = \sum_{L \ll M} L$. Notice that very often we make use of the second isomorphism theorem [22].

Lemma 3. *Let M be a hypermodule and K, L two subhypermodules such that L is a supplement of K in M.*

1. *If U is a subhypermodule of L, then $\frac{L}{U}$ is not small in $\frac{M}{U}$.*
2. *If U is a subhypermodule of L and U is a small subhypermodule in M, then U is a small subhypermodule in L.*
3. *$Rad(L) = L \cap Rad(M)$,*
4. *$Rad(\frac{M}{K}) = \frac{Rad(M)+K}{K}$.*
5. *$Rad(M) = (L + Rad(M)) \cap (K + Rad(M)) = (L \cap Rad(M)) + (K \cap Rad(M))$.*

Proof. (1) Let U be a subhypermodule of L. If $\frac{L}{U}$ is small in $\frac{M}{U}$, i.e., $\frac{L}{U} \ll \frac{M}{U}$, then, by Proposition 1, it follows that $K + U = M$, which contradicts with the minimality of L as a supplement of K. Thus, $\frac{L}{U}$ is not small in $\frac{M}{U}$.

(2) Suppose that $U + T = L$, for some subhypermodule T of L. Then $(U + T) + K = L + K = M$. Therefore $U + (T + K) = M$, and since $U \ll M$, it follows that $T + K = M$, with L a supplement of K in M. Thus, by the minimality of L, we have $T = L$. Hence, $U \ll L$.

(3) It is clear that $Rad(L) \subseteq L \cap Rad(M)$. Conversely, let $a \in L \cap Rad(M)$. Since $Rad(M)$ is the sum of all small subhypermodules of M, it follows that $Ra \ll M$. Then, by (2), we obtain $Ra \ll L$, i.e., $a \in Rad(L)$. Thus, $L \cap Rad(M) \subseteq Rad(L)$, and therefore $Rad(L) = L \cap Rad(M)$.

(4) Since L is a supplement of K in M, the canonical map $L \longrightarrow \frac{M}{K}$ is a small strong epimorphism. From $\frac{L}{L \cap K} \cong \frac{M}{K}$, we have that $Rad(\frac{L}{L \cap K}) \cong Rad(\frac{M}{K})$. Since $K \cap L \subseteq Rad(L)$, it follows that $Rad(\frac{L}{L \cap K}) = \frac{Rad(L)}{L \cap K}$. Therefore, every maximal subhypermodule of L contains

$K \cap L$. In addition, we have $\frac{M}{K} = \frac{K+L}{K} \cong \frac{L}{K \cap L}$ which implies $Rad(\frac{M}{K}) = \frac{Rad(L)+K}{K}$. By using the canonical strong epimorphism $M \longrightarrow \frac{M}{K}$, on one side we have $\frac{Rad(M)+K}{K} \leq \frac{Rad(L)+K}{K}$. On the other side, $Rad(L) + K \leq Rad(M) + K$, and therefore $Rad(\frac{M}{K}) = \frac{Rad(M)+K}{K}$.

(5) Let $N = Rad(M)$ and $\psi : M \longrightarrow \frac{M}{K}$ be the strong canonical epimorphism. Since
$$\psi(Rad(L)) = \frac{Rad(L)+K}{K} \cong \frac{Rad(L)}{K \cap Rad(L)} = \frac{Rad(L)}{K \cap L \cap Rad(M)} = \frac{Rad(L)}{K \cap L} = Rad(\frac{L}{K \cap L}) \cong Rad(\frac{M}{K})$$
and knowing (4), it follows that $\frac{Rad(M)+K}{K} = \frac{Rad(L)+K}{K}$. Thus, we can write

$$N + K = Rad(M) + K = Rad(L) + K = (L \cap N) + K.$$

Then, $N + (N \cap K) = N \cap (N + K) = N \cap [(L \cap N) + K]$, which implies that $N = (L \cap N) + (K \cap N)$, meaning that $Rad(M) = (L \cap Rad(M)) + (K \cap Rad(M))$. It remains to prove the first part of the formula. Again we use the modularity law and we obtain $L \cap (N + K) = L \cap (L \cap N + K) = (L \cap N) + (L \cap K) = L \cap N$. Therefore, $(N + K) \cap (N + L) = N + ((N + K) \cap L) = N + (L \cap N) = N$, meaning that

$$Rad(M) = (L + Rad(M)) \cap (K + Rad(M)).$$

Now the proof is completed. □

Recall from [6] that an R-hypermodule P is *normal A-projective* if, for every strong epimorphism $g \in Hom_R(A, B)$ and every strong homomorphism $f \in Hom_R(P, B)$, there exists $\overline{f} \in Hom_R(P, A)$ such that $g \circ \overline{f} = f$. If P is normal A-projective in the category Hmod for every hypermodule A, then P is called a *normal projective* hypermodule. In addition, from [21], we know that, for any hypermodules M and N, a strong epimorphism $g : M \longrightarrow N$ is a small strong epimorphism if and only if for every strong homomorphism f; if $g \circ f$ is a strong epimorphism, then f is a strong epimorphism, too. Moreover, if $f : P \longrightarrow M$ is a small strong epimorphism and P is a projective R-hypermodule, then P is called a *projective cover* of M.

Some fundamental results of supplements related to homomorphisms and projective covers are gathered in the next result.

Lemma 4. 1. *In the following commutative diagram, suppose that γ and θ are strong epimorphisms, while α is a small strong epimorphism related to the hypermodules U, V, W, S.*

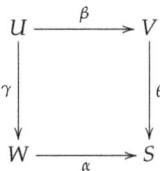

If X is a supplement of $ker(\gamma)$ in U, then $\beta(X)$ is a supplement of $ker(\theta)$ in V.
2. *If X is a subhypermodule of the hypermodule M and $\frac{M}{X}$ has a projective cover, then X has a supplement in the hypermodule M.*
3. *If L is a supplement of K in a hypermodule M and $\eta : M \longrightarrow M$ is a strong endomorphism with $Im(1 - \eta)$ a subhypermodule of K, then $\eta(L)$ is a supplement of K in M.*
4. *If L is a supplement of K in a hypermodule M and X is a subhypermodule of K, then $\frac{L+X}{X}$ is a supplement of $\frac{K}{X}$ in $\frac{M}{X}$.*

Proof. (1) By the hypothesis, we have $X + ker(\gamma) = U$ and $X \cap ker(\gamma) \ll X$. Let us consider the following short exact sequence constructed with the hypermodules and their strong homomorphisms: $X \longrightarrow \frac{U}{ker(\gamma)} \longrightarrow W \longrightarrow S \equiv U \longrightarrow \beta(X) \longrightarrow \frac{V}{ker(\theta)} \longrightarrow S$. Since

$\beta(X) + \ker(\theta) = V$ and $\beta(X) \cap \ker(\theta) \ll \beta(X)$, it follows that $\beta(X)$ is a supplement of $\ker(\theta)$ in V.

(2) Let P be a projective cover of $\frac{M}{X}$, i.e., the function $f : P \longrightarrow \frac{M}{X}$ is a strong epimorphism and P is a projective hypermodule. Then, for the strong epimorphism $h \in Hom_R(M, \frac{M}{X})$, there exists $\beta \in Hom_R(P, M)$ such that $g \circ \beta = f$, i.e., the following diagram commutes.

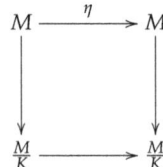

Since $\ker(id) = \{0_P\}$, it follows that P is a supplement of $\{0_P\} = \ker(id)$ in P and by item (1) it results that $\beta(P)$ is a supplement of $X = \ker(g)$.

(3) Let L be a supplement of K in the R-hypermodule M. Since $Im(1 - \eta)$ is a subhypermodule of K, it follows by item (1) that the following diagram

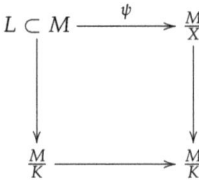

is commutative and $\eta(L)$ is a supplement of K in M.

(4) The statement follows by applying item (1) to the following diagram

$$L \subset M \xrightarrow{\psi} \frac{M}{X}$$
$$\downarrow \qquad \downarrow \alpha$$
$$\frac{M}{K} \longrightarrow \frac{M}{K}$$

where $\psi(L) = \frac{L+X}{X}$ and $Ker\alpha = \frac{K}{X}$. □

The last item of Lemma 4 can be written as follows.

Theorem 1. *Every quotient hypermodule of a supplemented hypermodule is supplemented, too.*

In order to characterize the sum of supplemented hypermodules, we first prove the following auxiliary result.

Lemma 5. *Let M be an R-hypermodule.*
1. *Let N, K, L be three subhypermodules of M such that $N + K + L = M$. If N is a supplement of $K + L$ in M and K is a supplement of $N + L$ in M, then $N + K$ is a supplement of L in M.*
2. *Let N and K be two subhypermodules of M such that N is supplemented. If $N + K$ has a supplement in M, then K has a supplement in M, too.*

Proof. (1) Since N is a supplement of $K + L$ in M, it follows that $(K + L) \cap N \ll N$ and, similarly, $(N + L) \cap K \ll K$. We will prove that $L \cap (N + K) \ll N + K$.

By the modularity law we have $L \cap (N + K) = N + (L \cap K)$ and $K \cap (N + L) = N + (K \cap L)$. Therefore, $L \cap (N + K) \subseteq [N \cap (L + K)] + [K \cap (L + N)]$ and since the sum of small subhypermodules is a small subhypermodule, we have that $L \cap (N + K) \ll N + K$.

(2) Let X be a supplement of $N + K$ in M. Thus, $N + K + X = M$ and $(N + K) \cap X \ll X$. We know that N is supplemented, therefore $N \cap (K + X)$ has a supplement Y in N, i.e., $N \cap (K + X) + Y = N$ and $N \cap (K + X) \cap Y = (K + X) \cap Y \ll Y$. Then we have

$$M = N + K + X = N \cap (K + X) + Y + (K + X) = K + X + Y$$

and

$$K \cap (X + Y) \subseteq [X \cap (K + Y)] + [Y \cap (K + X)] \subseteq [X \cap (K + N)] + [Y \cap (K + X)].$$

Since $X \cap (K + N) \ll X$ and $Y \cap (K + X) \ll Y$, it follows that $K \cap (X + Y) \ll X + Y$ (the sum of small subhypermodules is a small subhypermodule). Thus, $X + Y$ is a supplement of K in M. □

Theorem 2. *The sum of two supplemented hypermodules is supplemented, too.*

Proof. Let M_1 and M_2 be two supplemented hypermodules. We will prove that $M = M_1 + M_2$ is supplemented, too. Let U be a subhypermodule of M. Since M_2 is supplemented, it follows that its subhypermodule $(M_1 + U) \cap M_2$ has a supplement V in M_2. Then $M = M_1 + M_2 = M_1 + (M_1 + U) \cap M_2 + V = M_1 + U + V$. In addition, since V is a supplement of $(M_1 + U) \cap M_2$ in M_2, we have $(M_1 + U) \cap V = ((M_1 + U) \cap M_2) \cap V \ll V$. This means that V is a supplement of $M_1 + U$ in M. Since M_1 is supplemented, by Lemma 5 (2), it follows that U has a supplement in M. Therefore, M is supplemented. □

Corollary 1. *If in the exact sequence $0 \longrightarrow U \longrightarrow M \longrightarrow \frac{M}{U} \longrightarrow 0$ of hypermodules U and $\frac{M}{U}$ are supplemented and U has a supplement in every subhypermodule X, with $U < X < M$, then the hypermodule M is supplemented.*

Proof. Let V be a subhypermodule of M, $\frac{X}{U}$ be a supplement of $\frac{V+U}{U}$ in $\frac{M}{U}$, and Y be a supplement of U in X. We have $U + Y = X$, $U \cap Y \ll Y$, $\frac{V+U}{U} + \frac{X}{U} = \frac{M}{U}$ and $\frac{V+U}{U} \cap \frac{X}{U} \ll \frac{X}{U}$. Hence $V + U + X = M$, $(V + U) \cap Y \leq (V + U) \cap X$, so $\frac{(V+U) \cap Y}{U} \leq \frac{(V+U) \cap X}{U} \ll \frac{X}{U}$. Thus, we suppose that there exists a subhypermodule T of Y such that $(V + U) \cap Y + T = Y$. Then $\frac{(V+U) \cap Y}{U} + \frac{U+T}{U} = \frac{X}{U}$. By using $\frac{(V+U) \cap Y}{U} \ll \frac{X}{U}$, it follows that $\frac{U+T}{U} = \frac{X}{U}$. Thus, $U + T = X$. Since Y is a supplement of U in X, we have $T = Y$. Therefore, Y is a supplement of $V + U$ in M, i.e., $Y \cap (V + U) \ll Y$. Then, by Lemma 5 (2), we conclude that V has a supplement in M. □

Recall that an R-hypermodule M is local if and only if M is hollow and $Rad(M) \neq M$ [10]. It can be easily seen here that if a hypermodule M is a hollow and $Rad(M) \neq M$, then M is cyclic and $Rad(M)$ is the largest subhypermodule of M.

Theorem 3. *If M is a direct sum of hollow hypermodules and $Rad(M)$ is small in M, then M is supplemented.*

Proof. Let $M = \oplus_{\gamma \in \Omega} M_\gamma$, with M_γ a hollow hypermodule and $Rad(M) \ll M$. Defining $\overline{M_\gamma} = \frac{M_\gamma + Rad(M)}{Rad(M)}$, we obtain $\overline{M_\gamma} \cong \frac{M_\gamma}{M_\gamma \cap Rad(M)} = \frac{M_\gamma}{Rad(M_\gamma)}$ for every $\gamma \in \Omega$. Since M_γ is a hollow hypermodule for every $\gamma \in \Omega$, it follows that $\frac{M_\gamma}{Rad(M_\gamma)}$ is hollow, too, accordingly with [21], Proposition 2.4. Then $Rad(M) = \oplus_{\gamma \in \Omega} Rad(M_\gamma)$ and $Rad(M) \ll M$. Moreover, since M_γ is a hollow hypermodule and $Rad(M_\gamma) \leq M_\gamma$ for every $\gamma \in \Omega$, it follows that $Rad(M_\gamma) \ll M_\gamma$. Thus, $Rad(M_\gamma) \neq M_\gamma$ for every $\gamma \in \Omega$ and $Rad(M_\gamma)$ is the largest subhypermodule of M_γ for every $\gamma \in \Omega$. Therefore, $\frac{M_\gamma}{Rad(M_\gamma)}$ is simple for every $\gamma \in \Omega$. This implies that $\overline{M} = \frac{M}{Rad(M)} = \oplus_{\gamma \in \Omega} \frac{M_\gamma}{Rad(M_\gamma)} \cong \oplus_{\gamma \in \Omega} \overline{M_\gamma}$. Therefore, for an arbitrary subhypermodule U of M, there exists $\Phi \subset \Omega$ with $\overline{M} = (\oplus_{\gamma \in \Phi} \frac{M_\gamma}{Rad(M_\gamma)}) \oplus \overline{U}$. Let

$V = \oplus_{\gamma \in \Phi} M_\gamma$. Then, $\overline{M} = \overline{U} \oplus \overline{V}$ and $U \cap V \leq Rad(M)$. So $U \cap V \ll M$. Because $Rad(M)$ is small in M, we have $U \cap V \ll M$ and since V is a direct summand of M, we conclude that $U \cap V \ll V$. Therefore, V is a supplement of U in M. Hence M is supplemented. □

Theorem 4. *For a finitely generated hypermodule M, the following statements are equivalent:*

(a) *M is supplemented.*
(b) *Every maximal subhypermodule of M has a supplement in M.*
(c) *M is a sum of hollow subhypermodules.*

Proof. $(a) \Rightarrow (b)$ This implication is clear.

$(b) \Rightarrow (c)$ Let $S = \sum \{U \leq M \mid U \text{ is a hollow subhypermodule of } M\}$. Then $S \subseteq M$. Now suppose $S \subset M$. Since M is finitely generated, by Zorn's lemma we know that S is contained in a maximal subhypermodule N of M. By hypothesis (b), N has a supplement K in M, i.e., $M = N + K$ and $N \cap K \ll K$. Since $\frac{M}{N} = \frac{N+K}{N} \cong \frac{K}{N \cap K}$, it follows that $N \cap K$ is a maximal subhypermodule of K and $N \cap K \ll K$. Thus, K is local with the largest subhypermodule $N \cap K$. From $K < S < N$ it follows that $M = N + K = N$, which is a contradiction. Then $S = M$.

$(c) \Rightarrow (a)$ We know that M is finitely generated and $M = \sum_{\gamma \in \Omega} M_\gamma$, with Ω a finite set, where each M_γ is a hollow subhypermodule and $Rad(M) \ll M$. Let K be any proper subhypermodule of M. We can write $\frac{M}{Rad(M)} = \sum_{\gamma \in \Omega} \frac{M_\gamma + Rad(M)}{Rad(M)}$. Since $Rad(M_\gamma) \subseteq M_\gamma \cap Rad(M)$ and $\frac{M_\gamma + Rad(M)}{Rad(M)} \cong \frac{M_\gamma}{M_\gamma \cap Rad(M)}$, these factors are simple or zero. We gain the equation $\frac{M}{Rad(M)} = \oplus_{\theta \in \Omega'} \frac{M_\theta + Rad(M)}{Rad(M)}$, and since $Rad(M) \ll M$, we conclude that $M = \sum_{\theta \in \Omega'} M_\theta$ with local subhypermodules M_θ for any $\theta \in \Omega' \subset \Omega$. Thus, K is contained in a maximal one, and K has a supplement in M, as we saw in Theorem 3, so M is supplemented. □

Example 2 (See [10], Example 2.4). *Let $(\mathbb{Z}_2 \times \mathbb{Z}_4, *, \diamond)$ be a hypermodule over the hyperring $(\mathbb{Z}, \oplus, \odot)$, where $(a,b) * (c,d) = \{(a,b), (c,d)\}$, $n \diamond (a,b) = \{n(a,b)\}$, $n \oplus m = \{n, m\}$ and $n \odot m = \{nm\}$ for all $(a,b), (c,d) \in \mathbb{Z}_2 \times \mathbb{Z}_4$ and $n, m \in \mathbb{Z}$. Since every proper subhypermodule of $(\mathbb{Z}_2 \times \mathbb{Z}_4, *, \diamond)$ is small, it follows that $(\mathbb{Z}_2 \times \mathbb{Z}_4, *, \diamond)$ is a hollow. By using Theorem 4, we conclude that $(\mathbb{Z}_2 \times \mathbb{Z}_4, *, \diamond)$ is also supplemented.*

We conclude this section with some characterizations of amply supplemented hypermodules.

Theorem 5. *For a hypermodule M, the following statements are equivalent.*

(a) *M is amply supplemented.*
(b) *Every subhypermodule N of M is of the form $N = N_1 + N_2$ with N_1 supplemented and $N_2 \ll M$.*
(c) *For every proper subhypermodule N of M, there exists a supplemented proper subhypermodule N_1 of N with $\frac{N}{N_1} \ll \frac{M}{N_1}$.*

Proof. $(a) \Rightarrow (b)$ Let M be an amply supplemented hypermodule and N be a proper subhypermodule of M. Then N has an ample supplement K in M, i.e., $M = K + N$ and there exists a supplement N_1 of K in M which lies in N. It follows that $N \cap (K + N_1) = N \cap M = N$, while by the modular law we have $N \cap (K + N_1) = N_1 + (K \cap N)$. Thus, $N_1 + (K \cap N) = N$. Denote $N_2 = K \cap N$, which is small in M. It remains to be shown that N_1 is supplemented. By the hypothesis for a subhypermodule A of N_1, let L be a supplement of $A + K$ in M that is contained in N_1. Then L is also a supplement of A in N_1 because $L \cap A \ll L$, and from the minimality of N_1, it follows that $L + A = N_1$.

$(b) \Rightarrow (c)$ If $N = N_1 + N_2$ with $N_2 \ll M$, it follows immediately that $\frac{N}{N_1} \ll \frac{M}{N_1}$.

$(c) \Rightarrow (a)$ Let N be a subhypermodule of N. By hypothesis, there exists a supplemented subhypermodule N_1 of N with $\frac{N}{N_1} \ll \frac{M}{N_1}$. It follows that $U + N_1 = M$, and if N' is a supplement of $U \cap N_1$ in N_1, then using the small strong epimorphism $N' \longrightarrow \frac{N_1}{U \cap N_1} \cong \frac{M}{U}$, we conclude that N' is a supplement of U in M and it is contained in N_1. Thus, N has an ample supplement in M. □

Theorem 6. *A finitely generated hypermodule M is amply supplemented if and only if every maximal subhypermodule has ample supplements in M.*

Proof. For an arbitrary ample supplemented hypermodule M, first we prove the following property. If $A + B = M$ and both subhypermodules A and B have ample supplements in M, then so has $A \cap B$. Indeed, from $(A \cap B) + C = M$, it follows that $A + (B \cap C) = M = B + (A \cap C)$, and since M is ample supplemented, we have a supplement $B' < B \cap C$ of A and a supplement $A' < A \cap C$ of B in M. It follows that $A' + B' < C$ is a supplement of $A \cap B$ in M.

Suppose now that M is finitely generated and every maximal subhypermodule has ample supplements in M. By Theorem 4, we know that M is supplemented, hence $\frac{M}{Rad(M)}$ is semisimple. Thereby, for every subhypermodule U of M, the factor hypermodule $\frac{M}{Rad(M)+U}$ is semisimple and finitely generated. Since $\frac{M}{Rad(M)+U}$ is semisimple, it follows that $Rad(\frac{M}{Rad(M)+U}) = 0$. In addition, $Rad(\frac{M}{Rad(M)+U}) = \cap_{i \in I} \frac{X_i}{Rad(M)+U} = \frac{\cap_{i \in I} X_i}{Rad(M)+U}$ for every maximal subhypermodule $\frac{X_i}{Rad(M)+U}$ of $\frac{M}{Rad(M)+U}$. Thus, $Rad(M) + U = \cap_{i \in I} X_i$ for all maximal subhypermodules X_i of M. Since $\frac{M}{Rad(M)+U}$ is finitely generated, there exists a finite subset I' of I such that $Rad(M) + U = \cap_{i \in I'} X_i$. Thus, by the first part of the proof, we conclude that $Rad(M) + U$ has ample supplements in M, so also U. □

4. Normal π-Projective Hypermodules

The aim of this section is to introduce the notion of normal π-projective hypermodule, to find its properties related to direct summands and supplements, and to provide a relationship between direct summands and supplements for this particular case of hypermodules.

Definition 1. *An R-hypermodule M is called* **normal π-projective** *if for every pair (U, V) of subhypermodules of M satisfying $U + V = M$, there exists a strong homomorphism $\eta : M \longrightarrow M$ with $Im(\eta) \leq U$ and $Im(1 - \eta) \leq V$, where 1 denotes the identity strong homomorphism of M.*

Subhypermodules U and V are called **normal mutually-projective** *if U is normal V-projective and V is normal U-projective* [6].

Lemma 6. *For a normal π-projective hypermodule M, the following statements hold:*
1. *If $U + V = M$ and U is a direct summand in M, there exists a subhypermodule V' of V with $U \oplus V' = M$.*
2. *If $U + V = M$ and U and V are direct summands in M, then so is $U \cap V$.*
3. *If $U \oplus V = M$ and $\alpha : U \longrightarrow V$ is a strong homomorphism with a direct summand $Im(\alpha)$ in V, then $ker(\alpha)$ is a direct summand in U.*
4. *If $U \oplus V = M$ and a subhypermodule U' of U exists such that $\frac{U}{U'}$ is isomorphic to a direct summand in V, then U' is a direct summand in U.*

Proof. (1) Let $M = U + V$ and $M = U \oplus X$ for some subhypermodule X of M. Since M is a normal π-projective hypermodule, there exists a strong homomorphism $\eta : M = V + U \longrightarrow M$ with $Im(1 - \eta) \leq U$ and $Im(\eta) \leq V$. Therefore $\eta(X) \leq \eta(M) \leq V$, meaning that $\eta(X)$ is a subhypermodule of V. Then, it follows that $M = U \oplus \eta(X)$. Thus, there exists a subhypermodule $V' = \eta(X)$ of V with $U \oplus V' = M$.

(2) Suppose that $U + V = M$ and U and V are direct summands in M. Then, by (1), there exist a subhypermodule U' of U and a subhypermodule V' of V such that $M = U \oplus V' = U' \oplus V$. It follows that $M = (U \cap V) \oplus (U' + V')$.

(3) Suppose that $U \oplus V = M$ and $Im(\alpha)$ is a direct summand in V. Then there exists a subhypermodule V' of V such that $Im(\alpha) \oplus V' = V$. Let $A = U + V'$ and $B = \{u + \alpha(u) \mid u \in U\}$. Thus $M = A + B = A \oplus Im(\alpha) = B \oplus V$ and $A \cap B = ker(\alpha)$, so applying (2), we obtain that $ker(\alpha)$ is a direct summand in M and also in U.

(4) Suppose that $U \oplus V = M$, and $\frac{U}{U'}$ is isomorphic to a direct summand in V, where U' is a subhypermodule of U. Therefore there exists a strong injective homomorphism $\beta : \frac{U}{U'} \longrightarrow V$ such that $Im(\beta)$ is a direct summand in V. Now consider the strong canonical epimorphism $\pi : U \longrightarrow \frac{U}{U'}$ and let $\alpha = \beta \circ \pi : U \longrightarrow V$. By (3), we obtain that $ker(\alpha) = U'$ is a direct summand in U. □

Example 3. Let I and J be right hyperideals in a hyperring R, with $I \subset J \subseteq I'$, where I' is the intersection of all maximal hyperideals containing I. Consider the hypermodule $M := \frac{R}{I} \times \frac{R}{J}$ and the subhypermodules $A = R \cdot (1,0)$, $C = R \cdot (1,1)$ and $C = R \cdot (0,1)$. Since $I \subset J$, it follows immediately that $M = A + B = A \oplus C = B \oplus C$ and $A \cap B = \{0_R\} \cdot \frac{J}{I}$. Because $J \subseteq I'$, it follows that $\frac{J}{I} \subseteq Rad(\frac{R}{I})$, thus $A \cap B \ll M$ and therefore $A \cap B \neq \{0_M\}$ is not a direct summand in M. Moreover, the subhypermodules A and B are mutual supplements in M, that is $M = A + B$, $A \cap B \ll B$ and $A \cap B \ll A$.

Lemma 7. If $M = U \oplus V$ is a normal π-projective hypermodule, then the subhypermodules U and V are normal π-projective, too. In addition, they are normal mutually-projective.

Proof. To show the normal π-projectivity of U, suppose that $X + Y = U$, where X and Y are subhypermodules of U. Since $X + (Y + V) = M$ and M is a normal π-projective hypermodule, it follows that there exists a strong endomorphism α of M such that $Im(\alpha)$ is a subhypermodule of X and $Im(1 - \alpha)$ is a subhypermodule of $Y + V$. This induces a map $\eta : U \longrightarrow U$ defined by $\eta(u) = \alpha(u)$, for each $u \in U$. Then we have $Im(\eta) = \alpha(U) \leq X$ and $Im(1 - \eta) = Im(1 - \alpha) \leq Y$, since $U \cap V = \{0\}$. Therefore, U is a normal π-projective subhypermodule, and similarly we can prove the assertion for V.

It remains to be proved that V is U-projective. For this, for an arbitrary hypermodule Q, consider an arbitrary strong epimorphism $\beta : U \longrightarrow Q$ and an arbitrary strong homomorphism $\Phi : V \longrightarrow Q$. Therefore $Y = \{u - v \mid u \in U, v \in V \text{ and } \beta(u) = \Phi(v)\}$ is a subhypermodule of M such that $U + Y = M$. Hence, since M is a π-projective hypermodule, a strong endomorphism α of M exists such that $Im(\alpha) \leq U$ and $Im(1 - \alpha) \leq Y$. Therefore, the map $\gamma : V \longrightarrow U$ induced by α, i.e., $\gamma(v) = \alpha(v)$, for any $v \in V$, the equality $\beta\gamma = \Phi$ holds. □

Lemma 8. For a normal π-projective hypermodule M, the following statements hold:

(1) If $U + V = M$ and U has a supplement in M, then U has a supplement contained in V.
(2) If $U + V = M$ and U and V have supplements in M, then $U \cap V$ also has a supplement in M.
(3) If $U + V = M$ and V is a fully invariant subhypermodule in M, then every supplement of U lies in V.
(4) If U and V are mutual supplements in M, then $M = U \oplus V$.

Proof. (1) By hypothesis, the hypermodule $M = U + V$ is π-projective, so there exists a strong endomorphism α of M such that $Im\alpha \leq V$ and $Im(1 - \alpha) \leq U$. Since U has a supplement W in M, by Lemma 4 (3) it follows that $\alpha(W)$ is a supplement of U and $\alpha(W) \leq V$.

(2) Accordingly with point (1), the subhypermodule U has a supplement V' in M, with $V' \leq V$, and the subhypermodule V has a supplement U' in M, with $U' \leq U$.

Therefore, $M = U + V' = V + U'$, with $U \cap V' \ll V'$ and $V \cap U' \ll U'$. By the modularity law, we can write $U = U \cap M = U \cap (V + U') = (U \cap V) + U'$ and similarly, $V = (U \cap V) + V'$. Therefore,

$$M = U + V = [(U \cap V) + U'] + [(U \cap V) + V'] = U \cap V + (U' + V')$$

and

$$\begin{aligned}(U' + V') \cap (U \cap V) &= [(U' + V') \cap U] \cap V \\ &= (U' + V' \cap U) \cap V \\ &= (U' \cap V) + (V' \cap U) \\ &\ll U' + V'.\end{aligned}$$

It follows that $U' + V'$ is a supplement of $U \cap V$ in M.

(3) Let W be a supplement of U in M. Since M is a normal π-projective hypermodule, there exists a strong endomorphism $\alpha : M = W + U \longrightarrow M$, with $Im(1 - \alpha) \leq W$ and $Im(\alpha) \leq U$. Therefore, taking $\eta = 1 - \alpha$, we obtain that $\eta(V) = W \leq V$, since V is a fully invariant subhypermodule of M.

(4) Let U and V be mutual supplements in M. It is enough to show that $U \cap V = 0$, since clearly, $M = U + V$. Consider the strong epimorphisms $\alpha : U \times V \longrightarrow \frac{M}{U} \times \frac{M}{V}$, defined by $\alpha(u,v) = (v + U, u + V)$, for all $(u,v) \in U \times V$, $\beta : U \times V \longrightarrow M$, defined as $\beta(u,v) = u + v$, for all $(u,v) \in U \times V$ and $\pi : M \longrightarrow \frac{M}{U} \times \frac{M}{V}$, with the definition law $\pi(m) = (m + U, m + V)$, for all $m \in M$. Since

$$\begin{aligned}(\pi\beta)(u,v) &= \pi(u+v) = ((u+v) + U, (u+v) + V) = (v + U, u + V) \\ &= \alpha(u,v),\end{aligned}$$

it follows that the following diagram

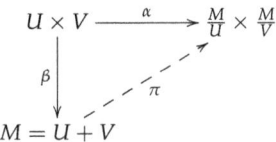

is commutative. It can be seen that $ker(\alpha) = (U \cap V) \times (U \cap V)$. Since $U \cap V \ll U$ and $U \cap V \ll V$, we obtain that $ker(\alpha)$ is small in $U \times V$. It means that α is a small strong epimorphism. Since M is normal π-projective, there exists a strong homomorphism $\eta : M \longrightarrow M$ with $Im(\eta) \leq U$ and $Im(1 - \eta) \leq V$. Let $f : M \longrightarrow U \times V$ be defined by $f(m) = (\eta(m), (1 - \eta)(m))$, for all $m \in M$. Then $(\beta f)(m) = \beta(f(m)) = \beta(\eta(m), (1 - \eta)(m)) = \eta(m) + (1 - \eta)(m) = m = I_M(m)$ and so β splits. It means that $ker(\beta)$ is a direct summand of $U \times V$. Therefore $ker(\beta) \leq ker(\alpha)$. It follows that $ker(\beta) \ll U \times V$ and so $ker(\beta) = 0$. Hence $U \cap V = 0$. □

Proposition 2. *For a normal π-projective hypermodule M, the following assertions are equivalent.*

1. *If $U + V = M$ and $U \cap V$ has a supplement in M, then U and V have a supplement in M, too.*
2. *If $U + V = M$ and $U \cap V$ has a supplement in M, there exist $U' \leq U$ and $V' \leq V$ with $U' \oplus V' = M$.*

   Moreover, if $Rad(M) \ll M$, then these two assertions are further equivalent to the next three, where $\overline{M} = \frac{M}{Rad(M)}$.
3. *If $U < M$ and $\overline{U}$ is a direct summand in $\overline{M}$, then U has a supplement in M.*
4. *Every direct summand of $\overline{M}$ is the image of a direct summand in M.*
5. *Every decomposition of $\overline{M}$ is induced by a decomposition of M.*

Proof. (1) ⇒ (2) By hypothesis, U has a supplement in M. Thus, accordingly to Lemma 6 (1), there exists $V' \leq V$ such that $U + V' = M$ and $U \cap V' \ll V'$, so U has a supplement V' in M. Similarly, V' has a supplement $U' \leq U$, and therefore $U' \oplus V' = M$ by Lemma 8 (4).

(2) ⇒ (1) Let $U + V = M$ and W be a supplement of $U \cap V$ in M. Therefore, $M = (U \cap V) + W$. Based on the modularity law, we can write $V = M \cap V = [(U \cap V) + W] \cap V = (U \cap V) + (V \cap W)$ and similarly, $U = (U \cap V) + (U \cap W)$. Therefore,

$$\begin{aligned} M &= U + V = [(U \cap V) + (V \cap W)] + [(U \cap V) + (U \cap W)] \\ &= U \cap V + V \cap W + U \cap W \\ &= U + (V \cap W). \end{aligned}$$

Since W is a supplement of $U \cap V$ in M, it follows that $(U \cap V) \cap W = U \cap (V \cap W)$ is a small subhypermodule of M. By hypothesis, there exist subhypermodules $U' \leq U$ and $V' \leq V \cap W$ such that $U' \oplus V' = M$. Now it is clear that $M = U + V' = V + U'$. Since $U \cap V' \leq U \cap (V \cap W)$ is a small subhypermodule of M and V' is a direct summand of M, we obtain that $U \cap V'$ is a small subhypermodule of V'. Hence V' is a supplement of U in M. In the same way, it can be shown that U' is a supplement of V in M.

Suppose now that $Rad(M) \ll M$.

(2) ⇒ (5) If $\overline{U} \oplus \overline{V} = \overline{M}$ with $Rad(M) \leq U$ and $V \leq M$, then there exist $U' \leq U$ and $V' \leq V$ with $U' \oplus V' = M$ by the hypothesis, and hence it follows that $\overline{U'} = \overline{U}$ and $\overline{V'} = \overline{V}$.

(5) ⇒ (4) Clear.

(4) ⇒ (3) For $\overline{W} \oplus \overline{U} = \overline{M}$, there exists a direct summand V of M with $\overline{V} = \overline{W}$ by the hypothesis. It follows that V is a supplement of U in M.

(3) ⇒ (1) Let $U + V = M$ and W be a supplement of $U \cap V$ in M. It follows for $V_1 := V \cap W$ that $U + V_1 = M$ and $U \cap V_1 \subseteq Rad(M)$. Because M is normal π-projective and $Rad(M)$ is a fully invariant subhypermodule in M, it can be shown that $(U + Rad(M)) \cap (V_1 + Rad(M)) = Rad(M)$, that is, $\overline{U} \oplus \overline{V_1} = \overline{M}$, so U has a supplement in M by the hypothesis. Similarly, the property holds for V. □

As a direct consequence of Proposition 2, we state the following necessary and sufficient condition for a normal π-projective hypermodule with small radical to be supplemented.

Corollary 2. *A normal π-projective hypermodule M with small radical is supplemented if and only if the quotient hypermodule $\overline{M} = \frac{M}{Rad(M)}$ is semisimple and every direct summand of $\overline{M}$ is the image of a direct summand in M.*

5. Conclusions

In classical algebra there is a unique concept of module over a ring, while in hypercompositional algebra we must distinguish between the general hypermodule and the Krasner hypermodule, depending on their additive structure: if the additive part is a canonical hypergroup, then we talk about a Krasner hypermodule. Thus, some properties hold only in Krasner hypermodules and not in general ones, such as, for example, the following one. The sum of two arbitrary Krasner subhypermodules is always a Krasner subhypermodule, whereas, the sum of subhypermodules of a general hypermodule may not be a subhypermodule. As a consequence, $Rad(M)$, which is the sum of all small subhypermodules of a hypermodule M (a general one or a Krasner hypermodule), plays a fundamental role in the characterization of hollow hypermodules. These are hypermodules with the property that every subhypermodule is small.

In this article, we have focused on Krasner hypermodules and in particular we have related the notions of supplement and direct summand to normal projectivity. Especially, we have proved that the class of supplemented Krasner hypermodules is closed under finite sums and under quotients. In addition, we have showed that a finitely generated Krasner hypermodule is supplemented if and only if it is a sum of hollow subhypermodules. Some characterizations of amply supplemented Krasner subhypermodules have been provided. One of them says that a finitely generated hypermodule M is amply supplemented if and only if every maximal subhypermodule has ample supplements in M. After presenting some fundamental properties of normal π-projective hypermodules related to the behavior of direct summands and supplements, we have concluded our study with a necessary and sufficient condition for a normal π-projective hypermodule M with small radical $Rad(M)$ to be supplemented.

We believe that this study could open new lines of research, one being related with embeddings. It would be useful to know that any Krasner R-hypermodule is embedding in a normal π-projective hypermodule, because then we can easily work with the characterizations provided in this article for normal π-projective hypermodules. Another future research idea could be related with the category of Krasner R-hypermodules. If we consider a normal π-projective R-hypermodule M with strong endomorphism hyperring $S = End(M)$, then we may ask about the relationship between the class $hom_R^S(M,N)$ of all strong R-homomorphisms from M to an arbitrary subhypermodule N and S as an S-subhypermodule.

Author Contributions: Conceptualization, B.N.T. and I.C.; methodology, B.N.T., H.B. and I.C.; investigation, B.N.T., H.B. and I.C.; writing—original draft preparation, B.N.T.; writing—review and editing, B.N.T., H.B. and I.C.; funding acquisition, I.C. All authors have read and agreed to the published version of the manuscript.

Funding: The third author acknowledges the financial support of the Slovenian Research Agency (research core funding No. P1-0285).

Institutional Review Board Statement: Not applicable.

Informed Consent Statement: Not applicable.

Data Availability Statement: Not applicable.

Conflicts of Interest: The authors declare no conflicts of interest.

References

1. Krasner, M. A class of hyperrings and hyperfields. *Int. J. Math. Math. Sci.* **1999**, *6*, 307–311. [CrossRef]
2. Massouros, C.G. Free and cyclic hypermodules. *Ann. Mat. Pura Appl.* **1988**, *4*, 153–166. [CrossRef]
3. Nakassis, A. Expository and survey article: Recent results in hyperring and hyperfield theory. *Int. J. Math. Math. Sci.* **1988**, *11*, 209–220. [CrossRef]
4. Anvariyeh, S.M.; Mirvakili, S.; Davvaz, B. θ^*-Relation on hypermodules and fundamental modules over commutative fundamental rings. *Commun. Algebra* **2008**, *36*, 622–631. [CrossRef]
5. Anvariyeh, S.M.; Mirvakili, S.; Davvaz, B. Transitivity of θ^*-relation on hypermodules. *Iran. J. Sci. Technol. Trans. A* **2008**, *32*, 188–205.
6. Ameri, R.; Shojaei, H. Projective and Injective Krasner Hypermodules. *J. Algebra Appl.* **2021**, *20*, 21501863. [CrossRef]
7. Bordbar, H.; Cristea, I. Height of prime hyperideals in Krasner hyperrings. *Filomat* **2017**, *31*, 6153–6163. [CrossRef]
8. Bordbar, H.; Cristea, I.; Novak, M. Height of hyperideals in Noetherian Krasner hyperrings. *Univ. Politeh. Buchar. Sci. Bull.-Ser. Math. Phys.* **2017**, *79*, 31–42.
9. Bordbar, H.; Novak, M.; Cristea, I. A note on the support of a hypermodule. *J. Algebra Appl.* **2020**, *19*, 2050019. [CrossRef]
10. Hamzekolaee, A.R.M.; Norouzi, M.; Leoreanu-Fotea, V. A new approach to smallness in hypermodules. *Algebr. Struct. Appl.* **2021**, *8*, 131–145.
11. Bass, H. Finitistic dimension and a homological generalization of semi-primary rings. *Trans. Am. Math. Soc.* **1960**, *95*, 466–488. [CrossRef]
12. Leonard, W.W. Small modules. *Proc. Am. Math. Soc.* **1966**, *17*, 527–531. [CrossRef]
13. Clark, J.; Lomp, C.; Vanaja, N.; Wisbauer, R. *Lifting modules: Supplements and Projectivity in Module Theory*; Birkhauser Verlag: Basel, Switzerland; Boston, MA, USA; Berlin, Germany, 2006.
14. Bordbar, H.; Cristea, I. About the normal projectivity and injectivity of Krasner hypermodules. *Axioms* **2021**, *10*, 83. [CrossRef]
15. Corsini, P. *Prolegomena of Hypergroup Theory*, 2nd ed.; Aviani Editore: Tricesimo, Italy, 1993.
16. Davvaz, B.; Leoreanu-Fotea, V. *Hyperring Theory and Applications*; International Academic Press: Palm Harbor, FL, USA, 2007.
17. Massouros, G.; Massouros, C. Hypercompositional Algebra, Computer Science and Geometry. *Mathematics* **2020**, *8*, 1338. [CrossRef]
18. Massouros, C.; Massouros, G. An Overview of the Foundations of the Hypergroup Theory. *Mathematics* **2021**, *9*, 1014. [CrossRef]

19. Wisbauer, R. *Foundations of Module and Ring Theory*; Gordon and Breach: Amsterdam, The Netherlands, 1991.
20. Mahjoob, R.; Ghaffari, V. Zariski topology for second subhypermodules. *Ital. J. Pure Appl. Math.* **2018**, *39*, 554–568.
21. Talaee, B. Small subhypermodules and their applications. *Rom. J. Math. Comput. Sci.* **2013**, *3*, 5–14.
22. Zhan, J.M. Isomorphism Theorems of Hypermodules. *Acta Math. Sin. Chin. Ser.* **2007**, *50*, 909–914.

Article

A Note on Lagrange Interpolation of $|x|$ on the Chebyshev and Chebyshev–Lobatto Nodal Systems: The Even Cases

Elías Berriochoa [1,*,†], Alicia Cachafeiro [1,*,†], Héctor García-Rábade [2,†] and José Manuel García-Amor [3,†]

1. Departamento de Matemática Aplicada I, Universidad de Vigo, 36310 Vigo, Spain
2. Departamento de Matemática Aplicada II, Universidad de Vigo, 32004 Ourense, Spain; hector.garcia.rabade@uvigo.es
3. Xunta de Galicia, Instituto E. S. Valle Inclán, 36001 Pontevedra, Spain; garciaamor@edu.xunta.gal
* Correspondence: esnaola@uvigo.es (E.B.); acachafe@uvigo.es (A.C.); Tel.: +34-988-387216 (E.B.); +34-986-812138 (A.C.)
† These authors contributed equally to this work.

Abstract: Throughout this study, we continue the analysis of a recently found out Gibbs–Wilbraham phenomenon, being related to the behavior of the Lagrange interpolation polynomials of the continuous absolute value function. Our study establishes the error of the Lagrange polynomial interpolants of the function $|x|$ on $[-1,1]$, using Chebyshev and Chebyshev–Lobatto nodal systems with an even number of points. Moreover, with respect to the odd cases, relevant changes in the shape and the extrema of the error are given.

Keywords: Lagrange interpolation; Chebyshev nodal systems; Chebyshev–Lobatto nodal systems; absolute value approximation; rate of convergence; Gibbs–Wilbraham phenomena

MSC: 41A05; 65D05; 42C05

1. Introduction

The Gibbs–Wilbraham phenomenon, introduced in [1], is an important topic in function approximation and attracts much interest amongst researchers. It appears in different types of approximations, with its specific characteristics linked to each one. In brief, we can describe the phenomenon as the peculiar behavior of the approximations of a function with a jump discontinuity, using the usual Fourier series or different types of interpolation polynomials. Near the singularity, we have a large oscillation, and far away from the singularity, we have uniform convergence. Refs. [2–9] are devoted to researching the Gibbs–Wilbraham phenomena; however, all of them, though in different contexts, only refer to functions with jump discontinuities. A complete view of the recent research is reflected in [10].

In the recent article [11], we have studied the behavior of the Lagrange interpolators of $|x|$ based on the Chebyshev and Chebyshev–Lobatto nodal systems with an odd number of nodal points, or if preferred, when 0 is part of the nodal system. The approximation of $|x|$ by polynomials is an important topic since the paper of S. Bernstein, see [12]. We must refer to the introduction of this paper for the relevance of the problem and its possible development. The most relevant result, studied in depth, is that the approximations present a new Gibbs–Wilbraham phenomenon case. Indeed, we establish where and when the phenomenon occurs and give an accuracy approximation.

At least using interpolation, when we have the Gibbs–Wilbraham phenomenon, it is usual that minor changes in the nodal system have no effect on the shape of the phenomenon nor on its amplitudes, (see [3]). Therefore, we assumed that the study of the same interpolation problem changing the parity of the nodal systems had no interest, but we found that this was a mistake. In the present piece of work, we study the behavior of the Lagrange interpolators of $|x|$ based on the Chebyshev and Chebyshev–Lobatto nodal systems

with even order and, in the end, we conclude that the Gibbs–Wilbraham phenomena are strongly different in shape and amplitude.

This piece of work maintains a close logical connection with [11], even though we have reformulated its structure to make it less extensive and easier to read. For instance, we have recovered some interesting sums. We want to point out the key role of Lemma 2, which is an important advance with respect to the methods developed in that paper.

The article is structured as follows:

1. After this introductory section, in Section 2, we present two Lagrange interpolatory problems in the unit circle $\mathbb{T}$, $\mathbb{T} = \{z \in \mathbb{T} : |z| = 1\}$, related to the function $F(z) = \left|\frac{z+\frac{1}{z}}{2}\right|$. We must point out that we do not justify the interest of these problems in this section. The results obtained here will be translated in a well-known and short way to the real problem in Section 3, which is devoted to the problem and its results on the real line.
2. In Section 4, we present some numerical examples and the corresponding graphs.
3. Finally, in Section 5, we present the conclusions and further developments.

2. On the Unit Circle

As we have said, we consider two different nodal systems on the unit circle. One of them, N_T, is constituted by the $2n$ roots of -1 with $n = 2p$ (p a natural number), being the related nodal polynomial, that we denote by $W_{2n,T}(z)$, just $W_{2n,T}(z) = z^{2n} + 1$. The other one, N_U, is constituted by the $2n$ roots of 1 with $n = 2p+1$ (p a natural number), being the related nodal polynomial, that we denote $W_{2n,U}(z)$, just $W_{2n,U}(z) = z^{2n} - 1$. An important feature that N_T and N_U have in common is that i does not belong to them. Indeed, i is exactly the middle of the arc between two consecutive nodal points. Moreover, we can denote the systems in a common way by $\{\alpha_k\}_{k=0}^{2n-1}$; both are equidistributed nodal systems on $\mathbb{T}$ and we can think that α_0 is $ie^{-i\frac{\pi}{2n}}$ and that the system is clockwise ordered (see Figure 1 below). The reasons for these choices and the notation will be seen clearly in Section 3. We use these nodal systems to interpolate the function $F(z) = \left|\frac{z+\frac{1}{z}}{2}\right|$, which is the translation to $\mathbb{T}$ of $|x|$ through the Joukowsky transformation (see [13] for details).

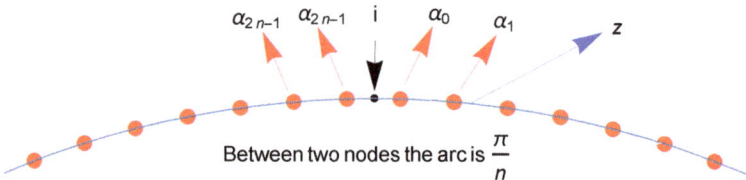

Figure 1. A common view of N_T and N_U near i.

The interpolation on the unit circle is not usually performed on the algebraic polynomial spaces. Instead of this, we use, due to completeness reasons, interpolation in subspaces of the space of Laurent polynomials $\Lambda[z] = \mathbb{P}[z] \oplus \mathbb{P}[\frac{1}{z}]$ and usually balanced spaces are used. Thus, in our case, we interpolate $F(z)$ in the space $\Lambda_{-n,n-1}[z] = \mathbb{P}_{n-1}[z] \oplus \mathbb{P}_n[\frac{1}{z}]$ and we denote the corresponding interpolating polynomials by $\mathcal{L}_{-n,n-1}(F,z,T)$ and $\mathcal{L}_{-n,n-1}(F,z,U)$, that is, corresponding to N_T and N_U, respectively. This problem is well-known, and in [3], we have given expressions for the interpolation polynomial in a quite general situation. Next, we translate some of them to our particular conditions.

1. The Laurent polynomials $\mathcal{L}_{-n,n-1}(F,z,T)$ and $\mathcal{L}_{-n,n-1}(F,z,U)$ have the following expressions

$$\mathcal{L}_{-n,n-1}(F,z,T) = \frac{W_{2n,T}(z)}{2n\, z^n} \sum_{j=0}^{2n-1} \frac{1}{\alpha_j^{n-1}(z-\alpha_j)} F(\alpha_j), \qquad (1)$$

and

$$\mathcal{L}_{-n,n-1}(F,z,U) = \frac{W_{2n,U}(z)}{2n\,z^n} \sum_{j=0}^{2n-1} \frac{1}{\alpha_j^{n-1}(z-\alpha_j)} F(\alpha_j). \qquad (2)$$

2. The barycentric formulae of type II for $\mathcal{L}_{-n,n-1}(F,z,T)$ and $\mathcal{L}_{-n,n-1}(F,z,U)$ are

$$\mathcal{L}_{-n,n-1}(F,z,T) = \frac{\sum_{j=0}^{2n-1} \frac{1}{\alpha_j^{n-1}(z-\alpha_j)} F(\alpha_j)}{\sum_{j=0}^{2n-1} \frac{1}{\alpha_j^{n-1}(z-\alpha_j)}} \text{ and } \mathcal{L}_{-n,n-1}(F,z,U) = \frac{\sum_{j=0}^{2n-1} \frac{1}{\alpha_j^{n-1}(z-\alpha_j)} F(\alpha_j)}{\sum_{j=0}^{2n-1} \frac{1}{\alpha_j^{n-1}(z-\alpha_j)}}. \qquad (3)$$

Barycentric formulae are easy to use and numerically stable in the sense of [14] in these cases.

Using exactly the same ideas as in [11], we can obtain an expression for the error between $F(z)$ and its interpolants when z is an element of $\mathbb{T}$ with $\Re(z), \Im(z) \geq 0$. We obtain

$$\mathcal{E}(F,z,T) = F(z) - \sum_{j=0}^{2n-1} F(\alpha_j) \frac{1}{z^n} \frac{W_{2n,T}(z)}{2n\alpha_j^{n-1}(z-\alpha_j)} = -2 \sum_{j=n}^{2n-1} F(\alpha_j) \frac{W_{2n,T}(z)}{z^n 2n} \frac{1}{\alpha_j^{n-1}(z-\alpha_j)},$$

and

$$\mathcal{E}(F,z,U) = F(z) - \sum_{j=0}^{2n-1} F(\alpha_j) \frac{1}{z^n} \frac{W_{2n,U}(z)}{2n\alpha_j^{n-1}(z-\alpha_j)} = -2 \sum_{j=n}^{2n-1} F(\alpha_j) \frac{W_{2n,U}(z)}{z^n 2n} \frac{1}{\alpha_j^{n-1}(z-\alpha_j)}.$$

We know that this error is, at most, of order $\frac{1}{2n}$ and we therefore study $2n\mathcal{E}(F,z,T)$ and $2n\mathcal{E}(F,z,U)$. After changing the index of the summation, we obtain:

$$2n\mathcal{E}(F,z,T) = -2\frac{W_{2n,T}(z)}{i^n z^n} \sum_{\ell=1}^{n} F(\alpha_{2n-\ell}) \frac{i^n}{\alpha_{2n-\ell}^{n-1}(z-\alpha_{2n-\ell})}, \qquad (4)$$

and

$$2n\mathcal{E}(F,z,U) = -2\frac{W_{2n,U}(z)}{i^n z^n} \sum_{\ell=1}^{n} F(\alpha_{2n-\ell}) \frac{i^n}{\alpha_{2n-\ell}^{n-1}(z-\alpha_{2n-\ell})}. \qquad (5)$$

Notice that the only, but relevant, differences between (4) and (5) and the expressions stated in [11] are just the superior limit of the summation and the corresponding nodal polynomials.

We can describe z as $z = ie^{-i\frac{\pi d}{n}}$. Taking into account the previous description of the nodal system, we have $\alpha_\ell = ie^{-i\frac{\pi(\ell+\frac{1}{2})}{n}}$ and $\alpha_{2n-\ell} = ie^{i\frac{\pi(\ell-\frac{1}{2})}{n}}$ (see Figure 1). These choices make the reinterpretation of the previous expressions possible. Indeed, it is easy to obtain $\frac{W_{2n,T}(z)}{i^n z^n} = 2\cos d\pi$ when n is even and newly $\frac{W_{2n,U}(z)}{i^n z^n} = 2\cos d\pi$ when n is odd.

On the other hand, $F(\alpha_{2n-\ell}) = -\frac{\alpha_{2n-\ell} + \frac{1}{\alpha_{2n-\ell}}}{2} = -\frac{ie^{i\frac{\pi(\ell-\frac{1}{2})}{n}} + \frac{1}{ie^{i\frac{\pi(\ell-\frac{1}{2})}{n}}}}{2} = -\Re(ie^{i\frac{\pi\ell}{n}}) = \sin\frac{(\ell-\frac{1}{2})\pi}{n}$ and

$$\frac{i^n}{\alpha_{2n-\ell}^{n-1}(z-\alpha_{2n-\ell})} = \frac{i^n}{\alpha_{2n-\ell}^n} \frac{1}{\frac{z}{\alpha_{2n-\ell}}-1} = \frac{i^n}{i^n\left(e^{i\frac{\pi(\ell-\frac{1}{2})}{n}}\right)^n} \frac{1}{\frac{ie^{-i\frac{\pi d}{n}}}{ie^{i\frac{\pi(\ell-\frac{1}{2})}{n}}}-1} =$$

$$i\frac{(-1)^\ell}{e^{-i\frac{\pi(d+\ell-\frac{1}{2})}{n}}-1} = i(-1)^\ell\left(-\frac{1}{2}+i\frac{\cos\frac{\pi(d+\ell-\frac{1}{2})}{2n}}{2\sin\frac{\pi(d+\ell-\frac{1}{2})}{2n}}\right). \tag{6}$$

For the last equality, we have used $\frac{1}{e^{-ix}-1} = -\frac{1}{2}+i\frac{\cos\frac{x}{2}}{2\sin\frac{x}{2}}$ (see [11] for details).

Hence, we have for $z = ie^{-i\frac{\pi d}{n}}$

$$2n\mathcal{E}(F,z,T) = -4\cos d\pi \sum_{\ell=1}^n i(-1)^\ell \left(-\frac{1}{2}+i\frac{\cos\frac{\pi(d+\ell-\frac{1}{2})}{2n}}{2\sin\frac{\pi(d+\ell-\frac{1}{2})}{2n}}\right)\sin\frac{(\ell-\frac{1}{2})\pi}{n} =$$

$$4\cos d\pi \sum_{\ell=1}^n (-1)^\ell \frac{\cos\frac{\pi(d+\ell-\frac{1}{2})}{2n}}{2\sin\frac{\pi(d+\ell-\frac{1}{2})}{2n}}\sin\frac{(\ell-\frac{1}{2})\pi}{n} + 2i\cos d\pi \sum_{\ell=1}^n (-1)^\ell \sin\frac{(\ell-\frac{1}{2})\pi}{n}, \tag{7}$$

and the expression is also true for $2n\mathcal{E}(F,z,U)$.

Lemma 1. *It holds*

(i) $\sum_{\ell=1}^n (-1)^\ell \sin\frac{(\ell-\frac{1}{2})\pi}{n} = -\frac{1}{2}\sin(n-1)\pi \sec\frac{\pi}{2n} = 0.$

(ii) $\sum_{\ell=1}^{n-1} (-1)^\ell \cos\frac{(\ell-\frac{1}{2})\pi}{n} = \frac{1}{2}\sec\frac{\pi}{2n}\left(\cos(n-1)\pi-1\right).$

Proof. All the sums that we gather in this lemma can be reconsidered as a sum of different geometric progressions by taking into account that $\sin\theta = \frac{e^{i\theta}-e^{-i\theta}}{2i}$ and $\cos\theta = \frac{e^{i\theta}+e^{-i\theta}}{2}$. Thus, the different problems can be confidently solved by a symbolic calculator. We have used Mathematica® 12.2 (Wolfram, Champaign, IL, USA) in all cases and made some elementary simplifications when necessary. □

Proposition 1. *For $z = ie^{-i\frac{\pi d}{n}}$, it holds*

$$2n\mathcal{E}(F,z,T) = 4\cos d\pi \sum_{\ell=1}^n (-1)^\ell \frac{\cos\frac{\pi(d+\ell-\frac{1}{2})}{2n}}{2\sin\frac{\pi(d+\ell-\frac{1}{2})}{2n}}\sin\frac{(\ell-\frac{1}{2})\pi}{n} \text{ and}$$

$$2n\mathcal{E}(F,z,U) = 4\cos d\pi \sum_{\ell=1}^n (-1)^\ell \frac{\cos\frac{\pi(d+\ell-\frac{1}{2})}{2n}}{2\sin\frac{\pi(d+\ell-\frac{1}{2})}{2n}}\sin\frac{(\ell-\frac{1}{2})\pi}{n}. \tag{8}$$

Proof. We can neglect the imaginary part of $2n\mathcal{E}(F,z,T)$ in (7) as a consequence of Lemma 1 (i). We obtain the same result for $2n\mathcal{E}(F,z,U)$ because (7) is valid for it too. We must point out that the same expression is correct for both errors although we have the difference in the parity of n, which we need to take into account. □

In the next Lemma, we present an auxiliary result, which represents an important advance in the methods developed in [11].

Lemma 2. *It holds*

$$\sum_{\ell=1}^{n}(-1)^\ell \frac{\cos\frac{(d+\ell-\frac{1}{2})\pi}{2n}}{2\sin\frac{(d+\ell-\frac{1}{2})\pi}{2n}} \sin\frac{(\ell-\frac{1}{2})\pi}{n} = Q_{1,n}(d) + Q_{2,n}(d) \text{ with}$$

$$Q_{1,n}(d) = \begin{cases} -\frac{1}{2}\sec\frac{\pi}{2n} & \text{if } n \text{ even} \\ -\frac{1}{2}\cos\frac{d\pi}{n} & \text{if } n \text{ odd} \end{cases} \text{ and} \tag{9}$$

$$Q_{2,n}(d) = -\frac{1}{2}\sin\frac{d\pi}{n}\sum_{\ell=1}^{n}(-1)^\ell \cot\frac{(d+\ell-\frac{1}{2})\pi}{2n}. \tag{10}$$

Proof. We use $\ell_1 = \ell - \frac{1}{2}$ to simplify the exposition. Because

$$\sin\frac{\ell_1\pi}{n} = \sin\left(\frac{(d+\ell_1)\pi}{n} - \frac{d\pi}{n}\right) = \sin\frac{(d+\ell_1)\pi}{n}\cos\frac{-d\pi}{n} + \cos\frac{(d+\ell_1)\pi}{n}\sin\frac{-d\pi}{n} =$$

$$2\sin\frac{(d+\ell_1)\pi}{2n}\cos\frac{(d+\ell_1)\pi}{2n}\cos\frac{d\pi}{n} - \left(\cos^2\frac{(d+\ell_1)\pi}{2n} - \sin^2\frac{(d+\ell_1)\pi}{2n}\right)\sin\frac{d\pi}{n} =$$

$$2\sin\frac{(d+\ell_1)\pi}{2n}\cos\frac{(d+\ell_1)\pi}{2n}\cos\frac{d\pi}{n} + 2\sin^2\frac{(d+\ell_1)\pi}{2n}\sin\frac{d\pi}{n} - \sin\frac{d\pi}{n}.$$

we have, taking $\ell_1 = \ell - \frac{1}{2}$,

$$\sum_{\ell=1}^{n}(-1)^\ell \frac{\cos\frac{(d+\ell_1)\pi}{2n}}{2\sin\frac{(d+\ell_1)\pi}{2n}} \sin\frac{\ell_1\pi}{n} =$$

$$\frac{1}{2}\sum_{\ell=1}^{n}(-1)^\ell \frac{\cos\frac{(d+\ell_1)\pi}{2n}}{\sin\frac{(d+\ell_1)\pi}{2n}}\left(2\sin\frac{(d+\ell_1)\pi}{2n}\cos\frac{(d+\ell_1)\pi}{2n}\cos\frac{d\pi}{n} + 2\sin^2\frac{(d+\ell_1)\pi}{2n}\sin\frac{d\pi}{n}\right) +$$

$$\left(-\frac{1}{2}\right)\sin\frac{d\pi}{n}\sum_{\ell=1}^{n}(-1)^\ell \frac{\cos\frac{(d+\ell_1)\pi}{2n}}{\sin\frac{(d+\ell_1)\pi}{2n}}.$$

Thus, we can define $Q_{2,n}(d) = -\frac{1}{2}\sin\frac{d\pi}{n}\sum_{\ell=1}^{n}(-1)^\ell \frac{\cos\frac{(d+\ell-\frac{1}{2})\pi}{2n}}{\sin\frac{(d+\ell-\frac{1}{2})\pi}{2n}}$, that is, as in (10), and we can also take

$$Q_{1,n}(d) =$$

$$\frac{1}{2}\sum_{\ell=1}^{n}(-1)^\ell \frac{\cos\frac{(d+\ell_1)\pi}{2n}}{\sin\frac{(d+\ell_1)\pi}{2n}}\left(2\sin\frac{(d+\ell_1)\pi}{2n}\cos\frac{(d+\ell_1)\pi}{2n}\cos\frac{d\pi}{n} + 2\sin^2\frac{(d+\ell_1)\pi}{2n}\sin\frac{d\pi}{n}\right) =$$

$$\frac{1}{2}\sum_{\ell=1}^{n}(-1)^\ell \left(2\cos^2\frac{(d+\ell_1)\pi}{2n}\cos\frac{d\pi}{n} + 2\sin\frac{(d+\ell_1)\pi}{2n}\cos\frac{(d+\ell_1)\pi}{2n}\sin\frac{d\pi}{n}\right) =$$

$$\frac{1}{2}\sum_{\ell=1}^{n}(-1)^\ell \left(\left(1+\cos\frac{(d+\ell_1)\pi}{n}\right)\cos\frac{d\pi}{n} + \sin\frac{(d+\ell_1)\pi}{n}\sin\frac{d\pi}{n}\right) =$$

$$\frac{1}{2}\left(\cos\frac{d\pi}{n}\sum_{\ell=1}^{n}(-1)^\ell + \sum_{\ell=1}^{n}(-1)^\ell \cos\frac{\ell_1\pi}{n}\right).$$

After using Lemma 1 (ii), we obtain for $Q_{1,n}(d)$ the expression

$$Q_{1,n}(d) = \frac{1}{2}\left(\cos\frac{d\pi}{n}\sum_{\ell=1}^{n}(-1)^{\ell} + \frac{1}{2}\sec\frac{\pi}{2n}(\cos(\pi(n-1))-1)\right).$$

Notice that $Q_{1,n}(d)$ is affected by the parity of n, and we conclude (9) because, when n is even, we have $Q_{1,n}(d) = -\frac{1}{2}\sec\frac{\pi}{2n}$, and when n is odd, we have $Q_{1,n}(d) = -\frac{1}{2}\cos\frac{d\pi}{n}$. □

In the sequel, we use the special function Phi of Hurwitz–Lerch with -1 as first argument, that is, $HurwitzLerchPhi[-1,s,d]$. It is defined by

$$HurwitzLerchPhi[-1,s,d] = \sum_{k=0}^{\infty}\frac{(-1)^k}{(k+d)^s}.$$

Moreover, in our case, $s = 1$. Thus, we use $HurwitzLerchPhi[-1,1,d]$, which we denote by $\eta(d)$ (see [15] for the details).

To obtain the main results of this section, we need some intermediate statements that we gather in Lemmas 3 and 4.

In [11], we have considered the expression $P_{2,n}(d) = -\frac{1}{2}\sin\frac{d\pi}{n}\sum_{\ell=1}^{n-1}(-1)^{\ell}\frac{\cos\frac{(d+\ell)\pi}{2n}}{\sin\frac{(d+\ell)\pi}{2n}}$ closely related to $Q_{2,n}(d)$. Next, we obtain some results about $P_{2,n}(d)$ based on that paper.

Lemma 3. *It holds:*

(i) *If* $-\frac{1}{2} \leq d \leq \sqrt{n}$, *then* $P_{2,n}(d) = d\eta(d+1) + \mathcal{O}\left(\frac{1}{\sqrt{n}}\right)$, *for all n.*

(ii) *If* $\sqrt{n} - \frac{1}{2} \leq d \leq \frac{n}{2} + \frac{1}{2}$, *then* $P_{2,n}(d) = \frac{1}{2}\cos\frac{d\pi}{n} + \mathcal{O}\left(\frac{1}{\sqrt{n}}\right)$, *when n is even.*

(iii) *If* $\sqrt{n} - \frac{1}{2} \leq d \leq \frac{n}{2} + \frac{1}{2}$, *then* $P_{2,n}(d) = \frac{1}{2} + \mathcal{O}\left(\frac{1}{\sqrt{n}}\right)$, *when n is odd.*

Proof. (i), (ii) and (iii) are, respectively, consequences of Propositions 5–7 (ii) of the last cited paper. Although the limits for d are different (they do not contain $\frac{1}{2}$), the behaviors do not change. □

Lemma 4. *If* $0 \leq d \leq \frac{n}{2}$, *it holds*

(i) $\sin\frac{d\pi}{2n}\sin\frac{(d-\frac{1}{2})\pi}{2n} = \frac{1}{2}\left(1-\cos\frac{d\pi}{n}\right) + \mathcal{O}\left(\frac{1}{n}\right).$

(ii) $\dfrac{\cos\frac{d\pi}{2n}}{\cos\frac{(d-\frac{1}{2})\pi}{2n}} = 1 + \mathcal{O}\left(\frac{1}{n}\right).$

(iii) $\sin\frac{d\pi}{n}\tan\frac{(d-\frac{1}{2})\pi}{2n} = 1 - \cos\frac{d\pi}{n} + \mathcal{O}\left(\frac{1}{n}\right).$

(iv) *If* $\sqrt{n} \leq d \leq \frac{n}{2}$, *then* $\dfrac{\sin\frac{d\pi}{n}}{\sin\frac{(d-\frac{1}{2})\pi}{2n}} = 1 + \mathcal{O}\left(\frac{1}{\sqrt{n}}\right).$

Proof. (i) It is obtained thanks to the Mean Value Theorem (MVT). It is verified that

$$\sin\frac{d\pi}{2n}\sin\frac{(d-\frac{1}{2})\pi}{2n} = \sin\frac{d\pi}{2n}\left(\sin\frac{d\pi}{2n} - \cos\xi\frac{\pi}{4n}\right) = \sin^2\frac{d\pi}{2n} + \mathcal{O}\left(\frac{1}{n}\right) =$$

$$\frac{1}{2}\left(1 - \cos\frac{d\pi}{n}\right) + \mathcal{O}\left(\frac{1}{n}\right).$$

We obtain (ii) newly applying the MVT. It is verified that

$$\frac{\cos\frac{d\pi}{2n}}{\cos\frac{(d-\frac{1}{2})\pi}{2n}} = \frac{\cos\frac{(d-\frac{1}{2})\pi}{2n} - \sin\zeta\frac{\pi}{4n}}{\cos\frac{(d-\frac{1}{2})\pi}{2n}} = 1 + \mathcal{O}\left(\frac{1}{n}\right).$$

Note that $\cos\frac{(d-\frac{1}{2})\pi}{2n} \geq \cos\frac{\pi}{4}$ as $0 \leq d \leq \frac{n}{2}$.

(iii) It is a consequence of (i) and (ii) because

$$\sin\frac{d\pi}{n}\tan\frac{(d-\frac{1}{2})\pi}{2n} = 2\sin\frac{d\pi}{2n}\sin\frac{(d-\frac{1}{2})\pi}{2n}\frac{\cos\frac{d\pi}{2n}}{\cos\frac{(d-\frac{1}{2})\pi}{2n}} =$$

$$2\left(\frac{1}{2}\left(1-\cos\frac{d\pi}{n}\right) + \mathcal{O}\left(\frac{1}{n}\right)\right)\left(1+\mathcal{O}\left(\frac{1}{n}\right)\right) = 1 - \cos\frac{d\pi}{n} + \mathcal{O}\left(\frac{1}{n}\right).$$

(iv) It can be proved in the same way as (ii). □

Theorem 1. *Let $z = ie^{-i\frac{\pi d}{n}}$. If $\sqrt{n} \leq d \leq \frac{n}{2}$, then $2n\mathcal{E}(F,z,T) = \mathcal{O}(\frac{1}{\sqrt{n}})$ and $2n\mathcal{E}(F,z,U) = \mathcal{O}(\frac{1}{\sqrt{n}})$.*

Proof. First, we prove our thesis for $2n\mathcal{E}(F,z,T)$, that is, when n is even. We know that $2n\mathcal{E}(F,z,T) = 4\cos d\pi(Q_{1,n}(d) + Q_{2,n}(d))$, with $Q_{1,n}(d), Q_{2,n}(d))$ given in (9) and (10). We can write

$$Q_{2,n}(d) = -\frac{1}{2}\sin\frac{d\pi}{n}\sum_{\ell=1}^{n}(-1)^\ell \cot\frac{(d+\ell-\frac{1}{2})\pi}{2n} =$$

$$-\frac{1}{2}\sin\frac{d\pi}{n}\sum_{\ell=1}^{n-1}(-1)^\ell \cot\frac{(d+\ell-\frac{1}{2})\pi}{2n} - \frac{1}{2}\sin\frac{d\pi}{n}(-1)^n \cot\frac{(d+n-\frac{1}{2})\pi}{2n} =$$

$$\frac{\sin\frac{d\pi}{n}}{\sin\frac{(d-\frac{1}{2})\pi}{n}}\underbrace{\left(-\frac{1}{2}\sin\frac{(d-\frac{1}{2})\pi}{n}\sum_{\ell=1}^{n-1}(-1)^\ell \cot\frac{(d+\ell-\frac{1}{2})\pi}{2n}\right)}_{*} + \underbrace{\frac{1}{2}\sin\frac{d\pi}{n}\tan\frac{(d-\frac{1}{2})\pi}{2n}}_{**}. \quad (11)$$

This expression is more complex, but it is convenient as we can see that

$$* = \left(1 + \mathcal{O}\left(\frac{1}{\sqrt{n}}\right)\right)\left(\frac{1}{2}\cos\frac{d\pi}{n} + \mathcal{O}\left(\frac{1}{\sqrt{n}}\right)\right)$$

(see Lemma 3 (ii) and Lemma 4 (iv)) and

$$** = \frac{1}{2}\left(1 - \cos\frac{d\pi}{n}\right) + \mathcal{O}\left(\frac{1}{\sqrt{n}}\right)$$

(see Lemma 4 (iii)). Thus, we have $Q_{2,n}(d) = \frac{1}{2} + \mathcal{O}(\frac{1}{\sqrt{n}})$. Taking into account that $Q_{1,n}(d) = -\frac{1}{2}\sec\frac{\pi}{2n}$, we have the result for $2n\mathcal{E}(F,z,T)$.

We use the same ideas for $2n\mathcal{E}(F,z,U)$, that is, when n is odd, and we obtain

$$* = (1 + \mathcal{O}\left(\frac{1}{\sqrt{n}}\right))\left(\frac{1}{2} + \mathcal{O}\left(\frac{1}{\sqrt{n}}\right)\right)$$

and

$$** = -\frac{1}{2}\left(1 - \cos\frac{d\pi}{n}\right) + \mathcal{O}\left(\frac{1}{\sqrt{n}}\right)$$

and $Q_{1,n}(d) = -\frac{1}{2}\cos\frac{d\pi}{n}$. These elements lead us to the same result for $2n\mathcal{E}(F,z,U)$. □

Lemma 5. *If $0 \leq d \leq \sqrt{n}$, then* $\sin\frac{d\pi}{n}\frac{\sin(d-\frac{1}{2})\pi}{\sin\frac{(d-\frac{1}{2})\pi}{n}} = \mathcal{O}(1)$.

Proof. Let us suppose that $d \geq 1$. In this case, we write $\left|\frac{\sin\frac{d\pi}{n}\sin(d-\frac{1}{2})\pi}{\sin\frac{(d-\frac{1}{2})\pi}{n}}\right| \leq \frac{\frac{d\pi}{n}}{\frac{2}{\pi}\frac{(d-\frac{1}{2})\pi}{n}} =$
$\mathcal{O}(1)$. When $0 \leq d \leq 1$ and $d \neq \frac{1}{2}$, we obtain $\left|\frac{\sin\frac{d\pi}{n}\sin(d-\frac{1}{2})\pi}{\sin\frac{(d-\frac{1}{2})\pi}{n}}\right| \leq \frac{\frac{d\pi}{n}(d-\frac{1}{2})\pi}{\frac{2}{\pi}\frac{(d-\frac{1}{2})\pi}{n}} =$
$\mathcal{O}(1)$. □

Lemma 6. *If $0 \leq d \leq \sqrt{n}$, it holds*

$$\cos d\pi\, Q_{2,n}(d) = \cos d\pi \left(-\frac{1}{2}\sin\frac{d\pi}{n}\sum_{\ell=1}^{n}(-1)^\ell \frac{\cos\frac{(d+\ell-\frac{1}{2})\pi}{2n}}{\sin\frac{(d+\ell-\frac{1}{2})\pi}{2n}}\right) = \cos(d\pi)\,d\,\eta(d+\frac{1}{2}) + \mathcal{O}\left(\frac{1}{\sqrt{n}}\right) \quad (12)$$

Proof. Considering (11), we have

$$\cos d\pi\, Q_{2,n}(d) =$$

$$\underbrace{\cos d\pi \frac{\sin\frac{d\pi}{n}}{\sin\frac{(d-\frac{1}{2})\pi}{n}}\left(-\frac{1}{2}\sin\frac{(d-\frac{1}{2})\pi}{n}\sum_{\ell=1}^{n-1}(-1)^\ell \cot\frac{(d+\ell-\frac{1}{2})\pi}{2n}\right)}_{*} +$$

$$\underbrace{\cos d\pi \frac{1}{2}\sin\frac{d\pi}{n}\tan\frac{(d-\frac{1}{2})\pi}{2n}}_{**}. \quad (13)$$

The term ** of (13) is, in our case, $\mathcal{O}\left(\frac{1}{n}\right)$. For the other term, which is the relevant one, and taking into account that $\cos d\pi = -\sin(d-1/2)\pi$, Lemma 3 (i) and Lemma 5, we obtain

$$* = \cos d\pi \frac{\sin\frac{d\pi}{n}}{\sin\frac{(d-\frac{1}{2})\pi}{n}}\left(-\frac{1}{2}\sin\frac{(d-\frac{1}{2})\pi}{n}\sum_{\ell=1}^{n-1}(-1)^\ell \cot\frac{(d+\ell-\frac{1}{2})\pi}{2n}\right) =$$

$$-\sin\frac{d\pi}{n}\frac{\sin(d-1/2)\pi}{\sin\frac{(d-1/2)\pi}{n}}\left((d-\frac{1}{2})\eta(d+\frac{1}{2}) + \mathcal{O}\left(\frac{1}{\sqrt{n}}\right)\right) =$$

$$-\sin\frac{d\pi}{n}\frac{\sin(d-1/2)\pi}{\sin\frac{(d-1/2)\pi}{n}}(d-\frac{1}{2})\eta(d+\frac{1}{2}) + \mathcal{O}(1)\mathcal{O}\left(\frac{1}{\sqrt{n}}\right).$$

Therefore, using newly $\cos d\pi = -\sin(d-1/2)\pi$, we obtain

$$* = \cos d\pi \frac{\sin \frac{d\pi}{n}}{\sin \frac{(d-\frac{1}{2})\pi}{n}} (d - \frac{1}{2}) \eta(d + \frac{1}{2}) + \mathcal{O}\left(\frac{1}{\sqrt{n}}\right) =$$

$$\cos d\pi \frac{\sin \frac{d\pi}{n}}{\frac{d\pi}{n}} \frac{\frac{(d-\frac{1}{2})\pi}{n}}{\sin \frac{(d-1/2)\pi}{n}} d\, \eta(d + \frac{1}{2}) + \mathcal{O}\left(\frac{1}{\sqrt{n}}\right) =$$

$$\cos(d\pi)\, d\, \eta(d + \frac{1}{2}) \left(1 + \mathcal{O}\left(\frac{1}{n^2}\right)\right) \left(1 + \mathcal{O}\left(\frac{1}{n^2}\right)\right) + \mathcal{O}\left(\frac{1}{\sqrt{n}}\right). \quad (14)$$

For the last equality of (14), we have used the well-known facts that $\frac{x}{\sin x}$ and $\frac{\sin x}{x}$ are both $1 + \mathcal{O}(x^2)$, when x is small. Thus, we can conclude (12). □

Theorem 2. *Let $z = ie^{-i\frac{\pi d}{n}}$ and $0 \leq d \leq \sqrt{n}$.*

(i) *If n is even, then $2n\mathcal{E}(F, z, T) = 4\cos d\pi \left(d\, \eta(d + \frac{1}{2}) - \frac{1}{2} \sec \frac{\pi}{2n}\right) + \mathcal{O}\left(\frac{1}{\sqrt{n}}\right)$. Moreover, for n large enough, $2n\mathcal{E}(F, z, T)$ behaves like $4\cos d\pi \left(d\, \eta(d + \frac{1}{2}) - \frac{1}{2}\right)$ and the error is $\mathcal{O}\left(\frac{1}{\sqrt{n}}\right)$.*

(ii) *If n is odd, then $2n\mathcal{E}(F, z, U) = 4\cos d\pi \left(d\, \eta(d + \frac{1}{2}) - \frac{1}{2} \cos \frac{d\pi}{n}\right) + \mathcal{O}\left(\frac{1}{\sqrt{n}}\right)$. Moreover, for n large enough, $2n\mathcal{E}(F, z, U)$ behaves like $4\cos d\pi \left(d\, \eta(d + \frac{1}{2}) - \frac{1}{2}\right)$ and the error is $\mathcal{O}\left(\frac{1}{\sqrt{n}}\right)$.*

Proof. Both facts are straightforward consequences of Proposition 1 and Lemmas 2 and 6. Both expressions can be approximated by $4\cos d\pi \left(d\, \eta(d + \frac{1}{2}) - \frac{1}{2}\right) + \mathcal{O}\left(\frac{1}{\sqrt{n}}\right)$. □

We can conclude the following:

1. It appears a Gibbs–Wilbraham phenomenon. Theorem 1 states $2n\mathcal{E}(F, z, T)$ and $2n\mathcal{E}(F, z, U)$ converge uniformly to 0 far from i but, as a consequence of Theorem 2, they present a strong oscillation close to i. The limits for these behaviors are clearly stated.
2. An important consequence of Theorem 2 is that we can asymptotically approximate $2n\mathcal{E}(F, z, T)$ (or $2n\mathcal{E}(F, z, U)$) near i by $4\cos d\pi \left(d\, \eta(d + \frac{1}{2}) - \frac{1}{2}\right)$. Notice that the extrema of the error must be asymptotically near the extrema of the approximation. It is easy to obtain these last extrema. We have done this by using the sequence of Mathematica® commands gathered in the extremaerror file of https://github.com/eberriochoa/Absolute-value-interpolation-The-even-cases (accessed on 2 June 2022). The results are presented in Table 1.
3. Finally, the more relevant result is that the Gibbs–Wilbraham phenomenon is completely different with the corresponding phenomenon when i belongs to the nodal systems (see [11]). This can be appreciated in shapes and extrema.

Table 1. Extrema of $4\cos d\pi \left(d\, \eta(d + \frac{1}{2}) - \frac{1}{2}\right)$.

In the Interval	The Extremum is Attained at (d Value)	Being the Extremum
$[0, \frac{1}{2}]$	0	-2
$[\frac{1}{2}, \frac{3}{2}]$	0.864497	0.310441
$[\frac{3}{2}, \frac{5}{2}]$	1.91506	-0.103946
$[\frac{5}{2}, \frac{7}{2}]$	2.93871	0.0504843
$[\frac{7}{2}, \frac{9}{2}]$	3.95233	-0.0294926
$[\frac{9}{2}, \frac{11}{2}]$	4.96111	-0.179272

3. Interpolation of $|x|$ on Chebyshev and Chebyshev–Lobatto Nodal Systems with Even Nodes

In the sequel, $\ell_{m-1}(|x|, x, T_m)$ denotes the Lagrange interpolation polynomial which interpolates $|x|$ on the Chebyshev nodal system constituted by the m roots of $T_m(x)$, the Chebyshev polynomial of degree m. Similarly, $\ell_{m+1}(|x|, x, U_m)$ denotes the Lagrange interpolation polynomial which interpolates $|x|$ on the Chebyshev–Lobatto nodal system constituted by the m roots of $U_m(x)$, the Chebyshev polynomial of degree m, plus ± 1. In both cases, we consider m even. Classical references about Chebyshev polynomials are [16,17]. Taking into account the symmetry of the problem, it is immediate that $\ell_{m-1}(|x|, -x, T_m) = \ell_{m-1}(|x|, x, T_m)$. Thus, $\ell_{m-1}(|x|, x, T_m)$ cannot have odd monomials, and it is a polynomial of degree $m-2$ at most. Similarly, $\ell_{m+1}(|x|, x, U_m)$ is a polynomial of degree m at most. If we consider the Joukowsky–Szegő transformation with x and z related to $x = \frac{z + \frac{1}{z}}{2}$, we have that the Chebyshev nodes are related to N_T (the $2m$ roots of -1) and the Chebyshev–Lobatto nodes are related to N_U (the $2m + 2$ roots of 1). Moreover, $\ell_{m-1}(|x|, \frac{z+\frac{1}{z}}{2}, T_m)$ interpolates $F(z) = |\frac{z+\frac{1}{z}}{2}|$ on N_T. As $\ell_{m-1}(|x|, \frac{z+\frac{1}{z}}{2}, T_m)$ belongs to $\Lambda_{-m,m-1}[z]$, we can conclude that $\ell_{m-1}(|x|, \frac{z+\frac{1}{z}}{2}, T_m) = \mathcal{L}_{-n,n-1}(F, z, T)$. Furthermore, as this is a roundtrip, we know the behavior of $|x| - \ell_{m-1}(|x|, x, T_m)$, taking into account the behavior of $|\frac{z+\frac{1}{z}}{2}| - \mathcal{L}_{-m,m-1}(F, z, T)$. A similar affirmation is true for $\ell_{m+1}(|x|, x, U_m)$. Thus, we can state the next theorems.

Theorem 3. *For $x = \sin \frac{d\pi}{m}$, it holds*

1. *If $\sqrt{m} \le d \le \frac{m}{2}$, then*
    $$2m(|x| - \ell_{m-1}(|x|, x, T_m)) = \mathcal{O}\left(\frac{1}{\sqrt{m}}\right) \text{ and}$$
    $$2(m+1)(|x| - \ell_{m+1}(|x|, x, U_m)) = \mathcal{O}\left(\frac{1}{\sqrt{m}}\right).$$

2. *If $0 \le d \le \frac{m}{2}$, then*
    $$2m(|x| - \ell_{m-1}(|x|, x, T_m)) = 4 \cos d\pi \left(d\eta(d+\tfrac{1}{2}) - \tfrac{1}{2}\right) + \mathcal{O}\left(\frac{1}{\sqrt{m}}\right) \text{ and}$$
    $$2(m+1)(|x| - \ell_{m+1}(|x|, x, U_m)) = 4 \cos d\pi \left(d\eta(d+\tfrac{1}{2}) - \tfrac{1}{2}\right) + \mathcal{O}\left(\frac{1}{\sqrt{m}}\right).$$

Proof. Take into account the preceding paragraph and Theorems 1 and 2. □

4. Numerical Experiments and Graphs

All the graphs which can be seen below have been obtained by using a sequence of commands of Mathematica® 12.2. We share these codes and the graphs through the link https://github.com/eberriochoa/Absolute-value-interpolation-The-even-cases (accessed on 2 June 2022). The representations are always related to the function $F(z) = |\frac{z+\frac{1}{z}}{2}|$ and the interpolation polynomial $\mathcal{L}_{-n,n-1}(F, z, T)$ for $n = 200$. For simplicity, we use the variable θ, with $z = e^{i\theta}$, in the plots.

We have tested that the graphs for other values of n do not present changes.

Figure 2 presents a general view of the interpolation on the left-hand side. On the right-hand side, we have the representation considering both functions multiplied by $2n$, and we can appreciate that the interpolation has problems near i, or equivalently $\theta = \frac{\pi}{2}$.

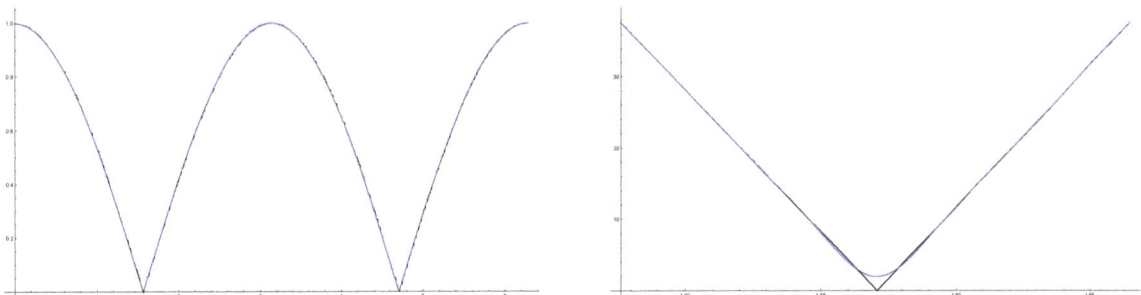

Figure 2. A general view of $F(z)$ and $\mathcal{L}_{-200,199}(F,z,T)$ on the left and a detailed view of both scaled functions near i on the right.

Figure 3 gives a good idea of the Gibbs–Wilbraham phenomenon. It presents the difference between $F(z)$ and $\mathcal{L}_{-200,199}(F,z,T)$ multiplied by $2n$, that is, $2n\mathcal{E}(F,z,T)$. It is clear that far enough from $\pm i$, this difference is close to 0. On the other hand, when we are near the singularities, the function presents an oscillatory behavior. This behavior is more pronounced the closer we get to the singularities.

Figure 3. A neat view of the Gibbs–Wilbraham phenomena. The representation of $2n\mathcal{E}(F,z,T)$ along $\mathbb{T}$ for $n = 200$.

Figure 4 gives a good idea of the behavior near i. The figure presents $2n\mathcal{E}(F,z,T)$ and the approximation given in Theorem 2 along 30 arcs centered in i. We must point out that the functions are indistinguishable.

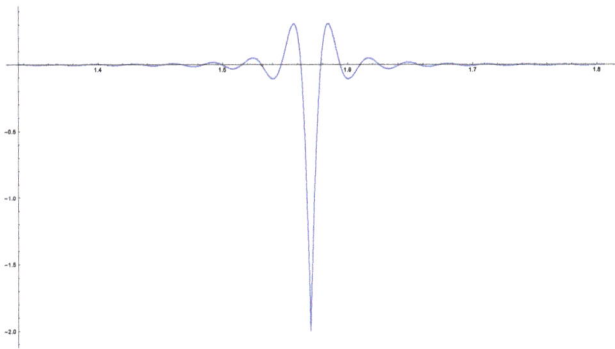

Figure 4. A detailed view of the Gibbs–Wilbraham phenomena. The representation of $2n\mathcal{E}(F,z,T)$ along 30 arcs near i for $n = 200$.

Figure 5 is a detail of Figure 4. $2n\mathcal{E}(F, z, T)$ and the approximation given in Theorem 2 along 30 arcs centered in i are presented. We must point out that the functions are indistinguishable.

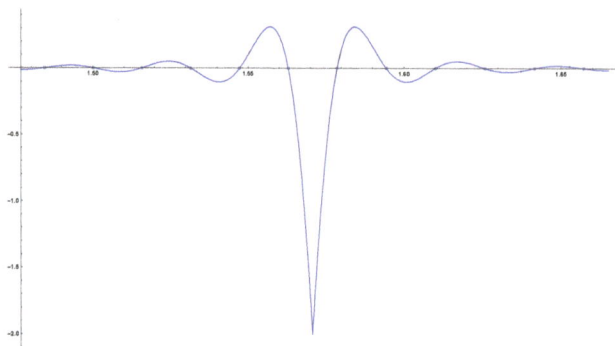

Figure 5. A detailed view of the Gibbs–Wilbraham phenomena. The representation of $2n\mathcal{E}(F, z, T)$ along 12 arcs near i for $n = 200$.

Figure 6 shows us an important difference between the Gibbs–Wilbraham phenomenon in the interpolation of the jump function, defined by $F(z) = \begin{cases} 1 & z \in \mathbb{T}, \Re(z) \geq 0 \\ -1 & z \in \mathbb{T}, \Re(z) < 0 \end{cases}$, and the Gibbs–Wilbraham phenomenon in the interpolation of the absolute value function. The Gibbs–Wilbraham phenomenon does not depend on the parity of the nodal system in the first case; meanwhile, it depends on the parity in the second one.

In Figure 6 (at the left), we represent the Lagrange interpolation polynomials of the jump function based on the roots of $T_{200}(x)$ (in black) and on the roots of $T_{201}(x)$ (in blue); it is remarkable that the Gibbs–Wilbraham phenomena are similar in shape and extrema.

On the other hand, Figure 6 (at the right) presents the Lagrange interpolation polynomials of the absolute value based on the roots of $T_{200}(x)$ (in black) and on the roots of $T_{201}(x)$ (in blue); it is remarkable that the Gibbs–Wilbraham phenomena are completely different in shape and extrema.

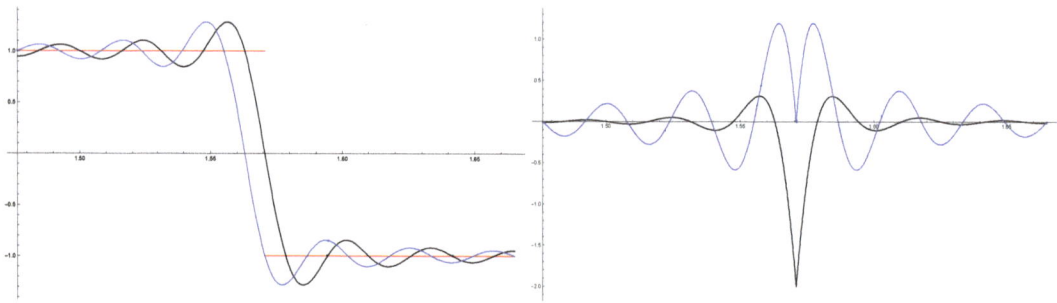

Figure 6. Left: Noninfluence of the parity on the error, n odd and even and Lagrange interpolation of jump function. **Right**: Influence of parity on error, n odd and even and Lagrange interpolation of $|x|$.

5. Conclusions and Future Work

The objective of this work is not to suppress the Gibbs–Wilbraham phenomena, but a better knowledge of them could help to develop the research with this goal. Refs. [18,19] are interesting papers of this research line.

We think that there is a lot of possible future work related to the Gibbs–Wilbraham phenomena for functions with very local singularities.

First of all, we have evidence about the phenomenon when the singularity is 0 (or $\pm i$ thinking in $\mathbb{T}$). Therefore, we must perform some work to extend our knowledge to problems related to arbitrary points.

A second point of interest is the order of the derivative which has the singularity. We have evidence only for 0 (Jump function) and 1 (absolute value), but it is clear that the same problem for derivatives of greater order could be of interest. In this sense, we want to emphasize the role that Lemma 2, a key point in this article, could play in the development of this research.

6. Materials and Methods

To perform the numerical experiments included in this piece of work, we have used the notation and formulae included in the paper. We created three programs which can be obtained at the url https://github.com/eberriochoa/Absolute-value-interpolation-The-even-cases (accessed on 2 June 2022). These files are the text of notebooks elaborated with Mathematica® 12.2. These programs (notebooks) should run correctly with recent previous versions and future versions because we use only simple commands. Furthermore, we do not use compiled routines.

7. Discussion

Recently, we have published the paper [11], which presents the behavior of the Lagrange interpolation polynomial of the continuous absolute value function, using Chebyshev and Chebyshev–Lobatto systems with an odd number of points.

The aim of the present piece of work is to continue the analysis of this new Gibbs–Wilbraham phenomenon. Our study establishes the error of the Lagrange polynomial interpolants of the function $|x|$ on the bounded interval $[-1, 1]$, using Chebyshev and Chebyshev–Lobatto nodal systems with an even number of points.

It could be thought that there is no novelty in this approach. Indeed, at the beginning, we thought that the results would have to be the same or quite similar. Nevertheless, as we said in our introduction, this is a presumed idea. Moreover, relevant changes with respect to the odd cases in the shape and the extrema of the error are given. This is an important difference with the usual Gibbs–Wilbraham phenomenon related to the Lagrange interpolation of functions with jump discontinuities.

We think that the findings presented in our paper would be useful for applied mathematicians and numerical analysts interested in the reconstruction of a function using Lagrange interpolation and approximation theory.

Author Contributions: Conceptualization, E.B., A.C., H.G.-R. and J.M.G.-A.; investigation, E.B., A.C., H.G.-R. and J.M.G.-A.; software, E.B., A.C., H.G.R. and J.M.G.-A.; writing—original draft, E.B., A.C., H.G.-R. and J.M.G.-A. All authors have read and agreed to the published version of the manuscript.

Funding: This document is the result of a research project partially funded (first two authors) by the Ministerio de Ciencia e Innovación under grant PID2020-116764RB-I00.

Institutional Review Board Statement: Not applicable.

Informed Consent Statement: Not applicable.

Data Availability Statement: Not applicable.

Conflicts of Interest: The authors declare no conflict of interest.

References

1. Gibbs, J.W. Fourier's series. *Nature* **1898**, *59*, 606. [CrossRef]
2. Berriochoa, E.; Cachafeiro, A.; Díaz, J. Gibbs phenomenon in the Hermite interpolation on the circle. *Appl. Math. Comput.* **2015**, *253*, 274–286. [CrossRef]
3. Berriochoa, E.; Cachafeiro, A.; García Amor, J.M. Gibbs-Wilbraham phenomenon on Lagrange interpolation based on analytic weights on the unit circle. *J. Comput. Appl. Math.* **2020**, *365*, 17. [CrossRef]

4. Davis, J.M.; Hagelstein, P. Gibbs phenomena for some classical orthogonal polynomials. *J. Math. Anal. Appl.* **2022**, *505*, 14. [CrossRef]
5. Helmberg, G. The Gibbs phenomenon for Fourier interpolation. *J. Approx. Theory* **1994**, *78*, 41–63. [CrossRef]
6. Helmberg, G. A limit function for equidistant Fourier interpolation. *J. Approx. Theory* **1995**, *81*, 389–396. [CrossRef]
7. Helmberg, G.; Wagner, P. Manipulating Gibbs phenomenon for Fourier interpolation. *J. Approx. Theory* **1997**, *89*, 308–320. [CrossRef]
8. Hewitt, E.; Hewitt, R. The Gibbs-Wilbraham phenomenon: An episode in Fourier analysis. *Arch. Hist. Exact Sci.* **1980**, *21*, 129–160. [CrossRef]
9. Trefethen, L.N. *Approximation Theory and Approximation Practice*; Society for Industrial and Applied Mathematics (SIAM): Philadelphia, PA, USA, 2013.
10. Jerri, A.J. (Ed.) *Advances in The Gibbs Phenomenon*, 1st ed.; Σ Sampling Publishing: Potsdam, NY, USA, 2007.
11. Berriochoa, E.; Cachafeiro, A.; García Amor, J.M.; García Rábade, H. The Gibbs–Wilbraham phenomenon in the approximation of $|x|$ by using Lagrange interpolation on the Chebyshev–Lobatto nodal systems. *J. Comput. Appl. Math.* **2022**, *414*, 22. [CrossRef]
12. Bernstein, S. Sur la meilleure approximation de $|x|$ par des polynômes de degrés donnés. *Acta Math.* **1914**, *37*, 1–57. [CrossRef]
13. Szegő, G. *Orthogonal Polynomials*, 4th ed.; American Mathematical Society: Providence, RI, USA, 1975; Volume 23.
14. Higham, N.J. The numerical stability of barycentric Lagrange interpolation. *IMA J. Numer. Anal.* **2004**, *24*, 547–556. [CrossRef]
15. Erdélyi, A.; Magnus, W.; Oberhettinger, F.; Tricomi, F.G. *Higher Transcendental Functions*; R.E. Krieger Publishing Co., Inc.: Melbourne, VI, USA, 1981; Volume 1.
16. Mason, J.C.; Handscomb, D.C. *Chebyshev Polynomials*; Chapman & Hall/CRC: Boca Raton, FL, USA, 2003.
17. Rivlin, T. The Chebyshev polynomials. In *Pure and Applied Mathematics*; John Wiley & Sons: New York, NY, USA, 1974.
18. Adcock, B.; Platte, R.B. A mapped polynomial method for high-accuracy approximations on arbitrary grids. *SIAM J. Numer. Anal.* **2016**, *54*, 2256–2281. [CrossRef]
19. De Marchi, S.; Marchetti, F.; Perracchione, E.; Poggiali, D. Polynomial interpolation via mapped bases without resampling. *Comput. Appl. Math.* **2020**, *364*, 112347. [CrossRef]

Article

An Interval-Simplex Approach to Determine Technological Parameters from Experimental Data

Ilia Beloglazov * and Kirill Krylov

Department of Automation of Technological Processes and Production, Saint Petersburg Mining University, 199106 Saint Petersburg, Russia
* Correspondence: beloglazov_ii@pers.spmi.ru

Abstract: Statistical equations are widely used to describe the laws of various chemical technological processes. The values of constants and parameters included in these equations are determined by various methods. Methods that can determine the values of equation parameters using a limited amount of experimental data are of particular practical interest. In this manuscript, we propose a method to obtain simplex-interval equations. The proposed approach can be effectively used to control the values of technological process parameters. In this paper, we consider examples of chemical kinetics equation transformations and heterogeneous processes of solid particle dissolution. In addition, we describes mathematical model transformations, including equations for functions of the residence time distribution (RTD) of apparatus particles, the distribution of particles by size, etc. Finally, we apply the proposed approach to an example involving modeling of the calcination of coke in a tubular rotary kiln.

Keywords: kinetic equations; chemical process; simplex method; interval method; metallurgical process; residence time distribution; mathematical modeling; tubular rotary kiln

MSC: 65G30

Citation: Beloglazov, I.; Krylov, K. An Interval-Simplex Approach to Determine Technological Parameters from Experimental Data. *Mathematics* 2022, *10*, 2959. https://doi.org/10.3390/math10162959

Academic Editors: Irina Cristea, Yuriy Rogovchenko, Justo Puerto, Gintautas Dzemyda and Patrick Siarry

Received: 4 August 2022
Accepted: 12 August 2022
Published: 16 August 2022

Publisher's Note: MDPI stays neutral with regard to jurisdictional claims in published maps and institutional affiliations.

Copyright: © 2022 by the authors. Licensee MDPI, Basel, Switzerland. This article is an open access article distributed under the terms and conditions of the Creative Commons Attribution (CC BY) license (https://creativecommons.org/licenses/by/4.0/).

1. Introduction

Fundamental analytical dependencies are necessary to determine performance indicators of technological processes. Adequate mathematical models can be created by considering the peculiarities of chemical reactions and mass transfer course. In engineering practice, differential equations of various orders are used to create mathematical models. The numerical solution of such equations is difficult in most cases. Therefore, when a direct solution is impossible, equations and their boundary conditions are analyzed in order to formulate approximate solutions in the form of a similarity criteria general function. Similarity criteria are usually derived either by analyzing differential equations, describing the process under study and their boundary conditions, or using the dimensional analysis method.

The method of dimensional analysis is supplemented by expert assessment to increase the reliability of obtained characteristics of complex processes in engineering design practice [1–3]. The disadvantages of these methods ultimately lead to attainment of approximate equations describing the process, limiting their applicability in engineering calculation practice [4].

In connection with the approximate nature of the criterion equations obtained by this method, the development of a method for transforming equations into a criterial form is of practical and theoretical interest. Therefore, in this article, we propose a new approach using the simplex method.

The efficiency of chemical and metallurgical apparatus depends not only on the technological mode but also on design features, which determine the final result [5,6]. To determine the optimal design and dimensions of an apparatus, it is necessary to take into consideration the chemical reactions rates, heat and mass transfer, and the hydrodynamic mode or flow behavior of the apparatus.

Optimization methods, such as artificial neural networks [7–9], the simplex method [10–13], and genetic algorithms [14–16], as well as various combinations thereof [17,18], provide effective means of determining the optimal values of process parameters, leading to optimal conditions. Such methods differ in terms of the height of the determined optimum, the number of experiments, and the required time.

Batch, semi-periodic, and continuous reactors are commonly used in modern industrial chains. Continuous reactors are most effective due to superior unit productivity and continuous automated operation and control ability. Batch units are usually used only in industries with small reaction phase flows. The economic efficiency of the latter mostly depends on appropriate configuration of technological reactor and process parameter values [3,13,15,19,20].

Residence time distribution modeling is used for various chemical engineering processes, for example, to describe the full cycle of a continuous production line or the complex behavior of a single unit in a technological chain. Mathematical models of multiple connected ideal or non-ideal reactors with a known analytical RTD are used in major cases. The most common types are continuous stirred tank reactors (CSTRs) and plug flow reactors (PFRs). However, these reactor types are too idealized for correct modeling of the behavior of real processes. Therefore, a combination of various models takes into account the characteristics of fluid flow, including effects such as dead zones, non-ideal back mixing, and bypassing effects. Furthermore, the determination of combined model parameters is complicated. Non-linear programming methods are used for such task. The proposed approach of RTD modeling is used, for example, in the development of chemical reactions, metallurgy, pharmaceuticals, water purification processes, etc. [21–24].

The main factors influencing any type of apparatus operation include:

(1) Thermodynamic factors: constants of chemical and phase equilibrium. This group of factors determines the reaction direction and technological parameters and affects the rate and selectivity of the entire process [25];
(2) Kinetic factors: rate constants and activation energies of the main and side reactions, as well as the reaction's true and apparent orders [4,25];
(3) Mass transfer factors: mass transfer coefficients of initial and intermediate substances and final reaction products [6,26];
(4) Heat exchange factors: heat transfer coefficients within phases and between the medium and heat exchange devices, as well as the external heat exchange surface size [15];
(5) Hydrodynamic factors: interface characteristics and mixing in continuous and dispersed phases [3,25].

The last factor in the above list plays the main role, as the hydrodynamic environment decisively affects the heat rate and mass transfer processes, as well as the chemical process rate [4,26].

The operation of technological equipment is characterized by close connections between productivity, quality, and production cost. The latter depends on the optimal time of the raw material's actual stay in the apparatus. With an unjustified delay of raw materials in the apparatus, the equipment's overall performance decreases, production cost increases, and in some cases, the product quality can also decrease [26,27]. Although an unjustified reduction in RTD increases the overall performance of the equipment, it reduces the efficiency of the raw processing material, leading to a deterioration in product quality.

To determine the mathematical model parameters for a continuous reactor, it is first necessary to consider the RTD of the material in the apparatus, which will ultimately improve the economic efficiency of the process under consideration. Information about RTD in the apparatus enables evaluation of the efficiency of the apparatus itself, which determines the proportion of the apparatus volume occupied by particles within a given time interval [28–30].

Various methods have been applied to analyze complex systems of differential equations, describing the phenomenon or process under study. The methods used with respect to similarity theory are of the most practical interest. As an example, consider the possibility of using simplex-interval methods for equations of chemical kinetics; heterogeneous processes of dissolution of solid particles; and transformations of mathematical models, including equations for the RTD functions of particles in an apparatus, equations for particles size distribution, etc. [31–35]. The interval method affords simplex-interval equations. It can be effectively used to control the values of technological and chemical process parameters [36–38].

In this paper, we consider the use of the simplex-interval method to convert statistical equations of varying complexity into a convenient form for practical engineering calculations. To that end, it is necessary to determine the values of constants and parameters included in these equations. In the future, such a method could enable the development of an automatic control system using model-predictive controllers in a dynamic mode [39,40].

2. Materials and Methods

According to the simplex-interval method, statistical equations describing the kinetics of chemical and metallurgical processes can be converted to a dimensionless form through similarity simplices corresponding to several values of y_i and x_i selected on the experimental curve $y_i = \varphi(x_i)$ describing the investigated process. For example, any two values of the functions y_i and y_{i+1} corresponding to two values of the arguments x_i and x_{i+1} determined from an experimental curve can be expressed as [41]:

(1) For the value of the argument x_i, $x_i = \varphi(y_i)$; and
(2) For the value of the argument x_{i+1}, $x_{i+1} = \varphi(y_{i+1})$.

For the interval considered above, $\Delta x = x_{i+1} - x_i$, the form of the functional dependence Δx, S_x, X_a, X_g and others can be determined from y_i and y_{i+1}, where Δx is the value of the interval used to calculate the parameters of the equation; X_a and X_g are the arithmetic mean and geometric mean of x_i and x_{i+1}, respectively; and S_x is the similarity simplex.

The equation system solution affords a simplex-interval dependence that describes the investigated technological process laws.

The simplex-interval equation can also be obtained using the following interval characteristics: Δy, S_y, $y_a = (y_{i+1} \cdot y_i)/2$ and $y_g = \sqrt{y_{i+1} \cdot y_i}$, as determined for the interval of variation of the value $\Delta y = y_i - y_{i+1}$. To determine the characteristics $\Delta y / \Delta x = f(x_i; x_{i+1})$ and $\Delta y \cdot \Delta x = f(x_i; x_{i+1})$, it is necessary to identify expressions that afford a generalized description.

The proposed simplex-interval method makes it possible to determine the values of the parameters of the equations using a limited number of experimental points (for example, with two or three values of x_i corresponding to two or three values of y_i), provided that

For the interval Δx, the form of the functional dependence $\Delta x = \varphi(y)$ and similarity simplex $S_y = \varphi(y)$ can be expressed as:

$$\Delta x = x_{i+1} - x_i = \phi_1(y; y_{i+1}), \tag{1}$$

$$S_y = x_{i+1}/x_i = \phi_2(y_i; y_{i+1}), \tag{2}$$

The joint solution of Equations (1) and (2) affords a simplex-criteria dependence describing the laws of the process under study. The possibility of applying the simplex-interval method to transform equations describing metallurgical and chemical process laws is illustrated by the examples in presented in the Results section.

3. Results

3.1. Simplex-Interval Method Examples

For a reaction of zero order, the laws of which are described by the kinetic equation ($n = 0$):

$$\frac{c}{c_0} = 1 - k_0 \frac{\tau}{c_0}, \qquad (3)$$

where c_0 and c are the concentration of the target component at time $\tau = 0$ and τ, respectively; and k_0 is the specific reaction rate of the zero order.

We define the interval characteristics as $\Delta \tau$ and Δc. The simplex-criteria equation for the case under consideration will have the form

$$-\frac{\Delta c}{\Delta \tau} = k_0, \qquad (4)$$

For a first order reaction ($n = 1$)

$$\frac{c}{c_0} = exp(-k_1 \tau), \qquad (5)$$

where k_1—the first-order reaction rate.

The values of the interval characteristics $\Delta \tau$, Δc, S_τ, and S_c for any two points lying on the kinetic curve can be determined by the following formulae:

$$\Delta \tau = (1/k_1) ln S_c^{-1}, \qquad (6)$$

where is the similarity simplex for concentration matter.

And

$$\Delta c = c_0 \left(S_c^{\frac{S_\tau}{S_\tau - 1}} - S_c^{\frac{1}{S_\tau - 1}} \right), \qquad (7)$$

where S_τ is similarity simplex for time.

Combining dependences (6) and (7) result in:

$$-\frac{\Delta c}{\Delta \tau} = k_1 c_0 \left(S_c^{\frac{S_\tau}{S_\tau - 1}} - S_c^{1/(S_\tau - 1)} \right) / ln S_c, \qquad (8)$$

For a second-order reaction ($n = 2$)

$$\frac{c}{c_0} = \frac{1}{1 + c_0 k_1 \tau}, \qquad (9)$$

where k_2 is the second-order reaction rate.

Similarly, the values of the interval characteristics are related by the following dependencies:

$$\Delta \tau = \left(\frac{1}{k_2 c_0} \right) \frac{(1 - S_c)(S_\tau - 1)}{S_c S_\tau - 1}, \qquad (10)$$

and

$$\Delta c = c_0 \left(\frac{(S_c S_\tau - 1)(S_\tau - 1)}{S_c (S_\tau - 1)} \right), \qquad (11)$$

The ratio $\Delta c / \Delta \tau$ in this case is determined by:

$$-\frac{\Delta c}{\Delta \tau} = k_2 c_0^2 \frac{(S_c S_\tau - 1)^2}{S_c (S_\tau - 1)^2}, \qquad (12)$$

In the general case, for reactions of order ($n > 1$)

$$\frac{c}{c_0} = \left(\frac{1}{1 + (n-1)k_n c_0^{n-1} \tau}\right)^{1/(n-1)}, \quad (13)$$

where n is the reaction order, and k_n is the n-th-order reaction rate, which can be represented as:

$$\Delta \tau = \left[1/(n-1)k_n c_0^{n-1}\right] \frac{(1 - S_c^{n-1})(S_\tau - 1)}{S_\tau S_c^{n-1} - 1}, \quad (14)$$

and

$$\Delta c = c_0 \frac{(S_\tau S_c^{n-1} - 1)^{1/(n-1)}(S_c - 1)}{(S_\tau - 1)^{1/(n-1)} S_c}, \quad (15)$$

Accordingly, $\Delta c / \Delta \tau$ is determined by the following equation:

$$-\frac{\Delta c}{\Delta \tau} = (n-1)k_n c_0^n \frac{(S_\tau S_c^{n-1} - 1)^{n/(n-1)}(1 - S_c)}{(S_\tau - 1)^{n/(n-1)} \left(1 - S_c^{n-1}\right) S_c}, \quad (16)$$

In expressions (4), (12), and (16), the values of the constants are equal to $k_0 = M_0$, $k_1 c_0 = M_1$, and $(n-1)k_n c_0^n = M_n$, respectively, where $M_0, M_1 \ldots M_n$ are the modules of reactions of the n-th order.

The introduced simplex-interval dependences can be used to determine the value of the initial concentration of the target component (c_0), as well as to calculate the values of the reaction rates (k_n).

To determine the value of C_0 and the order of a reaction (n), it is more convenient to use Equation (14), which, for any two intervals ($\Delta \tau_i$ and $\Delta \tau_j$), can be written as:

$$n = 1 + \frac{1}{\ln S_c} \ln \left[\frac{S_{\Delta \tau}(S_{\tau_i} - 1) - \left(S_{\tau_j} - 1\right)}{S_{\Delta \tau} S_{\tau_j}(S_{\tau_i} - 1) - S_{\tau_j}\left(S_{\tau_j} - 1\right)}\right], \quad (17)$$

where $S_{\Delta \tau}$ is the simplicity of time similarity for two intervals ($\Delta \tau_i$ and $\Delta \tau_j$).

According to analysis of dependences (4), (12), and (16), it can be argued that they can be easily transformed into dependences traditionally used to describe the laws of the kinetics of chemical reactions, provided that $\tau_i = 0$, $C_i = 0$ и $\tau = \tau_{i+1}$, $C = C_{i+1}$.

The value of the parameter n can be determined using the following equation:

$$-\frac{dc}{d\tau} = k_n c^n, \quad (18)$$

which can be represented in simplex form using the following logarithmic transformation:

$$\ln S_c = \ln(k_n \Delta \tau) + (n-1)\ln c, \quad (19)$$

Another method can be used to calculate the parameter n, involving the combination of dependencies (14) and (15):

$$(n-1)k_n \Delta \tau \Delta C^{n-1} = \left(1 - S_c^{n-1}\right)\left(\frac{S_c - 1}{S_c}\right)^{n-1}, \quad (20)$$

If $\Delta \tau_i \neq \Delta \tau_j$ $\Delta c_i \neq \Delta c_j$ and $S_{c_i} \neq S_{c_j}$:

$$n = 1 + \frac{\ln S_{\Delta \tau}}{\ln S_{\Delta c}}, \quad (21)$$

The concentration value (c_0) can be determined by the following equation:

$$c_0 = \frac{\Delta c S_c (S_\tau - 1)^{1/(n-1)}}{(S_c - 1)\left(S_\tau S_c^{n-1} - 1\right)^{1/(n-1)}}, \qquad (22)$$

The specific reaction rate (k_n) can be calculated using dependence (14).

The equation describing the laws of kinetics of the heterogeneous process of dissolution of solid particles

$$\frac{c_i}{c_0} = (1 - T_i)^n = (1 - \tau_i/\tau_0)^n, \qquad (23)$$

where $T_i = \tau_i/\tau_0$ is the relative time equal to the ratio of the absolute time (τ_i) to the time of complete (or conditionally complete) completion of the process (τ_0); and c_0 and c_i are the content of the extracted component at time instants $\tau = 0$ and τ_i, respectively.

The simplex-criteria equation is expressed as:

$$\frac{\tau_0}{\Delta \tau} = \frac{S_\tau - S_c^{1/n}}{\left(1 - S_c^{1/n}\right)(S_\tau - 1)}, \qquad (24)$$

$$\frac{\Delta c}{c_0} = \frac{(S_c - 1)(1 - S_\tau)^n}{\left(S_c^{1/n} - S\right)^n}, \qquad (25)$$

The value of $\Delta c/\Delta \tau$ is determined by the following formula:

$$\frac{\Delta c}{\Delta \tau} = \frac{c_0}{\tau_0} \frac{(S_\tau - 1)(1 - S_c)^{n-1}}{\left(1 - S_c^{1/n}\right)\left(S_c^{1/n} - S_\tau\right)^{n-1}}, \qquad (26)$$

3.2. Mathematical Modeling Examples

3.2.1. CSTR Model

In this section, we describe the mathematical modeling of mass transfer processes. The model is presented using simplex-criteria equations describing the patterns of fluid flow in a tubular reactor.

We use the CSTR model to describe mass transfer in a tubular reactor. The main parameter of the CSTR in-series model (tanks-in-series model) is the number of reactors (N). Various approaches are used to determine the optimal value of reactor number and other mathematical model parameters. The practical application of existing calculation methods is usually associated with a large number of computational operations and the difficulty of determining the distribution functions of the complete profile. Particular difficulties are associated with the study of industrial apparatus with a high reaction volume and a low volumetric flow rate [42,43].

For a circulating flow reactor (CSTR with back mixing), part of the flow is withdrawn outside the reactor or part of it before being put back and mixed with the incoming stream at the inlet of the reactor or in some of its zones. A suitable industrial example of such behavior is tube furnaces for calcination of feedstock, particularly for coke calcination [35]. Therefore, in the general case, if there is a complex fluid and solid flows in the investigated tubular reactor, due to mixing zones, perfect flows, dead zones, bypass, etc., Equation (19) takes the following form to calculate the concentration of a substance in the reactor:

$$\ln\left(\prod_1^j S_C^a\right) = C \sum_1^j Ho_j \qquad (27)$$

where S_c is the concentration similarity simplex (c_{i-1}/c_i), j is the number of elementary streams in the device, $H_0 = \Delta\tau/\bar{\tau} = \Delta\tau Q/V_0$ is the homochronicity number, C is the constant, and a is the exponent.

For the CSTR in-series model, Equation (27) can be written as:

$$lnS_c S_\tau^{1-N} = Ho, \qquad (28)$$

where N is the number of reactors.

For any two considered time instants, τ_i and τ_{i+1} can be written as:

$$lnS_c = H_0 + (N-1)lnS_\tau, \qquad (29)$$

To determine the number of reactors in the case of a tubular rotary kiln for coke calcination, we will use the data processing results obtained during the experiment. A tubular rotary kiln consists of three zones, serving as an example of the CSTR in-series model (Figure 1) parameter determination method described in [43].

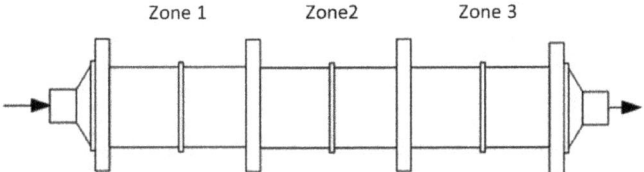

Figure 1. CSTR in-series model for a tubular rotary kiln.

The indicator concentration at the outlet of the reactors cascade for various periods of time is introduced in Table 1.

Table 1. Indicator concentration in the CSTR in series for various time intervals.

Parameter, τ, s	0	10	20	30	40	50	60	70	80	90	100	110	120	130	140
$\tau/\bar{\tau}$	0	0.2	0.4	0.6	0.8	1.0	1.2	1.4	1.6	1.8	2.0	2.2	2.4	2.6	2.8
lnS	—	0.693	0.405	0.288	0.223	0.176	0.154	0.134	0.118	0.105	0.094	0.088	0.070	0.074	0.069
C_i ($N=1$)	1.000	0.219	0.676	0.649	0.449	0.0368	0.301	0.247	0.202	0.165	0.135	0.111	0.091	0.074	0.061
lnS_c	1.222	1.222	1.222	1.222	1.222	1.222	1.222	1.222	1.222	1.221	1.223	1.222	1.222	1.222	1.222
C_i ($N=2$)	0	0.164	0.268	0.329	0.360	0.368	0.361	0.345	0.323	0.298	0.224	0.274	0.218	0.193	0.170
lnS_c	—	−0.471	−0.205	−0.088	−0.020	+0.020	+0.048	+0.067	+0.086	+0.095	+0.104	+0.113	+0.122	+0.122	+0.137
C_i ($N=3$)	0	0.016	0.054	0.099	0.144	0.184	0.217	0.242	0.258	0.268	0.271	0.268	0.261	0.251	0.238
lnS_c	—	−1.184	−0.612	−0.375	−0.246	−0.165	−0.067	−0.037	−0.037	−0.011	+0.010	+0.030	+0.040	+0.049	0.050

We use the equation to process the experimental data (29). The experimental data are represented on the logarithmic scale, $lnS_c = \varphi(lnS_\tau)$. The number of reactors is determined by the tangent of the slope of the straight lines (Figure 2) according to the following equation: $N = 1 + tg\alpha$ or $N = (lnS_c - H_0)/lnS_\tau + 1$. As a result, we obtain $N = 1$ for the first straight line, $N = 2$ for the second straight line, and $N = 3$ for the third straight line. Therefore, such a cascade model can be calculated using the proposed approach.

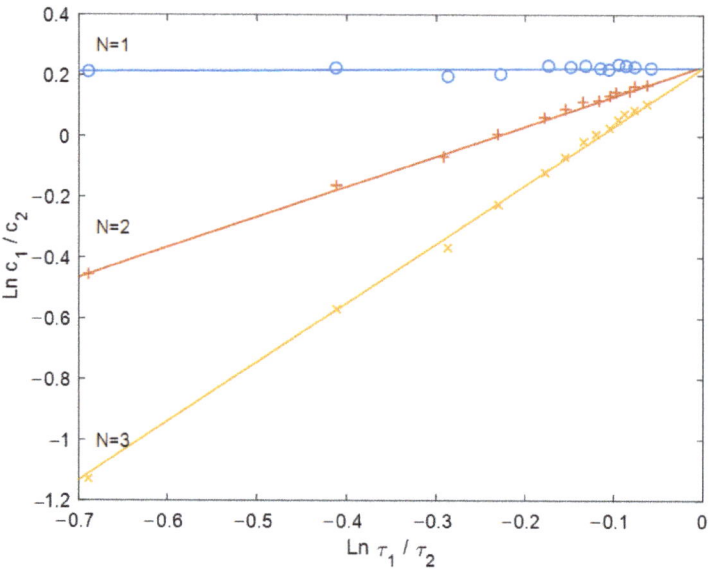

Figure 2. The dependence of $lnS_c = \varphi(lnS_\tau)$ for a cascade of perfect mixing reactors.

3.2.2. Dispersion Model

A dispersion (diffusion) model is used for to model non-ideal plug-flow reactors and is written in the form of a dimensionless partial differential equation [44]. The main parameter of the dispersion model is the value of the Bodenstein number (Bo). The Bodenstein number, as well as the average particle residence time ($\overline{\tau}$) is usually determined based on the calculation of the probability characteristics of the distribution curve or other methods [45–48]. The Bodenstein number (Bo) and the Peclet number (Pe) are sometimes used interchangeably in this context, although the numbers have a slightly different meaning [44].

We transform equations of the diffusion model into the criterial form using dependences (1) and (2). The PFR model is used in the simplest case for the tubular reactor, affording $C/\Delta_\tau = -\omega lnS_C/\Delta x$; then, $lnS_C = 1$, where ω is the flow rate. Similarly, for a one-parameter diffusion model of a tubular reactor:

$$lnS_C = \frac{2\omega \Delta x}{D_L} = 2Bo_L \quad (30)$$

For a two-parameter diffusion model:

$$lnS_C = \frac{(2Bo_A - lnS_A)Bo_L}{Bo_L + Bo_A} \quad (31)$$

where Bo_A is the Bodenstein number for the case of axial mixing, and Bo_L is the Bodenstein number for longitudinal mixing.

When $Bo_L \gg Bo_R$, Equation (30) takes the form of dependence (31).

To reduce the time required for an experiment to determine the shape of the curve of the distribution function and verify the adequacy of the investigated reactor with the complex model, it is necessary to obtain the values of $\overline{\tau}$, the average residence time, using the time-similarity simplex from (28).

$$lnS_c S_\tau^T = Bo \cdot T^2 \sum_1^2 H_{0x}, \quad (32)$$

where $T = \tau_L/\bar{\tau}$ is a constant, τ_L is the flow time along the axis of the tubular reactor, $\bar{\tau}$ is the average residence time, $H_{01} = \Delta\tau Q/V_0$ is homochronicity number for a flow with perfect mixing, and $H_{02} = \Delta\tau Q V_0/V^2/V$ is the homochronicity number for a flow with a dead zone.

For a one-parameter diffusion model of a tubular apparatus, $T = 0.5$.

$$lnS_n S_\tau^{0,5} = Bo \cdot 0.5^2 Ho - \frac{(S_r - 1)^2}{HoS_\tau}, \tag{33}$$

$$lnS_c S_\tau^{0,5} = \frac{Bo\Delta\tau}{4\bar{\tau}}\left(1 - \frac{\bar{\tau}^2}{\tau_i \cdot \tau_{i+1}}\right), \tag{34}$$

or

$$lnS_c S_\tau^{0,5} = A - B\left(\frac{1}{\tau_i \cdot \tau_{i+1}}\right) \tag{35}$$

where A and B are constant value, and $A = \frac{Bo\Delta\tau}{4\bar{\tau}}$, $B = \frac{Bo\Delta\tau}{4} \cdot \bar{\tau}$.

The experimental data on the RTD of coke particles in a tubular rotary kiln in the corresponding coordinate system lie on a straight line. To find the values of $\bar{\tau}$ and Bo, the constants A and B are determined; then, the calculations are carried out according to the following formulae: $\bar{\tau} = \sqrt{B/A}$, $Bo = 4\sqrt{A \cdot B}/\Delta\tau$.

As an example, Figure 3 shows the results of processing the experimental data given in [49]. Experimental data on the RTD of particles in the apparatus are obtained under the condition of a tracer impulse added at the inlet. The RTD of the process can be observed as a tracer concentration profile at the outlet. The data obtained during the experiment should lie on a straight line in the appropriate coordinate system. As shown in Figure 3, the experimental points for two cases are close to a straight line. Their scatter is obviously associated with errors that occurred when determining the indicator concentration at the beginning and end of the experiment, when its value decreased significantly. The difference between the calculated values of the parameters from the data given in [35,49] is less than 2%.

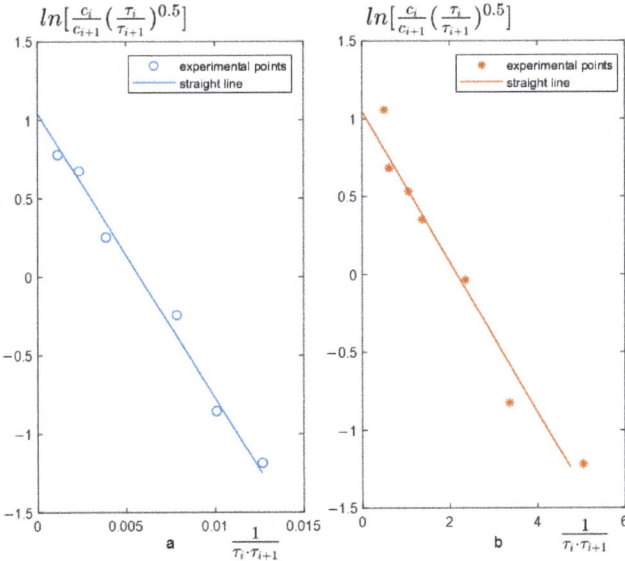

Figure 3. The dependence of $lnS_c = \varphi(1/\tau_i \cdot \tau_{i+1})$ for the dispersion model for two experimental data points (**a**,**b**).

4. Conclusions

Analyzing the simplex-interval equations above, we can conclude that the proposed method can be used to determine the parameters of various technological processes. The type of curves obtained depends on the nature of the kinetic process and the mathematical equation type used to describe it. The considered equations allow for calculation on different intervals. As a result, they can describe both differential and integral dependencies. The simplex-interval method provides calculations of process parameters using a limited number of experimental points. Therefore, simplex-interval dependencies can be widely used in engineering calculations to effectively monitor the progress of an investigated process.

In addition to solving the various problems considered in the present manuscript, the simplices and similarity criteria can be used to carry out a more detailed study of various chemical and metallurgical apparatus operational features with a complex flow structure. Thus, in this work, a new approach is proposed for calculating the operational parameters of various models wherein reactions of the n-th order take place. This approach can represent calculations with the direct use of experimental data without a preliminary determination of the parameters of the kinetic model or the distribution function. The proposed method can be extended to cascade reactors that can be described by a complex tanks-in-series model, particularly when the reaction order differs from the stoichiometric order.

Another topic of interest is that the extension of mathematical models obtained on the basis of the simplex method can serve as the basis for the development of model-predictive controllers.

Author Contributions: Conceptualization, I.B.; formal analysis, I.B.; methodology, I.B.; project administration, I.B.; resources, I.B.; software, I.B. and K.K.; validation, I.B.; visualization, I.B. and K.K.; writing—original draft, I.B.; writing—review and editing, I.B. All authors have read and agreed to the published version of the manuscript.

Funding: The research was performed at the expense of the subsidy for the state assignment in the field of scientific activity for 2021 №FSRW-2020-0014.

Institutional Review Board Statement: Not applicable.

Informed Consent Statement: Not applicable.

Data Availability Statement: Not applicable.

Conflicts of Interest: The authors declare no conflict of interest.

References

1. Carlson, R.; Carlson, J.E. *Design and Optimization in Organic Synthesis: Second Revised and Enlarged Edition*; Elsevier Science: Amsterdam, The Netherlands, 2005; ISBN 9780080455273.
2. Bonvin, D.; Georgakis, C.; Pantelides, C.C.; Barolo, M.; Grover, M.A.; Rodrigues, D.; Schneider, R.; Dochain, D. Linking Models and Experiments. *Ind. Eng. Chem. Res.* **2016**, *55*, 6891–6903. [CrossRef]
3. Li, S. Reaction Engineering. In *Handbook of Heterogeneous Catalysis*; Wiley: Hoboken, NJ, USA, 2017; pp. 1–664. [CrossRef]
4. Carr, R.W. Modeling of Chemical Reactions. In *Comprehensive Chemical Kinetics*; Elsevier: Amsterdam, The Netherlands, 2007; p. 297.
5. Bueno, M.P.; Kojovic, T.; Powell, M.S.; Shi, F. Multi-Component AG/SAG Mill Model. *Miner. Eng.* **2013**, *43–44*, 12–21. [CrossRef]
6. Cameron, I.; Gani, R. *Product and Process Modelling*; Elsevier: Amsterdam, The Netherlands, 2011; p. 571. [CrossRef]
7. Quaglio, M.; Roberts, L.; bin Jaapar, M.S.; Fraga, E.S.; Dua, V.; Galvanin, F. An Artificial Neural Network Approach to Recognise Kinetic Models from Experimental Data. *Comput. Chem. Eng.* **2020**, *135*, 106759. [CrossRef]
8. Zhang, L.; Li, L.; Wang, S.; Zhu, B. Optimization of LPDC Process Parameters Using the Combination of Artificial Neural Network and Genetic Algorithm Method. *J. Mater. Eng. Perform.* **2012**, *21*, 492–499. [CrossRef]
9. Chi, C.; Janiga, G.; Thévenin, D. On-the-Fly Artificial Neural Network for Chemical Kinetics in Direct Numerical Simulations of Premixed Combustion. *Combust. Flame* **2021**, *226*, 467–477. [CrossRef]
10. Nelder, J.A.; Mead, R. A Simplex Method for Function Minimization. *Comput. J.* **1965**, *7*, 308–313. [CrossRef]
11. Morgan, S.L.; Deming, S.N. Simplex Optimization of Analytical Chemical Methods. *Anal. Chem.* **1974**, *46*, 1170–1181. [CrossRef]
12. Olsson, D.M.; Nelson, L.S. The Nelder-Mead Simplex Procedure for Function Minimization. *Technometrics* **1975**, *17*, 45–51. [CrossRef]

13. Spendley, W.; Hext, G.R.; Himsworth, F.R. Sequential Application of Simplex Designs in Optimisation and Evolutionary Operation. *Technometrics* **1962**, *4*, 441. [CrossRef]
14. Li, H.; Nalim, R.; Haldi, P.A. Thermal-Economic Optimization of a Distributed Multi-Generation Energy System—A Case Study of Beijing. *Appl. Therm. Eng.* **2006**, *26*, 709–719. [CrossRef]
15. Hu, H.; Zhu, Y.; Peng, H.; Ding, G.; Sun, S. Effect of Tube Diameter on Pressure Drop Characteristics of Refrigerant-Oil Mixture Flow Boiling inside Metal-Foam Filled Tubes. *Appl. Therm. Eng.* **2013**, *61*, 433–443. [CrossRef]
16. Wang, J.J.; Jing, Y.Y.; Zhang, C.F. Optimization of Capacity and Operation for CCHP System by Genetic Algorithm. *Appl. Energy* **2010**, *87*, 1325–1335. [CrossRef]
17. Fan, S.K.S.; Liang, Y.C.; Zahara, E. A Genetic Algorithm and a Particle Swarm Optimizer Hybridized with Nelder–Mead Simplex Search. *Comput. Ind. Eng.* **2006**, *50*, 401–425. [CrossRef]
18. Lin, H.; Yamashita, K. Hybrid Simplex Genetic Algorithm for Blind Equalization Using RBF Networks. *Math. Comput. Simul.* **2002**, *59*, 293–304. [CrossRef]
19. Li, S.; Xin, F.; Li, L. Fluidized Bed Reactor. In *Reaction Engineering*; Elsevier: Amsterdam, The Netherlands, 2017; pp. 369–403.
20. Burton, K.W.C.; Nickless, G. Optimisation via Simplex. Part I. Background, Definitions and a Simple Application. *Chemom. Intell. Lab. Syst.* **1987**, *1*, 135–149. [CrossRef]
21. Liotta, F.; Chatellier, P.; Esposito, G.; Fabbricino, M.; Van Hullebusch, E.D.; Lens, P.N.L. Hydrodynamic Mathematical Modelling of Aerobic Plug Flow and Nonideal Flow Reactors: A Critical and Historical Review. *Crit. Rev. Environ. Sci. Technol.* **2014**, *44*, 2642–2673. [CrossRef]
22. Toson, P.; Doshi, P.; Jajcevic, D. Explicit Residence Time Distribution of a Generalised Cascade of Continuous Stirred Tank Reactors for a Description of Short Recirculation Time (Bypassing). *Processes* **2019**, *7*, 615. [CrossRef]
23. Gorzalski, A.S.; Harrington, G.W.; Coronell, O. Modeling Water Treatment Reactor Hydraulics Using Reactor Networks. *J. Am. Water Work. Assoc.* **2018**, *110*, 13–29. [CrossRef]
24. Sheoran, M.; Chandra, A.; Bhunia, H.; Bajpai, P.K.; Pant, H.J. Residence time distribution studies using radiotracers in chemical industry—A review. *Chem. Eng. Commun.* **2018**, *205*, 739–758. [CrossRef]
25. Vyazovkin, S.V.; Goryachko, V.I.; Lesnikovich, A.I. An Approach to the Solution of the Inverse Kinetic Problem in the Case of Complex Processes. Part III. Parallel Independent Reactions. *Thermochim. Acta* **1992**, *197*, 41–51. [CrossRef]
26. Braun, R.L.; Burnham, A.K. Analysis of Chemical Reaction Kinetics Using a Distribution of Activation Energies and Simpler Models. *Energy Fuels* **1987**, *1*, 153–161. [CrossRef]
27. Levin, V.I. Optimization in terms of interval uncertainty: The determinization method. *Autom. Control. Comput. Sci.* **2012**, *46*, 157–163. [CrossRef]
28. Gorlanov, E.S.; Brichkin, V.N. Polyakov Electrolytic production of aluminium: Review. part 1. conventional areas of development. *Tsvetnye Met.* **2020**, *2*, 36–41. [CrossRef]
29. Savchenkov, S.A.; Bazhin, V.Y.; Brichkin, V.N.; Povarov, V.G.; Ugolkov, V.L.; Kasymova, D.R. Synthesis of magnesium-zinc-yttrium master alloy. *Lett. Mater.* **2019**, *9*, 339–343. [CrossRef]
30. Savchenkov, S.A.; Bazhin, V.Y.; Brichkin, V.N.; Kosov, Y.I.; Ugolkov, V.L. Production Features of Magnesium-Neodymium Master Alloy Synthesis. *Metallurgist* **2019**, *63*, 394–402. [CrossRef]
31. Cleary, P.W.; Monaghan, J.J. Conduction Modelling Using Smoothed Particle Hydrodynamics. *J. Comput. Phys.* **1999**, *148*, 227–264. [CrossRef]
32. Kondrasheva, N.K.; Rudko, V.A.; Ancheyta, J. Thermogravimetric Determination of the Kinetics of Petroleum Needle Coke Formation by Decantoil Thermolysis. *ACS Omega* **2020**, *5*, 29570–29576. [CrossRef]
33. Beloglazov, I.N.; Beloglazov, N.K. The Simplex Method to Describe Hydrometallurgical Processes. *Miner. Process. Extr. Metall. Rev.* **1995**, *15*, 139. [CrossRef]
34. Smol'nikov, A.D.; Sharikov, Y.V. Simulation of the Aluminum Electrolysis Process in a High-Current Electrolytic Cell in Modern Software. *Metallurgist* **2020**, *63*, 1313–1320. [CrossRef]
35. Sharikov, F.Y.; Sharikov, Y.V.; Krylov, K.A. Selection of key parameters for green coke calcination in a tubular rotary kiln to produce anode petcoke. *ARPN J. Eng. Appl. Sci.* **2020**, *15*, 2904–2912.
36. Cheremisina, O.V.; Cheremisina, E.A.; Ponomareva, M.A.; Fedorov, A.T. Sorption of rare earth coordination compounds. *J. Min. Inst.* **2020**, *244*, 474–481. [CrossRef]
37. Cheremisina, E.; Cheremisina, O.; Ponomareva, M.; Bolotov, V.; Fedorov, A. Kinetic Features of the Hydrogen Sulfide Sorption on the Ferro-Manganese Material. *Metals* **2021**, *11*, 90. [CrossRef]
38. Kondrasheva, N.K.; Rudko, V.A.; Nazarenko, M.Y.; Gabdulkhakov, R.R. Influence of parameters of delayed asphalt coking process on yield and quality of liquid and solid-phase products. *J. Min. Inst.* **2020**, *241*, 97. [CrossRef]
39. Rehrl, J.; Kruisz, J.; Sacher, S.; Khinast, J.; Horn, M. Optimized continuous pharmaceutical manufacturing via model-predictive control. *Int. J. Pharm.* **2016**, *510*, 100–115. [CrossRef] [PubMed]
40. Tsai, H.-H.; Fuh, C.-C.; Ho, J.-R.; Lin, C.-K. Design of Optimal Controllers for Unknown Dynamic Systems through the Nelder–Mead Simplex Method. *Mathematics* **2021**, *9*, 2013. [CrossRef]
41. Visuthirattanamanee, R.; Sinapiromsaran, K.; Boonperm, A. Self-Regulating Artificial-Free Linear Programming Solver Using a Jump and Simplex Method. *Mathematics* **2020**, *8*, 356. [CrossRef]

42. Gutierrez, C.G.C.C.; Dias, E.F.T.S.; Gut, J.A.W. Residence time distribution in holding tubes using generalized convection model and numerical convolution for non-ideal tracer detection. *J. Food Eng.* **2010**, *98*, 248–256. [CrossRef]
43. Islamov, S.R.; Bondarenko, A.V.; Mardashov, D.V. Substantiation of a Well Killing Technology for Fractured Carbonate Reservoirs. In *Youth Technical Sessions Proceedings*; CRC Press: Boca Raton, FL, USA, 2019; pp. 256–264. [CrossRef]
44. Levenspiel, O.; Smith, W.K. Notes on the diffusion-type model for the longitudinal mixing of fluids in flow. *Chem. Eng. Sci.* **1957**, *6*, 227–235. [CrossRef]
45. Dittrich, E.; Klincsik, M. Analysis of conservative tracer measurement results using the Frechet distribution at planted horizontal subsurface flow constructed wetlands filled with coarse gravel and showing the effect of clogging processes. *Environ. Sci. Pollut. Res.* **2015**, *22*, 17104–17122. [CrossRef]
46. Braga, B.M.; Tavares, R.P. Description of a New Tundish Model for Treating RTD Data and Discussion of the Communication "New Insight into Combined Model and Revised Model for RTD Curves in a Multi-strand Tundish" by Lei. *Met. Mater. Trans. A* **2018**, *49*, 2128–2132. [CrossRef]
47. Dryer, F.L.; Haas, F.M.; Santner, J.; Farouk, T.I.; Chaos, M. Interpreting chemical kinetics from complex reaction–advection–diffusion systems: Modeling of flow reactors and related experiments. *Prog. Energy Combust. Sci.* **2014**, *44*, 19–39. [CrossRef]
48. Shestakov, A.K.; Sadykov, R.M.; Petrov, P.A. Multifunctional crust breaker for automatic alumina feeding system of aluminum reduction cell. *E3S Web Conf.* **2021**, *266*, 09002. [CrossRef]
49. Sharikov, Y.V.; Sharikov, F.Y.; Krylov, K.A. Mathematical Model of Optimum Control for Petroleum Coke Production in a Rotary Tube Kiln. *Theor. Found. Chem. Eng.* **2021**, *55*, 711–719. [CrossRef]

Article
WSA-Supplements and Proper Classes

Yılmaz Mehmet Demirci [1,*] and Ergül Türkmen [2]

[1] Department of Engineering Science, Faculty of Engineering, Abdullah Gül University, Kocasinan, Kayseri 38080, Turkey
[2] Department of Mathematics, Sciences and Arts Faculty, Amasya University, Ipekköy, Amasya 05100, Turkey
* Correspondence: yilmaz.demirci@agu.edu.tr

Abstract: In this paper, we introduce the concept of wsa-supplements and investigate the objects of the class of short exact sequences determined by wsa-supplement submodules, where a submodule U of a module M is called a wsa-supplement in M if there is a submodule V of M with $U + V = M$ and $U \cap V$ is weakly semiartinian. We prove that a module M is weakly semiartinian if and only if every submodule of M is a wsa-supplement in M. We introduce CC-rings as a generalization of C-rings and show that a ring is a right CC-ring if and only if every singular right module has a crumbling submodule. The class of all short exact sequences determined by wsa-supplement submodules is shown to be a proper class which is both injectively and co-injectively generated. We investigate the homological objects of this proper class along with its relation to CC-rings.

Keywords: proper class of short exact sequences; wsa-supplement submodule; weakly semiartinian module; C-ring; CC-ring

MSC: 16D10; 18G25

1. Introduction

Throughout this study, all rings considered are associative with an identity element and all modules at hand are right and unital. Given such a module M, we use the notations $E(M)$, $\text{Soc}(M)$, $Z(M)$, $\text{Rad}(M)$ for the injective hull, socle, singular submodule, and radical of M, respectively. The notation $(N \lneq M)$ $N \leq M$ means that N is a (proper) submodule of M. $\text{Mod} - R$ denotes the category of all right R-modules over a ring R. For the terminology and notations used in this work we refer the reader to [1–3].

For any $M \in Mod - R$, we denote the injectivity domain of M by $\mathfrak{In}^{-1}(M)$. It is clear that M is injective if and only if its injectivity domain is as large as it can be, that is, $\mathfrak{In}^{-1}(M) = Mod - R$. It is well known that every module is injective relative to any semisimple module. In [4], the authors introduced modules M whose injectivity domain $\mathfrak{In}^{-1}(M)$ is minimal possible, namely the class of all semisimple modules and called such modules *poor*. This definition gives a natural homological opposite to injectivity of modules since only injective modules have the class of all modules as their injectivity domain. It is proved in [5] (Proposition 1) that every ring has a poor module. However, semisimple poor modules need not exist over an arbitrary ring. Recall that a module M is said to *crumble* (or be a *crumbling* module) if $\text{Soc}(M/N)$ is a direct summand of M/N for every submodule N of M. It follows from [5] (Corollary 2) that a module M crumbles if and only if it is a locally noetherian V-module. It is shown in [5] (Theorem 1) that a ring R has a semisimple poor module if and only if every right crumbling R-module is semisimple. Clearly, a ring R crumbles if and only if it is a right SSI-ring, that is, every semisimple right R-module is injective.

Following [6], we denote the sum of all submodules of a module M that crumble by $C(M)$. By [6] (Propositions 3.1 and 3.4), $C(M)$ is the largest submodule of M that crumbles and $\text{Soc}(M) \leq C(M)$. A module M is called *semiartinian* if $\text{Soc}(M/N) \neq 0$ for every proper

submodule N of M. As a proper generalization of artinian modules, the class of semiartinian modules are extensively studied in the literature. In [6], the authors considered modules of which factor modules have a nonzero crumbling submodule. A module M is called *weakly semiartinian* if $C(M/N) \neq 0$ for every proper submodule N of M. The sum of all weakly semiartinian submodules of a module M is the largest weakly semiartinian submodule of M which we denote by wsa(M). Clearly, semiartinian modules and crumbling modules are examples of weakly semiartinian modules. A weakly semiartinian module need not be semiartinian, in general. An example of a weakly semiartinian module which is not semiartinian can be found in [6] (Remark 2). Various properties of weakly semiartinian modules are given in the same work.

It is well known that a module is semisimple if and only if its submodules are direct summands. As a generalization of direct summands, supplement submodules are defined as follows. Let M be a module and $U, V \leq M$. V is called a *supplement* of U in M if it is minimal with respect to $M = U + V$, equivalently if $M = U + V$ and $U \cap V$ is small in V. Here a submodule S of a module M is called *small* in M, denoted by $S \ll M$, if $M \neq S + L$ for every proper submodule L of M. A module M is called *supplemented* if every one of its submodules has a supplement in M. Supplement submodules play an important role in ring theory and relative homological algebra. In recent years, types of supplement submodules are extensively studied by many authors. In a series of books and articles [1–3,7,8], the authors have obtained detailed information about variations of supplement submodules and related rings.

In [9], the author introduced proper classes to axiomatize conditions under which a class of short exact sequences of modules can be computed as Ext groups corresponding to a certain relative cohomology. The class $\mathcal{S}plit$ of all splitting short exact sequences of right R-modules and the class $\mathcal{A}bs$ of all short exact sequences of right R-modules are trivial examples of proper classes. It follows from [1] (20.7) that the class $\mathcal{S}upp$ of all short exact sequences $0 \longrightarrow M \xrightarrow{\psi} N \longrightarrow K \longrightarrow 0$ such that Imψ is a supplement in N is a proper class. Examples and properties of proper classes, especially related to supplements can be found in [10–12].

Recently defined type of supplement submodules is as follows. A submodule V of a module M is called an *sa-supplement* of U in M if $M = U + V$ and $U \cap V$ is semiartinian (see [7]). It is shown in [7] that the class $\mathcal{SAS}$ of all short exact sequences $0 \longrightarrow M \xrightarrow{\psi} N \longrightarrow K \longrightarrow 0$ such that Imψ is an sa-supplement in N is a proper class. Since semiartinian modules are weakly semiartinian, it is of interest to investigate a new type of supplement submodules by replacing the property of being "semiartinian" by being "weakly semiartinian". The purpose of this paper is to introduce the concept of wsa-supplement submodules and investigate the objects of the proper class determined by wsa-supplement submodules in relative homological algebra.

The paper is organized as follows. In Section 2, we prove that a module M is weakly semiartinian if and only if every submodule of M is a wsa-supplement in M. In particular, a ring R is weakly semiartinian if and only if every right maximal ideal of R is a wsa-supplement in R.

We introduce right CC-rings as a generalization of C-rings and give some characterizations of such rings in Section 3. We show that a ring R is a right CC-ring if and only if every singular right R-module has a crumbling submodule. A semilocal right CC-ring is a right C-ring. A right noetherian and a right WV-ring is a right CC-ring.

In Section 4, we show that, over an arbitrary ring, the class of all short exact sequences $0 \longrightarrow M \xrightarrow{\psi} N \longrightarrow K \longrightarrow 0$ such that Imψ is a wsa-supplement in N is a proper class. We study the objects of this class, which we call $\mathcal{WSS}$. We show that a module M is $\mathcal{WSS}$-co-injective if and only if it is a wsa-supplement $E(M)$. Over a right CC-ring, a projective module P is $\mathcal{WSS}$-co-injective if and only if $P/\text{wsa}(P)$ is injective. A ring R is weakly semiartinian if and only if every right R-module is $\mathcal{WSS}$-co-injective.

Finally, we show that over a crumbling-free ring $\mathcal{WSS}$-coprojective modules are only the projective modules.

2. Weakly Semiartinian Modules

In this section, we give a characterization of weakly semiartinian modules via wsa-supplement submodules. Firstly, let us start by giving the closure properties.

Proposition 1 ([6] (Proposition 3.1)). *If $f : M \longrightarrow N$ is a homomorphism of modules, then $f(C(M) \subseteq C(N)$.*

Proposition 2. *The class of weakly semiartinian modules is closed under submodules, factor modules, direct sums, sums and extensions.*

Proof. By [6] (Propositions 3.1 and 3.4), we get that the class of weakly semiartinian modules is closed under submodules, factor modules, direct sums and sums. Let B be a module and A be a submodule of B with A and B/A weakly semiartinian. Assume that $C(B/X) = 0$ for some $X \lneq B$. By Proposition 1, we have $C(A/A \cap X) \cong C((A+X)/X) \leq C(B/X) = 0$. Since A is weakly semiartinian, $A/A \cap X) = 0$ so that $A \leq X$. $B/X \cong (B/A)/(X/A)$ is weakly semiartinian which implies that $C(B/X) \neq 0$, a contradiction. Hence, B is weakly semiartinian. □

The sum of all weakly semiartinian submodules of a module M is denoted by $\mathrm{wsa}(M)$. By Proposition 2, $\mathrm{wsa}(M)$ is weakly semiartinian. Therefore M is weakly semiartinian if and only if $\mathrm{wsa}(M) = M$. Using this fact and Proposition 2, we have the following result.

Corollary 1. *For any module M, $\mathrm{wsa}(M/\mathrm{wsa}(M)) = 0$.*

Proof. Let $N \leq M$ containing $\mathrm{wsa}(M)$ such that $N/\mathrm{wsa}(M) \leq \mathrm{wsa}(M/\mathrm{wsa}(M))$. It follows from Proposition 2 that $N/\mathrm{wsa}(M)$ is weakly semiartinian. Since $\mathrm{wsa}(M)$ is weakly semiartinian, applying Proposition 2 once again, we obtain that N is weakly semiartinian. Therefore $N \subseteq \mathrm{wsa}(M)$. This means that $N/\mathrm{wsa}(M) = 0$. □

Let M be a module and $U \leq M$. We say that U is (has) a *weakly semiartinian supplement* (*wsa-supplement* for short) in M if there exists $V \leq M$ such that $U + V = M$ and $U \cap V$ is a weakly semiartinian module.

Theorem 1. *An R-module M is weakly semiartinian if and only if every submodule of M is a wsa-supplement in M.*

Proof. Necessity follows from Proposition 2. For sufficiency, suppose that $C(mR) = 0$ for some $m \in M$. Let U be any submodule of mR. By the assumption, there exists a submodule V of M such that $M = U + V$ and $U \cap V$ is weakly semiartinian. Using modular law, we have $mR = U + V \cap mR$. Note that $C(U \cap V) = C(U \cap mR \cap V) \subseteq C(mR) = 0$. It means that U is a direct summand of mR and so mR is semisimple. Therefore $mR = \mathrm{Soc}(mR) = C(mR) = 0$, and hence $m = 0$. This completes the proof. □

A module M is said to be *crumbling-free* if $C(M) = 0$. A ring R is called crumbling-free if R_R is crumbling free. Let R be a ring and A and B be R-modules. Recall that A is *B-injective* if for any submodule X of B, any homomorphism $f : X \to A$ extends to a homomorphism $g : B \to A$.

Proposition 3. *An R-module M is weakly semiartinian if and only if every crumbling-free R-module is M-injective.*

Proof. Necessity is clear since $C(U) \neq 0$ for every submodule U of M. For sufficiency, suppose that N is a submodule of M with $C(N) = 0$. Let $U \leq N$. Since N is crumbling-free, U is crumbling-free and so, by the hypothesis, U is M-injective. So we can write $M = U \oplus V$, where V is a submodule of M. By the modular law, we get $N = U \oplus N \cap V$. This means that $N = \text{Soc}(N) = C(N) = 0$. Hence M is weakly semiartinian. □

Proposition 4. *Let M be a module and U be a submodule of M with M/U weakly semiartinian. A submodule V of M is a wsa-supplement of U in M if and only if $M = U + V$ and V is weakly semiartinian.*

Proof. Let V be a wsa-supplement of U in M. Then $V/(U \cap V) \cong M/U$ is weakly semiartinian. Since $U \cap V$ is also weakly semiartinian, it follows from Proposition 2 that V is weakly semiartinian. The converse is clear by again Proposition 2. □

Since for a maximal submodule U of M we have M/U is simple, therefore weakly semiartinian, the following result is a consequence of Proposition 4.

Corollary 2. *Let M be a module and U be a maximal submodule of M. A submodule V of M is a wsa-supplement of U in M if and only if $M = U + V$ and V is weakly semiartinian.*

Recall that a module M is *coatomic* if every proper submodule of M is contained in a maximal submodule of M.

Corollary 3. *Let M be a coatomic module. Then M is weakly semiartinian if and only if every maximal submodule of M is a wsa-supplement in M.*

Proof. Necessity follows from Proposition 1. For sufficiency, assume that M is not weakly semiartinian, that is, $\text{wsa}(M) \neq M$. Let N be a maximal submodule of M that contains $\text{wsa}(M)$ and K be a wsa-supplement of N in M. Then K is weakly semiartinian by Corollary 2 and we have $K \leq \text{wsa}(M) \leq N$ which implies $M = N + K \leq N$, contradicting the maximality of N. □

It is well known that a ring R is semisimple artinian if and only if every maximal right ideal of R is a direct summand of R. Now we give an analogous characterization of this fact for right weakly semiartinian rings.

Corollary 4. *A ring R is right weakly semiartinian if and only if every maximal right ideal of R is a wsa-supplement in R.*

3. A Generalization of C-Rings

In [1] (10.10), a ring R is called *a right C-ring* if for every right R-module M and for every proper essential submodule N of M, $\text{Soc}(M/N) \neq 0$, that is M/N has a simple submodule. The class of right C-rings is studied by many authors in homological algebra. Semiartinian rings and Dedekind domains are examples right C-rings. Since semiartinian rings are weakly semiartinian, motivated by this fact, it is natural to introduce right CC-rings as follows: A ring R is called a right CC-ring if for every right R-module M and for every proper essential submodule N of M, $C(M/N) \neq 0$, that is M/N has a cyclic crumbling submodule.

Proposition 5. *The following statements are equivalent for a ring R.*
1. *R is a right CC-ring;*
2. *Every singular right R-module has a cyclic crumbling submodule;*
3. *For every proper essential right ideal I of R, $C(R/I) \neq 0$.*

Proof. (1 ⇒ 2): Let M be a singular right R-module and $0 \neq m \in M$. Now consider the isomorphism $f : R/\text{ann}(m) \longrightarrow mR$. Since M is singular, $\text{ann}(m)$ is a non-zero proper essential right ideal of R. Then, $R/\text{ann}(m)$ has a cyclic crumbling submodule, that is

$C(R/\operatorname{ann}(m)) \neq 0$. It follows from Proposition 1 that $C(mR) \neq 0$. This completes the proof of $(1 \Rightarrow 2)$.

$(2 \Rightarrow 3)$ is clear since R/I is a singular right R-module for every proper essential right ideal I of R.

$(3 \Rightarrow 1)$: Let M be an R-module and N be a proper essential submodule of M. We shall show that $C(M/N) \neq 0$. Let $0 \neq m + N \in M/N$. Since M/N is singular, $\operatorname{ann}(m + N)$ is a proper essential right ideal of R. By assumption, $R/\operatorname{ann}(m+N)$ has a cyclic crumbling submodule. Applying Proposition 1, we obtain that $C(R(m+N)) \neq 0$ and so $C(M/N) \neq 0$. It means that R is a right CC-ring. □

As a consequence of Proposition 5, we have the following result.

Corollary 5. *Let R be commutative domain. Then the following statements are equivalent.*
1. *R is a right CC-ring;*
2. *Every torsion right R-module has a cyclic crumbling submodule.*

A ring R is called *a right weakly-V-ring* (WV-ring for short) if every simple right R-module is R/I-injective for any right ideal I of R such that R/I is proper. Clearly, every right V-ring is a right WV-ring. Since a right WV-ring need not be right noetherian; in general, the authors investigated when a right WV-ring is right noetherian in [13] and showed that a right WV-ring R is right noetherian if and only if every cyclic right R-module can be written as a direct sum of a projective module and a module which is either CS or right noetherian.

Proposition 6. *A right noetherian and a right WV-ring is a right CC-ring.*

Proof. Let R be a right noetherian and a right WV-ring. Suppose that N is a proper essential submodule of an R-module M. Let $0 \neq m + N \in M/N$. Then there exists a proper essential right ideal I of R such that $R/I \cong R(m+N)$. Clearly, $R(m+N)$ is noetherian. Since R is a right WV-ring, R/I is a V-module. It means that $R(m+N)$ crumbles and so M/N has a cyclic crumbling submodule. □

Proposition 7. *Let R be a ring with $R/\operatorname{Soc}(R_R)$ weakly semiartinian. Then R is a right CC-ring.*

Proof. By Proposition 5, it suffices to show that $C(R/I) \neq 0$ for every proper essential right ideal I of R. Since $\operatorname{Soc}(R_R)$ is the intersection of all essential right ideals of R, $\operatorname{Soc}(R_R) \subseteq I$ and so $R/I \cong (R/\operatorname{Soc}(R_R))/(I/\operatorname{Soc}(R_R))$ is a weakly semiartinian R-module by Proposition 2. This means that $C(R/I) \neq 0$. Hence R is a right CC-ring. □

A ring R is called *semilocal* if $R/\operatorname{Rad}(R)$ is semisimple. The class of semilocal rings properly contains the class of semiperfect rings. Note that over a semilocal ring a module with zero radical is semisimple (see [1]).

Proposition 8. *A semilocal and a right CC-ring is a right C-ring.*

Proof. Let I be a proper essential right ideal of R. Since R is a right CC-ring, we can write $C(R/I) \neq 0$. Note also by [6] (Lemma 4) that $\operatorname{Rad}(C(R/I)) = 0$. By [1] (17.2-3), we obtain that $\operatorname{Soc}(R/I) = C(R/I) \neq 0$ since the ring is semilocal. This means that R is a right C-ring. □

Theorem 2. *Let R be a right CC-ring. Then an R-module M is semisimple if and only if $\operatorname{Soc}(M) = \operatorname{wsa}(M)$ and every essential submodule of M is a wsa-supplement in M.*

Proof. Necessity part is clear. For sufficiency, let U be a proper essential submodule of M. Then there is a wsa-supplement V of U in M, that is $U + V = M$ and $U \cap V$ is weakly semiartinian. Since R is a right CC-ring, $V/(U \cap V) \cong M/U$ is weakly semiartinian. Then V is weakly semiartinian by Proposition 2 and we have $V \leq \text{wsa}(M) = \text{Soc}(M) \leq U$. This implies $U = M$, a contradiction. Therefore, M has no proper essential submodules. Hence M is semisimple. □

4. The Objects of the Proper Class $\mathcal{WSS}$

In this section, we consider the class of short exact sequences determined by wsa-supplement submodules. Before doing so, here we give the definition of a proper class which plays a key role in relative homological algebra in terms of examining classes of short exact sequences along with their homological objects (see [9] for an equivalent definition of a proper class).

Definition 1. *Let $\mathcal{P}$ be a class of short exact sequences of right R-modules and R-module homomorphisms. If a short exact sequence $\mathbb{E} : 0 \longrightarrow K \xrightarrow{f} L \xrightarrow{g} M \longrightarrow 0$ belongs to $\mathcal{P}$, then f is said to be a $\mathcal{P}$-monomorphism and g is said to be a $\mathcal{P}$-epimorphism.*

A subfunctor $\mathcal{P}$ of Ext is said to be a proper class if $\mathcal{P}(M, N)$ is a subgroup of $\text{Ext}(M, N)$ for every R-modules M, N, and one of the following conditions is satisfied.

1. The composition of two $\mathcal{P}$-monomorphisms is a $\mathcal{P}$-monomorphism whenever this composition is defined;
2. The composition of two $\mathcal{P}$-epimorphisms is a $\mathcal{P}$-epimorphism whenever this composition is defined.

Let R be a ring and $\mathcal{P}$ be a proper class of right R-modules. An R-module M is said to be $\mathcal{P}$-injective (resp., $\mathcal{P}$-co-injective) if $\text{Ext}_{\mathcal{P}}(K, M) = 0$ (resp., $\text{Ext}_{\mathcal{P}}(K, M) = \text{Ext}_R(K, M)$) for all right R-modules K. The smallest proper class for which every module from the class of modules $\mathcal{P}$ is co-injective is called *co-injectively generated* by $\mathcal{P}$.

A short exact sequence $0 \longrightarrow A \xrightarrow{f} B \longrightarrow C \longrightarrow 0$ is called WSS if $\text{Im } f$ is a wsa-supplement submodule of B. We denote the class of all WSS sequences by $\mathcal{WSS}$. The next result shows that the class $\mathcal{WSS}$ is a proper class over an arbitrary ring.

Proposition 9. *The class $\mathcal{WSS}$ is the proper class co-injectively generated by the class of weakly semiartinian modules.*

Proof. It follows from Proposition 2 and [14] (Theorem 2). □

Proposition 10. *The class $\mathcal{WSS}$ is injectively generated by the class of crumbling-free modules.*

Proof. Let $E : 0 \longrightarrow A \longrightarrow B \longrightarrow C \longrightarrow 0 \in \mathcal{WSS}$, M be a crumbling-free module and $\alpha : A \longrightarrow M$ a homomorphism. Then $\alpha_* E : 0 \longrightarrow M \longrightarrow D \longrightarrow C \longrightarrow 0 \in \mathcal{WSS}$ since $\mathcal{WSS}$ is a proper class. Then there is a submodule K of D such that $M + K = D$ and $M \cap K$ is weakly semiartinian. By Proposition 1, we have $C(M \cap K) \leq C(M) = 0$ so that $\alpha_* E$ splits. Therefore, M is $\mathcal{WSS}$-injective.

Now let $F : 0 \longrightarrow X \longrightarrow Y \longrightarrow Z \longrightarrow 0$ be a short exact sequence such that every crumbling-free module is F-injective. Since $C(X/\text{wsa}(X)) = 0$, there is a submodule L of Y with $\text{wsa}(X) \leq L$ and $X/\text{wsa}(X) \oplus L/\text{wsa}(X) = Y/\text{wsa}(X)$. Then we have $X + L = Y$ and $X \cap L = \text{wsa}(X)$. Hence $F \in \mathcal{WSS}$. □

We call a module M $\mathcal{WSS}$-*co-injective*, if every short exact sequence,

$$0 \longrightarrow M \longrightarrow N \longrightarrow K \longrightarrow 0,$$

of right R-modules starting with the module M is in the proper class $\mathcal{WSS}$. It follows that a module M is $\mathcal{WSS}$-co-injective if and only if it is a wsa-supplement in every extension.

It is clear that injective modules, semiartinian modules and wsa-supplementing modules are examples of $\mathcal{WSS}$-co-injective modules. Proposition 10 implies that a crumbling-free module is $\mathcal{WSS}$-co-injective if and only if it is injective. Recall that we denote the injective hull of a module M by $E(M)$.

Theorem 3. *The following statements are equivalent for a module M.*
1. M is $\mathcal{WSS}$-co-injective;
2. M is a wsa-supplement in $E(M)$.

Proof. $(1 \Rightarrow 2)$ is clear.

$(2 \Rightarrow 1)$: Let M be a wsa-supplement in $E(M)$ and let N be a module containing M. Since $E(M) \subseteq E(N)$, there exists a submodule $U \subseteq E(N)$ such that $E(N) = E(M) \oplus U$. Since M is a wsa-supplement in $E(M)$, M is a wsa-supplement in $E(N)$. Hence there exists a submodule V of $E(N)$ such that $E(N) = M + V$ and $M \cap V$ is weakly semiartinian. By modular law, we can write $N = N \cap E(N) = N \cap (M+V) = M + N \cap V$ and $M \cap (N \cap V) = (M \cap N) \cap V = M \cap V$ is weakly semiartinian. It means that M is $\mathcal{WSS}$-co-injective. □

The following result is a consequence of Theorem 3.

Corollary 6. *Let M be a module with $M/\operatorname{wsa}(M)$ injective. Then M is $\mathcal{WSS}$-co-injective.*

Proof. By the assumption, there exists a submodule K of $E(M)$ containing $\operatorname{wsa}(M)$ such that $M/\operatorname{wsa}(M) \oplus K/\operatorname{wsa}(M) = E(M)/\operatorname{wsa}(M)$. Therefore $M + K = E(M)$ and $M \cap K \subseteq \operatorname{wsa}(M)$. Applying Proposition 2, $M \cap K$ is weakly semiartinian and so M is a wsa-supplement in $E(M)$. It follows from Theorem 3 that M is $\mathcal{WSS}$-co-injective. □

The next result shows that the class of $\mathcal{WSS}$-co-injective modules is closed under extensions.

Proposition 11. *Let $0 \longrightarrow M \longrightarrow N \longrightarrow K \longrightarrow 0$ be a short exact sequence of modules. If M and K are $\mathcal{WSS}$-co-injective, then so is N.*

Proof. By [15] (Proposition 1.9 and 1.14). □

Corollary 7. *Every finite direct sum of $\mathcal{WSS}$-co-injective modules is $\mathcal{WSS}$-co-injective.*

Proof. Let $n \in \mathbb{Z}^+$ and M_i $(1 \leq i \leq n)$ be any finite collection of $\mathcal{WSS}$-co-injective modules. Let $M = M_1 \oplus M_2 \oplus \ldots \oplus M_n$. Suppose that $n = 2$, that is, $M = M_1 \oplus M_2$. Then $0 \longrightarrow M_1 \longrightarrow M \longrightarrow M_2 \longrightarrow 0$ is a short exact sequence. Applying Proposition 11, we have that M is $\mathcal{WSS}$-co-injective. The proof is completed by induction on n. □

We do not know if any direct sum of $\mathcal{WSS}$-co-injective modules is $\mathcal{WSS}$-co-injective. Nevertheless, over right noetherian rings, we show that the class of $\mathcal{WSS}$-co-injective modules is closed under direct sums.

Theorem 4. *Let R be a right noetherian ring and $\{M_i\}_{i \in I}$ be a collection of $\mathcal{WSS}$-co-injective R-modules. Then $\bigoplus_{i \in I} M_i$ is $\mathcal{WSS}$-co-injective.*

Proof. Put $M = \bigoplus_{i \in I} M_i$. It is easy to see that $\operatorname{wsa}(M) = \bigoplus_{i \in I} \operatorname{wsa}(M_i)$. Since R is a right noetherian ring, $E(M)$ is the direct sum of $E(M_i)$ for each $i \in I$. Note that $E(M)/\operatorname{wsa}(M) = \bigoplus_{i \in I} E(M_i)/\bigoplus_{i \in I} \operatorname{wsa}(M_i) \cong \bigoplus_{i \in I}(E(M_i)/\operatorname{wsa}(M_i))$. Using Theorem 3, we can write $E(M_i)/\operatorname{wsa}(M_i) = (M_i/\operatorname{wsa}(M_i)) \oplus (K_i/\operatorname{wsa}(M_i))$ for some submodule $K_i/\operatorname{wsa}(M_i)$ of $E(M_i)/\operatorname{wsa}(M_i)$ $(i \in I)$. Let $K/\operatorname{wsa}(M) = \bigoplus_{i \in I} K_i/\operatorname{wsa}(M_i)$. Therefore $E(M)/\operatorname{wsa}(M) = M/\operatorname{wsa}(M) \oplus K/\operatorname{wsa}(M)$. This means that M is a wsa-supplement in $E(M)$. Applying Theorem 3 once again, we obtain that M is $\mathcal{WSS}$-co-injective. □

In general, a submodule of a $\mathcal{WSS}$-co-injective module need not be $\mathcal{WSS}$-co-injective. For example, the submodule $\mathbb{Z}_\mathbb{Z}$ of the $\mathcal{WSS}$-co-injective module $\mathbb{Q}_\mathbb{Z}$ is not $\mathcal{WSS}$-co-injective. We prove that every wsa-supplement submodule of a $\mathcal{WSS}$-co-injective module is $\mathcal{WSS}$-co-injective.

Proposition 12. *Let M be a $\mathcal{WSS}$-co-injective module and V be a wsa-supplement submodule of M. Then V is $\mathcal{WSS}$-co-injective.*

Proof. Let V be a wsa-supplement in M. Then $\mathbb{E} : 0 \longrightarrow V \longrightarrow M \longrightarrow M/V \longrightarrow 0$ is a short exact sequence in $\mathcal{WSS}$, that is, $U + V = M$ and $U \cap V$ is weakly semiartinian for some submodule U of M. Therefore by [15] (Proposition 1.8) V is $\mathcal{WSS}$-co-injective. □

The following fact is direct consequence of Proposition 12.

Corollary 8. *Every direct summand of a $\mathcal{WSS}$-co-injective module is $\mathcal{WSS}$-co-injective.*

We call a ring R weakly semiartinian if R_R is weakly semiartinian, or equivalently, if every R-module is weakly semiartinian.

Proposition 13. *The following statements are equivalent for a ring R.*
1. *R is right weakly semiartinian;*
2. *Every $\mathcal{WSS}$-co-injective R-module is weakly semiartinian;*
3. *Every injective R-module is weakly semiartinian.*

Proof. $(1 \Rightarrow 2)$ and $(2 \Rightarrow 3)$ are trivial.
$(3 \Rightarrow 1)$: R_R is a submodule of $E(R_R)$ which is weakly semiartinian by assumption. Proposition 2 completes the proof. □

A ring R is called *right hereditary* if every factor module of an injective module is injective. Now we prove that over right hereditary rings every factor module of a $\mathcal{WSS}$-co-injective module is $\mathcal{WSS}$-co-injective. Firstly, we need the following result.

Proposition 14. *$\mathcal{WSS}$-co-injective modules are closed under quotients if and only if quotients of injective modules are $\mathcal{WSS}$-co-injective.*

Proof. The necessity part follows from the fact that injective modules are $\mathcal{WSS}$-co-injective. For sufficiency, let M be a $\mathcal{WSS}$-co-injective module and N be a submodule of M. We have the commutative diagram:

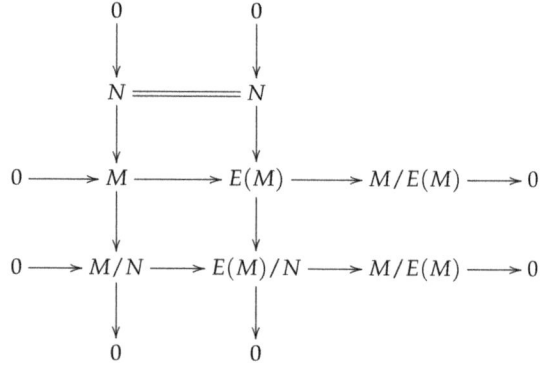

with exact rows and columns. Since M is $\mathcal{WSS}$-co-injective it has a wsa-supplement in $E(M)$. $\mathcal{WSS}$ being a proper class implies that M/N has a wsa-supplement in $E(M)/N$

which is $\mathcal{WSS}$-co-injective by assumption. By [15] (Proposition 1.8) M/N is $\mathcal{WSS}$-co-injective module. □

Corollary 9. *Let R be a right hereditary ring and M be a $\mathcal{WSS}$-co-injective R-module. Then every factor module of M is $\mathcal{WSS}$-co-injective.*

Proposition 15. *Let M be a $\mathcal{WSS}$-co-injective module. Then the following are equivalent:*
1. *$M/\operatorname{wsa}(M)$ is $\mathcal{WSS}$-co-injective;*
2. *$M/\operatorname{wsa}(M)$ is injective;*
3. *M/N is $\mathcal{WSS}$-co-injective for each weakly semiartinian submodule N of M;*
4. *M/N is $\mathcal{WSS}$-co-injective for each wsa-supplement submodule N of M.*

Proof. $(1 \Rightarrow 2)$ follows from Corollary 1.

$(2 \Rightarrow 3)$: Let N be a weakly semiartinian submodule of M. We have the short exact sequence $0 \longrightarrow \operatorname{wsa}(M)/N \longrightarrow M/N \longrightarrow M/\operatorname{wsa}(M) \longrightarrow 0$ with $M/\operatorname{wsa}(M)$ injective, hence $\mathcal{WSS}$-co-injective. By Proposition 2, weakly semiartinian modules are closed under quotients and so $\operatorname{wsa}(M)/N$ is $\mathcal{WSS}$-co-injective. By Proposition 11, M/N is also $\mathcal{WSS}$-co-injective.

$(3 \Rightarrow 4)$: Let N be a wsa-supplement submodule of M. Then there exists $K \leq M$ such that $N + K = M$ and $N \cap K$ is weakly semiartinian. Since $N \cap K \leq \operatorname{wsa}(M)$, we have the short exact sequence

$$0 \longrightarrow \operatorname{wsa}(M)/(N \cap K) \longrightarrow M/N \cap K \longrightarrow M/\operatorname{wsa}(M) \longrightarrow 0.$$

By Proposition 2, $\operatorname{wsa}(M)/(N \cap K)$ is $\mathcal{WSS}$-co-injective. $M/\operatorname{wsa}(M)$ is $\mathcal{WSS}$-co-injective by assumption. By Proposition 11, $M/(N \cap K)$ is also $\mathcal{WSS}$-co-injective. Since M/N is isomorphic to a direct summand of $M/(N \cap K)$, M/N is $\mathcal{WSS}$-co-injective module.

$(4 \Rightarrow 1)$ follows from the fact that $\operatorname{wsa}(M)$ is a wsa-supplement of M in M. By assumption $M/\operatorname{wsa}(M)$ is $\mathcal{WSS}$-co-injective. □

Corollary 10. *The following statements are equivalent:*
1. *$I/\operatorname{wsa}(I)$ is injective for every injective module I;*
2. *$M/\operatorname{wsa}(M)$ is injective for every $\mathcal{WSS}$-co-injective module M;*
3. *The class of $\mathcal{WSS}$-co-injective modules is closed under wsa-supplement quotients.*

Proof. The equivalence of 2 and 3 is given in Proposition 15 and $(2 \Rightarrow 1)$ is clear.

$(1 \Rightarrow 2)$: Let M be a $\mathcal{WSS}$-co-injective module. Then M has a wsa-supplement N in injective hull $E(M)$ of M. Since $M + N = E(M)$ and $M \cap N$ is weakly semiartinian, we have $M \cap N \leq \operatorname{wsa}(M)$ and hence $E(M)/\operatorname{wsa}(M) = [M/\operatorname{wsa}(M)] \oplus [(N + \operatorname{wsa}(M))/\operatorname{wsa}(M)]$. By Proposition 15, $E(M)/\operatorname{wsa}(M)$ is a $\mathcal{WSS}$-co-injective module and so is $M/\operatorname{wsa}(M)$ as a direct summand of $E(M)/\operatorname{wsa}(M)$. Corollary 8 completes the proof. □

Corollary 11. *Let R be a right CC-ring. Then the class of $\mathcal{WSS}$-co-injective modules is closed under wsa-supplement quotients.*

Proof. Let R be a right CC-ring and I be an injective module. Then every singular module is weakly semiartinian which implies that every crumbling-free module is nonsingular. Since $I/\operatorname{wsa}(I)$ is crumbling-free, it is nonsingular and it follows from [16] (Lemma 2.3) that $\operatorname{wsa}(I)$ is closed I. We have $I \cong \operatorname{wsa}(I) \oplus [I/\operatorname{wsa}(I)]$ and so $I/\operatorname{wsa}(I)$ is injective. The rest of the proof follows from Corollary 10. □

Proposition 16. *The following statements are equivalent for a projective module P.*
1. *P is $\mathcal{WSS}$-co-injective;*

2. $P/\operatorname{wsa}(P)$ is a homomorphic image of an injective module;
3. There exists a weakly semiartinian submodule M of P such that P/M is a homomorphic image of an injective module.

Proof. $(1 \Rightarrow 2)$: Let $\alpha : P \to E(P)$ be the inclusion and $\pi : P \to P/\operatorname{wsa}(P)$ the canonical epimorphism. Then we have the diagram

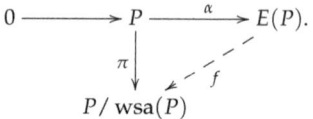

Since P is $\mathcal{WSS}$-co-injective and $P/\operatorname{wsa}(P)$ is crumbling-free, it follows from Proposition 10 that there exists a homomorphism $f : E(P) \to P/\operatorname{wsa}(P)$ such that $f\alpha = \pi$. Since π is an epimorphism, then so is f. Hence $P/\operatorname{wsa}(P) = f(E(P))$.

$(2 \Rightarrow 3)$: Since $\operatorname{wsa}(P)$ is weakly semiartinian, taking $M = \operatorname{wsa}(P)$ yields the result by assumption.

$(3 \Rightarrow 1)$: Let M be a weakly semiartinian submodule of P such that there is an epimorhism $f : I \to P/M$ with I injective. Consider the diagram

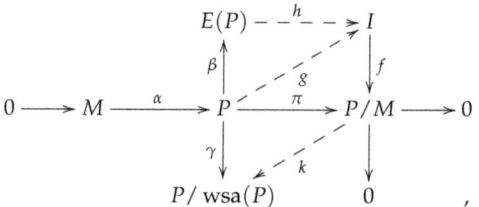

where $\alpha : M \to P$ and $\beta : P \to E(P)$ are inclusions and $\pi : P \to P/M$ and $\gamma : P \to P/\operatorname{wsa}(P)$ are canonical epimorphisms. Since M is weakly semiartinian, there is a homomorphism $k : P/M \to P/\operatorname{wsa}(P)$ such that $k\pi = \gamma$. Since f is an epimorphism and P is projective, there is a homomorphism $g : P \to I$ such that $fg = \pi$. Since β is a monomorphism and I is injective, there is a homomorphism $h : E(P) \to I$ such that $h\beta = g$. We have that the homomorphism $kfh : E(P) \to P/\operatorname{wsa}(P)$ satisfies $(kfh)\beta = k(f(h\beta)) = k(fg) = k\pi = \gamma$.

Now let F be a crumbling-free module and $\theta : P \to F$ be a homomorphism. Since $\operatorname{wsa}(P) \leq \operatorname{Ker}\theta$, by Factor Theorem there is homomorphism $u : P/\operatorname{wsa}(P) \to F$ such that $u\gamma = \theta$. Then, we have the diagram,

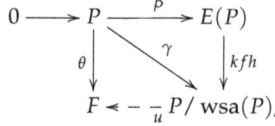

with the homomorphism $ukfh : E(P) \to F$ that satisfies $(ukfh)\beta = u((kfh)\beta) = u\gamma = \theta$ which implies by Proposition 10 that P is $\mathcal{WSS}$-co-injective. □

Corollary 12. *Every projective module is $\mathcal{WSS}$-co-injective if and only if every crumbling-free module is a homomorphic image of an injective module.*

Proof. For necessity let M be a crumbling-free module. There is an epimorphism $f : P \to M$ with P projective. Let $E(P)$ be the injective hull of P and $\alpha : P \to E(P)$ be the inclusion. Since P is $\mathcal{WSS}$-co-injective, it follows from Proposition 10 that there is a homomorphism

$g : E(P) \to M$ such that $g\alpha = f$. Clearly, f is an epimorphism. Sufficiency follows from Proposition 16. □

Corollary 13. *Over a right CC-ring, a projective module P is $\mathcal{WSS}$-co-injective if and only if $P/\operatorname{wsa}(P)$ is injective.*

Proof. For necessity, let P be a $\mathcal{WSS}$-co-injective module. Then, by Proposition 16, there is an epimorphism $f : I \to P$ for some injective module I. Since $P/\operatorname{wsa}(P)$ is a crumbling-free module over a right CC-ring, it is nonsingular. By [16] (Lemma 2.3), $\operatorname{Ker} f$ is closed in I, and so $\operatorname{Ker} f \oplus [P/\operatorname{wsa}(P)] \cong I$. Hence $P/\operatorname{wsa}(P)$ is injective. Sufficiency follows from the fact that $\mathcal{WSS}$-co-injective modules are closed under extensions. □

Proposition 17. *A ring R is right weakly semiartinian if and only if every right R-module is $\mathcal{WSS}$-co-injective.*

Proof. Necessity is clear. For sufficiency, it is enough to show that $C(M) \neq 0$ for every nonzero R-module M. Let N be a crumbling-free module. Then any submodule K of N is also crumbling-free. It follows from Proposition 10 that K is injective, therefore a direct summand of N. This shows that N is semisimple. Then we have $N = \operatorname{Soc} N \leq C(N) = 0$. Hence R is right weakly semiartinian. □

A ring R is called a right SSI-ring if all semisimple right R-modules are injective. It is known that a ring R is a right noetherian right V-ring if and only if it is a right SSI-ring.

Theorem 5. *The following statements are equivalent for a ring R.*
1. *Every $\mathcal{WSS}$-co-injective R-module is injective;*
2. *Every weakly semiartinian R-module is injective;*
3. *R is semisimple artinian.*

Proof. $(1 \Rightarrow 2)$ and $(3 \Rightarrow 1)$ are clear.

$(2 \Rightarrow 3)$: Every semisimple module is weakly semiartinian, hence injective by assumption and so R is a right SSI-ring. Then every module crumbles by [6] (Theorem 3). Since crumbling modules are weakly semiartinian, R is semisimple artinian by assumption. □

An R-module K is called $\mathcal{WSS}$-coprojective if every short exact sequence,

$$0 \longrightarrow M \longrightarrow N \longrightarrow K \longrightarrow 0,$$

of right R-modules ending with the module K is in the proper class $\mathcal{WSS}$. For an arbitrary ring R, let $C(R) = C(R_R)$.

Proposition 18. *Let R be a crumbling-free ring. Then $\mathcal{WSS}$-coprojective R-modules are only projective modules.*

Proof. Let M be a $\mathcal{WSS}$-coprojective R-module. Since every R-module is a factor module of a free R-module, there exist a free R-module F and an epimorphism $\psi : F \longrightarrow M$. Put $U = \operatorname{Ker}(\psi)$. Now we consider the short exact sequence $0 \longrightarrow U \overset{\iota}{\longrightarrow} F \overset{\psi}{\longrightarrow} M \longrightarrow 0$, where ι is the canonical injection. By the hypothesis, there exists a submodule V of F such that $F = U + V$ and $U \cap V$ is weakly semiartinian. Since $C(R) = 0$, it follows from [6] (Corollary 8) that $C(F) = C(R)F = 0$, and so $C(U \cap V) \subseteq C(F) = 0$. It means that the short exact sequence $0 \longrightarrow U \overset{\iota}{\longrightarrow} F \overset{\psi}{\longrightarrow} M \longrightarrow 0$ splits. Hence M is projective. □

Recall that a module M is *flat* if every short exact sequence of the form,

$$0 \longrightarrow M \overset{\psi}{\longrightarrow} N \longrightarrow K \longrightarrow 0,$$

is pure exact, that is, Im ψ is a pure submodule of N. Clearly, every projective module is flat.

Theorem 6. *Over a commutative C-ring $\mathcal{WSS}$-projective modules are flat.*

Proof. This follows from [7] (Theorem 3.9) and the fact that $\mathcal{SAS} \subseteq \mathcal{WSS}$. □

Author Contributions: Conceptualization, Y.M.D. and E.T.; methodology, Y.M.D. and E.T.; investigation, Y.M.D. and E.T.; writing–original draft preparation, Y.M.D. and E.T.; writing–review and editing, Y.M.D. All authors have read and agreed to the published version of the manuscript.

Funding: This research received no external funding.

Institutional Review Board Statement: Not applicable.

Informed Consent Statement: Not applicable.

Data Availability Statement: Not applicable.

Acknowledgments: The authors would like to thank the reviewers for valuable comments and suggestions that improved the presentation of the paper.

Conflicts of Interest: The authors declare no conflict of interest.

References

1. Clark, J.; Lomp, C.; Vanaja, N.; Wisbauer, R. *Lifting Modules. Supplements and Projectivity in Module Theory*; Frontiers in Mathematics; Birkhäuser: Basel, Switzerland, 2006. [CrossRef]
2. Dung, N.V.; Van Huynh, D.; Smith, P.F.; Wisbauer, R. *Extending Modules*; Chapman & Hall/CRC Research Notes in Mathematics Series; Taylor & Francis: Abingdon, UK, 1994; Volume 313. [CrossRef]
3. Wisbauer, R. *Foundations of Module and Ring Theory*; Algebra, Logic and Applications; Gordon and Breach Science Publishers: Philadelphia, PA, USA, 1991; Volume 3. [CrossRef]
4. Alahmadi, A.N.; Alkan, M.; López-Permouth, S. Poor modules: The opposite of injectivity. *Glasg. Math. J.* **2010**, *52*, 7–17. [CrossRef]
5. Er, N.; López-Permouth, S.; Sökmez, N. Rings whose modules have maximal or minimal injectivity domains. *J. Algebra* **2011**, *330*, 404–417. [CrossRef]
6. Alizade, R.; Demirci, Y.M.; Nişancı Türkmen, B.; Türkmen, E. On rings with one middle class of injectivity domains. *Math. Commun.* **2022**, *27*, 109–126.
7. Durğun, Y. sa-supplement submodules. *Bull. Korean Math. Soc.* **2021**, *58*, 147–161. [CrossRef]
8. Koşan, M.T. δ-lifting and δ-supplemented modules. *Algebra Colloq.* **2007**, *14*, 53–60. [CrossRef]
9. Buchsbaum, D.A. A note on homology in categories. *Ann. Math.* **1959**, *69*, 66–74. [CrossRef]
10. Alizade, R.; Büyükaşık, E.; Durğun, Y. Small supplements, weak supplements and proper classes. *Hacet. J. Math. Stat.* **2016**, *45*, 649–661. [CrossRef]
11. Alizade, R.; Demirci, Y.M.; Durğun, Y.; Pusat, D. The proper class generated by weak supplements. *Commun. Algebra* **2014**, *42*, 56–72. [CrossRef]
12. Durğun, Y. Extended S-supplement submodules. *Turk. J. Math.* **2019**, *43*, 2833–2841. [CrossRef]
13. Holston, C.; Jain, S.; Leroy, A. Rings Over Which Cyclics are Direct Sums of Projective and CS or Noetherian. *Glasg. Math. J.* **2010**, *52*, 103–110. [CrossRef]
14. Alizade, R.G. Proper Kepka Classes. *Mat. Zametki* **1985**, *37*, 268–273. [CrossRef]
15. Mišina, A.P.; Skornjakov, L.A. *Abelevy Gruppy i Moduli*; Izdat. "Nauka": Moscow, Russia, 1969.
16. Sandomierski, F.L. Nonsingular rings. *Proc. Am. Math. Soc.* **1968**, *19*, 225–230. [CrossRef]

Article

Applications of a Group Theoretical Method on Biomagnetic Fluid Flow and Heat Transfer for Different Shapes of Fe₃O₄ Magnetic Particles under the Influence of Thermal Radiation and a Magnetic Dipole over a Cylinder

Jahangir Alam [1], Ghulam Murtaza [2], Eugenia N. Petropoulou [3], Efstratios Em. Tzirtzilakis [4,*] and Mohammad Ferdows [1]

[1] Research Group of Fluid Flow Modeling and Simulation, Department of Applied Mathematics, University of Dhaka, Dhaka 1000, Bangladesh
[2] Department of Mathematics, Comilla University, Cumilla 3506, Bangladesh
[3] Geotechnical Engineering Laboratory, Department of Civil Engineering, University of Patras, 26500 Patras, Greece
[4] Fluid Mechanics and Turbomachinery Laboratory, Department of Mechanical Engineering, University of the Peloponnese, 26334 Patras, Greece
* Correspondence: etzirtzilakis@uop.gr

Citation: Alam, J.; Murtaza, G.; Petropoulou, E.N.; Tzirtzilakis, E.E.; Ferdows, M. Applications of a Group Theoretical Method on Biomagnetic Fluid Flow and Heat Transfer for Different Shapes of Fe₃O₄ Magnetic Particles under the Influence of Thermal Radiation and a Magnetic Dipole over a Cylinder. *Mathematics* **2022**, *10*, 3520. https://doi.org/10.3390/math10193520

Academic Editors: Irina Cristea, Yuriy Rogovchenko, Justo Puerto, Gintautas Dzemyda and Patrick Siarry

Received: 29 August 2022
Accepted: 21 September 2022
Published: 27 September 2022

Publisher's Note: MDPI stays neutral with regard to jurisdictional claims in published maps and institutional affiliations.

Copyright: © 2022 by the authors. Licensee MDPI, Basel, Switzerland. This article is an open access article distributed under the terms and conditions of the Creative Commons Attribution (CC BY) license (https://creativecommons.org/licenses/by/4.0/).

Abstract: The flow and heat characteristics of an unsteady, laminar biomagnetic fluid, namely blood containing Fe₃O₄ magnetic particles, under the influence of thermal radiation and a magnetic dipole over a cylinder with controlled boundary conditions using a group theory method are investigated in the present study. The mathematical formulation of the problem is constructed with the aid of biomagnetic fluid dynamics (BFD) which combines principles of ferrohydrodynamics (FHD) and magnetohydrodynamics (MHD). It is assumed that blood exhibits polarization as well as electrical conductivity. Additionally, the shape of the magnetic particles, namely cylindrical and spherical, is also considered. Moreover, in this model, a group theoretical transformation, namely a two-parameter group technique, is applied. By applying this group transformation, the governing system of partial differential equations (PDEs) along with applicable boundary conditions are reduced to one independent variable and, consequently, converted into a system of ordinary differential equations (ODEs) with suitable boundary conditions. An efficient numerical technique is applied to solve the resultant ODEs and this technique is based on three essential features, namely (i) a common finite differences method with central differencing, (ii) tridiagonal matrix manipulation and (iii) an iterative procedure. The flow and heat characteristics of blood-Fe₃O₄ are found to be dependent on some physical parameters such as the particle volume fraction, the ferromagnetic interaction parameter, the magnetic field parameter, and the thermal radiation parameter. An ample parametric study is accomplished to narrate the influences of such physical parameters on velocity, temperature distributions as well as the coefficient of skin friction and rate of heat transfer. From the numerical results, it is deduced that the fluid velocity is enhanced for the ferromagnetic number and the temperature profile is decreased as the ferromagnetic number is gradually increased. It is also obtained that for the cylindrical shape of magnetic particles, the fluid temperature is more enhanced than that of the spherical shape. Both the skin friction coefficient and the local Nusselt number are increased for increasing values of the ferromagnetic interaction parameter, where the heat transfer rate of blood-Fe₃O₄ is significantly increased by approximately 33.2% compared to that of pure blood, whereas the coefficient of skin friction is reduced by approximately 6.82%.

Keywords: group theoretical method; biomagnetic fluid dynamics (BFD); blood; magnetic particles; cylinder; magnetic dipole; finite differences method

MSC: 35Q35; 76M20; 76M55; 76W05

1. Introduction

From a theoretical and practical point of view, the studies of biomagnetic fluid dynamics (BFD), which consists of the ideas of ferrohydrodynamics (FHD) and magnetohydrodynamics (MHD), exhibit much interest to researchers due to their variety of applications in biomedical and bio-engineering areas as reported early in [1–4] such as drug and gene delivery performed by magnetic particles, magnetic resonance imaging (MRI) for imaging, the reduction in blood during surgeries, cancer treatment, and injury treatment. For researchers in fluid dynamics, BFD is a comparatively new area, where the effect of the magnetic field on the biological fluid is studied. In the recent past, this area has received tremendous attention from researchers since it is directly related to non-invasive applications for treating human body-related diseases and disorders. Moreover, blood is considered as one of the peculiarities of BFD due to the presence of ions. Blood could be considered to behave as a Newtonian or non-Newtonian fluid. When blood flows at high shear rates through arteries, blood can be considered as a Newtonian fluid as mentioned by Chien et al. [5] and the true non-Newtonian nature of blood should be considered when shear rates are very low according to the study of Bhatti et al. [6].

The influence of a magnetic field is incorporated in the study of bio-fluids and that is why the concepts of FHD and MHD need to be introduced. Basically, in ferrohydrodynamics (FHD), fluid is considered electrically non-conducting, where fluid flows are influenced in the presence of magnetization by the polarization effect. Specifically, when a magnetic field is exposed to a magnetic fluid such as blood, a measurement of the magnetization can be made in order to determine how much is affected by the applied magnetic field. Magnetization can be described mathematically by involving the magnetic field strength intensity and/or temperature. On the other hand, in magnetohydrodynamics (MHD), the influence of magnetization is negligible and fluid flows like an electrically conducting magnetic fluid. Based on the above-mentioned concept, a mathematical study of BFD considering the FHD principles was initiated by Haik et al. [7], where fluid is considered as a Newtonian fluid. The authors found that in the presence of high-gradient magnetic fields, the flow of a biomagnetic fluid is significantly affected. This mathematical model was extended by Tzirtzilakis [8], where both principles, namely MHD and FHD, are considered simultaneously. The behavior of MHD blood flow under the effect of temperature-dependent fluid viscosity and thermal conductivity was investigated by Sharma et al. [9]. The impact of temperature-dependent magnetization on a non-Newtonian biomagnetic fluid using viscoelastic fluid property over a stretching sheet was studied by Misra et al. [10] and the numerical solution was obtained by using a finite differences technique. The influence of thermal radiation and slip conditions on time-dependent blood flow and heat transfer over an inclined permeable stretching surface was studied by Koppu et al. [11]. The dual behavior of blood flow and heat transfer in the quadratic stretched surface under the influence of a magnetic dipole was investigated by Murtaza et al. [12] and the authors reveal that, in a particular range of the suction parameter and stretching/shrinking sheet, the physical solutions, i.e., stable and unstable solutions, are present. Recently, the study of a biomagnetic fluid under the influence of a magnetic dipole was studied by Murtaza et al. [13], where it was shown that the combination of MHD and FHD, i.e., BFD flow, is comparatively more significant than that of MHD, FHD, or pure hydrodynamics flow alone.

In the recent past, many researchers investigated the study of different regular fluids (water, blood, etc.) by adding different types of nanoparticles (magnetic/non-magnetic). This is because the heat transfer of a base fluid like blood is significantly improved when nanoparticles are mixed with a base fluid and this improvement is more effective than conventional heat transfer in fluids where the size of nanoparticles is usually 1–100 nm. When nanoparticles are mixed with a base fluid, this is known as a nanofluid, initially introduced by Choi [14]. As far as cylinder flows have been concerned, Alsenafi and Ferdows [15] showed that depending on the systems' parameters, dual solutions exist in opposing flow beyond a critical point where both solutions are connected. The forced convection of a Al_2O_3-water nanofluid over a circular cylinder inside a magnetic field was studied by

Nikelham et al. [16]. In that study, an experimental model as a function of the temperature, nanoparticle diameter, and volume fraction of the nanofluid was utilized to calculate the nanofluid's viscosity and conductivity coefficient. It was found that the model of the nanofluids is important, and the values of the Nusselt numbers in the experimental model are different than the Brinkman–Maxwell analytical one. Aminian et al. [17] numerically studied the MHD forced convection effects of Al_2O_3–CuO–water nanofluid inside a partitioned cylinder within a porous medium. Nanofluid flow was modeled as a two-phase flow using a two-phase mixture model, and the Darcy–Brinkman–Forchheimer equation was employed to model fluid flow in porous media. They demonstrated that incorporation of nanoparticles to the base fluid increased the performance evaluation criteria in all cases. The MHD flow of water-based nanofluids across a horizontal circular cylinder was numerically investigated by Tlili et al. [18]. It was found that skin friction and the local Nusselt numbers are strong functions of Reynolds and Hartmann numbers, whereas the local Sherwood number is a strong function of nanofluids parameters. The impact of heat source/sink along with suction/injection on steady, two-dimensional MHD flow through a stretched cylinder was developed by Elbashbeshy et al. [19]. Finally, the unsteady magnetohydrodynamic mixed convection flow of an incompressible hybrid nanofluid (Cu-Al_2O_3/water) past an isothermal cylinder with thermal radiation effect has been studied by Roy and Akter [20]. The corresponding results revealed that the hybrid nanofluid (Cu-Al_2O_3/water) enhances the heat transfer by approximately 28.28% in comparison to the Al_2O_3-water nanofluid and by approximately 51.15% more than in the pure fluid. Contrary to this, the heat transfer of hybrid nanofluid is augmented by approximately 41.76% more than the Cu-water nanofluid and by 71.41% more than the base fluid. The significance of melting in the presence of thermal radiation on Cattaneo–Christov-aligned MHD nanofluid flows together with microorganism to leading edge is investigated by Ali et al. [21] with an approaching FEM technique. An analysis of H_2O-Al_2O_3 nanofluid flow over a stretching sheet subject to prescribed heat flux in the presence of thermal radiation is studied by Kumar et al. [22]. They found that the coefficient of skin friction and thermal boundary layer decreases as the radius of nanoparticles is enhanced. Dawar et al. [23] examined the effects of Brownian motion and thermophoresis on MHD water-based nanofluid with copper and copper oxide nanoparticles between two parallel plates. It was found that the heat transfer rate is increased by approximately 1% between two blade-shaped nanoparticles as Cu and CuO when the values of volume fraction $\phi = 0.02$ and $\phi = 0.03$. Bilal et al. [24] inspected the $C_2H_6O_2$-H_2O hybrid nanofluid flow with three different nanoparticles—TiO_2, SiO_2, and Al_2O_3—with activation energy across two infinite parallel plates. They reported that when nanoparticles are added to a base fluid, the fluid velocity and the heat transfer rate increase. Souayeh et al. [25] performed a numerical analysis of the flow and heat transfer of water-silver/gold nanofluid flow through an electromagnetohydrodynamic (EMHD) peristaltic channel in the presence of activation energy and radiation and microorganisms. Alwawi et al. [26] applied the Keller box method solutions to recapitulate human blood and water with CuO, Al, Au nanoparticles assuming a constant surface heat flux subject to a circular cylinder. The authors reported that gold particles gave better numerical results compared to Aluminum and copper. The impact of a magnetic dipole on the flow and heat transfer of blood-$MnZnFe_2O_4$ over a cylinder is discussed by Alam et al. [27] with the help of a group theoretical method approach.

However, from the above-mentioned studies, the authors of the present paper observed that most of the research has been conducted with regular fluid by mixing non-magnetic particles. To the best of the authors' knowledge, although there are numerous studies on stretching sheet and stretching cylinder flows, there are not many studies on unsteady cylinder flow, where the base fluid (human blood) contains magnetic particles. The reason behind choosing magnetic particles rather than non-magnetic particles is the use of magnetic particles in medical applications, which is explained in [28–31]. The proposed mathematical model is that of BFD, which incorporates two principles, namely MHD and FHD, where blood is electrically conducting magnetic fluid which also exhibits magnetization. These two terms are interconnected. In most of the studies, researchers on the blood flow model only consider the magnetization effect, where the fluid is considered as an electrically non-conducting fluid. From a practical point of view, if we want to destroy the tumor cells from our body without harming good cells, we can apply a strong magnetic field in that particular tumor area and determine how much fluid is affected by this applied magnetic field, which is measured by the mathematical term known as magnetization. To solve such fluid mechanics problems, several transformation techniques have been proposed by various researchers. In this paper, a group theoretical method, namely a two-parameter group method, is applied to solve the blood-based magnetic particles problem over a cylinder under the influence of a magnetic dipole. By applying this two-parameter group theoretical method, we can find a group of solutions in terms of various conditions. Meanwhile, we are frequently in contact with previously derived analogous solutions and the two-parameter group restores many of these forms and we will find some completely new ones. Such group theoretical methodology, i.e., the one/two parameter group method, has been analyzed in [32–36]. By using this systematic method, the number of independent variables is reduced by one and, consequently, the governing partial differential equations (PDEs) are transformed into a set of ordinary differential equations (ODEs) along with suitable boundary conditions which are later numerically solved by applying an efficient numerical technique, based on a common finite differences method with tridiagonal matrix manipulation and an iterative procedure. The significant impact of involving parameters such as the ferromagnetic parameter, the magnetic particle volume fraction, the magnetic field parameter, thermal radiation, temperature profiles as well as the skin friction coefficient and the rate of heat transfer is discussed with their respective graphical outcomes. Two cases are considered for the obtained numerical solutions: the first case concerns the behavior of pure blood and blood-Fe_3O_4, whereas the second solution examines the effect of particle shape on blood-Fe_3O_4 flow and heat transfer, which is also the key objective of the present study.

Furthermore, in this study, the maximum temperature for the human body is considered to be 41 °C, which is reasonable for applications in cancer treatment and moreover noticeable for enzyme function and the function of other proteins of the human body. Therefore, the current study could be applicable to biomedical sciences especially in drug administration, cancer therapy, reducing the flow of blood during surgeries, etc. Since, this study relates to human body related diseases and disorders, it is hoped that it will be important not only for understanding flow mechanisms but also for taking prevention measures.

2. Mathematical and Physical Formulation

The schematic representation of the governing co-ordinate system considered in this study is presented in Figure 1. The fluid considered (blood) contains magnetic particles (Fe_3O_4) and flows through a two-dimensional cylinder along the $\bar{x}$-axis, where L is the characteristic length of the cylinder. The flow is considered as unsteady, and the cylinder has a radius $\bar{R}$ and the $\bar{r}$-axis is the normal direction of the cylinder. The temperature of the cylinder surface is T_w and the ambient fluid temperature is T_c situated far away from the surface, with $T_w < T_c$. A magnetic dipole which is assumed to be located below the sheet maintaining a distance c, propagates a magnetic field of strength $\bar{H}$. Moreover, due to the presence of FHD principles, the base fluid (blood) exhibits the polarization effect, where the applied magnetic field is supposed to be strong enough, to attain the equilibrium of magnetization.

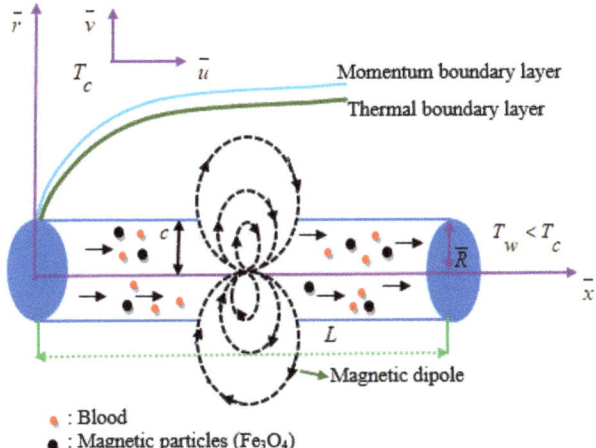

Figure 1. Schematic representation of geometry.

Due to the aforementioned assumptions and following [8,37], the governing continuity, momentum, and energy equations in cylindrical coordinates can be written as follows:

Continuity equation:
$$\frac{\partial \bar{u}}{\partial \bar{x}} + \frac{\bar{v}}{\bar{r}} + \frac{\partial \bar{v}}{\partial \bar{r}} = 0. \tag{1}$$

Momentum equation:
$$\frac{\partial \bar{u}}{\partial \bar{t}} + \bar{u}\frac{\partial \bar{u}}{\partial \bar{x}} + \bar{v}\frac{\partial \bar{u}}{\partial \bar{r}} = \frac{\mu_{mf}}{\rho_{mf}}\left(\frac{\partial^2 \bar{u}}{\partial \bar{r}^2} + \frac{1}{\bar{r}}\frac{\partial \bar{u}}{\partial \bar{r}}\right) - \frac{\sigma_{mf} B^2 \bar{u}}{\rho_{mf}} + \frac{\mu_0}{\rho_{mf}} M \frac{\partial \bar{H}}{\partial \bar{x}}. \tag{2}$$

Energy equation:
$$(\rho C_p)_{mf}\left(\frac{\partial \bar{T}}{\partial \bar{t}} + \bar{u}\frac{\partial \bar{T}}{\partial \bar{x}} + \bar{v}\frac{\partial \bar{T}}{\partial \bar{r}}\right) + \mu_0 \bar{T}\frac{\partial M}{\partial \bar{T}}\left(\bar{u}\frac{\partial \bar{H}}{\partial \bar{x}} + \bar{v}\frac{\partial \bar{H}}{\partial \bar{r}}\right) = \kappa_{mf}\left(\frac{\partial^2 \bar{T}}{\partial \bar{r}^2} + \frac{1}{\bar{r}}\frac{\partial \bar{T}}{\partial \bar{r}}\right) - \frac{\partial q_r}{\partial \bar{r}}. \tag{3}$$

The boundary conditions accompanying (1)–(3) are [27,35,37]:
$$\begin{aligned}\bar{r} &= \bar{R}: \bar{u} = 0, \bar{v} = 0, \bar{T} = T_w, \\ \bar{r} &\to \infty : \bar{u} = 0, \bar{T} = T_c.\end{aligned} \tag{4}$$

Here, $\bar{u}$ and $\bar{v}$ are the dimensional velocity components along the axis, respectively. Further, the symbols κ, ρ, C_p, μ, μ_0, $M, \sigma, \bar{H}, q_r$ are known as blood thermal conductivity, density, specific heat at constant pressure, dynamic viscosity, magnetic permeability, magnetization, electrical conductivity, magnetic field strength, and radiative heat flux, respectively. Additionally, $B \;(= \mu_0 \bar{H})$ is the magnetic induction and the subscript symbol $(\;)_{mf}$ means magnetic fluid. The bar above the quantities indicates that the quantities are dimensional.

Due to the electrical conductivity of the fluid, the term $-\frac{\sigma_{mf} B^2 \bar{u}}{\rho_{mf}}$ arising in Equation (2), represents the Lorentz force per unit volume along the $\bar{x}$ axis. This term is known from MHD studies [8,13]. From FHD studies [38–40], the component of the magnetic force per unit volume is defined by the term $\frac{\mu_0}{\rho_{mf}} M\frac{\partial \bar{H}}{\partial \bar{x}}$, arising in Equation (2) and depends on the existence of the magnetic gradients on the corresponding $\bar{x}$ axis, while the thermal power per unit volume due to the magnetocaloric effect, is represented by the term $\mu_0 \bar{T}\frac{\partial M}{\partial \bar{T}}\left(\bar{u}\frac{\partial \bar{H}}{\partial \bar{x}} + \bar{v}\frac{\partial \bar{H}}{\partial \bar{r}}\right)$ arising in Equation (3).

Raptis [41,42] described the radiative heat flux q_r using Rosseland approximation in such a way that:

$$q_r = -\frac{4\sigma_1}{3\chi}\frac{\partial \overline{T}^4}{\partial \overline{r}}, \qquad (5)$$

where σ_1 is the Stefan–Boltzmann constant and χ is the mean absorption coefficient. The fluid temperature differences within the flow are supposed to be sufficiently small. Then, the temperature term $\overline{T}^4$ may be expressed as a linear function of the temperature, by expanding $\overline{T}^4$ in a Taylor series about T_c and neglecting higher-order terms yielding the expression

$$\overline{T}^4 \cong 4T_c^3 \overline{T} - 3T_c^4. \qquad (6)$$

Thus, the local radiant absorption is given by

$$\frac{\partial q_r}{\partial \overline{r}} = -\frac{16\sigma_1 T_c^3}{3\chi}\frac{\partial^2 \overline{T}}{\partial \overline{r}^2}. \qquad (7)$$

Substituting (7) into Equation (3) yields

$$(\rho C_p)_{mf}\left(\frac{\partial \overline{T}}{\partial t} + \overline{u}\frac{\partial \overline{T}}{\partial \overline{x}} + \overline{v}\frac{\partial \overline{T}}{\partial \overline{r}}\right) + \mu_0 \overline{T}\frac{\partial M}{\partial \overline{T}}\left(\overline{u}\frac{\partial \overline{H}}{\partial \overline{x}} + \overline{v}\frac{\partial \overline{H}}{\partial \overline{r}}\right) = \kappa_{mf}\left(\frac{\partial^2 \overline{T}}{\partial \overline{r}^2} + \frac{1}{\overline{r}}\frac{\partial \overline{T}}{\partial \overline{r}}\right) + \frac{16\sigma_1 T_c^3}{3\chi}\frac{\partial^2 \overline{T}}{\partial \overline{r}^2} \qquad (8)$$

According to [43,44], the components $\overline{H}_x$ and $\overline{H}_r$ of the magnetic field $\vec{\overline{H}} = (\overline{H}_x, \overline{H}_r)$, due to the magnetic dipole may be written as follows:

$$\overline{H}_x(\overline{x},\overline{r}) = -\frac{\partial V}{\partial \overline{x}} = \frac{\gamma}{2\pi}\frac{\overline{x}^2 - (\overline{r}+c)^2}{(\overline{x}^2 + (\overline{r}+c)^2)^2}, \qquad (9)$$

$$\overline{H}_r(\overline{x},\overline{r}) = -\frac{\partial V}{\partial \overline{r}} = \frac{\gamma}{2\pi}\frac{2\overline{x}(\overline{r}+c)}{(\overline{x}^2 + (\overline{r}+c)^2)^2}, \qquad (10)$$

where the scalar potential of the magnetic dipole is defined by $V(\overline{x},\overline{r}) = \frac{\gamma}{2\pi}\frac{\overline{x}}{\overline{x}^2+(\overline{r}+c)^2}$ and γ is the strength of the magnetic field at the source position. The magnetic field strength intensity $\overline{H}$ is given by

$$\overline{H}(\overline{x},\overline{r}) = \sqrt{\overline{H}_x^2 + \overline{H}_r^2} = \frac{\gamma}{2\pi}\frac{1}{\overline{x}^2+(\overline{r}+c)^2}, \qquad (11)$$

and the gradients of the magnetic field intensity are obtained by the above relation by expanding $\overline{H}$ in powers of $\overline{x}$ and retaining terms up to $\overline{x}^2$, taking eventually the form

$$\frac{\partial \overline{H}}{\partial \overline{x}} = -\frac{\gamma}{2\pi}\frac{2\overline{x}}{(\overline{r}+c)^4}, \qquad (12)$$

$$\frac{\partial \overline{H}}{\partial \overline{r}} = -\frac{\gamma}{2\pi}\left(\frac{-2}{(\overline{r}+c)^3} + \frac{4\overline{x}^2}{(\overline{r}+c)^5}\right). \qquad (13)$$

Moreover, Matsuki et al. [45] experimentally showed that the magnetization M can be expressed as a function of the temperature $\overline{T}$ and the magnetic field strength intensity $\overline{H}$ is given by

$$M = K\overline{H}(T_c - \overline{T}), \qquad (14)$$

where K is the pyromagnetic coefficient and T_c is the Curie temperature.

The thermophysical properties of the base fluid and magnetic particles are introduced according to the studies of Makinde [46], Lin et al. [47] and Kandasamy et al. [48] and presented in Table 1.

Table 1. Thermophysical properties of the magnetic fluid model [46–48].

Magnetic Fluid Properties	Applied Model
Density	$\rho_{mf} = (1-\phi)\rho_f + \phi\rho_s$
Dynamic viscosity	$\mu_{mf} = \mu_f (1-\phi)^{-2.5}$
Electrical conductivity	$\frac{\sigma_{mf}}{\sigma_f} = 1 + \frac{3\left(\frac{\sigma_s}{\sigma_f}-1\right)\phi}{\left(\frac{\sigma_s}{\sigma_f}+1\right)-\left(\frac{\sigma_s}{\sigma_f}-1\right)\phi}$
Heat capacitance	$(\rho C_p)_{mf} = (1-\phi)(\rho C_p)_f + \phi(\rho C_p)_s$
Thermal conductivity	$\frac{\kappa_{mf}}{\kappa_f} = \frac{(\kappa_s+(m-1)\kappa_f)-(m-1)\phi(\kappa_f-\kappa_s)}{(\kappa_s+(m-1)\kappa_f)+\phi(\kappa_f-\kappa_s)}$

Here, ϕ denotes the magnetic particle volume fraction and m is the magnetic particle shape factor such that when $m = 3$ and $m = 6.3698$ represent that the particles have spherical and cylindrical shape, respectively. Further, the notations $(\ )_f$ and $(\ )_s$ stand for the base fluid and the magnetic particles, respectively. When $\phi = 0$, all corresponding equations are transformed into a regular fluid model. In this paper, blood is considered as the base fluid and Fe_3O_4 as the magnetic particles and their corresponding thermophysical properties are tabulated in Table 2 according to previous studies [49–51].

Table 2. The values of thermophysical properties of blood and Fe_3O_4 [49–51].

Physical properties	C_p (jkg^{-1}K^{-1})	ρ (kgm^{-3})	σ (sm^{-1})	κ (Wm^{-1}K^{-1})
Blood	3.9×10^3	1050	0.8	0.5
Fe$_3$O$_4$	670	5180	0.74×10^6	9.7

In order to proceed with the solution of the problem, Equations (1), (2) and (8) together with the boundary conditions (4) are transformed into dimensionless form by using the following transformations [27,35,37]:

$$x = \frac{\bar{x}}{R}, r = \frac{\bar{r}}{R}, u = \frac{\bar{u}R}{v_f}, v = \frac{\bar{v}R}{v_f}, t = \frac{\bar{t}v_f}{R^2}, H = \frac{\bar{H}}{H_0}, \theta = \frac{T_c - \bar{T}}{T_c - T_w}, \quad (15)$$

where v_f is the kinematic viscosity of the fluid and H_0 is the reference magnetic field strength intensity. Hence, the reduced dimensionless form of the corresponding equations with boundary conditions are:

$$\frac{\partial u}{\partial x} + \frac{v}{r} + \frac{\partial v}{\partial r} = 0, \quad (16)$$

$$A_1\left(\frac{\partial u}{\partial t} + u\frac{\partial u}{\partial x} + v\frac{\partial u}{\partial r}\right) = \frac{\partial^2 u}{\partial r^2} + \frac{1}{r}\frac{\partial u}{\partial r} - A_2 MnH^2 u + A_3\beta H\theta\frac{\partial H}{\partial x}, \quad (17)$$

$$A_4 Pr\left(\frac{\partial \theta}{\partial t} + u\frac{\partial \theta}{\partial x} + v\frac{\partial \theta}{\partial r}\right) + A_5\beta EcH(\varepsilon - \theta)\left(u\frac{\partial H}{\partial x} + v\frac{\partial H}{\partial r}\right) = (1 + NrA_5)\frac{\partial^2 \theta}{\partial r^2} + \frac{1}{r}\frac{\partial \theta}{\partial r}, \quad (18)$$

$$\begin{array}{l} r = 1 : u = 0, v = 0, \theta = 1 \\ r \to \infty : u = 0, \theta = 0 \end{array} \quad (19)$$

where

$$A_1 = (1-\phi)^{2.5}\left(1-\phi+\phi\frac{\rho_s}{\rho_f}\right), \quad A_2 = (1-\phi)^{2.5}\left[1+\frac{3\left(\frac{\sigma_s}{\sigma_f}-1\right)\phi}{\left(\frac{\sigma_s}{\sigma_f}+1\right)-\left(\frac{\sigma_s}{\sigma_f}-1\right)\phi}\right],$$
$$A_3 = (1-\phi)^{2.5}, \quad A_4 = \frac{\kappa_f}{\kappa_{mf}}\left(1-\phi+\phi\frac{(\rho C_p)_s}{(\rho C_p)_f}\right), \quad A_5 = \frac{\kappa_f}{\kappa_{mf}}$$
(20)

Here, $\beta = \frac{\mu_0 K H_0^2 (T_c - T_w) \overline{R}^2 \rho_f}{\mu_f^2}$ is the ferromagnetic interaction parameter, $Mn = \frac{\sigma_f \mu_0^2 H_0^2 \overline{R}^2}{\mu_f}$ is the magnetic field parameter, $Nr = \frac{16\sigma_1 T_c^3}{3\chi \kappa_f}$, is the thermal radiation parameter, $Pr = \frac{(\mu C_p)_f}{\kappa_f}$, is the Prandtl number, $\varepsilon = \frac{T_c}{T_c - T_w}$ is the dimensionless Curie temperature and $Ec = \frac{\mu_f^3}{\rho_f^2 \kappa_f \overline{R}^2 (T_c - T_w)}$ is the Eckert number.

If the stream function ψ formulation is adopted, i.e., define the velocity components as

$$u = \frac{1}{r}\frac{\partial \psi}{\partial r}, v = -\frac{1}{r}\frac{\partial \psi}{\partial x}$$

Equation (16) is automatically satisfied and Equations (17) and (18) take the form:

$$A_1\left[r^2\frac{\partial^2 \psi}{\partial t \partial r} + r\frac{\partial \psi}{\partial r}\frac{\partial^2 \psi}{\partial x \partial r} + \frac{\partial \psi}{\partial x}\left(\frac{\partial \psi}{\partial r} - r\frac{\partial^2 \psi}{\partial r^2}\right)\right] = r^2\frac{\partial^3 \psi}{\partial r^3} - r\frac{\partial^2 \psi}{\partial r^2} + \frac{\partial \psi}{\partial r} \\ - A_2 M n H^2 r^2 \frac{\partial \psi}{\partial r} + A_3 \beta \, Hr^3 \theta \frac{\partial H}{\partial x}$$
(21)

$$A_4 Pr\left(r\frac{\partial \theta}{\partial t} + \frac{\partial \psi}{\partial r}\frac{\partial \theta}{\partial x} - \frac{\partial \psi}{\partial x}\frac{\partial \theta}{\partial r}\right) + A_5 \beta Ec H(\varepsilon - \theta)\left(\frac{\partial \psi}{\partial r}\frac{\partial H}{\partial x} - \frac{\partial \psi}{\partial x}\frac{\partial H}{\partial r}\right) = (1 + NrA_5)\, r\frac{\partial^2 \theta}{\partial r^2} + \frac{\partial \theta}{\partial r},$$
(22)

along with the boundary conditions:

$$r = 1: \frac{\partial \psi}{\partial r} = 0, \frac{\partial \psi}{\partial x} = 0, \theta = 1 \\ r \to \infty: \frac{\partial \psi}{\partial r} = 0, \theta = 0$$
(23)

3. The Group of Transformations

To identify all symmetries of a given differential equation (DE), group method analysis is the only rigorous mathematical method and for that no prior knowledge or exceptional assumptions of the given boundary layer equations under inquisition is needed. In physical standpoint, the boundary layer equations are very interesting due to their potency to admit a huge number of analytic solutions, i.e., invariant solutions. Here, invariant solutions mean the reduction of PDEs to simpler ODEs. Basically, the researchers in the fluid mechanics field, try to obtain similarity solutions by proposing a general similarity transformation with unknown parameters into the DE and as a result get an algebraic system. Then, the solution of this system, if it exists, determines the values of the unknown parameters. From this point of view, we believe that it is better to attack any problem of similarity solutions from the outset; that is, to find out the full list of symmetries of the problem and then study which of them are appropriate to provide group-invariant solutions more specifically similarity solutions. The two-parameter method that we applied in this model provided a group of solutions which is one of the major advantages of this group method. However, few limitations of this method also hold, such as the large number of arbitrary coefficients appearing in the obtained ODEs. It is quite difficult to determine numerical solutions to the problem.

In this section, a group theoretical method is applied to the system of PDEs (21)–(22) along with the boundary conditions (23). More precisely, a two-parameter transformation group is applied, which reduces the number of independent variables by one. Consequently, the set of PDEs (21)–(22) is converted into a system of ODEs.

3.1. The Group Systematic Formulation

The procedure is initiated with a class G of two-parameter (a_1, a_2) transformation group of the form

$$G : \overline{S} = C^S(a_1, a_2) \, S + K^S(a_1, a_2), \tag{24}$$

where C^S and K^S are real values and at least differentiable in each argument (a_1, a_2) and the symbol S stands for x, r, t, ψ, θ, H. Relation (24) may be further expressed in the following way:

$$G : \begin{cases} \overline{S} : \begin{cases} \overline{x} = C^x(a_1, a_2) \, x + K^x(a_1, a_2) \\ \overline{r} = C^r(a_1, a_2) \, r + K^r(a_1, a_2) \\ \overline{t} = C^t(a_1, a_2) \, t + K^t(a_1, a_2) \end{cases} \\ \overline{\psi} = C^\psi(a_1, a_2) \, \psi + K^\psi(a_1, a_2) \\ \overline{\theta} = C^\theta(a_1, a_2) \, \theta + K^\theta(a_1, a_2) \\ \overline{H} = C^H(a_1, a_2) \, H + K^H(a_1, a_2) \end{cases}, \tag{25}$$

which possesses complete sets of absolute invariants $\eta \, (x, r, t)$ and $\xi_i \, (x, r, t, \psi, \theta, H)$, $i = 1, 2, 3$ where ξ_i are the three absolute invariants corresponding to ψ, θ, H. If η is the absolute invariant of the independent variables, then $\xi_i = F_i(\eta), i = 1, 2, 3$. For more details one may refer to [52] or [53].

3.2. The Invariance Analysis

The transformation for the derivatives appearing in Equations (21) to (23), are directly gained from G via chain-rule operations and are

$$\frac{\partial \overline{S}}{\partial \overline{i}} = \frac{C^S}{C^i} \frac{\partial S}{\partial i}, \frac{\partial^2 \overline{S}}{\partial \overline{i}^2} = \frac{C^S}{(C^i)^2} \frac{\partial^2 S}{\partial i^2}, \frac{\partial^3 \overline{S}}{\partial \overline{i}^3} = \frac{C^S}{(C^i)^3} \frac{\partial^3 S}{\partial i^3}, \frac{\partial^2 \overline{S}}{\partial \overline{i} \partial \overline{j}} = \frac{C^S}{C^i C^j} \frac{\partial^2 S}{\partial i \partial j}, \tag{26}$$

where $S = \psi, \theta, H$ and $i, j = x, r, t$.

Equation (21) is said to be invariantly transformed under (25) and (26), whenever

$$A_1 \left\{ \overline{r}^2 \frac{\partial^2 \overline{\psi}}{\partial \overline{t} \partial \overline{r}} + \overline{r} \frac{\partial \overline{\psi}}{\partial \overline{r}} \frac{\partial^2 \overline{\psi}}{\partial \overline{x} \partial \overline{r}} + \frac{\partial \overline{\psi}}{\partial \overline{x}} \left(\frac{\partial \overline{\psi}}{\partial \overline{r}} - \overline{r} \frac{\partial^2 \overline{\psi}}{\partial \overline{r}^2} \right) \right\} - \frac{\partial \overline{\psi}}{\partial \overline{r}} + \overline{r} \frac{\partial^2 \overline{\psi}}{\partial \overline{r}^2} - \overline{r}^2 \frac{\partial^3 \overline{\psi}}{\partial \overline{r}^3} + A_2 Mn \overline{H}^2 \overline{r}^2 \frac{\partial \overline{\psi}}{\partial \overline{r}}$$
$$- A_3 \beta \overline{H} \overline{r}^3 \theta \frac{\partial \overline{H}}{\partial \overline{x}} = I_1(a_1, a_2) \left[\begin{array}{c} A_1 \left\{ r^2 \frac{\partial^2 \psi}{\partial t \partial r} + r \frac{\partial \psi}{\partial r} \frac{\partial^2 \psi}{\partial x \partial r} + \frac{\partial \psi}{\partial x} \left(\frac{\partial \psi}{\partial r} - r \frac{\partial^2 \psi}{\partial r^2} \right) \right\} \\ -\frac{\partial \psi}{\partial r} + r \frac{\partial^2 \psi}{\partial r^2} - r^2 \frac{\partial^3 \psi}{\partial r^3} + A_2 Mn H^2 r^2 \frac{\partial \psi}{\partial r} - A_3 \beta H r^3 \theta \frac{\partial H}{\partial x} \end{array} \right] \tag{27}$$

for some function $I_1(a_1, a_2)$ which may be constant. The terms defined in (25) together with the corresponding derivatives from (26) are substituted into the left side of Equation (27), yielding

$$A_1 \left[\frac{C^\psi C^r}{C^t} r^2 \frac{\partial^2 \psi}{\partial t \partial r} + \frac{(C^\psi)^2}{C^x C^r} r \frac{\partial \psi}{\partial r} \frac{\partial^2 \psi}{\partial x \partial r} + \frac{(C^\psi)^2}{C^x C^r} \frac{\partial \psi}{\partial x} \left(\frac{\partial \psi}{\partial r} - r \frac{\partial^2 \psi}{\partial r^2} \right) \right] - \frac{C^\psi}{C^r} \frac{\partial \psi}{\partial r}$$
$$+ \frac{C^\psi}{C^r} r \frac{\partial^2 \psi}{\partial r^2} - \frac{C^\psi}{C^r} r^2 \frac{\partial^3 \psi}{\partial r^3} + A_2 C^\psi C^r \left(C^H \right)^2 Mn H^2 r^2 \frac{\partial \psi}{\partial r} - A_3 \frac{C^\theta (C^H)^2 (C^r)^3}{C^x}$$
$$\beta H r^3 \theta \frac{\partial H}{\partial x} + R_1(a_1, a_2) = I_1(a_1, a_2) \left[A_1 \left\{ r^2 \frac{\partial^2 \psi}{\partial t \partial r} + r \frac{\partial \psi}{\partial r} \frac{\partial^2 \psi}{\partial x \partial r} + \frac{\partial \psi}{\partial x} \left(\frac{\partial \psi}{\partial r} - r \frac{\partial^2 \psi}{\partial r^2} \right) \right\} \right.$$
$$\left. - \frac{\partial \psi}{\partial r} + r \frac{\partial^2 \psi}{\partial r^2} - r^2 \frac{\partial^3 \psi}{\partial r^3} + A_2 Mn H^2 r^2 \frac{\partial \psi}{\partial r} - A_3 \beta H r^3 \theta \frac{\partial H}{\partial x} \right] \tag{28}$$

where

$$R_1(a_1,a_2) = A_1\left[\left\{2C^rK^rr+(K^r)^2\right\}\frac{C^\psi}{C^tC^r}\frac{\partial^2\psi}{\partial t\partial r} + \frac{(C^\psi)^2}{C^x(C^r)^2}K^r\frac{\partial\psi}{\partial r}\frac{\partial^2\psi}{\partial x\partial r} - \frac{(C^\psi)^2}{C^x(C^r)^2}K^r\frac{\partial\psi}{\partial x}\frac{\partial^2\psi}{\partial r^2}\right] + \frac{C^\psi}{(C^r)^2}$$

$$K^r\frac{\partial^2\psi}{\partial r^2} - \left\{2C^rK^rr+(K^r)^2\right\}\frac{C^\psi}{(C^r)^3}\frac{\partial^3\psi}{\partial r^3} + A_2Mn\left[\left\{2C^rK^rr+(K^r)^2\right\}\frac{C^\psi(C^H)^2}{C^r}H^2\frac{\partial\psi}{\partial r}+\right.$$

$$\left\{2C^HK^HH+\left(K^H\right)^2\right\}\left\{C^\psi C^r r^2\frac{\partial\psi}{\partial r}+\left\{2C^rK^rr+(K^r)^2\right\}\frac{C^\psi}{C^r}\frac{\partial\psi}{\partial r}\right\}\right] - \frac{(C^r)^3C^\theta C^H}{C^x}K^H A_3\beta r^3\theta\frac{\partial H}{\partial x} \quad (29)$$

$$-\frac{(C^r)^3(C^H)^2}{C^x}K^\theta A_3H\beta r^3\frac{\partial H}{\partial x} - \frac{(C^r)^3 C^H K^\theta}{C^x}K^H A_3\beta r^3\frac{\partial H}{\partial x} - \left[3(C^r r)^2K^r + 3C^r r(K^r)^2 + (K^r)^3\right]$$

$$\left[\frac{(C^H)^2 C^\theta}{C^x}A_3\beta H\theta\frac{\partial H}{\partial x} + \frac{C^\theta C^H}{C^x}K^H A_3\beta\theta\frac{\partial H}{\partial x} + \frac{(C^H)^2 K^\theta}{C^x}A_3\beta H\frac{\partial H}{\partial x} + \frac{C^H K^\theta}{C^x}K^H A_3\beta\frac{\partial H}{\partial x}\right].$$

From the form of Equation (28), it is obvious that (28) is invariantly transformed whenever

$$I_1(a_1,a_2) = \frac{C^\psi C^r}{C^t} = \frac{(C^\psi)^2}{C^x C^r} = \frac{C^\psi}{C^r} = C^\psi C^r\left(C^H\right)^2 = \frac{C^\theta(C^H)^2(C^r)^3}{C^x}, \quad (30)$$

and $R_1(a_1,a_2) \equiv 0$, which implies

$$K^r \equiv K^H \equiv K^\theta \equiv 0. \quad (31)$$

Similarly, Equation (22) is invariantly transformed under (25) and (26), by assuming that for some function $I_2(a_1,a_2)$, which may be constant the following holds:

$$A_4\Pr\left(\bar{r}\frac{\partial\bar{\theta}}{\partial\bar{t}} + \frac{\partial\bar{\psi}}{\partial\bar{r}}\frac{\partial\bar{\theta}}{\partial\bar{x}} - \frac{\partial\bar{\psi}}{\partial\bar{x}}\frac{\partial\bar{\theta}}{\partial\bar{r}}\right) + A_5\beta Ec\varepsilon\overline{H}\left(\frac{\partial\bar{\psi}}{\partial\bar{r}}\frac{\partial\overline{H}}{\partial\bar{x}} - \frac{\partial\bar{\psi}}{\partial\bar{x}}\frac{\partial\overline{H}}{\partial\bar{r}}\right)$$

$$-A_5\beta Ec\overline{H\theta}\left(\frac{\partial\bar{\psi}}{\partial\bar{r}}\frac{\partial\overline{H}}{\partial\bar{x}} - \frac{\partial\bar{\psi}}{\partial\bar{x}}\frac{\partial\overline{H}}{\partial\bar{r}}\right) - \left\{(1+NrA_5)\bar{r}\frac{\partial^2\bar{\theta}}{\partial\bar{r}^2} + \frac{\partial\bar{\theta}}{\partial\bar{r}}\right\}$$

$$= I_2(a_1,a_2)\left[\begin{array}{c} A_4\Pr\left(r\frac{\partial\theta}{\partial t} + \frac{\partial\psi}{\partial r}\frac{\partial\theta}{\partial x} - \frac{\partial\psi}{\partial x}\frac{\partial\theta}{\partial r}\right) + A_5\beta Ec\varepsilon H\left(\frac{\partial\psi}{\partial r}\frac{\partial H}{\partial x} - \frac{\partial\psi}{\partial x}\frac{\partial H}{\partial r}\right) \\ -A_5\beta EcH\theta\left(\frac{\partial\psi}{\partial r}\frac{\partial H}{\partial x} - \frac{\partial\psi}{\partial x}\frac{\partial H}{\partial r}\right) - \left\{(1+NrA_5)r\frac{\partial^2\theta}{\partial r^2} + \frac{\partial\theta}{\partial r}\right\} \end{array}\right] \quad (32)$$

Substitution of (24)–(26) into the left side of Equation (32) gives

$$A_4\Pr\left[\frac{C^r C^\theta}{C^t}r\frac{\partial\theta}{\partial t} + \frac{C^\psi C^\theta}{C^r C^x}\left(\frac{\partial\psi}{\partial r}\frac{\partial\theta}{\partial x} - \frac{\partial\psi}{\partial x}\frac{\partial\theta}{\partial r}\right)\right] + \frac{C^\psi(C^H)^2}{C^r C^x}A_5\beta Ec\varepsilon H\left(\frac{\partial\psi}{\partial r}\frac{\partial H}{\partial x} - \frac{\partial\psi}{\partial x}\frac{\partial H}{\partial r}\right)$$

$$-\frac{C^\psi C^\theta(C^H)^2}{C^r C^x}A_5\beta EcH\theta\left(\frac{\partial\psi}{\partial r}\frac{\partial H}{\partial x} - \frac{\partial\psi}{\partial x}\frac{\partial H}{\partial r}\right) - \frac{C^\theta}{C^r}\left\{(1+NrA_5)r\frac{\partial^2\theta}{\partial r^2} + \frac{\partial\theta}{\partial r}\right\} + R_2(a_1,a_2)$$

$$= I_2(a_1,a_2)\left[\begin{array}{c} A_4\Pr\left(r\frac{\partial\theta}{\partial t} + \frac{\partial\psi}{\partial r}\frac{\partial\theta}{\partial x} - \frac{\partial\psi}{\partial x}\frac{\partial\theta}{\partial r}\right) + A_5\beta Ec\varepsilon H\left(\frac{\partial\psi}{\partial r}\frac{\partial H}{\partial x} - \frac{\partial\psi}{\partial x}\frac{\partial H}{\partial r}\right) \\ -A_5\beta EcH\theta\left(\frac{\partial\psi}{\partial r}\frac{\partial H}{\partial x} - \frac{\partial\psi}{\partial x}\frac{\partial H}{\partial r}\right) - \left\{(1+NrA_5)r\frac{\partial^2\theta}{\partial r^2} + \frac{\partial\theta}{\partial r}\right\} \end{array}\right], \quad (33)$$

where

$$R_2(a_1,a_2) = A_4\Pr\frac{C^\theta K^r}{C^t}r\frac{\partial\theta}{\partial t} + \frac{C^\psi C^H K^H}{C^r C^x}A_5\beta Ec\varepsilon\left(\frac{\partial\psi}{\partial r}\frac{\partial H}{\partial x} - \frac{\partial\psi}{\partial x}\frac{\partial H}{\partial r}\right)$$

$$-A_5\beta Ec\left[\frac{C^\psi K^\theta(C^H)^2}{C^r C^x}H + \frac{C^\psi C^\theta C^H K^\theta}{C^x C^r}\theta + \frac{C^\psi C^H K^H K^\theta}{C^x C^r}\right] \quad (34)$$

$$\left(\frac{\partial\psi}{\partial r}\frac{\partial H}{\partial x} - \frac{\partial\psi}{\partial x}\frac{\partial H}{\partial r}\right) - \frac{C^\theta}{(C^r)^2}K^r(1+NrA_5)\frac{\partial^2\theta}{\partial r^2}.$$

From (33), it is obvious that it is invariantly transformed whenever

$$I_2(a_1, a_2) = \frac{C^\theta C^r}{C^t} = \frac{C^\theta C^\psi}{C^x C^r} = \frac{C^\theta}{C^r} = \frac{C^\psi (C^H)^2}{C^x C^r} = \frac{C^\theta C^\psi (C^H)^2}{C^x C^r}, \tag{35}$$

and $R_2(a_1, a_2) \equiv 0$, which implies

$$K^r \equiv K^H \equiv K^\theta \equiv 0. \tag{36}$$

Finally, the boundary conditions (23) must also be invariant under the same transformations, which yields

$$C^r = 1 \text{ and } C^\theta = 1. \tag{37}$$

Combining Equations (30) and (35) and taking into account (31), (36), and (37), it was found that:

$$C^t = 1 \text{ and } C^x = C^H = C^\psi = 1. \tag{38}$$

Hence, the two-parameter group G, which invariantly transforms Equations (21) and (22), and the boundary condition (23) takes the form

$$G : \begin{cases} \overline{S} : \begin{cases} \overline{x} = x + K^x(a_1, a_2) \\ \overline{r} = r \\ \overline{t} = t + K^t(a_1, a_2) \end{cases} \\ \overline{\psi} = \psi + K^\psi(a_1, a_2) \\ \overline{\theta} = \theta \\ \overline{H} = H \end{cases} \tag{39}$$

3.3. The Complete Set of Absolute Invariants

The basic tool of this technique is the application of a general theorem from group theory, so that the problem under consideration is described by ODEs (similarity representation) in an independent variable (similarity variable). Herein, the complete sets of absolute invariants include two types of absolute invariants, namely (i) the absolute invariants of independent variables (x, r, t), which are $\eta = \eta(x, r, t)$, and (ii) the absolute invariants of dependent variables (ψ, θ, H). This general theorem for the case of a two-parameter group (e.g., [54,55]), states that a function $\eta = \eta(x, r, t)$ is an absolute invariant of a two-parameter group of the form

$$\overline{S} : \begin{array}{l} [\overline{x} = C^x(a_1, a_2) \, x + K^x(a_1, a_2), \\ \overline{r} = C^r(a_1, a_2) \, r + K^r(a_1, a_2), \\ \overline{t} = C^t(a_1, a_2) \, t + K^t(a_1, a_2)]. \end{array} \tag{40}$$

If and only if η satisfies the first order linear PDEs:

$$\begin{array}{l} (\alpha_1 x + \alpha_2) \frac{\partial \eta}{\partial x} + (\alpha_3 r + \alpha_4) \frac{\partial \eta}{\partial r} + (\alpha_5 t + \alpha_6) \frac{\partial \eta}{\partial t} = 0, \\ (\delta_1 x + \delta_2) \frac{\partial \eta}{\partial x} + (\delta_3 r + \delta_4) \frac{\partial \eta}{\partial r} + (\delta_5 t + \delta_6) \frac{\partial \eta}{\partial t} = 0, \end{array} \tag{41}$$

where

$$\alpha_1 = \frac{\partial C^x}{\partial a_1}(a_1^0, a_2^0), \alpha_2 = \frac{\partial K^x}{\partial a_1}(a_1^0, a_2^0), \alpha_3 = \frac{\partial C^r}{\partial a_1}(a_1^0, a_2^0), \alpha_4 = \frac{\partial K^r}{\partial a_1}(a_1^0, a_2^0),$$

$$\alpha_5 = \frac{\partial C^t}{\partial a_1}(a_1^0, a_2^0), \alpha_6 = \frac{\partial K^t}{\partial a_1}(a_1^0, a_2^0), \delta_1 = \frac{\partial C^x}{\partial a_2}(a_1^0, a_2^0), \delta_2 = \frac{\partial K^x}{\partial a_2}(a_1^0, a_2^0),$$

$$\delta_3 = \frac{\partial C^r}{\partial a_2}(a_1^0, a_2^0), \delta_4 = \frac{\partial K^r}{\partial a_2}(a_1^0, a_2^0), \delta_5 = \frac{\partial C^t}{\partial a_2}(a_1^0, a_2^0), \delta_6 = \frac{\partial K^t}{\partial a_2}(a_1^0, a_2^0).$$

and (a_1^0, a_2^0) denote the values of a_1 and a_2, which yield the identity: $\overline{x} = x, \overline{r} = r, \overline{t} = t$ according to [55]. By definition, there is one functionally independent solution to (41). Additionally, if η, is a non-constant solution to (41) for a group S, then every other solution to (41), for S, is given in the form $J(\eta)$ where J is a differentiable function. From (41) and the definitions of the constants α_i, δ_i, it can be seen that distinctions between group S are reflected by the $\alpha's$ and $\delta's$. This means that, in general, any particular group S owns a characteristic set of $\alpha's$ and $\delta's$ and, consequently, a characteristic absolute invariant η is yielded by (41).

Since $K^r \equiv 0$, it is $\alpha_4 = \delta_4 = 0$ and Equation (41) becomes:

$$\begin{aligned}(\alpha_1 x + \alpha_2)\frac{\partial \eta}{\partial x} + \alpha_3 r \frac{\partial \eta}{\partial r} + (\alpha_5 t + \alpha_6)\frac{\partial \eta}{\partial t} = 0, \\ (\delta_1 x + \delta_2)\frac{\partial \eta}{\partial x} + \delta_3 r \frac{\partial \eta}{\partial r} + (\delta_5 t + \delta_6)\frac{\partial \eta}{\partial t} = 0.\end{aligned} \quad (42)$$

4. Derivation of Distinct Complete Sets

In this section, the distinct complete sets of invariants will be derived.

Invariants for the independent variables

As already mentioned in the previous section, system (42) has one functionally independent solution, which means that the rank of the coefficient matrix for $\left\{\frac{\partial \eta}{\partial x}, \frac{\partial \eta}{\partial r}, \frac{\partial \eta}{\partial t}\right\}$ must be two. This is true whenever at least one of the following conditions is satisfied:

$$\lambda_{31} x + \lambda_{32} \neq 0 \text{ or } \lambda_{35} t + \lambda_{36} \neq 0 \text{ or } \lambda_{15} xt + \lambda_{16} x + \lambda_{25} t + \lambda_{26} \neq 0, \quad (43)$$

where

$$\lambda_{ij} = \alpha_i \delta_j - \alpha_j \delta_i, \qquad i,j = 1, 2, 3, 4, 5, 6$$

and it should be mentioned that from the definitions of $\alpha's, \delta's$ and $\lambda's$, as well as from the transformations (39), it can be found that:

$$\lambda_{31} = \lambda_{35} = \lambda_{15} = 0. \quad (44)$$

For convenience, (42) can be rewritten in terms of (43) in the form:

$$\begin{aligned}(\lambda_{31} x + \lambda_{32})\frac{\partial \eta}{\partial x} + (\lambda_{35} t + \lambda_{36})\frac{\partial \eta}{\partial t} = 0, \\ (\lambda_{31} x + \lambda_{32}) r \frac{\partial \eta}{\partial r} - (\lambda_{15} xt + \lambda_{16} x + \lambda_{25} t + \lambda_{26})\frac{\partial \eta}{\partial t} = 0.\end{aligned} \quad (45)$$

According to conditions (43), three main cases arise which will be studied in the following:

4.1. First Case: None of the Coefficients in (45) Vanish Identically

Assume that

$$\lambda_{31} x + \lambda_{32} \neq 0 \text{ and } \lambda_{35} t + \lambda_{36} \neq 0 \text{ and } \lambda_{15} xt + \lambda_{16} x + \lambda_{25} t + \lambda_{26} \neq 0,$$

or taking into consideration (44) that

$$\lambda_{32} \neq 0 \text{ and } \lambda_{36} \neq 0 \text{ and } \lambda_{16} x + \lambda_{25} t + \lambda_{26} \neq 0. \quad (46)$$

In this case, (45) becomes

$$\begin{aligned}\lambda_{32}\frac{\partial \eta}{\partial x} + \lambda_{36}\frac{\partial \eta}{\partial t} = 0 \\ \lambda_{32} r \frac{\partial \eta}{\partial r} - (\lambda_{16} x + \lambda_{25} t + \lambda_{26})\frac{\partial \eta}{\partial t} = 0.\end{aligned} \quad (47)$$

According to a standard technique for linear PDEs, the first equation of (47) has the general solution

$$\eta = f(r, \xi(x, t)), \quad (48)$$

where f is an arbitrary function and ξ is a function such that

$$\xi(x, t) = \lambda_{36} x - \lambda_{32} t = c, \quad (49)$$

where c constant. Substitution of (48) to the second equation of (47) gives

$$r\frac{\partial \eta}{\partial r} - \frac{\lambda_{16}x + \lambda_{25}t + \lambda_{26}}{\lambda_{32}}\frac{\partial \zeta}{\partial t}\frac{\partial f}{\partial \zeta} = 0. \tag{50}$$

Since ζ is independent of r, the coefficient of $\frac{\partial f}{\partial \zeta}$ in (50) must also be independent of r, i.e.,

$$\frac{\lambda_{16}x + \lambda_{25}t + \lambda_{26}}{\lambda_{32}}\frac{\partial \zeta}{\partial t} = g(\zeta),$$

which, after taking (49) into consideration, becomes

$$g(\zeta) = -(\lambda_{16}x + \lambda_{25}t + \lambda_{26}) \tag{51}$$

However, since g is a function of only ζ, it is

$$\left.\frac{\partial g}{\partial x}\right|_\zeta = \left.\frac{\partial g}{\partial x}\right|_t + \left.\frac{\partial g}{\partial t}\right|_x \left.\frac{\partial t}{\partial x}\right|_\zeta \equiv 0,$$

which, after using (49) and (51), gives

$$-\lambda_{16} = -\lambda_{16} - \lambda_{25}\frac{\lambda_{36}}{\lambda_{36}} = 0 \Rightarrow \begin{cases} \lambda_{16} = 0 \\ \lambda_{16} + \lambda_{25}\frac{\lambda_{36}}{\lambda_{36}} = 0 \end{cases} \Rightarrow \begin{cases} \lambda_{16} = 0 \\ \lambda_{25} = 0 \end{cases},$$

after taking (46) into consideration. However, due to the definitions of α's, δ's and λ's, as well as from the transformations (39), it is $\alpha_1 = \alpha_3$ and $\delta_1 = \delta_3$. Thus,

$$\lambda_{16} = 0 \Rightarrow \alpha_1\delta_6 - \alpha_6\delta_1 = 0 \Rightarrow \alpha_3\delta_6 - \alpha_6\delta_3 = 0 \Rightarrow \lambda_{36} = 0,$$

which contradicts the second assumption of (46). Consequently, this first case is not acceptable.

4.2. Second Case: Two of the Coefficients in (45) Vanish Identically

Sub-case 2-I: Assume that

$$\lambda_{31}x + \lambda_{32} \equiv 0,\ \lambda_{35}t + \lambda_{36} \equiv 0 \text{ and } \lambda_{15}xt + \lambda_{16}x + \lambda_{25}t + \lambda_{26} \neq 0.$$

In this case, (45) reduces to the following one equation

$$(\lambda_{15}xt + \lambda_{16}x + \lambda_{25}t + \lambda_{26})\frac{\partial \eta}{\partial t} = 0,$$

since the first equation of (45) is identically satisfied, from which it is deduced that

$$\frac{\partial \eta}{\partial t} = 0. \tag{52}$$

By substituting (52) into (42) and after some manipulations, the following equations are obtained:

$$\left.\begin{array}{l}(\lambda_{16}x + \lambda_{26})\frac{\partial \eta}{\partial x} + \lambda_{36}r\frac{\partial \eta}{\partial r} = 0 \\ (\lambda_{15}xt + \lambda_{25}t)\frac{\partial \eta}{\partial x} + \lambda_{35}rt\frac{\partial \eta}{\partial r} = 0\end{array}\right\},$$

which in turn yields the equation

$$(\lambda_{15}xt + \lambda_{16}x + \lambda_{25}t + \lambda_{26})\frac{\partial \eta}{\partial x} + (\lambda_{35}t + \lambda_{36})r\frac{\partial \eta}{\partial r} = 0 \Rightarrow \tag{53}$$

$$\Rightarrow \frac{\partial \eta}{\partial x} = 0. \tag{54}$$

From (52) and (53), it is obvious that η is an arbitrary function of r alone, which for reasons of simplicity can be assumed to have the form

$$\eta = r \tag{55}$$

Sub-case 2-II: Assume that

$$\lambda_{31}x + \lambda_{32} \neq 0, \lambda_{35}t + \lambda_{36} \equiv 0 \text{ and } \lambda_{15}xt + \lambda_{16}x + \lambda_{25}t + \lambda_{26} \equiv 0.$$

In this case, (45) becomes

$$\left.\begin{array}{l}(\lambda_{31}x + \lambda_{32})\frac{\partial \eta}{\partial x} = 0 \\ (\lambda_{31}x + \lambda_{32}) r\frac{\partial \eta}{\partial r} = 0\end{array}\right\} \Rightarrow \left.\begin{array}{l}\frac{\partial \eta}{\partial x} = 0 \\ \frac{\partial \eta}{\partial r} = 0\end{array}\right\},$$

from which it is deduced that η is not a function of r, which is unacceptable from the point of view of the boundary conditions.

Sub-case 2-III: Assume that

$$\lambda_{31}x + \lambda_{32} \equiv 0, \lambda_{35}t + \lambda_{36} \neq 0 \text{ and } \lambda_{15}xt + \lambda_{16}x + \lambda_{25}t + \lambda_{26} \equiv 0 \tag{56}$$

In this case, (45) reduces to the following one equation

$$(\lambda_{35}t + \lambda_{36})\frac{\partial \eta}{\partial t} = 0,$$

since the first equation of (45) is identically satisfied, from which it is deduced that

$$\frac{\partial \eta}{\partial t} = 0.$$

Following the same procedure as in sub-case 2-I, Equation (53) appears, which due to (56) now gives

$$\frac{\partial \eta}{\partial r} = 0$$

Thus, η is not a function of r, which is unacceptable from the point of view of the boundary conditions.

4.3. Third Case: Only One of the Coefficients in (45) Vanishes Identically

Sub-case 3-I: Assume that

$$\lambda_{31}x + \lambda_{32} = 0, \lambda_{35}t + \lambda_{36} \neq 0, \lambda_{15}xt + \lambda_{16}x + \lambda_{25}t + \lambda_{26} \neq 0.$$

In this case, (45) reduces to the following one equation

$$\frac{\partial \eta}{\partial t} = 0,$$

which means that $\eta = \eta(x, r)$ and (42) is simplified to

$$\left.\begin{array}{l}(\alpha_1 x + \alpha_2)\frac{\partial \eta}{\partial x} + \alpha_3 r\frac{\partial \eta}{\partial r} = 0 \\ (\delta_1 x + \delta_2)\frac{\partial \eta}{\partial x} + \delta_3 r\frac{\partial \eta}{\partial r} = 0\end{array}\right\},$$

a solution of which is found to be

$$\eta = r \left(Ax + B\right)^n, \tag{57}$$

where $n = -\frac{\alpha_3}{\alpha_1} = -\frac{\delta_3}{\delta_1}$, $A = \alpha_1 = \delta_1$, $B = \alpha_2 = \delta_2$.

Sub-case 3-II: Assume that

$$\lambda_{31}x + \lambda_{32} \neq 0, \ \lambda_{35}t + \lambda_{36} = 0, \ \lambda_{15}xt + \lambda_{16}x + \lambda_{25}t + \lambda_{26} \neq 0.$$

In this case, the first equation of (45) reduces to the following equation

$$(\lambda_{31}x + \lambda_{32})\frac{\partial \eta}{\partial x} = 0 \Rightarrow \frac{\partial \eta}{\partial x} = 0,$$

which means that $\eta = \eta(r, t)$ and (42) is simplified to

$$\alpha_3 r \frac{\partial \eta}{\partial r} + (\alpha_5 t + \alpha_6)\frac{\partial \eta}{\partial t} = 0,$$
$$\delta_3 r \frac{\partial \eta}{\partial r} + (\delta_5 t + \delta_6)\frac{\partial \eta}{\partial t} = 0,$$

a solution of which is found to be

$$\eta = r(Bt + A)^n, \tag{58}$$

where $n = \frac{\alpha_3}{\alpha_5} = \frac{\delta_3}{\delta_5}$, $A = \delta_6 = \alpha_6$, $B = \delta_5 = \alpha_5$.

Sub-case 3-III: Assume that

$$\lambda_{31}x + \lambda_{32} \neq 0, \ \lambda_{35}t + \lambda_{36} \neq 0, \ \lambda_{15}xt + \lambda_{16}x + \lambda_{25}t + \lambda_{26} = 0.$$

In this case, the second equation of (45) reduces to the following equation

$$(\lambda_{31}x + \lambda_{32})r\frac{\partial \eta}{\partial r} = 0 \Rightarrow \frac{\partial \eta}{\partial r} = 0,$$

from which it is deduced that η is not a function of r, which is unacceptable from the point of view of the boundary conditions.

Invariants for the dependent variables

The next step is to obtain the absolute invariants of the dependent variables ψ, H and θ. From (37), it is derived that θ is itself an absolute invariant. Thus,

$$X_1(x, r, t; \theta) = \theta(\eta).$$

A function $X_2(x, t; \psi)$ is said to be an absolute invariant of a two-parameter group only when it satisfies the following first order PDEs:

$$(\alpha_1 x + \alpha_2)\frac{\partial X_2}{\partial x} + (\alpha_3 t + \alpha_4)\frac{\partial X_2}{\partial t} + (\alpha_5 \psi + \alpha_6)\frac{\partial X_2}{\partial \psi} = 0$$
$$(\delta_1 x + \delta_2)\frac{\partial X_2}{\partial x} + (\delta_3 t + \delta_4)\frac{\partial X_2}{\partial t} + (\delta_5 \psi + \delta_6)\frac{\partial X_2}{\partial \psi} = 0,$$

a solution of which is

$$X_2(x, t; \psi) = \varphi_1\left(\frac{\psi}{\Gamma_1(x, t)}\right) = F(\eta). \tag{59}$$

In a similar way, the following is found

$$X_3(x, t; H) = \varphi_2\left(\frac{H}{\Gamma_2(x, t)}\right) = E(\eta). \tag{60}$$

In (59)–(60), the functions $\Gamma_1(x, t)$ and $\Gamma_2(x, t)$ are to be determined so that eventually the PDEs (21)–(22) are reduced to ODEs. Without loss of generality, the functions ϕ_1 and ϕ_2 in (59)–(60), can be selected as the identity functions. Therefore, the functions $\psi(x, r, t)$ and $H(x, t)$ can be rewritten in terms of $F(\eta)$ and $E(\eta)$ in the following way:

$$\psi(x, r, t) = \Gamma_1(x, t)F(\eta), \ H(x, t) = \Gamma_2(x, t)E(\eta). \tag{61}$$

Since $\Gamma_2(x,t)$ and $H(x,t)$ are independent of r and η depends on r, E must be a constant, say E_0. Thus

$$\psi(x,r,t) = \Gamma_1(x,t)F(\eta), \quad H(x,t) = E_0\Gamma_2(x,t). \tag{62}$$

5. The Reduction to Ordinary Differential Equations

Assume that $\eta = r\pi(x,t)$. Using (62), the PDEs (21)–(22) and the boundary conditions (23) are reduced to the following system of ODEs:

$$r^2 F''' - C_1 r F'' + C_2 F' - C_3 A_2 r^2 MnF' + C_4 A_3 \beta\, r^3 \theta \\ - A_1\left[C_5 r^2 F' + C_6 r^3 F'' + C_7 r^2 F' + 2C_8 r F'^2 - (rFF'' - rF'^2)C_9 + C_{10} FF'\right] = 0 \tag{63}$$

$$(1 + NrA_5)\, r\theta'' + C_1\theta' - A_4 \Pr\left[C_6 r^2\theta' - C_9 F\theta'\right] - C_{11} A_5 \beta\, Ec\, (\varepsilon - \theta)\, F' = 0, \tag{64}$$

with corresponding boundary conditions

$$\begin{aligned} r = 1: F = 0, F' = 0, \theta = 1, \\ r \to \infty: F' = 0, \theta = 0. \end{aligned} \tag{65}$$

where

$$C_1 = \tfrac{1}{\pi}, C_2 = \tfrac{1}{\pi^2}, C_3 = \tfrac{\Gamma_2^2 E_0^2}{\pi^2}, C_4 = \tfrac{\Gamma_2 E_0^2}{\Gamma_1 \pi^3}\tfrac{\partial \Gamma_2}{\partial x}, C_5 = \tfrac{1}{\pi^3}\tfrac{\partial \pi}{\partial t}, C_6 = \tfrac{1}{\pi^2}\tfrac{\partial \pi}{\partial t}, \\ C_7 = \tfrac{1}{\Gamma_1 \pi^2}\tfrac{\partial \Gamma_1}{\partial t}, C_8 = \tfrac{\Gamma_1}{\pi^2}\tfrac{\partial \pi}{\partial x}, C_9 = \tfrac{1}{\pi}\tfrac{\partial \Gamma_1}{\partial x}, C_{10} = \tfrac{1}{\pi^2}\tfrac{\partial \Gamma_1}{\partial x}, C_{11} = \tfrac{\Gamma_1 \Gamma_2 E_0^2}{\pi}\tfrac{\partial \Gamma_2}{\partial x}. \tag{66}$$

The $C's$ defined in (66) are constants to be determined for every individual case corresponding to every set of absolute invariants. For this, the following three cases are considered:

Case (a)

Consider $\eta = r\pi(x,t)$ as in (55), i.e., $\pi(x,t) = 1$ and $\Gamma_1 = \Gamma_1(x), \Gamma_2 = \Gamma_2(x)$. In this case and by further assuming C_3 to be unity, (66) gives

$$C_1 = C_2 = C_3 = 1, C_9 = C_{10}, C_5 = C_6 = C_7 = C_8 = 0, C_4 = \tfrac{C_{11}}{\Gamma_1^2}, \\ \Gamma_1 = C_9 x + K_1 = C_{10} x + K_2, \Gamma_2 = K_3(C_9 x + K_1)^{C_{11}/C_9} = K_3(C_{10} x + K_2)^{C_{11}/C_{10}},$$

where K_1, K_2, K_3 are constants of integration. Substitution of the aforementioned values into (63)–(64), gives:

$$r^2 F''' - rF'' + F' - A_2 r^2 MnF' - A_1\left((rF'^2 - rFF'')C_9 + C_9 FF'\right) + C_4 A_3 \beta\, r^3 \theta = 0, \tag{67}$$

$$(1 + NrA_5)\, r\theta'' + \theta' + A_4 C_9 \Pr F\theta' - C_{11} A_5 \beta\, Ec\, (\varepsilon - \theta)\, F' = 0. \tag{68}$$

Equations (67)–(68) are accompanied of course by the boundary conditions (65), i.e.,:

$$\begin{aligned} r = 1: F = 0, F' = 0, \theta = 1, \\ r \to \infty: F' = 0, \theta = 0. \end{aligned} \tag{69}$$

In this case, the functions ψ and H given by (62) take the form

$$\psi = (C_9 x + K_1)F(\eta) = (C_{10} x + K_2)F(\eta), \\ H = K_3(C_9 x + K_1)^{C_{11}/C_9} E_0 = K_3(C_{10} x + K_2)^{C_{11}/C_{10}} E_0, \tag{70}$$

and the corresponding velocity components are:

$$u = \tfrac{1}{r}\tfrac{\partial \psi}{\partial r} = (C_9 x + K_1)\tfrac{\pi}{r} F' = (C_{10} x + K_2)\tfrac{\pi}{r} F', \\ v = -\tfrac{1}{r}\tfrac{\partial \psi}{\partial x} = -\tfrac{C_9}{r} F = -\tfrac{C_{10}}{r} F. \tag{71}$$

Case (b)

Consider $\eta = r\pi(x,t)$ as in (57), i.e., $\pi(x,t) = (Ax+B)^n$ and $\Gamma_1 = \Gamma_1(x), \Gamma_2 = \Gamma_2(x)$. In this case and by further assuming C_3 to be unity, (66) gives

$C_1 = \frac{1}{(Ax+B)^n}, C_2 = C_1^2, C_3 = 1, C_4 = \frac{An}{K}(Ax+B)^{-2n-2}, C_5 = C_6 = C_7 = 0, C_8 = AKn,$
$C_9 = AK(n+1), C_{10} = \frac{AK(n+1)}{(Ax+B)^n}, C_{11} = AKn(Ax+B)^{2n},$

where K is a constant of integration. Substitution of the aforementioned values into (63)–(64), gives:

$$r^2 F''' - C_1 r F'' + C_1^2 F' - A_2 r^2 MnF' + C_4 A_3 \beta \, r^3 \theta \\ - A_1 \left[2C_8 r F'^2 - (rFF'' - rF'^2) C_9 + C_{10} FF' \right] = 0 \tag{72}$$

$$(1 + NrA_5) \, r\theta'' + C_1 \theta' + A_4 C_9 \Pr F\theta' - C_{11} A_5 \beta \, Ec \, (\varepsilon - \theta) \, F' = 0. \tag{73}$$

Equations (72)–(73) are accompanied of course by the boundary conditions (65), i.e.,:

$$r = 1: F = 0, F' = 0, \theta = 1, \\ r \to \infty : F' = 0, \theta = 0. \tag{74}$$

In this case, the functions ψ and H given by (62) take the form

$$\psi = K(Ax+B)^{n+1} F, \\ H = (Ax+B)^n, \tag{75}$$

and the corresponding velocity components are:

$$u = \frac{1}{r} \frac{\partial \psi}{\partial r} = \frac{K}{r}(Ax+B)^{2n+1} F', \\ v = -\frac{1}{r} \frac{\partial \psi}{\partial x} = -\Gamma_1 An(Ax+B)^{n-1} F - \frac{K}{r} A(n+1)(Ax+B)^n F. \tag{76}$$

Case (c)

Consider $\eta = r\pi(x,t)$ as in (58), i.e., where $\pi(x,t) = (Bt+A)^n$ for $n = -\frac{1}{2}$ and $\Gamma_1 = \Gamma_1(x,t), \Gamma_2 = \Gamma_2(x,t)$. In this case and by further assuming C_3 to be unity, (66) gives

$C_1 = \sqrt{Bt+A}, C_2 = Bt+A, C_3 = 1, C_4 = C_8 = C_{11} = 0, C_5 = -\frac{B}{2}, C_6 = -\frac{B}{2C_1},$
$C_7 = -\frac{B}{2}, C_{10} = C_1 C_9.$

Substitution of the aforementioned values into (63)–(64), gives:

$$r^2 F''' - C_1 r F'' + C_2 F' - A_2 r^2 MnF' - A_1 \left[-\frac{B}{2} r^2 F' - \frac{B}{2} \eta \, r^2 F'' - C_7 r^2 F' \right. \\ \left. + C_9 C_1 FF' - C_9 (rFF'' - rF'^2) \right] = 0, \tag{77}$$

$$(1 + NrA_5) \, r\theta'' + C_1 \theta' + A_4 \Pr \left[\frac{B}{2} \eta \, r\theta' - C_9 F\theta' \right] = 0. \tag{78}$$

Equations (77)–(78) are accompanied of course by the boundary conditions (65), i.e.,:

$$r = 1: F = 0, F' = 0, \theta = 1, \\ r \to \infty : F' = 0, \theta = 0. \tag{79}$$

In this case, the functions ψ and H given by (62) take the form

$$\psi = \frac{(x+K_1)}{\sqrt{Bt+A}} C_9 F, \\ H = \frac{1}{\sqrt{Bt+A}}, \tag{80}$$

where K_1 is a constant of integration, and the corresponding velocity components are:

$$u = \frac{1}{r}\frac{\partial \psi}{\partial r} = \frac{(x+K_1)}{(Bt+A)}C_9F',$$
$$v = -\frac{1}{r}\frac{\partial \psi}{\partial x} = -\frac{C_9}{r\sqrt{(Bt+A)}}.$$
(81)

It can be observed, that cases (a) and (b) the impacts of the ferromagnetic number and the magnetic field parameter in velocity and temperature profiles are significant compared to case (c), since, in case (c), the FHD parameter is absent. For these reasons, only cases (a) and (b) are numerically solved.

6. The Numerical Procedure

To numerically solve the fluid mechanics problem described by equations such as (63)–(65), several computational techniques have been proposed by many researchers. In this paper, an efficient numerical technique is employed based on the common finite differences method with central differencing, a tridiagonal matrix manipulation and an iterative procedure introduced in [56]. In this section, this technique will be described for case (b). First of all, the arbitrary coefficient constants in (72)–(73) are for reasons of simplicity, all assumed to be equal to one. Therefore, (72)–(73) are rewritten as:

$$r^2 F''' - rF'' + F' - A_2 r^2 MnF' + A_3 \beta\, r^3 \theta - A_1 \left[2rF'^2 - \left(rFF'' - rF'^2\right) + FF'\right] = 0, \quad (82)$$

$$(1 + NrA_5)\, r\theta'' + \theta' + A_4 \Pr F\theta' - A_5\beta\, Ec\,(\varepsilon - \theta)\, F' = 0. \quad (83)$$

Following [49], Equation (82) is written in the form

$$r^2 F''' + (A_1 rF - r)F'' + \left(1 - A_2 r^2 M - 2A_1 rF' - A_1 rF' - A_1 F\right)F' = -A_3\beta\, r^3\theta, \quad (84)$$

or

$$r^2 (F')'' + (A_1 rF - r)(F')' + \left(1 - A_2 r^2 Mn - 2A_1 rF' - A_1 rF' - A_1 F\right)F' = -A_3\beta\, r^3\theta, \quad (85)$$

and (83) in the form

$$(1 + NrA_5)\, r\theta'' + (1 + A_4 \Pr F)\theta' + A_5\beta\, EcF'\theta = A_5\beta\, Ec\, \varepsilon\, F'. \quad (86)$$

Both (85) and (86) are of the general form

$$Pg''(\eta) + Qg'(\eta) + Rg(\eta) = S \quad (87)$$

with

$$g = F'(\eta),\ P = r^2,\ Q = A_1 rF - r,\ R = 1 - A_2 r^2 Mn - 2A_1 rF' - A_1 rF' - A_1 F,\ S = -A_3\beta\, r^3\theta,$$

or Equation (85) and

$$g = \theta(\eta),\ P = (1 + NrA_5)\, r,\ Q = 1 + A_4 \Pr F,\ R = A_5\beta\, EcF',\ S = A_5\beta\, Ec\, \varepsilon\, F'$$

for Equation (86).

Equations (85)–(86) are solved by a common finite differences method based on central differencing and tridiagonal matrix manipulation. Before starting the solution procedure, it is necessary to assume an initial guess for $F'(\eta)$ and $\theta(\eta)$ between $\eta = 0$ and $\eta = \eta_\infty$ ($\eta \to \infty$) which satisfies the boundary conditions (74). Thus, it is assumed that

$$F(\eta) = \frac{\eta}{\eta_\infty},\quad F'(\eta) = \frac{\eta}{\eta_\infty},\quad \theta(\eta) = 1 - \frac{\eta}{\eta_\infty},$$

Therefore, the $F(\eta)$ distribution is obtained by integrating $F'(\eta)$. The function $\theta(\eta)$ is retained while a new estimation for $F'(\eta)$, say (F'_{new}), is determined by solving

(85) using the same technique. Thus, the $F(\eta)$ profile is updated by integrating the new $F'(\eta)$. These new distributions $F(\eta)$ and $F'(\eta)$ are then used for new inputs, etc. In this way, Equation (85) and, consequently, (72) is iteratively solved until the required convergence up to a small quantity ε_1 is attained. The converged profile of $F(\eta)$ is used to solve (86), using the same finite differences method, but without iteration, producing a new approximation for $\theta(\eta)$. In this way, the temperature profile $\theta(\eta)$ is obtained until the convergence ε_1 is attained.

This numerical scheme is continued until the trial convergence of the solution is performed. The applied step size used in this paper for case (b) is $h = \Delta \eta = 0.01$ for $\eta_{min} = 0$ and $\eta_{max} = 7$. The solution is convergent with an approximation to $\varepsilon_1 = 10^{-3}$. For case (a), the same step size is considered, i.e., $h = \Delta \eta = 0.01$, but for $\eta_{min} = 0$, $\eta_{max} = 12$ and $\varepsilon_1 = 10^{-3}$. The arbitrary constants C_4, C_9, C_{10} appearing in case (a) are also considered equal to one.

7. Results and Discussion

Before proceeding to the application of the above-mentioned method for the derivation of the numerical results, it is essential to check the accuracy of the applied numerical algorithm. For that, calculations were performed for partial cases of the present problem in order to perform comparisons with previously published results. For demonstration purposes, a graphical comparison is given in Figures 2 and 3 concerning results comparison obtained for the present case (b) with that obtained in [37] for the velocity and temperature distributions, respectively. From the relative figures as well as from all other comparisons performed, we found that the results are accurate and ensure the acceptability of the proposed numerical algorithm.

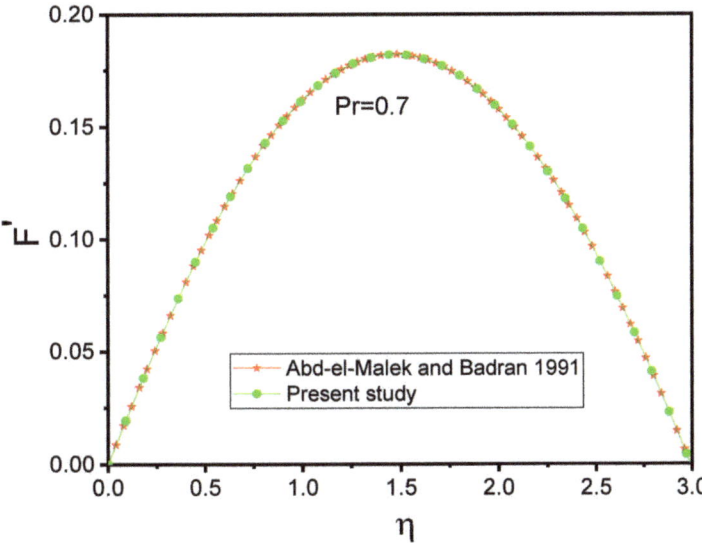

Figure 2. Comparison with [37] of F' for $Pr = 0.7$ with $\beta = Mn = Ec = Nr = \phi = 0$.

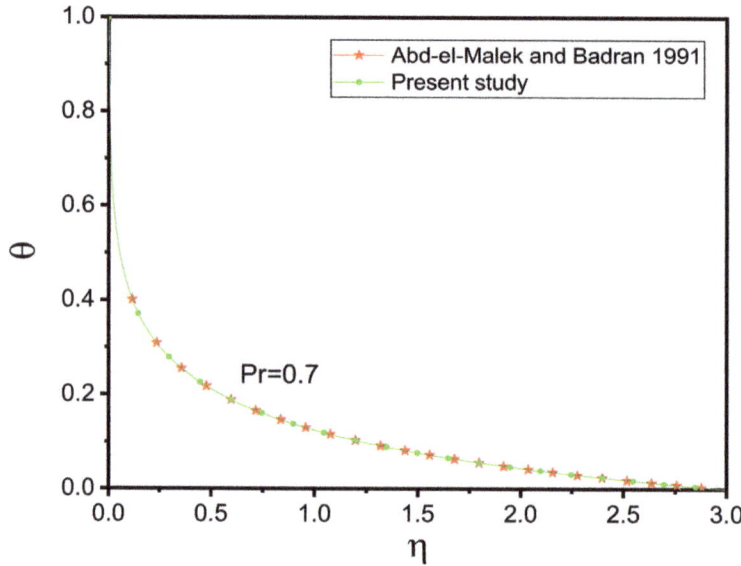

Figure 3. Comparison with [37] of θ for $Pr = 0.7$ with $\beta = Mn = Ec = Nr = \phi = 0$.

In the following, the numerical results in conjunction with the appearing parameters are discussed with their respective outcomes for the velocity, temperature profiles as well as the skin friction coefficient and the rate of heat transfer for both cases (a) and (b). Before moving on to the numerical procedure, we need to ensure the allocation of some realistic values of the respective parameter to ensure that the obtained results of the proposed model will be as realistic as possible. The consideration of realistic case scenarios has been made for similar physical BFD problems and thus the following values of the parameters are utilized for case (a) and case (b) as follows:

(i) The ferromagnetic interaction parameter $\beta = 0 - 10$ as in [12,13,39,40,49];
(ii) The magnetic field parameter $Mn = 1, 3, 5$ as in [13,40,49,57];
(iii) The Prandtl number $Pr = 21, 23, 25$ as in [13,40,49];
(iv) The radiation parameter $Nr = 0.1, 0.2, 0.5, 1, 1.5, 3$ as in [57];
(v) The Eckert number $Ec = 0.001, 0.002, 0.003, 0.01, 1$ as in [58];
(vi) The volume fraction $\phi = 0, 0.05, 0.1, 0.2$ as in [49].

Moreover, human body temperature is considered as $T_w = 37\,°C$ [13,41], and body Curie temperature as $T_c = 41\,°C$. For these values, the dimensionless temperature is turned out to be $\varepsilon = \frac{T_c}{T_c - T_w} = \frac{314}{314 - 310} = 78.5$ [39,40]. Hence, the required values of the Prandtl number for human blood is $Pr = \frac{(\mu C_p)_f}{\kappa_f} = \frac{3.2 \times 10^{-3} \times 3.9 \times 10^3}{0.5} \approx 25$.

For case (a), the graphical results are obtained for pure blood and blood-Fe_3O_4, where magnetic particles are assumed of cylindrical shape. In case (b), the effect of magnetic particle shape is compared for blood-Fe_3O_4 flow on a cylindrical surface.

Figures 4–7 present the typical profiles for the velocity and temperature for numerous values of the ferromagnetic interaction parameter. It is alluded that when the values of the ferromagnetic interaction parameter are increased, the velocity profile is reduced and, consequently, the temperature profile is also decreased. This is due to the presence of the Kelvin force which is also known as resistive force, and it appears because of the fluid polarization at the inflow region. Figures 4 and 5 show the behaviors of pure blood and blood-Fe_3O_4 and for that particular case, the magnetic particles are assumed as cylindrical. It is seen from those figures that when the magnetic particles are mixed with blood, blood velocity and temperature is slightly increased throughout to the boundary layer compared to the case when pure blood is considered. The more profound reduction in the velocity with the increment of the applied magnetic field strength is depicted at Figure 6 for the case b. This reduction in the velocity is immense for η—greater than approximately 1.5. Analogous suppression of the temperature distributions with the increment of the magnetic field strength, i.e., as β increases, are also observed at Figure 7. It is also noticed from the aforementioned figures (see Figure 7) that if the particle shape is cylindrical, then the blood temperature is more significantly increased than when the spherical shape is adopted. It is noted that in these figures the above behavior concerns the effect of increasing polarization for a given electrical conductivity effect, i.e., steady Mn.

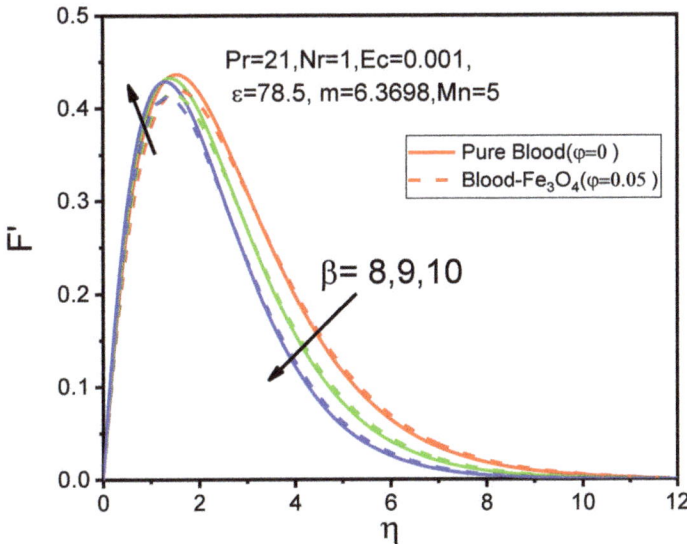

Figure 4. (Case a): Variations of F' for $\beta = 8$, 9, 10 against η.

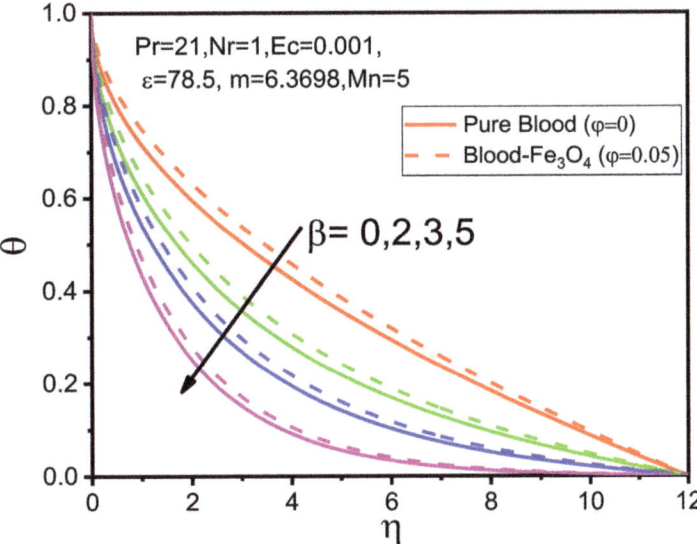

Figure 5. (Case a): Variations of θ for $\beta = 0$, 2, 3, 5 against η.

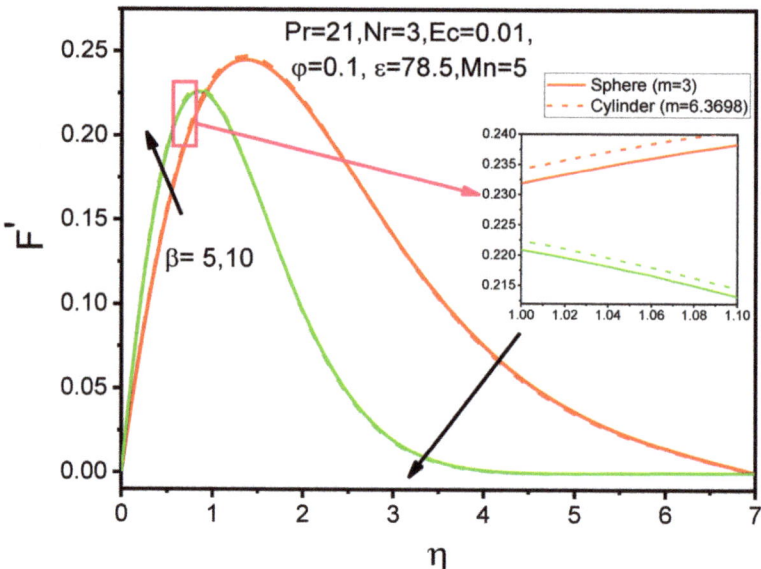

Figure 6. (Case b): Variations of F' for $\beta = 5, 10$ against η.

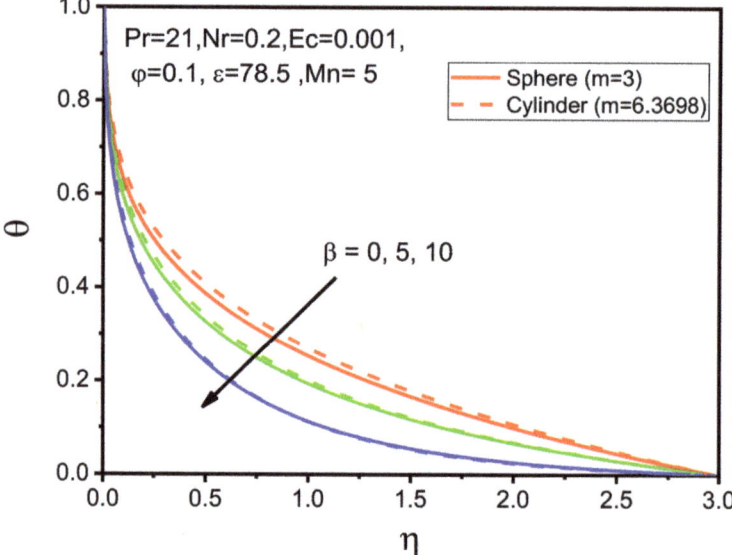

Figure 7. (Case b): Variations of θ for $\beta = 0, 5, 10$ against η.

The impact of the magnetic field parameter on the velocity and temperature distributions, for a steady ferromagnetic parameter β, are displayed in Figures 8 and 9. Figure 8 shows that blood velocity is decreased up to approximately $\eta \approx 1.9$ but then the fluid velocity is gradually increased. This is due to the application of the magnetic field which results to the arising of the Lorentz force, acting in the opposite direction to the fluid flow. As a result, for a given polarization effect, i.e., $\beta = 10$, when the values of the magnetic field parameter are increased, the temperature distribution is enhanced and that is clearly observed in Figure 9. A similar type of magnetic particle shape impact is also observed with the variation of the magnetic field parameter and the ferromagnetic number. Additionally, from Figure 10, we found that the temperature of blood-Fe$_3$O$_4$ is much better enhanced after adding magnetic particles rather than that occurring for pure blood.

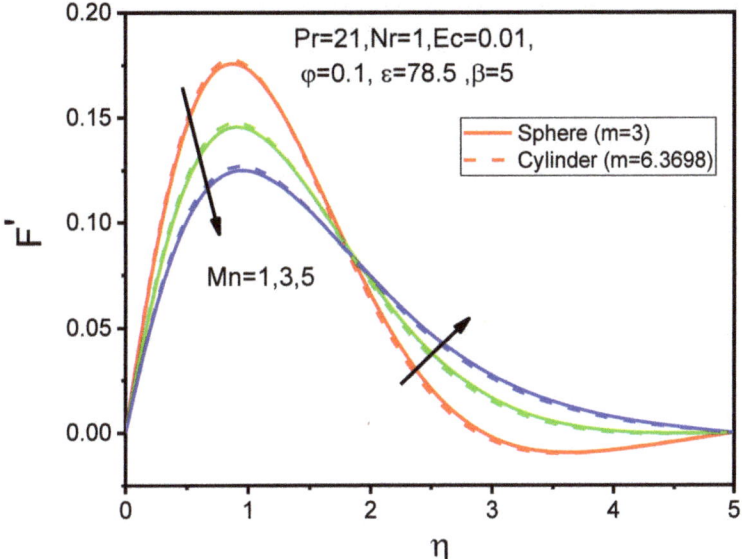

Figure 8. (Case b): Variations of F' for $Mn = 1, 3, 5$ against η.

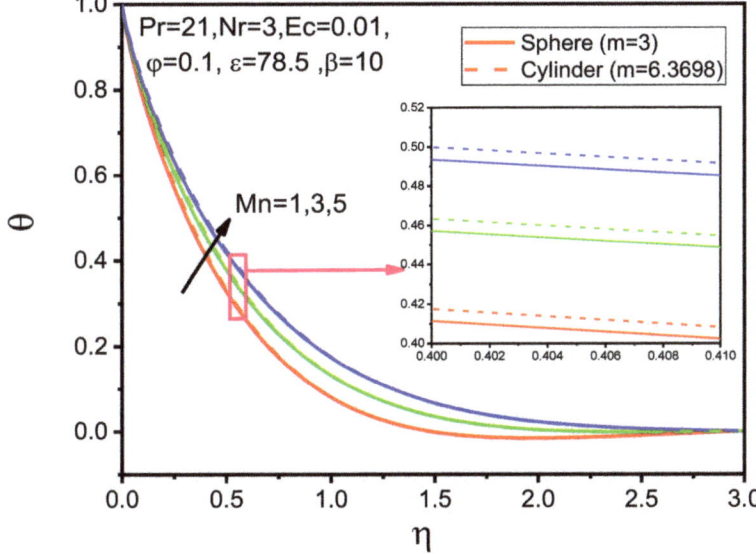

Figure 9. (Case b): Variations of θ for $Mn = 1, 3, 5$ against η.

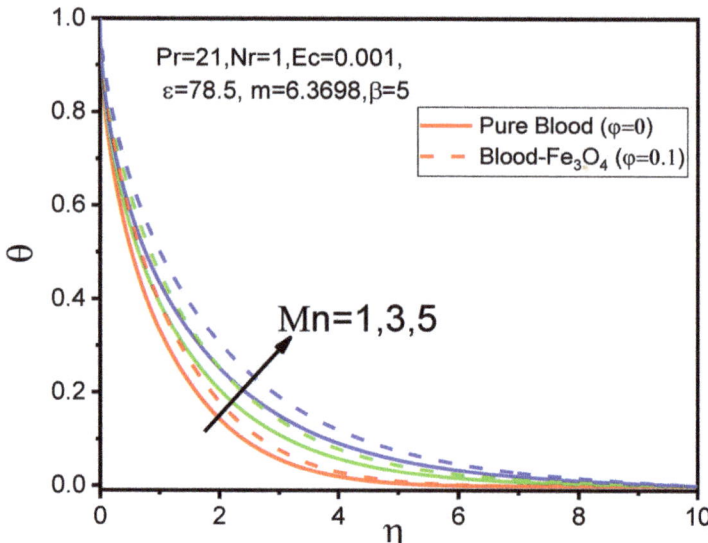

Figure 10. (Case a): Variations of θ for $Mn = 1, 3, 5$ against η.

Figures 11 and 12 present the effects of the magnetic particle volume fraction on the velocity and temperature profiles, respectively. It is evident that blood temperature is improved by the imposition of the magnetic particle volume fraction on blood (see Figure 12). It is also noticeable that it is more effective when particles are cylindrical rather than spherical. This is justified because of the large concentration of magnetic particles, which yields a higher proportion of thermal conductivity. From velocity profiles (Figure 11) two types of solutions are observed. Before the intersection of lines, it is observed that blood-Fe_3O_4 flow is decreased but after the intersection reverse trend is noticed as values of the magnetic particle volume fraction are enhanced. For both occasions, the magnetic particle shape factor plays a vital role, and their comparison is easily seen by observation of Figures 11 and 12.

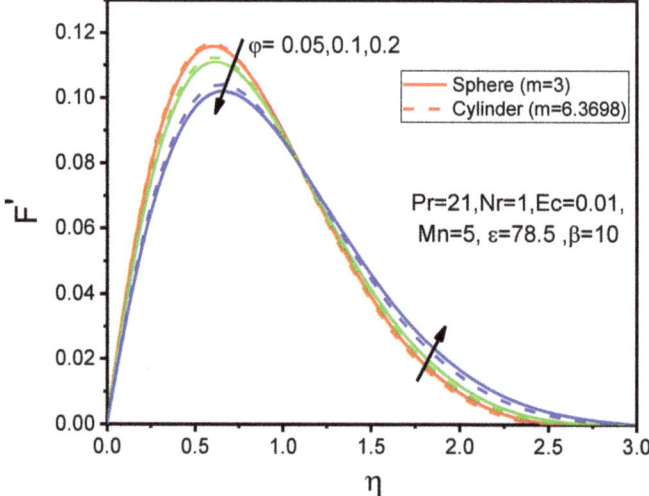

Figure 11. (Case b): Variations of F' for $\phi = 0.05, 0.1, 0.2$ against η.

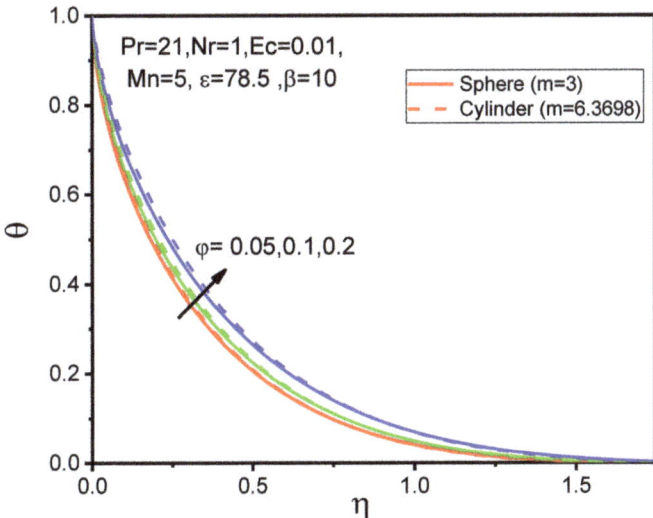

Figure 12. (Case b): Variations of θ for $\phi = 0.05, 0.1, 0.2$ against η.

The influence of the radiation parameter for various values on the velocity and temperature profiles, respectively, are plotted in Figures 13 and 14. From Figures 13 and 14, it is observed that, for a given magnetic field effect, i.e., Mn and β constants, as the values of the radiation parameter increase, both velocity and temperature distributions are increased. This is happening because heat energy is released from the fluid in the flow regime when the values of the radiation are gradually increased and as a result, the temperature of blood-Fe_3O_4 is enhanced.

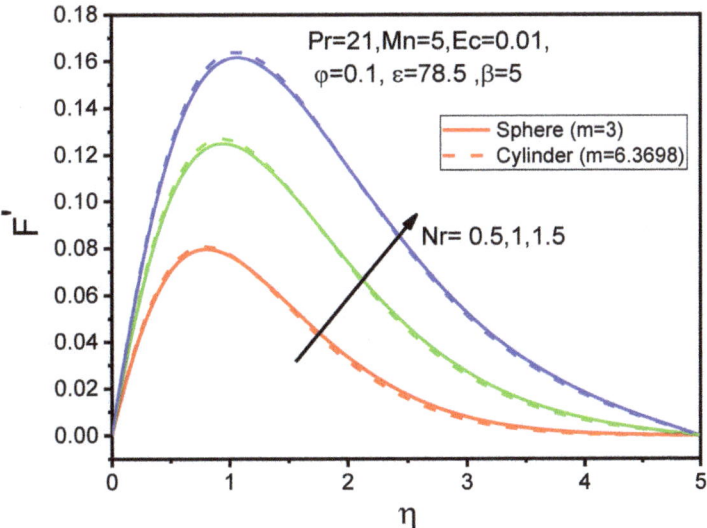

Figure 13. (Case b): Variations of F' for $Nr = 0.5, 1, 1.5$ against η.

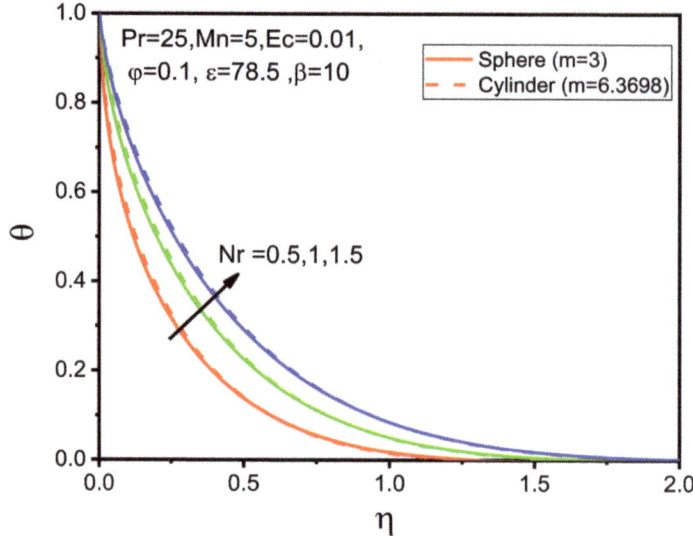

Figure 14. (Case b): Variations of θ for $Nr = 0.5, 1, 1.5$ against η.

Figures 15 and 16 represent the dimensionless velocity and temperature profiles, respectively, for various values of the Eckert number. As the Eckert number increases, both velocity and the temperature profiles are enhanced and especially the flow and heat of blood-Fe_3O_4 are remarkably increased compared to pure blood. Major temperature of fluid is attained for $Ec = 0.001$, which indicates that lower values of the Eckert number are responsible for enhancing temperature in fluid regime due to the combined effects of the magnetic field parameter and ferromagnetic number.

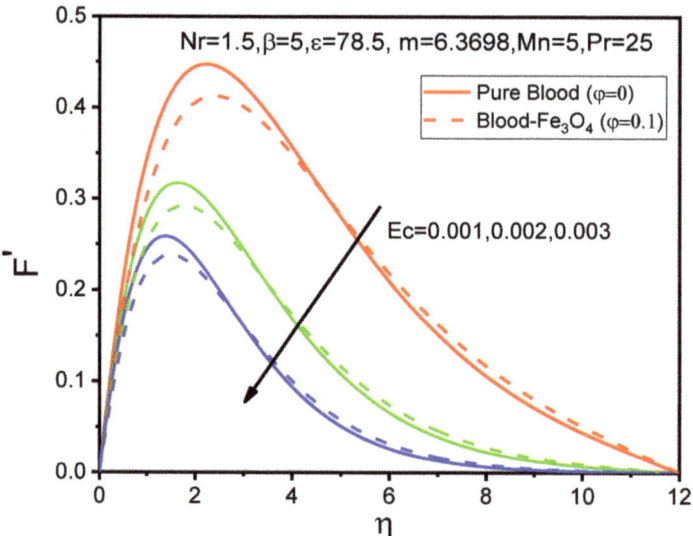

Figure 15. (Case a): Variations of F' for $Ec = 0.001, 0.002, 0.003$ against η.

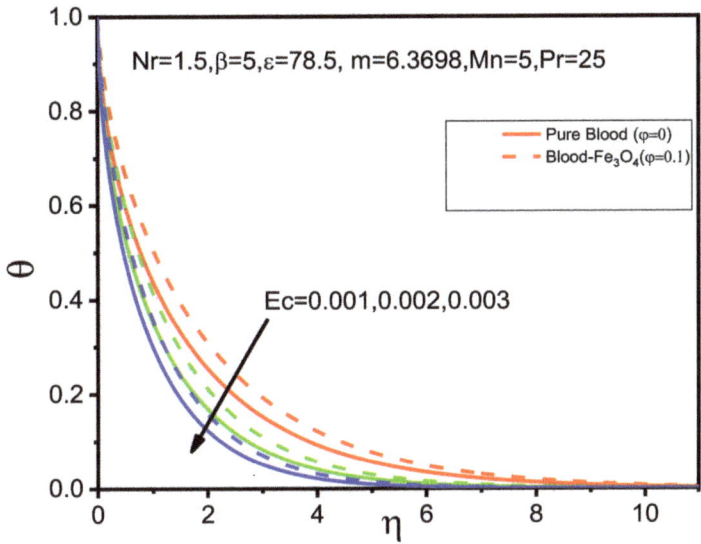

Figure 16. (Case a): Variations of θ for $Ec = 0.001, 0.002, 0.003$ against η.

Two quantities of great physical interest are the skin friction coefficient C_f and the rate of heat transfer Nu (local Nusselt number) which are defined by

$$C_f = \frac{2\,\tau_w}{\rho_f \left(\frac{u_0 \bar{x}}{L}\right)^2}, \qquad (88)$$

and

$$Nu = \frac{\bar{x}\, q_w}{\kappa_f (T_c - T_w)} \qquad (89)$$

where $\tau_w = \mu_{mf} \left(\frac{\partial \bar{u}}{\partial \bar{r}}\right)_{\bar{r}=\bar{R}}$ is the wall shear stress parameter and $q_w = \kappa_{mf} \left(\frac{\partial \bar{T}}{\partial \bar{r}}\right)_{\bar{r}=\bar{R}}$ is the wall heat transfer parameter. Therefore, relations (88) and (89) take the following form:

$$C_f = \frac{2\vartheta_f^2}{(1-\phi)^{2.5}\bar{R}^4 \left(\frac{u_0 x}{L}\right)^2} \left(\frac{\partial u}{\partial r}\right)_{r=1}, \qquad (90)$$

and

$$Nu = -\frac{x\kappa_{mf}}{\kappa_f} \left(\frac{\partial \theta}{\partial r}\right)_{r=1}, \qquad (91)$$

where $\vartheta_f^2 = \frac{\mu_f v_f}{\rho_f}$.

The skin friction coefficient and the local Nusselt number (the rate of heat transfer) are presented in Figures 17–22 for various values of the ferromagnetic interaction parameter, the magnetic particle volume fraction, the magnetic field parameter with regard to the magnetic field parameter, respectively. From Figures 17 and 18, we found that both the skin friction coefficient and the rate of heat transfer are increased for the ferromagnetic number with respect to the magnetic field parameter. It is noticeable from these figures that the rate of heat transfer of blood-Fe_3O_4 is significantly increased by approximately 33.2% compared to that of pure blood, whereas the reverse trend is observed in the skin friction coefficient and it is decreased by approximately 6.82% (see Figure 17). From Figure 19 to Figure 22, it is evident that both the skin friction coefficient and the Nusselt number are enhanced with the increment of the ferromagnetic interaction parameter, but the reverse trend is observed from Figures 21 and 22 as the particle volume fraction is increased. However, it is also noticed that the skin friction coefficient of blood-Fe_3O_4 is effectively increased for the cylindrical shape of magnetic particles comparable to that of spherical shape and it is increased by approximately 1.09%, whereas the local Nusselt number of blood-Fe_3O_4 is reduced 0.08% for cylindrical shape than that of spherical shape.

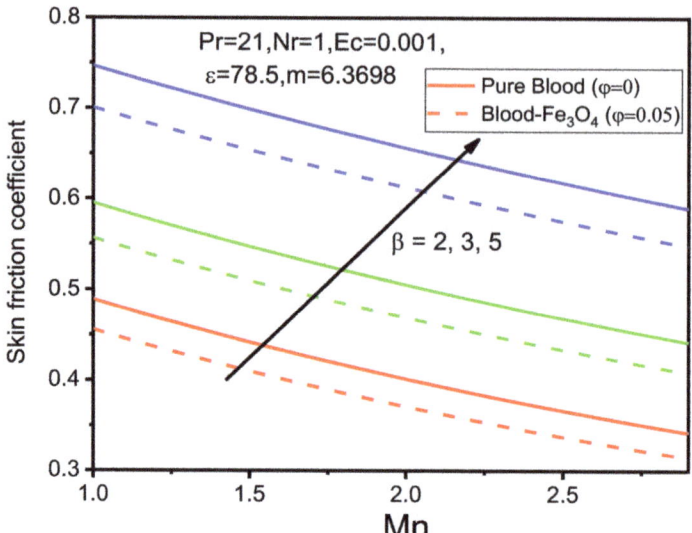

Figure 17. (Case a): Values of the skin friction coefficient for different values of β against Mn.

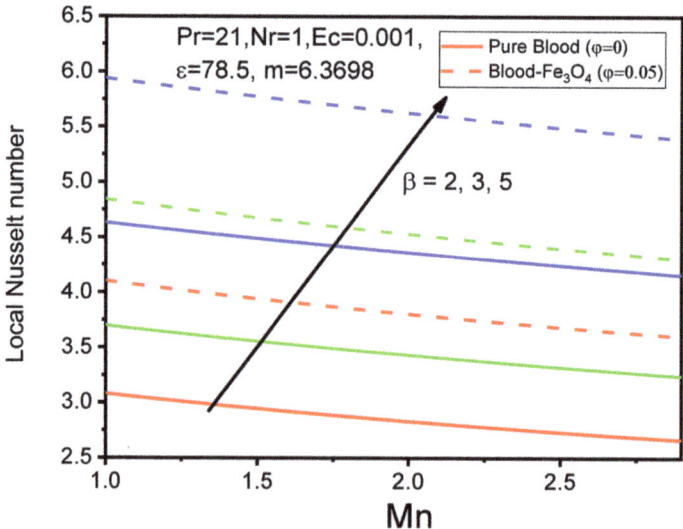

Figure 18. (Case a): Values of the local Nusselt number for different values of β against Mn.

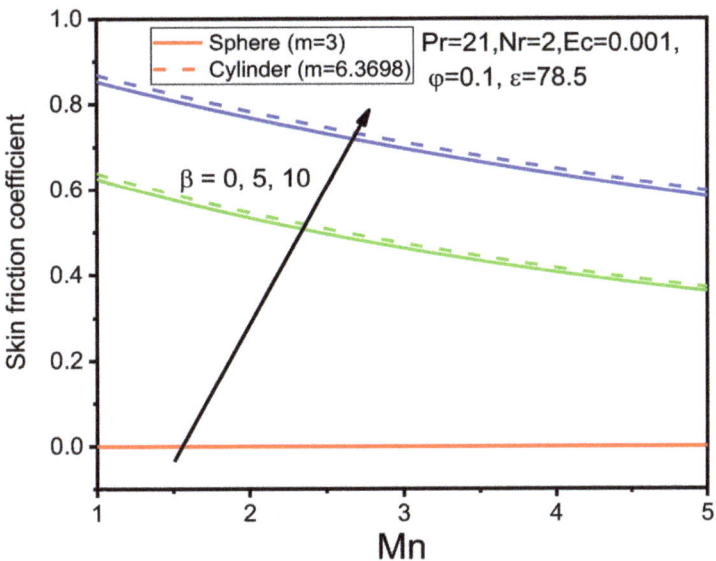

Figure 19. (Case b): Values of the skin friction coefficient for different values of β against Mn.

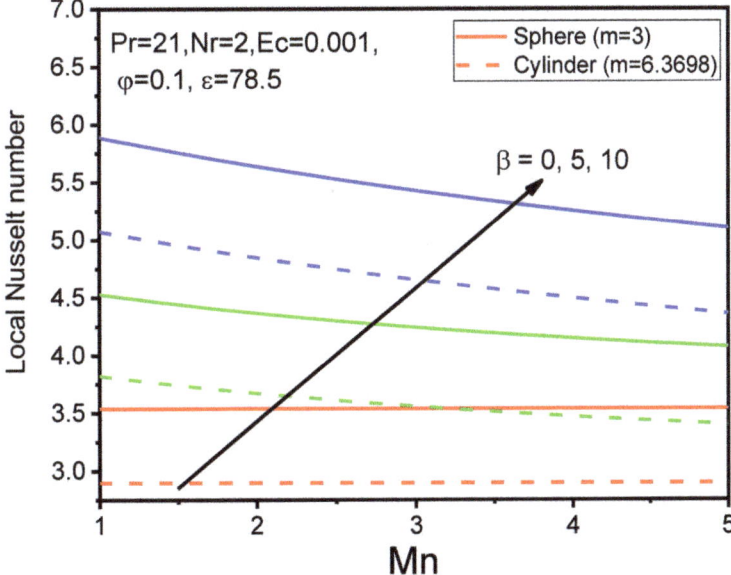

Figure 20. (Case b): Values of the local Nusselt number for different values of β against Mn.

For the ferromagnetic interaction parameter, the velocity profile is reduced and, consequently, the temperature profile is also decreased. This is due to the presence of the Kelvin force which is also known as resistive force, and it appears because of the fluid polarization at the inflow region (see Figures 4 and 5).

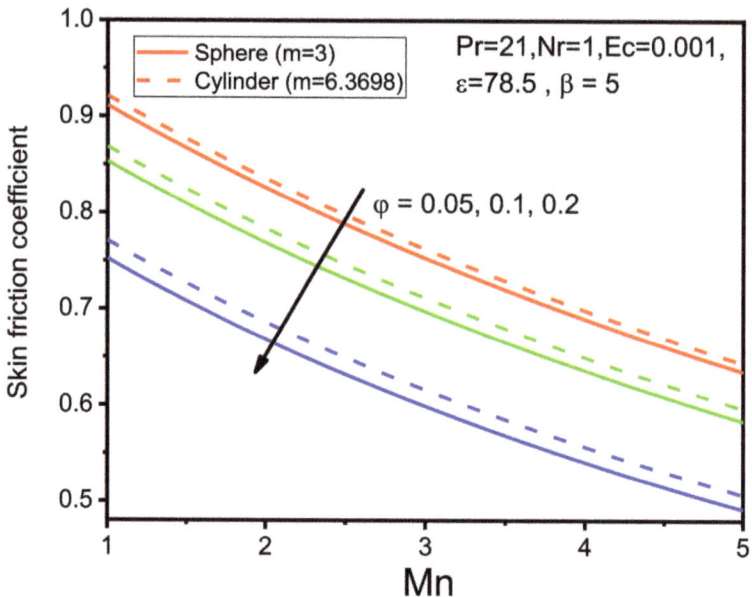

Figure 21. (Case b): Values of the skin friction coefficient for different values of ϕ against Mn.

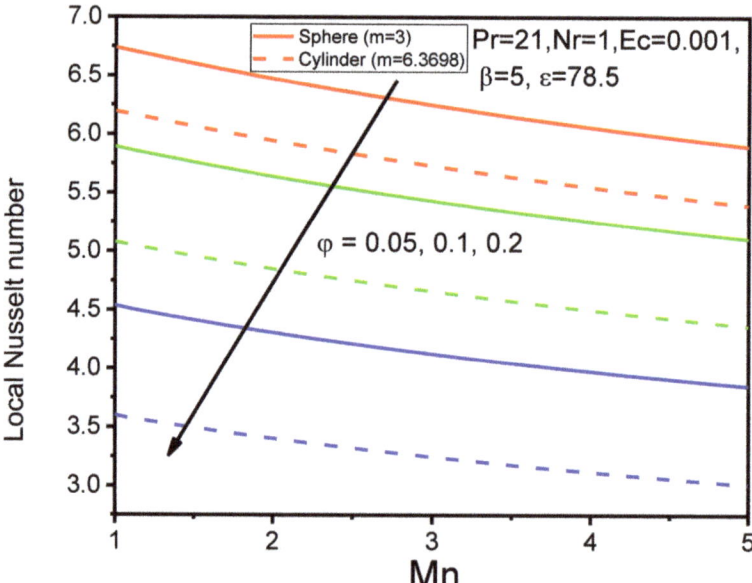

Figure 22. (Case b): Values of the local Nusselt number for different values of ϕ against Mn.

Fluid (blood) velocity decreases for enhancing values of the magnetic field parameter (Figure 8). This is due to the application of the magnetic field which results to the arising of the Lorentz force, acting in the opposite direction to the fluid flow.

Due to the large concentration of magnetic particles, which yields a higher proportion of thermal conductivity, blood temperature is enhanced (see Figure 12) and more significant in case of cylindrical shape.

Additionally, from graphs 17–22, it is observed that the heat transfer rate of blood-Fe_3O_4 is significantly increased by approximately 33.2% compared to that of pure blood, whereas the coefficient of skin friction is reduced by approximately 6.82%. Moreover, the coefficient of skin friction of blood-Fe_3O_4 is increased by approximately 1.09% when particles are in cylindrical shape compared to that of spherical shape, whereas the rate of heat transfer is enhanced 0.08% for spherical shape compared to that of cylindrical shape.

8. Concluding Remarks

In this paper, a BFD model is utilized to study blood flow with magnetic particles under consideration of FHD and MHD principles over a two-dimensional cylinder. The full form of a group theoretical method, namely a two-parameter group theory, is also applied. The effect of thermal radiation is also taken into consideration. With the application of the two-parameter group theory, the number of independent variables is reduced to one variable and, consequently, the set of PDEs is converted into a set of ODEs subject to corresponding boundary conditions. This resultant system of ODEs subject to analogous boundary conditions is numerically solved by applying an efficient numerical technique that consists of a common finite differences method with central differencing, tridiagonal matrix manipulation, and finally an iterative procedure. The significant impact of the variation of the appearing physical parameters is discussed and analogous graphical representations are also demonstrated. Moreover, a comparison of results with others, previously published, is performed to assure the accuracy of the applied numerical algorithm. From the above analysis, we found that:

1. The blood velocity is appreciably reduced, and temperature is significantly improved when magnetic particles are injected into a blood flow stream compared to that of pure blood, where the ferromagnetic interaction parameter plays a significant role.
2. The particle shape plays a vital role in the flow and heat characteristics of blood-Fe_3O_4, where a better temperature enhancement is observed for cylindrical shapes compared to that of spherical shapes.
3. An increase in the values of the magnetic field parameter and/or the volume of the fraction of the magnetic particles reduced the fluid velocity, whereas for the increment of the ferromagnetic interaction parameter, the fluid velocity was enhanced.
4. The temperature distributions of the fluids increased for all cases of the variation of parameters such as the ferromagnetic interaction parameter, the magnetic field parameter, and the magnetic particle volume fraction.
5. Both velocity and temperature profiles are increased as the values of the radiation parameter are enhanced, whereas the reverse trend is observed as the Eckert number is increased.
6. Both the skin friction coefficient and the rate of heat transfer are escalated with increasing values of the ferromagnetic interaction parameter. The heat transfer rate of blood-Fe_3O_4 is enhanced by approximately 33.2% compared to that of pure blood and the coefficient of skin friction is reduced by approximately 6.82%.
7. Both the coefficient of skin friction and the rate of heat transfer decrease with increasing values of the particle volume fraction. It was found that the skin friction coefficient is increased by approximately 1.09% for cylindrical shapes compared to that spherical shapes, while an 0.08% reduction is noticed for cylindrical shapes in the heat transfer rate compared to spherical shapes.

Author Contributions: Conceptualization, M.F.; Data curation, J.A.; Formal analysis, E.N.P.; Investigation, J.A.; Methodology, G.M. and M.F.; Project administration, E.E.T. and M.F.; Software, J.A., G.M. and E.E.T.; Supervision, E.E.T. and M.F.; Validation, G.M. and E.N.P.; Writing—original draft, J.A. and G.M.; Writing—review & editing, E.N.P. and E.E.T. All authors have read and agreed to the published version of the manuscript.

Funding: This research received no external funding.

Conflicts of Interest: The authors declare no conflict of interest.

List of Symbols

$(\bar{u}, \bar{v})$	Velocity components [m/s]	$\bar{H}$	Magnetic field strength [A/m]
$(\bar{x}, \bar{r})$	Components of the cartesian system [m]	I_1, I_2	Arbitrary function of two-parameter group
$\bar{R}$	Radius of the cylinder [m]		
c	Distance between the magnetic dipole and sheet [m]	A, B, C	Arbitrary constants
L	Characteristic length [m]	$\bar{T}$	Fluid temperature [K]
H_0	Reference magnetic field strength	T_w	Temperature of the cylinder surface [K]
t	Time [s]	T_c	Curie temperature [K]
C_p	Specific heat at constant pressure [J Kg^{-1} K^{-1}]	Mn	Magnetic field parameter
F'	Dimensionless velocity component	K	Pyromagnetic coefficient [K^{-1}]
γ	Strength of the magnetic field at the source position	Ec	Eckert number
Pr	Prandtl number	Nu	Local Nusselt number
α_i, δ_i	Arbitrary constants	C_f	Skin friction coefficient
q_r	Radiative heat flux	B	Magnetic induction
q_w	wall heat transfer parameter	V	Scalar potential of the magnetic dipole
ϕ	Dimensionless magnetic particle volume fraction	ψ	Stream function
η	Dimensionless similarity variable	ρ	Fluid density [Kg/m^3]
θ	Dimensionless temperature	μ	Dynamic viscosity [Kg/ms]
μ_0	Magnetic fluid permeability [NA^{-2}]	v	Kinematical viscosity [m^2/s]
ε_1	Convergence criteria	ε	Dimensionless Curie temperature
β	Ferromagnetic interaction parameter	κ	Thermal conductivity [J/m s K]
M	Magnetization	Nr	Thermal radiation parameter
τ_w	Wall shear stress	m	Magnetic particle's shape factor
σ_1	Stefan–Boltzmann constant	σ	Electrical conductivity
χ	Mean absorption coefficient	C_i	Arbitrary coefficient
$()_{mf}$	Magnetic fluid		Base fluid
$()_s$	Magnetic particles	$()'$	Differentiation with respect to η
$\overline{()}$	Dimensional quantities	v_f	Kinematic viscosity of the fluid

Abbreviations

BFD	Biomagnetic fluid dynamics
FHD	Ferrohydrodynamics
MHD	Magnetohydrodynamic
MRI	Magnetic resonance imaging
PDEs	Partial differential equations
ODEs	Ordinary differential equations

References

1. Stark, D.D.; Weissleder, R.; Elizondo, G.; Hahn, P.F.; Saini, S.; Todd, L.E.; Wittenberg, J.; Ferrucci, J.T. Superparamagnetic iron oxide: Clinical application as a contrast for MR imaging of the liver. *Radiology* **1988**, *168*, 297–301. [CrossRef]
2. Rugge, E.K.; Rusetski, A.N. Magnetic fluids as drug carries: Targeted transport of drugs by a magnetic field. *J. Magn. Magn. Mater.* **1993**, *122*, 335–339. [CrossRef]
3. Fiorentini, G.; Szasz, S. Hyperthermia today: Electric energy, a new opportunity in cancer treatment. *J. Cancer Res. Ther.* **2006**, *2*, 41–46. [CrossRef]
4. Misra, J.C.; Sinha, A.; Shit, G.C. Flow of a biomagnetic viscoelastic fluid: Application to estimation of blood flow in arteries during electromagnetic hyperthermia, a therapeutic procedure for cancer treatment. *Appl. Math. Mech.-Engl. Ed.* **2010**, *31*, 1405–1420. [CrossRef]
5. Chien, S.; Usami, S.; Skalsk, R. Blood flow in small tubes. In *American Physiological Society Handbook of Physiology*; Section 2, The Cardivascular System, 4; Renkins, E.M., Michel, C.C., Eds.; American Physiological Society: Bethesda, MD, USA, 1984; pp. 217–249.
6. Bhatti, M.M.; Abbas, M.A. Simultaneously effects of slip and MHD on peristaltic blood flow of Jeffrey fluid model through a porous medium. *Alex. Eng. J.* **2016**, *55*, 1017–1023. [CrossRef]
7. Haik, Y.; Chen, J.C.; Pai, V.M. Development of bio-magnetic fluid dynamics. In *Proceedings of the IX International Symposium on Transport Properties in Thermal Fluids Engineering, Singapore*; Winoto, S.H., Chew, Y.T., Wijeysundera, N.E., Eds.; Pacific Center of Thermal Fluid Engineering: Hawaii, HI, USA, 1996; pp. 121–126.

8. Tzirtzilakis, E.E. A mathematical model for blood flow in magnetic field. *Phys. Fluids* **2005**, *17*, 077103. [CrossRef]
9. BSharma, K.; Kumawat, C. Impact of temperature dependent viscosity and thermal conductivity on MHD blood flow through a stretching surface with ohmic effect and chemical reaction. *Nonlinear Eng.* **2021**, *10*, 255–271. [CrossRef]
10. Misra, J.C.; Shit, G.C. Biomagnetic viscoelastic fluid over a stretching sheet. *Appl. Math. Comput.* **2009**, *210*, 350–361. [CrossRef]
11. Koppu, S.; Pol, B.A.R.; Bhuvanagiri, S.R.V.P. Effects of chemical reaction and thermal radiation on MHD flow over an inclined permeable stretching surface with non-uniform heat source/sink: An application to the dynamics of blood flow. *J. Mech. Med. Biol.* **2014**, *14*, 1450067.
12. Murtaza, M.G.; Tzirtzilakis, E.E.; Ferdows, M. A duality of biomagnetic fluid flow and heat transfer over a quadratic stretched surface. *J. Power Technol.* **2021**, *101*, 154–162.
13. Murtaza, M.G.; Tzirtzilakis, E.E.; Ferdows, M. Effect of electrical conductivity and magnetization on the biomagnetic fluid flow over a stretching sheet. *Z. Angew. Math. Phys.* **2017**, *68*, 93. [CrossRef]
14. Choi, S.U.S.; Eastman, J.A. Enhancing thermal conductivity of fluids with nanoparticles. In *Developments and Applications of Non-Newtonian Flows*; Siginer, D.A., Wang, H.P., Eds.; ASME: New York, NY, USA, 1995; Volume 66, pp. 99–105.
15. Alsenafi, A.; Ferdows, M. Dual solution for double-diffusive mixed convection opposing flow through a vertical cylinder saturated in a Darcy porous media containing gyrotactic microorganisms. *Sci. Rep.* **2021**, *11*, 19918. [CrossRef]
16. Nikelham, A.; Enjilela, V.; Vaziri, N.; Moziraji, Z.P. The effects of magnetic-field direction and magnitude on forced convection of aluminum oxide–water nanofluid over a circular cylinder. *Int. J. Therm. Sci.* **2022**, *173*, 107398. [CrossRef]
17. Aminian, E.; Moghadasi, H.; Saffari, H. Magnetic field effects on forced convection flow of a hybrid nanofluid in a cylinder filled with porous media: A numerical study. *J. Therm. Anal Calorim.* **2020**, *141*, 2019–2031. [CrossRef]
18. Tlili, I.; Khan, W.A.; Ramadan, K. MHD flow of nanofluid flow across horizontal circular cylinder: Steady forced convection. *J. Nanofl.* **2019**, *8*, 179–186. [CrossRef]
19. Elbashbeshy, E.M.A.; Emam, T.G.; El-Azab, M.S.; Abdelgaber, K.M. Effect of magnetic field on flow and heat transfer over a stretching horizontal cylinder in the presence of a heat source/sink with suction/injection. *J. Appl. Mech. Eng.* **2012**, *1*, 1–5. [CrossRef]
20. Roy, N.; Akter, A. Heat transfer enhancement and boundary layer separations for a hybrid nanofluid flow past an isothermal cylinder. *J. Appl. Comput. Mech.* **2021**, *7*, 2096–2112.
21. Ali, L.; Ali, B.; Ghori, M.B. Melting effect on Cattaneo–Christov and thermal radiation features for aligned MHD nanofluid flow comprising microorganisms to the leading edge: FEM approach. *Comput. Math. Appl.* **2022**, *109*, 260–269. [CrossRef]
22. Kumar, P.; Poonia, H.; Ali, L.; Areekara, S. The numerical simulation of nanoparticle size and thermal radiation with the magnetic field effect based on tangent hyperbolic nanofluid flow. *Case Stud. Therm. Eng.* **2022**, *37*, 102247. [CrossRef]
23. Dawar, A.; Saeed, A.; Kumam, P. Magneto-hydrothermal analysis of copper and copper oxide nanoparticles between two parallel plates with Brownian motion and thermophoresis effects. *Int. Commun. Heat Mass Transf.* **2022**, *133*, 105982. [CrossRef]
24. Bilal, M.; El Ahmed, A.; El-Nabulsi, R.A.; Ahammad, N.A.; Alharbi, K.A.M.; Elkotb, M.A.; Anukool, W.; Zedan, A.S.A. Numerical analysis of an unsteady, Electroviscous, Tenary Hybrid nanofluid flow with chemical reaction and activation energy across. *Micromachines* **2022**, *13*, 874. [CrossRef] [PubMed]
25. Souayeh, B.; Ramesh, K.; Hdhiri, N.; Yasmin, E.; Alam, M.W.; Alfares, K.; Yasmin, A. Heat transfer attributes of Gold-Silver-Blood hybrid nanomaterial flow in an EMHD peristaltic channel with activation energy. *Nanomaterials* **2022**, *12*, 1615. [CrossRef]
26. Alwawi, F.A.; Swalmeh, M.Z.; Sulaiman, I.M.; Yaseen, N.; Alkasasbeh, H.T.; Al-Soub, T.F. Numerical investigation of heat transfer characteristics for blood/water-based nanofluids in free convection about a circular cylinder. *J. Mech. Eng. Sci.* **2022**, *16*, 8931–8942. [CrossRef]
27. Alam, J.; Murtaza, M.G.; Tzirtzilakis, E.E.; Ferdows, M. Group Method analysis for Blood-Mn-ZnFe$_2$O$_4$ flow and heat transfer under ferrohydrodynamics through a stretched cylinder. *Math. Methods Appl. Sci.* **2022**, 1–21. [CrossRef]
28. Shinkaj, M.; Ito, A. Functional magnetic particles for medical application. *Adv. Biochem. Engin./Biotechnol.* **2004**, *91*, 191–220.
29. Stueber, D.D.; Vilanova, J.; Aponte, I.; Xiao, Z.; Colvin, V.L. Magnetic nanoparticles in Biology and Medicine: Past, present and future trends. *Pharmaceutics* **2021**, *13*, 943. [CrossRef] [PubMed]
30. Ramanujan, V. Magnetic particles for biomedical applications. In *Biomedical Materials*; Narayan, R., Ed.; Sringer: Boston, MA, USA, 2009.
31. Baki, A.; Weikhorst, F.; Bleul, R. Advances in magnetic nanoparticles engineering for biomedical applications—A Review. *Bioengineering* **2021**, *8*, 134. [CrossRef] [PubMed]
32. Morgan, A.J.A. The reduction by one of the number of independent variables in systems of partial differential equations. *Quart. J. Math. Oxford Ser.* **1952**, *3*, 250–259. [CrossRef]
33. El-Kabeir, S.M.M.; El-Hakiem, M.A.; Rashad, A.M. Group method analysis for the effect of radiation on MHD coupled heat and mass transfer natural convection flow water vapor over a vertical cone through porous medium. *Int. J. Appl. Math Mech.* **2007**, *3*, 35–53.
34. Abd-el-Malek, M.B.; Badran, N.B. Group method analysis of unsteady free convective laminar boundary layer flow on a nonisothermal vertical circular cylinder. *Acta Mech.* **1990**, *85*, 193–206. [CrossRef]
35. Ibrahim, F.S.; Hamad, M.A.A. Group method analysis of mixed convection boundary-layer flow of a micropolar fluid near a stagnation point on a horizontal cylinder. *Acta Mech.* **2006**, *181*, 65–81. [CrossRef]

36. Rajput, G.R.; Krishnaprasad, J.S.V.R.; Timol, M.G. Group theoretic technique for MHD forced convection laminar boundary flow of nanofluid over a moving surface. *Int. J. Heat Tech.* **2016**, *34*, 1–6. [CrossRef]
37. Abd-el-Malek, M.B.; Badran, N.A. Group method analysis of steady free-convective laminar boundary-layer flow on a nonisothermal vertical circular cylinder. *J. Comput. Appl. Math.* **1991**, *36*, 227–238. [CrossRef]
38. Tzirtzilakis, E.E.; Kafoussias, N.G. Three-dimensional magnetic fluid boundary layer flow over a linearly stretching sheet. *J. Heat Transf.* **2010**, *132*, 011702. [CrossRef]
39. Tzirtzilakis, E.E.; Kafoussias, N.G. Biomagnetic fluid flow over a stretching sheet with non linear temperature dependent magnetization. *Z. Angew. Math. Phys.* **2003**, *54*, 551–565.
40. Tzirtzilakis, E.E.; Tanoudis, G.B. Numerical study of biomagnetic fluid flow over a stretching sheet with heat transfer. *Internat. J. Numer. Methods Heat Fluid Flow* **2003**, *13*, 830–848. [CrossRef]
41. Raptis, A. Flow of a micropolar fluid past a continuously moving plate by the presence of radiation. *Int. J. Heat Mass Tran.* **1998**, *41*, 2865–2866. [CrossRef]
42. Raptis, A. Radiation and free convection flow through a porous medium. *Int. Commun. Heat Mass Tran.* **1998**, *25*, 289–295. [CrossRef]
43. Andersson, H.I.; Valnes, O.A. Flow of a heated ferrofluid over a stretching sheet in the presence of a magnetic dipole. *Acta Mech.* **1998**, *128*, 39–47. [CrossRef]
44. Nadeem, S.; Ullah, N.; Khan, A.U.; Akbar, T. Effect of homogeneous-heterogeneous reactions on ferrofluid in the presence of magnetic dipole along a stretching cylinder. *Results Phys.* **2017**, *7*, 3574–3582. [CrossRef]
45. Matsuki, H.; Yamasawa, K.; Murakami, K. Experimental consideration on a new automatic cooling device using temperature sensitive magnetic fluid. *IEEE Trans. Magn.* **1997**, *13*, 1143–1145. [CrossRef]
46. Makinde, O.D. Stagnation point flow with heat transfer and temporal stability of ferrofluid past a permeable stretching/shrinking. *Defect Diffus. Forum* **2018**, *387*, 510–522. [CrossRef]
47. Lin, Y.; Zheng, L.; Chen, G. Unsteady flow and heat transfer of pseudo-plastic nano liquid in a finite thin film on a stretching surface with variable thermal conductivity and viscous dissipation. *Powder Technol.* **2015**, *274*, 324–332. [CrossRef]
48. Kandasamy, R.; Adnan, N.A.-b; Mohammad, R. Nanoparticles shape effects on squeezed MHD flow of water based on Cu, Al_2O_3 and SWCNTs over a porous sensor surface. *Alex. Eng. J.* **2018**, *57*, 1433–1445. [CrossRef]
49. Alam, J.; Murtaza, G.; Tzirtzilakis, E.E.; Ferdows, M. Biomagnetic fluid flow and heat transfer study of blood with gold nanoparticles over a stretching sheet in the presence of magnetic dipole. *Fluids* **2021**, *6*, 113. [CrossRef]
50. Aziz, A.; Jamshed, W.; Ali, Y.; Shams, M. Heat transfer and entropy analysis of Maxwell hybrid nanofluid including effects of an inclined magnetic field, Joule heating and thermal radiation. *Discrete Contin. Dyn. Syst. Ser. S* **2020**, *13*, 2667–2690. [CrossRef]
51. Reddy, S.R.R.; Reddy, P.B.A. Bio-mathematical analysis for the stagnation point flow over a non-linear stretching surface with the second order velocity slip and titanium alloy nanoparticle. *Front. Heat Mass Tran.* **2018**, *10*, 13.
52. Hassanien, I.A.; Salama, A.A.; Hosham, H.I. Group theoretic method analysis for unsteady boundary layer flow near a stagnation point. *Taiwanese J. Math.* **2005**, *9*, 639–660. [CrossRef]
53. Abd-el-Malek, M.B.; Boutros, Y.Z.; Badran, N.A. Group method analysis of unsteady free-convective laminar boundary-layer flow on a nonisothermal vertical flat plate. *J. Engrg. Math.* **1990**, *24*, 343–368. [CrossRef]
54. Moran, M.J.; Gaggioli, R.A. A new systematic formalism for similarity analysis with application to boundary layer flows. *U.S. Army Math. Res. Center Tech. Summ.* **1968**, *75*, AD0681404.
55. Moran, M.J.; Gaggioli, R.A. A new systematic formalism for similarity analysis. *J. Engrg. Math.* **1969**, *3*, 151–162. [CrossRef]
56. Kafoussias, N.G.; Williams, E.W. An improved approximation technique to obtain numerical solution of a class of two-point boundary value similarity problems in fluid mechanics. *Int. J. Numer. Meth. Fluids* **1993**, *17*, 145–162. [CrossRef]
57. Alam, M.J.; Murtaza, M.G.; Tzirtzilakis, E.E.; Ferdows, M. Effect of thermal radiation on biomagnetic fluid flow and heat transfer over an unsteady stretching sheet. *Comput. Assist. Meth. Eng. Sci. (CAMES)* **2021**, *28*, 81–104.
58. Fenuga, O.J.; Hasan, A.R.; Olanrewaju, P.O. Effects of radiation and Eckert number on MHD flow with heat transfer rate near a stagnation point over a non-linear vertical stretching sheet. *Int. J. Appl. Mech. Eng.* **2020**, *25*, 27–36. [CrossRef]

Article

Quantification of Aversion to Uncertainty in Intertemporal Choice through Subjective Perception of Time

Viviana Ventre and Roberta Martino *

Department of Mathematics and Physics, University of Campania Luigi Vanvitelli, Viale A. Lincoln, 5, 81100 Caserta, Italy
* Correspondence: roberta.martino@unicampania.it

Abstract: Intertemporal choices are those decisions structured over several periods in which the effects only manifest themselves with the passage of time. The main mathematical reference for studying the behavior of individuals with respect to this type of decision is the Discounted Utility Model which hypothesizes completely rational individuals. The empirical evidence that deviates from normative expectations has motivated the formulation of alternative models with the aim of better describing the behavior of individuals. The present paper investigates the characteristics behind hyperbolic discounting starting from the phenomenon of decision inconsistency, i.e., when individuals' preferences vary over time. The mechanisms of inconsistency will be explored through the physical concept of relative time, proving the importance of uncertainty aversion in the hyperbolic trend of the discount function. The analysis of the mathematical characteristics of hyperbolic discounting and the relationship between decision inconsistency and subjective perception of time defines the maximum distance between rational and non-rational preferences. An experimental part empirically proves the relationship between uncertainty aversion and time inconsistency. The present paper contributes to the literature by defining a new characteristic of hyperbolic discounting and quantifying the impact of the subjective perception of time in the decision-making process.

Keywords: hyperbolic discounting; intertemporal choice; impatience; inconsistency; subjective perception of time; uncertainty

MSC: 91E45; 91F99

Citation: Ventre, V.; Martino, R. Quantification of Aversion to Uncertainty in Intertemporal Choice through Subjective Perception of Time. *Mathematics* 2022, *10*, 4315. https://doi.org/10.3390/math10224315

Academic Editors: Irina Cristea, Yuriy Rogovchenko, Justo Puerto, Gintautas Dzemyda and Patrick Siarry

Received: 22 October 2022
Accepted: 11 November 2022
Published: 17 November 2022

Publisher's Note: MDPI stays neutral with regard to jurisdictional claims in published maps and institutional affiliations.

Copyright: © 2022 by the authors. Licensee MDPI, Basel, Switzerland. This article is an open access article distributed under the terms and conditions of the Creative Commons Attribution (CC BY) license (https:// creativecommons.org/licenses/by/ 4.0/).

1. Introduction

Recent studies in finance argue that asset pricing should consider both risk and uncertainty [1]. The decision-making context in which the present research is developed involves choices under uncertainty, particularly the kind of decisions in which alternatives are distributed over time, called intertemporal choices. The purpose of the research is to understand how individuals behave when they have to select an intertemporal prospect from those available. The reason why intertemporal choices are so complex and interesting comes down to two characteristics. First, precisely because alternatives are spread over multiple periods, the selection of later and more important outcomes necessarily involves foregoing a more imminent and modest outcome [2]. Moreover, even after selecting an alternative, it is not necessarily perceived over time always to be the optimal one [3]. The essential mathematical reference model for the study of behavior with respect to intertemporal choices was formalized by Samuelson [4,5]. The model predicts that the utility of an alternative was calculated as the product between its cardinal utility and the discount function evaluated at the time of receipt. From an operational point of view, the discount function determines a reduction in the present utility of the outcome based on how the individual perceives the indeterminacy of the future. The first formulation of the model predicted an exponential trend in the discount function, in line with the principles of economic rationality, which assumes a perfectly rational decision-maker capable of considering all components of the decision-making environment. Empirical evidence has over time motivated research to formulate alternative discount functions that could better describe the behavior of individuals. The hyperbolic model was formalized later in response to the discrepancy between the preferences predicted by the exponential model and the behavior of individuals. The main difference between the hyperbolic model and the exponential model is that in the former, the discount rate and the degree of impatience [6] are not constant but decrease over time [7,8]. Initially, this feature of hyperbolic discounting came to be associated with a kind of non-rationality of decision-making, characterizing nonexponential preferences with a negative connotation. In 1957, the concept of bounded rationality introduced by Simon [9] proposed the idea of a decision-maker with limited cognitive ability and resources. A decision-maker applies her rationality only after simplifying the available alternatives not being able to perceive, from a cognitive point of view, their full complexity. The consequence of this mechanism is that the decision-making satisfies adequacy criteria to determine a satisfactory solution rather than identifying the absolute best alternative. Later, a variety of works [10,11] clarified that decision-making is affected by systematic distortions associated with cognitive machinery and the emotional sphere. Since everyone is prone to certain biases, the work on strategic personalization proposed in Nudge theory [12] and in behavioral personalized finance [13,14] highlights the importance of behavioral attitudes in decision-making. At this point, it is even more interesting to investigate the characteristics of hyperbolic discounting since it is an expression of the cognitive and behavioral structure of the decision-maker.

This paper aims to understand whether the decreasing discount rate and impatience are sufficient to describe the mechanisms underlying hyperbolic discounting, or whether there are concepts within its structure that have not yet been formalized. To achieve the purpose, the object under consideration in the present paper is the phenomenon of time inconsistency, for which an individual's preferences vary over time. The idea is to describe the phenomenon of inconsistency by integrating within hyperbolic discounting the concept of subjective perception of time. Using a time transformation, a measure of inconsistency is defined to quantify the discrepancy between the exponential and hyperbolic models. The relationships between this new measure and the elements used so far to describe hyperbolic discounting (discount rate and impatience) will prove that it constitutes distinct and original elements from those found in the literature. A variety of works that operationally justify the present study [15–22] also lead one to associate the defined measure with an uncertainty aversion mechanism. The applicability of this research addresses the Markets in Financial Instruments Directive, 2014/65/UE (MiFID2), which emphasizes the need to create customer profiling to ensure personalized strategies and protection mechanisms. The quantification of bias through the concept of impatience [23] and the quantification of uncertainty aversion are two useful measures to define classes of behavioral investors. In fact, although this article is far from dealing with choices under risky conditions, uncertainty analysis is considered essential by some studies for asset pricing and entrepreneurship [24]. Therefore, any relationships between the measure presented in this article and risk aversion coefficients [25] could be topics for future research. Finally, the possibility of applying the measure presented in this paper to the strategic personalization and classification of individuals is supported by two well-known works in the literature: with respect to classification, [26] prove that there is a relationship between cognitive ability and hyperbolic discounting, with respect to customized strategic plans, on the other hand, [27] proves how it is possible to increase helper-control with techniques to reduce dynamically inconsistent preferences. This paper is organized as follows. After a brief presentation on the Discounted Utility Model, some studies are presented that justifies the introduction of a temporal transformation function in intertemporal choice theory. The problem of time inconsistency will shift from the trend of the discount function to the evaluation of perceived time. The new measure of inconsistency is characterized and discussed with respect to the discount factor and impatience exhibited by the function. An experimental part will empirically prove the formalized results. This is followed by a discussion and conclusion section.

2. Motivation and Mathematical Formalization

2.1. Discounted Utility Model and Time in Intertemporal Choice

Let $x_1, \ldots, x_n$ be n alternatives available at the times $t_1, \ldots, t_n$, respectively. An intertemporal prospect is the n-pla $(x_1, t_1; \ldots; x_n, t_n)$ of pairs (x_i, t_i) where $x_i \in \mathbb{R}$, $t_i \in \mathbb{R}^+$. If the individual accepts the prospect, then the outcome x_i will be received at time t_i. The Discounted Utility Model [4,5] states that:

$$U(x_1, t_1; \ldots; x_n, t_n) = \sum_{i=0}^{n} U(x_i) f(t_i)$$

where $U(x_i)$ is the cardinal utility of x_i and $f(t_i)$ is the discount function. By definition, the discount function is defined as $f : \mathbb{R} \to \mathbb{R}$ such that $f(0) = 1$, $f(t)$ monotonous decreasing and $\lim_{t \to \infty} f(t) = 0$. It is possible to prove that a discount function generates a relation, called preference relation $(\geq)$, of total order and vice versa [6]. From a practical point of view, given $(x_1, t_1; \ldots; x_n, t_n)$ and $(y_1, s_1; \ldots; y_n, s_n)$ two different prospects then $(x_1, t_1; \ldots; x_n, t_n) >_f (y_1, s_1; \ldots; y_m, s_m) \iff \sum_{i=0}^{n} U(x_i) f(t_i) > \sum_{i=0}^{m} U(y_i) f(s_i)$ and $(x_1, t_1; \ldots; x_n, t_n) \sim_f (y_1, s_1; \ldots; y_m, s_m) \iff \sum_{i=0}^{n} U(x_i) f(t_i) = \sum_{i=0}^{m} U(y_i) f(s_i)$: the first case indicates that the decision-making prefers to select the prospect $(x_1, t_1; \ldots; x_n, t_n)$; the second case indicates that the decision-making is indifferent with respect the two prospects.

Preferences in intertemporal choice theory are weak order, continuous, monotone, and impatient [7]. The performance of the discount function is decisive for preferences because it determines a reduction in the present utility of the outcome according to the time distance between evaluation and reception. Table 1 reports the common discount functions in intertemporal choice theory.

Table 1. Common discount functions in intertemporal choice reported by [8], p. 426.

Linear	$f(t) = 1 - rt$
Exponential	$f(t) = \left(\frac{1}{1+\rho}\right)^t$
Hyperbolic	Generalized $f(t) = (1 + \alpha t)^{-\frac{\beta}{\alpha}}$
	Quasi-hyperbolic $f(t) = \beta \left(\frac{1}{1+\rho}\right)^t$
	One parameter $f(t) = \left(\frac{1}{1+\rho t}\right)$

As can be seen from Table 1, all discount functions have a decreasing trend over time, which, from a behavioral point of view, is equivalent to saying that in the future the value of an asset decreases because it is more uncertain. The main difference between the linear, exponential, and hyperbolic discount functions is that the first two decrease with a constant rate. In general, empirical evidence proves that hyperbolic discounting has greater descriptive power of individuals' preferences than exponential discounting [28]. The psychological mechanisms underlying the decrease in the discount function are quantified by the discount rate and the degree of impatience. The discount rate, defined as $\rho(t) = -\frac{f'(t)}{f(t)}$, represents "the proportional variation of f over a standard period" [8] (p. 425). The impatience of investor, defined in $[t_i, t_j]$ is given by $1 - f(t_j)/f(t_i)$ and represents "the amount of money that the agent is willing to lose in exchange for anticipating the availability of a \$1 reward" [6] (p. 5). The main difference from a mathematical point of view between the exponential and hyperbolic formulation of the discount function lies in the fact that the discount rate and the degree of impatience are not constant over time in the hyperbolic discount. In particular, the degree with which impatience decreases represents the gap between preferring an event to occur and preferring an event to occur sooner [7].

Time is a concept that has attracted the curiosity of various fields of inquiry, such as philosophy and physics. Although the objective nature of time, associated with the chronological scanning of events, was obvious, the subjective perception of time is a dimension of human intuition that cannot be refuted. How the passage of time is perceived defines the cognitive, emotional, and motivational style of the individual [22,29]. As a result, decision-making is strongly influenced by the subjective perception of time. In intertemporal choices, in which the passage of time is critical to prospect evaluation, one must integrate the subjective perception of time into the dynamics responsible for the hyperbolic or exponential pattern of preferences. Regarding the key elements of the discounted Utility Model, a variety of studies prove the existence of a relationship between subjective perception of time, degree of impatience, and hyperbolic trends. Zauberman et al. [16] proved that the hyperbolic trend of the discount function decreases, considering the impact of subjective perception of time. Next, Nyberg et al. [17] verified that the decrease in impatience is correlated with a nonlinear perception of time. Among the mathematical formalization of the impact that the subjective perception of time has on decision-making, the discount function proposed by [30], named the general hyperbolic function, defines and includes the subjective time duration. The reference to a clear distinction between subjective time and physical time in intertemporal choice has been empirically proven by [31]. The present article, with respect to the cited literature, investigates the subjective perception of time as a physical component of hyperbolic discounting, determining a point of maximum temporal misperception that, to the best of our knowledge, had not yet been identified in the dynamics of decision inconsistency. This result also introduces the need to have to investigate the relationship that exists between impatience, discount rate (both decreasing over time), and temporal misperception since they have a different trends over time. From an operational point of view, the mathematical approach used in this paper is based on a time transformation function, referring to the theory of relativity. Dos Santos and Martinez [32] have already addressed inconsistency as the result of a subjective time dilation perception effect but unlike their study, the present work considers that time perceived by consistent functions is also a "proper time" different from objective time.

From a psychological perspective, the idea of introducing a time transformation to determine a measure of inconsistency that is associated with the subjective perception of time refers to the projection mechanism [18–21]. In practice, to evaluate the usefulness of an alternative available to a prospect, it is necessary to project the choice into the future. Therefore, defining a measure of inconsistency related to the subjective perception of time is equivalent to quantifying an individual's aversion to the uncertainty of the future.

2.2. Aversion to Uncertainty and Inconsistency Function

Temporal inconsistency is the phenomenon whereby preferences vary over time. In practice, if the decision-maker has to choose between a smaller sooner outcome (SS) and a larger later outcome (LL), the choice will depend only on the discount applied. From a theoretical perspective, it is rational to prefer SS or LL, assuming that this preference remains constant over time. Inconsistency is generated when the decision-maker prefers LL at first and SS at a later evaluation time. This mechanism generates an intersection point between the hyperbolic and exponential functions.

Definition 1. *Let $f(t)$ be a hyperbolic discount function. For each indifference pair of the type $(x, 0) \sim_f (y, t), y > x > 0$, the normative function is the exponential discount function $y(t)$ such that $(x, 0) \sim_y (y, t)$.*

Proposition 1. *Let $f(t)$ be a hyperbolic discount function whose indifference $(x, 0) \sim (y, T)$ is fixed. Then, there is a unique normative function.*

Proof. A generical exponential discount function can be expressed as $y(t) = e^{-zt}$, $z \in [0, +\infty)$ because $\forall \delta \epsilon (0,1) \exists! z \in [0, +\infty) : \delta = (1/e)^z$. As z varies in $[0, +\infty)$ there are infinite exponential discount functions. The only exponential normative function that verifies Definition 1 is the one for $z = -(\ln(x/y))/T$. □

Figure 1 shows the relationship between the hyperbolic discount function and the related normative function for a generic indifference pair fixed at the time instant T. We observe that by the continuity property of the preference relation, it is sufficient to fix the initial outcome x to determine for each time instant the unique normative function.

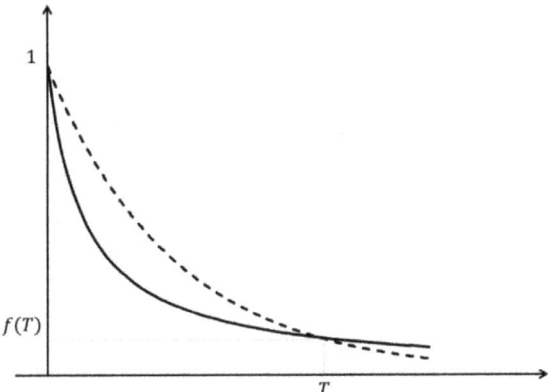

Figure 1. Representation of a hyperbolic discount function and the related empirical function.

Proposition 2. *Let $f(t)$ be an exponential discount function and $y(t)$ the respective exponential normative function then the time perceived by $f(t)$ is shorter than that perceived by $y(t) \forall t \in (0, T)$ and it is longer than that perceived by $(t) \forall t \in (T, +\infty)$.*

Proof. At the instant $t = 0$, $f(t) = y(t) = 1$. The existence of the point T such that $f(T) = y(T)$ and the hyperbolic character of $f(t)$ allows us to state that there exists at least one $R > 0$ in which $f(t)$ has a steeper decrement than $y(t)$ in a neighborhood $I_R(0)$ such that $(t) < y(t) \forall t \in (0, T)$. From the monotony of the discount function $\exists! \tilde{t} < t$ for which $f(\tilde{t}) = y(t)$. Thus, the generic instant t is perceived as if it were an instant closer to the origin, and the time perception of $f(t)$ is contracted with respect to that of $y(t)$. For the interval $(T, +\infty)$, the demonstration is analogous considering that $f(t) > y(t) \forall t \in (T, +\infty)$. □

Proposition 3. *Let $y_1(t)$ and $y_2(t)$ be two exponential normative functions of the hyperbolic discount function $f(t)$ with respect to two indifference pairs $(x_1, 0) \sim_{y_1} (y_1, T_1)$ and $(x_2, 0) \sim_{y_2} (y_2, T_2)$. If*

$$\ln\left(\frac{x_1}{y_1}\right)\Big/T_1 > \ln\left(\frac{x_2}{y_2}\right)\Big/T_2 \tag{1}$$

then the time perceived by $y_1(t)$ is longer than that perceived by $y_2(t)$.

Proof. If (1) then $z_1 < z_2$ and $\delta_1 > \delta_2$. What has been said is equivalent to state that $\forall t \in (0, +\infty), y_1(t) > y_2(t)$. For the monotony of the discount function exists a point $\tilde{t} < t$ such that $y_1(t) = y_2(\tilde{t})$. The thesis follows as in Proposition 2. □

Definition 2. Let $f(t)$ and $y(t)$ be a hyperbolic discount function and the respective exponential normative function. The time function between $f(t)$ and $y(t)$ is the function defined as:

$$\tilde{t}: [0,+\infty) \to [0,+\infty)$$
$$t \to \tilde{t}(t) = \tilde{t} \tag{2}$$

Proposition 4. Let $f(t)$ and $y(t)$ be a hyperbolic discount function and the respective exponential normative function, then $f(\tilde{t}(t)) = y(t)$ $\forall t \in (0,+\infty)$.

Proof. Follows by Proposition 2. □

Figure 2 highlights the contraction mechanism described by the function $\tilde{t}(t)$.

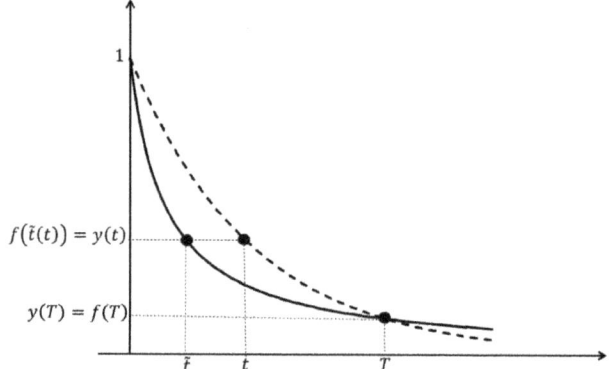

Figure 2. Correspondence between the function $\tilde{t}(t)$ and the time scanned by exponential discounting.

Proposition 5. Let $y_1(t)$ and $y_2(t)$ be two exponential normative functions of the hyperbolic discount function $f(t)$ respect to $(x_1, 0) \sim_{y_1} (y_1, t_1)$ and $(x_2, 0) \sim_{y_2} (y_2, t_2)$ then $\forall t \in (0,+\infty)$ $t - \tilde{t}_1(t) < t - \tilde{t}_2(t) \Leftrightarrow y_1(t) - f(t) < y_2(t) - f(t)$.

Proof. $\Leftarrow$ By hypothesis $y_1(t) < y_2(t)$. Let $\tilde{t}_1(t)$ and $\tilde{t}_2(t)$ be the time functions of $f(t)$ with respect to $y_1(t)$ and $y_2(t)$, respectively. $\forall t \in (0,+\infty) y_1(t) = f(\tilde{t}_1(t)) < f(\tilde{t}_2(t)) = y_2(t)$. For the monotony of $f(t) \tilde{t}_1(t) > \tilde{t}_2(t)$ and follows the thesis.
$\Longrightarrow$ By hypothesis $\tilde{t}_1(t) > \tilde{t}_2(t)$. The thesis follows from the monotony of $f(t)$. □

Definition 3. Let $f(t)$ and $y(t)$ be a hyperbolic discount function and the respective exponential normative function. The time misperception function $d_{\tilde{t}}$ and the empirical inconsistency function d_y are defined as:

$$d_{\tilde{t}}: [0,+\infty) \to \mathbb{R}$$
$$t \to t - \tilde{t} \tag{3}$$

$$d_y: [0,+\infty) \to \mathbb{R}$$
$$t \to y(t) - f(t) \tag{4}$$

Theorem 1. *Existence of maximum empirical inconsistency.* Let $f(t)$ and $y(t)$ be a hyperbolic discount function and the respective exponential normative function then $d_y(t)$ admits at least one point of maximum in the interval $[0, T)$.

Proof. By construction $d_y(0) = f(0) - y(0) = 0$ and $d_y(T) = y(T) - f(T) = 0$. As discussed in Proposition 2, $(t) < y(t) \forall t \in (0, T)$. It follows that $d_y(t)$ is a continuous and positive function in the interval $(0, T)$. The thesis follows by considering that

$$\lim_{t \to 0} d_y(t) = \lim_{t \to T} d_y(t) = 0 \tag{5}$$

and $d_y(t) > 0$ in $(0, T)$. □

Theorem 2. *Uniqueness of maximum empirical inconsistency. Let $f(t)$ and $y(t)$ be a hyperbolic discount function and the respective exponential normative function then $d_y(t)$ admits a unique point of maximum in the interval $[0, T)$.*

Proof. Absurdly $\dddot{t}_1$ and $\dddot{t}_2$ are two points of maximum for the function $d_y(t)$ and without loss of generality $\dddot{t}_1 < \dddot{t}_2$. By continuity of the function $d_y(t)$, there exists a point $\hat{t} : \dddot{t}_1 < \hat{t} < \dddot{t}_2$ in which $d_y(t)$ reaches a minimum value. Then, we obtained that $y'(t) > f'(t) \forall t \in (0, \dddot{t}_1)$, $y'(t) < f'(t) \forall t \in (\dddot{t}_1, \hat{t})$ and $y'(t) > f'(t) \forall t \in (\hat{t}, \dddot{t}_2)$. The above contradicts the nature of the discount functions considered. □

This paper does not discuss the case of the interval $[T, +\infty)$. Thus, although the properties of the discount function ensure the existence of a unique minimum m, it is not formalized.

Proposition 6. *Characterization of maximum empirical inconsistency. Let $f(t)$ and $y(t)$ be a hyperbolic discount function and the respective exponential normative function and let $\dddot{t} \in [0, T)$ the maximum point for $d_y(t)$. Denoted by $\rho_f = -f\prime(t)/f(t)$ and $\rho_y = -y\prime(t)/y(t)$ the discount rates of $f(t)$ and $y(t)$ then $\exists! \hat{t} : \dddot{t} < \hat{t} < T$ for which $\rho_f(t) > \rho_y(t) \forall t \in (0, \hat{t})$ and $\rho_f(t) < \rho_y(t) \forall t \in (\hat{t}, +\infty)$.*

Proof. By hypothesis $\dddot{t}$ is the point of maximum for $d_y(t)$, i.e., $\frac{d}{dt}(y(t) - f(t))_{t=\dddot{t}} = 0$. It follows that $y'(\dddot{t}) - f'(\dddot{t}) = 0$. Since Proposition 2 and from the monotony of $y'(t)$ and $f'(t)$ follows that $y'(t) - f'(t) > 0 \forall t \in (0, \dddot{t})$. In the interval $(0, \dddot{t})$, $y'(t) > f\prime(t)$ implies $-y\prime(t) < -f\prime(t)$ and considering that $d_y(t) > 0$ in $(0, T)$ follows:

$$\rho_f(t) = -\frac{f'(t)}{f(t)} > -\frac{y'(t)}{y(t)} = \rho_y(t) \tag{6}$$

By Theorem 2, $\prime(t) - f\prime(t) < 0 \forall t \in (\dddot{t}, m)$, with m the point of minimum of $d_y(t)$. Since $m > T$ then $\prime(t) - f\prime(t) < 0 \forall t \in (\dddot{t}, T]$, i.e., $y'(T) < f'(T)$. At the T-point, $f(T) = y(T)$:

$$\rho_f(T) = -\frac{f'(T)}{f(T)} < -\frac{y'(T)}{y(T)} = \rho_y(T) \tag{7}$$

Then, there exists a point $\hat{t} > \dddot{t}$ such that $\rho_f(\hat{t}) = \rho_y(\hat{t})$. The thesis follows considering that $\rho_y(t)$ is constant and $\rho_f(t)$ decreases. □

Proposition 7. *Let $f(t)$ and $y(t)$ be a hyperbolic discount function and the respective exponential normative function. The time misperception function $d_{\tilde{t}}$ increases (decreases) $\iff$ empirical inconsistency function d_y increases (decreases).*

Corollary 1. *Let $f(t)$ and $y(t)$ be a hyperbolic discount function and the respective exponential normative function then $\dddot{t} \in [0, +\infty)$ is a maximum (or minimum) point for $d_{\tilde{t}}(t) \iff \dddot{t} \in [0, +\infty)$ is a maximum (or minimum) point for $d_y(t)$.*

Corollary 2. *Let $f(t)$ and $y(t)$ be a hyperbolic discount function and the respective exponential normative function then the time misperception function $d_{\tilde{t}}$ admits a unique point of maximum.*

Proof. Follows by Theorem 1 and Theorem 2 and Corollary 1. □

Theorem 3. *Relationship between uncertainty and impatience. Let $f(t)$ and $y(t)$ be a hyperbolic discount function and the respective exponential normative function. Let $\dddot{t}$ be the point in which the time misperception function $d_{\tilde{t}}$ reaches the maximum value then $I_{f[t_i,t_j]} > I_{y[t_i,t_j]} \forall t \in [t_i,t_j] \subseteq [0,\dddot{t})$ and $I_{f[t_i,t_j]} < I_{y[t_i,t_j]} \forall t \in [t_i,t_j] \subseteq (\dddot{t},+\infty)$.*

Proof. By Proposition 6, $\forall t \in (0, \dddot{t})$ it is possible to state that $f'(t) < y\prime(t)$. Let $t_i < \dddot{t}$ and $h > 0$ be such that $t_i + h = t_j < \dddot{t}$, then

$$f'(t) = \lim_{h \to 0} \frac{f(t_i+h) - f(t_i)}{h} < \lim_{h \to 0} \frac{y(t_i+h) - y(t_i)}{h} = y\prime(t) \tag{8}$$

$$\frac{f(t_i) - f(t_i+h)}{f(t_i)} > \frac{f(t_i) - f(t_i+h)}{y(t_i)} > \frac{y(t_i) - y(t_i+h)}{y(t_i)} \tag{9}$$

$$I_{f[t_i,t_j]} = 1 - \frac{f(t_i+h)}{f(t_i)} > 1 - \frac{y(t_i+h)}{y(t_i)} = I_{y[t_i,t_j]} \tag{10}$$

The thesis follows from the assumption that $f'(\dddot{t}) = y\prime(\dddot{t})$, and $\lim_{t_i \to +\infty} I_{f[t_i,t_j]} = 0$. □

3. Materials and Methods

Among the results proved in Section 2.2, the experimental phase refers in particular to the following objectives: to find the expression of the best empirical exponential function starting from a fixed initial outcome x, to analyze the correspondence between $d_{\tilde{t}}$ and d_y function and their respective maximum points, to describe the variation of the sample's uncertainty aversion, and to analyze the impatience trend of the hyperbolic discount function versus the exponential discount function. The questionnaire was implemented with the creation of a web application, made available and freely accessible by all Italian individuals. In fact, the test was designed entirely in Italian and voluntarily submitted only to Italian individuals to avoid the influence of cultural differences. The responses were stored in a database and processed for data analysis using Python and Excel. When uploading the link, the respondent had to indicate age and gender. Table 2 shows the distribution of the sample with a total of 50 individuals with respect to the characteristics considered.

Table 2. Distribution of the sample with respect to age and gender.

Characteristic	Categories	Percentage
Sex	Male	59.09%
	Female	40.91%
Age	20–34	63.67%
	35–49	33.23%
	50–64	9.10%

The distribution of collected data is uneven with respect to age, probably due to the type of experimentation adopted (using a web app might be difficult or boring to an over-50 person). The distribution with respect to gender is uniform, but this article is not devoted to behavioral differences in the decision-making context between the two genders. This observation could be an additional line of development for the present research. After entering the characteristics shown in Table 2, the experiment includes an "INSTRUCTIONS" section, in which the response mode and the existence of time are briefly introduced. The questionnaire consists of two questions that alternate with each other: the first question is used to collect the values needed to construct the empirical discount function using the interpolation technique; the second question is used to elicit a sense of confusion. The first question answers the following:

"You have to receive $U(x(t_i))$ euros in t_i days, how much do you want to receive in t_{i+1} days to consider the offer equivalent?"

The second question, used as distraction, is like the previous one but leaves the figure constant over time as follows:

"You have to receive 100 euros today, how much do you want to receive in t_i days to consider the offer equivalent?"

In this way, it will be more difficult for respondents to keep track of the figures they write previously in response to the first question. Individuals undergoing the experimental phase did not actually receive the proposed figures but were asked to respond hypothetically. In this regard, from an experimental point of view [33] proves that decision-making processes may vary whether the money figures are real or hypothetical. However, because the application of the present article is especially directed toward empirical testing of theoretically proven results, it is not interested in investigating the influence of decision context in the proposed inconsistency measure, although this may be a future avenue of research. The initial outcome has been set as $U(x(0)) = $ €100, a moderate amount to enable individuals of all ages to realize the hypothesis in a practical way. For each question, the maximum time to answer was set at 20 s, and the countdown was constantly visible in a square placed below the question. In this way, each respondent had a constant perception of the limited passage of time. This dynamic was designed to elicit haste and agitation from each respondent. At the end of the countdown, if the question had not yet been submitted, the statement.

"Time's up! The time available to answer the question has expired. Please answer the question IMMEDIATELY without further thought."

Would appear on the website. The introductory display also points out that if the time expires more than 10 times, the sample analyzed will be disregarded. Fortunately, all individuals who participated fell within the imposed limit of 10 countdown deadlines.

The time instants for defining indifference pairs are $t = $ 0, 2, 4, 7, 10, 14, 20, 30, 45, 60, 90. The choice of heterogeneous intervals is related to the need to preserve homogeneity in the perception of the future (for example, the interval [4, 6] is perceived equivalently to the interval [4, 7] but the interval [6, 10] is not perceived as the interval [10, 14]).

The discount function was obtained by interpolating the median values of individual participants as:

$$f(t) = \begin{cases} f(0) = 1 \\ f(t_{i+1}) = \frac{f(t_i)*U(x(t_i))}{U(x(t_{i+1}))} \end{cases} \quad (11)$$

The choice of median depends on the high variability of the results obtained at the end of the interviews (e.g., $f(20) \in [0.000067; 33.33]$).

4. Results

Figure 3 represents the obtained discount function, in which a steeper initial discount, characteristic of the empirical evidence and hyperbolic discounting, is shown.

To determine the normative exponential function, instead of fixing a priori a point T needed for definition, the best exponential approximation of the empirical curve was evaluated with Excel, obtaining $T = 60$. Any other point chosen would still have defined a single normative exponential function, but this strategy minimizes the maximum discrepancy between the exponential and hyperbolic trends. The normative exponential function occurs for $z = 0.045$ and its trend is shown in Figure 4.

The function, representing the discrepancy between exponential preferences and hyperbolic trends, was calculated as in Definition 3. The graph is shown in Figure 5.

To check the correspondence between the point at which the maximum discrepancy occurs and the point at which the maximum contraction to the future occurs, identified by the point at which the maximum of the temporal misperception function occurs, the function $d_{\tilde{t}}(t)$ was calculated. The graph is shown in Figure 6.

For the construction of the graph of $d_{\tilde{t}}(t)$, it was assumed that the time perceived by the sample is that associated with the hyperbolic curve. Therefore, the time of the exponential discount function was calculated by the inverse formula:

$$\tilde{t}^{-1}(t) = -\frac{\ln(f(t))}{0.045} \qquad (12)$$

It is possible to observe that the point at which the functions $d_{\tilde{t}}(t)$ and $d_y(t)$ reach the maximum value is for both functions $t = 10$. The importance of $t = 10$ is also evident in Table 3, which confirms the result proved in Theorem 3. In fact, $I_{f[t_i,t_j]} > I_{y[t_i,t_j]}$ before the point $t = 10$ and then the situation changes. This result is an empirical evidence of the relationship between the quantities used so far to describe inconsistency and the measure proposed by this paper. In addition, this result confirms that individuals who apply hyperbolic discounting exhibit greater impatience in periods closer to the present than those who apply exponential discounting.

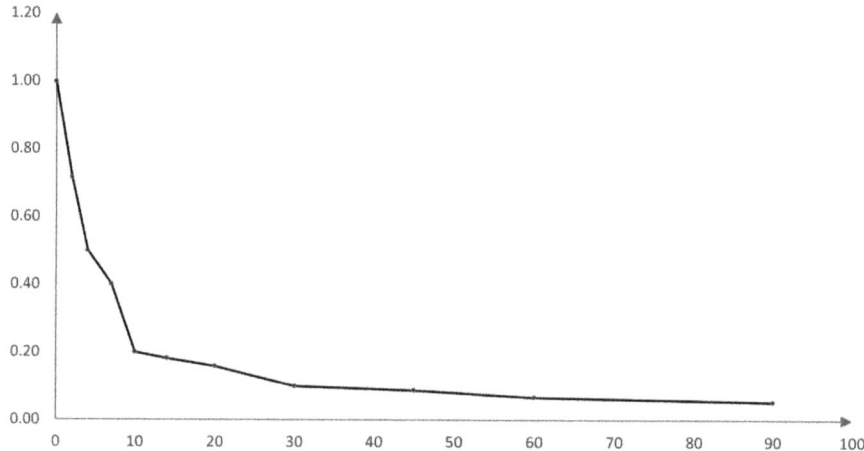

Figure 3. Discount function obtained from interview collection.

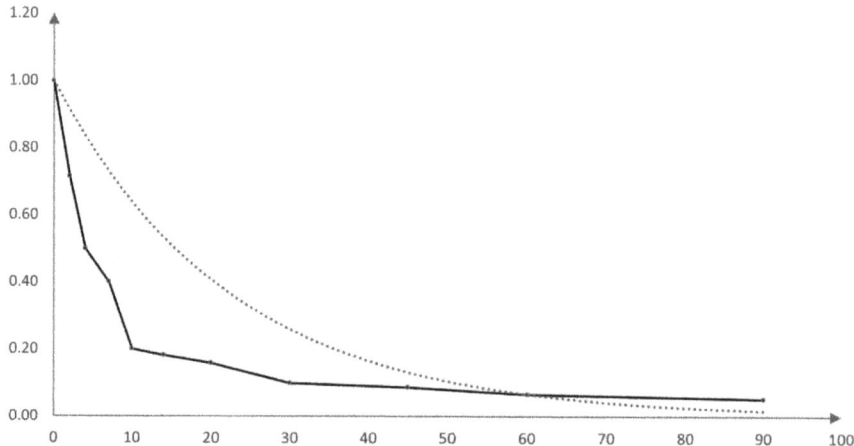

Figure 4. Empirical and normative functions.

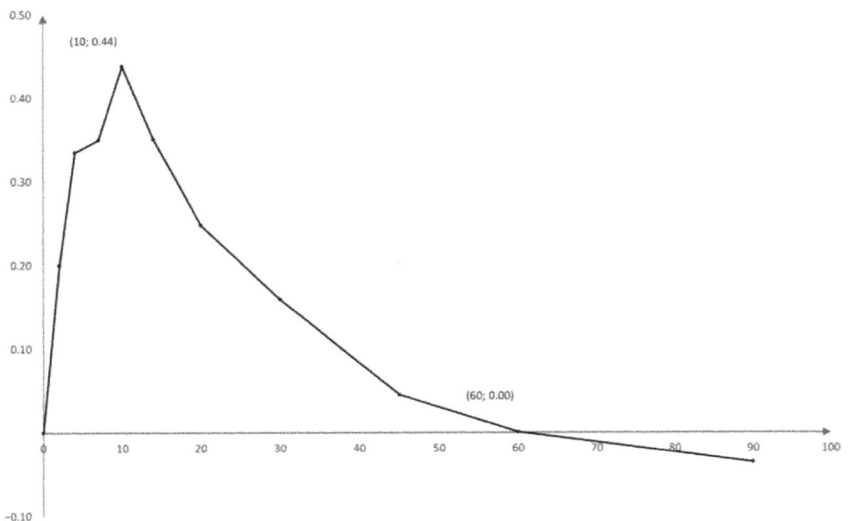

Figure 5. Graph of $d_y(t)$.

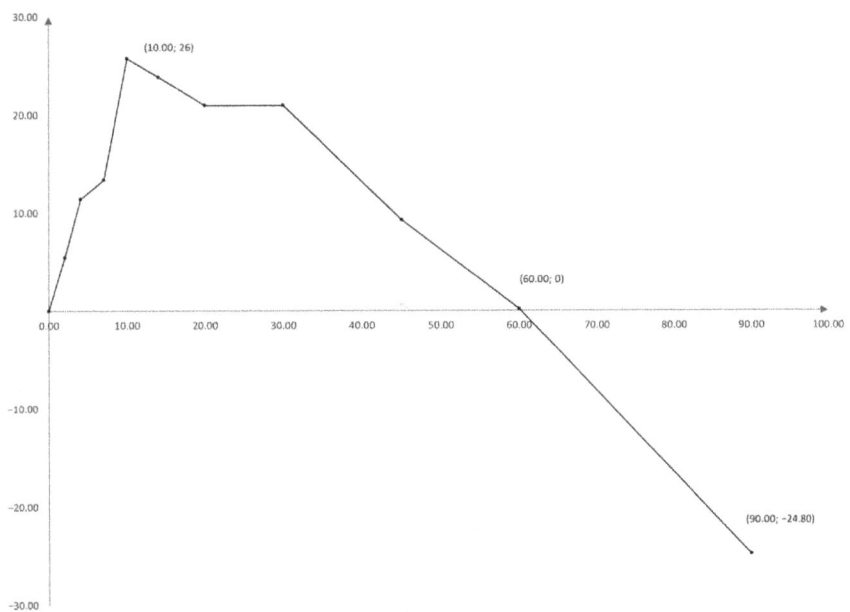

Figure 6. Graph of $d_{\bar{i}}(t)$.

Table 3. $I_{f[t_i,t_j]}$ and $I_{y[t_i,t_j]}$ for [0, 10] and [10, 90].

$I_{f[0, 10]}$	$I_{y[0, 10]}$	$I_{f[10, 90]}$	$I_{y[10,90]}$
0.80	0.36	0.73	0.97

5. Discussion

Intertemporal choices have a great influence on everyday life [34]. The discrepancy between the normative model and empirical evidence has motivated researchers to investigate the dynamics of decision-making when alternatives distributed over multiple periods are evaluated. The mechanisms of hyperbolic discounting, a reflection of the human rationality of the decision-maker, have so far been described through the discount factor and the degree of impatience.

This paper deepens the characteristics of hyperbolic discounting by adding a third element to the study of preference trends: time perception. The idea behind the definitions presented in Section 2.2 is to shift the problem of time inconsistency, a phenomenon associated with hyperbolic discount function performance, from curve performance to time perception. The transformation defined in Definition 2 made it possible to derive a new characteristic of hyperbolic discounting. In fact, although the two functions coincide punctually (Proposition 4), the discrepancy between hyperbolic and exponential preferences increases to a point of maximum. The existence of a maximum point is a feature not associated with either the degree of impatience or the discount rate, both of which assume a decreasing trend over time. The correspondence between the trend of the functions, proven in Corollary 1, justifies the idea of considering a psychological relationship between the two maximum points. In this regard, the present work addresses the mechanism of projection into the future that occurs when an intertemporal prospect is evaluated. The temporal contraction of perceived time invokes a dynamic of contraction that the individual feels with respect to the future. The aversion the decision-maker feels with respect to the future increases over time because it is more distant and because it is more difficult to imagine [35]. The existence of the maximum is when the individual becomes emotionally disinterested in a scenario that she cannot yet perceive (as if it were a future too far in the future to feel concerned and to imagine its projection sharply). Therefore, the degree of uncertainty aversion begins to decrease, and so the discrepancy between the hyperbolic and exponential functions does the same. The dynamic described is equivalent to saying that the decision-maker is more uncertainty averse, for example, to a future that is 10 days away, rather than 5 years away. Again, cognitive limitations and the emotional factor of the decision-maker are responsible for what is observed. The relationships tested with respect to the discount factor and impatience (Proposition 6 and Theorem 3) show that they are all distinct objects expressing three different dynamics: the discount factor expresses how much one prefers an event to happen, impatience expresses how much one prefers an event to happen sooner, and uncertainty aversion expresses how close one perceives the future to be.

The experimental phase empirically confirmed the results proven in Section 2. With respect to the implementation of the experiment, it is possible to observe how simple the construction of the proposed measure is. In fact, once the discount function is obtained through the interpolation technique, the construction of the best exponential function that approximates it is imminent even using simple Excel spreadsheets. Therefore, the proposed inconsistency measure lends itself to a very wide audience of researchers, who can investigate the dynamics of decision-making in intertemporal choices by varying the time instants considered, the lengths of the intervals, the initial digit, and so on, without necessarily making use of advanced implementation techniques. So far, the calculation of the degree of inconsistency of a discount function has always been a much-discussed problem, especially since [7] formalized the measure of the degree of decrease in impatience, defined as $DI(t) = -\frac{\ln(f(t))''}{\ln f(t)'}$. The proposed measure, in fact, is very difficult to calculate from an empirical point of view since it requires the calculation of the first and second derivatives of the logarithm. Subsequently, the following works deepened the tool proposed by [7] by improving its quantitative aspect: [36], through the introduction of time trade-off curves, generally simplified both qualitative and quantitative analysis of inconsistency; [37], on the other hand, formalized the concept of hyperbolic factor that provides the degree of decrease in impatience fixed an indifference pair.

The measure formalized in the present paper does not replace those mentioned but complements them because it conceptually differs from the psychological mechanisms incorporated in the concept of decreasing impatience, but still turns out to be a description of it, as proved in Theorem 3. Particularly important is the correspondence between Figures 5 and 6 and Table 3, in which the point $t = 10$ is critical. What has been observed should not be surprising considering that the same measure defined by Prelec, can be described as $DI(t) = -\ln(\rho(t))$. The expression is equivalent to saying that the rate at which the discount rate varies is related to the degree to which impatience decreases, and the way in which the discount rate varies, by definition, quantifies how the individual's perception of the indeterminacy of time changes. In conclusion, the novelty of the measure of inconsistency proposed by the present paper lies in being characterized by a maximum point that represents the boundary between the emotional drive and the detachment from it of the decision-maker.

6. Conclusions

This article refers to the investigation of the discrepancy between normative models and empirical evidence in the context of intertemporal choices. The characteristics of hyperbolic discounting, starting from inconsistency, were explored through the concept of subjective perception of time. A dynamic related to how the decision-maker perceives the remoteness of the future was quantified. This mechanism generates a contraction with respect to the time frames involved in the intertemporal prospect and contributes to the hyperbolic preference trend. An experimental phase empirically confirmed the proven results. The research conducted aims at three key concepts: anomaly, normalization, and personalization.

The term anomaly denotes those phenomena that are difficult to rationalize from a theoretical point of view. The anomalies of the Discounted Utility Model [38,39] are described by a hyperbolic trend of the discount function. The goal is the full description of the anomalies through a combination of the quantities mentioned throughout the paper (impatience, discount rate, uncertainty, and subjective time).

Quantifying the gap between the normative model and the empirical evidence allows the normalization of anomalous attitudes, defining the extent to which the decision-maker's bounded rationality respects economic rationality, also overcoming from a formal point of view the concept of non-rationality. These first two key concepts are unified in personalization: after understanding and quantifying non-rational preferences, these measures can be used to define classes of investors. The need to introduce personalized strategies is known from the work of Pompian [13,14] and Thaler [12]: the former refers to personalization by behavioral attitudes; the latter discusses systematic cognitive alterations in decision-making and projects them into a strategic architecture. In addition, the planning ability of individuals is not common to all decision-makers but is related to cognitive ability [26] and is critical to reducing the effects of myopic behavior in the future [27]. Therefore, quantifying the elements of the hyperbolic discount, which represents the expression of the individual's decision-making process, is a method for calibrating the personalized approach.

The need to concretize these tools responds to the Markets in Financial Instruments Directive, 2014/65/UE (MiFID2) which emphasizes the need to consider the client's needs, but also her behavioral attitudes with respect to available alternatives. Specifically, MiFID 2 can be seen as a tool to protect savers by requiring client assessment mechanisms. The main goal is to achieve a maximum fit between the individual's profile and the products offered. In assessing suitability, customer profiling addresses both objective and subjective characteristics of the individual: objective characteristics include, for example, criteria such as investment objectives, duration of service, and associated risks; subjective characteristics, on the other hand, are all behavioral and individual aspects of the customer such as risk tolerance, knowledge needed to understand portfolio assets, and financial situation. Only by increasing the details that describe the client's profile, recommendable financial instruments can be determined.

The measure proposed in the present paper refers to the subjective aspect of customer traits. First, quantifying the impact that subjective time has on intertemporal preferences can help investigate investor attitudes toward debt and investment dynamics [40], through the anomalies of the intertemporal choices [38,39]. The above could provide an additional criterion, in addition to personality traits [41,42], for the classification required by MiFID 2. With respect to the emotional sphere, on the other hand, the proposed measure of inconsistency, because it expresses the subjective perception of time, is linked related to emotional factors that interact with decision-making [43,44] and can help investigate the relationship between investor sentiment and financial activity [45]. For example, assuming risk as a feeling [46], assessing the influence of subjective time in the description of decision inconsistency can improve the description of risk aversion and perception of risk [47–49], elements on which MiFID 2 places so much emphasis on when designing customized plans. The transition between measurement and individualized plan design can be guided using decision support techniques, such as multicriteria methods [50,51].

From a conceptual point of view, one possible development of this paper is the introduction of another concept fundamental for calibrating strategies, financial inertia [52]. Inertia in finance, as in physics, is the force by which a body, in this case the investor, opposes a change in its motion. In this sense, inertia, as a force, helps delineate the geometric properties of the curve associated with the discount function. Finally, in addition to extending the formalization to the other anomalies of the Discounted Utility Model [38,39], it would be interesting to discuss the measure in a continuous, not discrete set of definitions. For although intertemporal choice is determined by precise instants of time, the concept of uncertainty aversion is continuous over time, and its extension in this sense could enhance its descriptive capabilities of the psychological mechanisms responsible.

Author Contributions: All authors contributed equally to this work. All authors have read and agreed to the published version of the manuscript.

Funding: This research received no external funding.

Institutional Review Board Statement: Not applicable.

Informed Consent Statement: Informed consent was obtained from all subjects involved in the study.

Data Availability Statement: Not applicable.

Conflicts of Interest: The authors declare no conflict of interest.

References

1. Anderson, E.W.; Ghysels, E.; Juergens, J.L. The impact of risk and uncertainty on expected returns. *J. Financ. Econ.* **2009**, *94*, 233–263. [CrossRef]
2. Noor, J. Intertemporal choice and the magnitude effect. *Games Econ. Behav.* **2011**, *72*, 255–270. [CrossRef]
3. Sayman, S.; Öncüler, A. An investigation of time inconsistency. *Manag. Sci.* **2009**, *55*, 470–482. [CrossRef]
4. Samuelson, P.A. A note on measurement of utility. *Rev. Econ. Stud.* **1937**, *4*, 155–161. [CrossRef]
5. Samuelson, P.A. Probability, utility, and the independence axiom. *Econom. J. Econom. Soc.* **1952**, *20*, 670–678. [CrossRef]
6. Cruz Rambaud, S.; Muñoz Torrecillas, M.J. Measuring impatience in intertemporal choice. *PLoS ONE* **2016**, *11*, e0149256. [CrossRef]
7. Prelec, D. Decreasing impatience: A criterion for Non-stationary time preference and "hyperbolic" discounting. *Scand. J. Econ.* **2004**, *106*, 511–532. [CrossRef]
8. Read, D. *Blackwell Handbook of Judgment and Decision Making*; John Wiley & Sons: Hoboken, NJ, USA, 2008; pp. 424–443.
9. Simon, H.A. *Models of Man, Social and Rational: Mathematical Essays on Rational Human Behavior in Society Setting*; Wiley: New York, NY, USA, 1957.
10. Kahneman, D. *Thinking, Fast and Slow*; Farrar, Straus and Giroux: New York, NY, USA, 2011.
11. Kahneman, D.; Tversky, A. Prospect theory: An analysis of decision under risk. In *Handbook of the Fundamentals of Financial Decision Making: Part I*; World Scientific: Singapore, 2013; pp. 99–127.
12. Thaler, R.H.; Sunstein, C.R. *Nudge: Improving Decisions about Health, Wealth, and Happiness*; Reviewed and Expanded Edition; Penguin Books: New York, NY, USA, 2009.
13. Pompian, M.M. Using behavioral investor types to build better relationships with your clients. *J. Financ. Plan.* **2008**, *21*, 64–76.
14. Pompian, M.M. *Behavioral Finance and Investor Types: Managing Behavior to Make Better Investment Decisions*; John Wiley & Sons: Hoboken, NJ, USA, 2012.
15. Agostino, C.S.; Claessens, P.M.E.; Balci, F.; Zana, Y. The role of time estimation in decreased impatience in intertemporal choice. *J. Neurosci. Psychol. Econ.* **2021**, *14*, 185. [CrossRef]

16. Zauberman, G.; Kim, B.K.; Malkoc, S.A.; Bettman, J.R. Discounting time and time discounting: Subjective time perception and intertemporal preferences. *J. Mark. Res.* **2009**, *46*, 543–556. [CrossRef]
17. Nyberg, L.; Kim, A.S.N.; Habib, R.; Levine, B.; Tulving, E. Consciousness of subjective time in the brain. *Proc. Natl. Acad. Sci. USA* **2010**, *107*, 22356–22359. [CrossRef] [PubMed]
18. Loewenstein, G. Out of control: Visceral influences on behavior. *Organ. Behav. Hum. Decis. Process.* **1996**, *65*, 272–292. [CrossRef]
19. Loewenstein, G.; O'Donoghue, T.; Rabin, M. Projection bias in predicting future utility. *Q. J. Econ.* **2003**, *118*, 1209–1248. [CrossRef]
20. Loewenstein, G.; Prelec, D.; Shatto, C. *Hot/Cold Intrapersonal Empathy Gaps and the under-Prediction of Curiosity*. Unpublished Manuscript; Carnegie-Mellon University: Pittsburgh, PA, USA, 1998.
21. Wheeler, M.A.; Stuss, D.T.; Tulving, E. Toward a theory of episodic memory: The frontal lobes and autonoetic consciousness. *Psychol. Bull.* **1997**, *121*, 331. [CrossRef] [PubMed]
22. Zimbardo, P.; Boyd, J. *The Time Paradox: The New Psychology of Time that Will Change Your Life*; Simon and Schuster: New York, NY, USA, 2008.
23. Ventre, V.; Rambaud, S.C.; Martino, R.; Maturo, F. An analysis of intertemporal inconsistency through the hyperbolic factor. *Qual. Quant.* **2022**, 1–28. [CrossRef]
24. Gifford, S. Risk and uncertainty. In *Handbook of Entrepreneurship Research*; Springer: Boston, MA, USA, 2003; pp. 37–53.
25. LeRoy, S.F.; Werner, J. *Principles of Financial Economics*; Cambridge University Press: Cambridge, MA, USA, 2014.
26. Da Silva, S.; De Faveri, D.; Correa, A.; Matsushita, R. High-income consumers may be less hyperbolic when discounting the future. *Economics Bulletin* **2017**, *37*, 1421–1434.
27. Laibson, D. Golden eggs and hyperbolic discounting. *Q. J. Econ.* **1997**, *112*, 443–478. [CrossRef]
28. Green, L.; Myerson, J.; McFadden, E. Rate of temporal discounting decreases with amount of reward. *Mem. Cogn.* **1997**, *25*, 715–723. [CrossRef]
29. Shipp, A.J.; Edwards, J.R.; Lambert, L.S. Conceptualization and measurement of temporal focus: The subjective experience of the past, present, and future. *Organ. Behav. Hum. Decis. Processes* **2009**, *110*, 1–22. [CrossRef]
30. Takahashi, T. Loss of self-control in intertemporal choice may be attributable to logarithmic time-perception. In *Behavioral Economics of Preferences, Choices, and Happiness*. *Med. Hypotheses* **2005**, *65*, 691–693. [CrossRef]
31. Han, R.; Takahashi, T. Psychophysics of time perception and valuation in temporal discounting of gain and loss. *Phys. A Stat. Mech. Its Appl.* **2012**, *391*, 6568–6576. [CrossRef]
32. Dos Santos, L.S.; Martinez, A.S. Inconsistency and subjective time dilation perception in intertemporal decision making. *Front. Appl. Math. Stat.* **2018**, *4*, 54. [CrossRef]
33. Xu, S.; Xiao, Z.; Rao, H. Hypothetical versus real monetary reward decrease the behavioral and affective effects in the Balloon Analogue Risk Task. *Exp. Psychol.* **2019**, *66*, a000447. [CrossRef] [PubMed]
34. Lu, Y.; Yang, C. Measuring impatience: Experiments of intertemporal choices. In *Education Management and Management Science*; CRC Press: Boca Raton, FL, USA, 2015; pp. 311–314.
35. Gilbert, D.T.; Gill, M.J.; Wilson, T.D. The future is now: Temporal correction in affective forecasting. *Organ. Behav. Hum. Decis. Processes* **2002**, *88*, 430–444. [CrossRef]
36. Attema, A.E.; Bleichrodt, H.; Rohde, K.I.; Wakker, P.P. Time-tradeoff sequences for analyzing discounting and time inconsistency. *Manag. Sci.* **2010**, *56*, 2015–2030. [CrossRef]
37. Rohde, K.I. The hyperbolic factor: A measure of time inconsistency. *J. Risk Uncertain.* **2010**, *41*, 125–140. [CrossRef]
38. Loewenstein, G.; Thaler, R.H. Anomalies: Intertemporal choice. *J. Econ. Perspect.* **1989**, *3*, 181–193. [CrossRef]
39. Loewenstein, G.; Prelec, D. Anomalies in intertemporal choice: Evidence and an interpretation. *Q. J. Econ.* **1992**, *107*, 573–597. [CrossRef]
40. Hoang, E.C.; Hoxha, I. Corporate payout smoothing: A variance decomposition approach. *J. Empir. Financ.* **2016**, *35*, 1–13. [CrossRef]
41. Conlin, A.; Kyröläinen, P.; Kaakinen, M.; Järvelin, M.R.; Perttunen, J.; Svento, R. Personality traits and stock market participation. *J. Empir. Financ.* **2015**, *33*, 34–50. [CrossRef]
42. Tauni, M.Z.; Fang, H.X.; Yousaf, S. The influence of investor personality traits on information acquisition and trading behavior: Evidence from Chinese futures exchange. *Personal. Individ. Differ.* **2015**, *87*, 248–255. [CrossRef]
43. McLoughlin, A. Factors Affecting Human Time Perception: Do Feelings of Rejection Increase the Rate of Subjective Timing? *Timing Time Percept.* **2019**, *7*, 131–147. [CrossRef]
44. Droit-Volet, S.; Meck, W.H. How emotions colour our perception of time. *Trends Cogn. Sci.* **2007**, *11*, 504–513. [CrossRef]
45. Schmeling, M. Investor sentiment and stock returns: Some international evidence. *J. Empir. Financ.* **2009**, *16*, 394–408. [CrossRef]
46. Loewenstein, G.F.; Weber, E.U.; Hsee, C.K.; Welch, N. Risk as feelings. *Psychol. Bull.* **2001**, *127*, 267. [CrossRef] [PubMed]
47. Wang, M.; Keller, C.; Siegrist, M. The less You know, the more You are afraid of—A survey on risk perceptions of investment products. *J. Behav. Financ.* **2011**, *12*, 9–19. [CrossRef]
48. Broihanne, M.H.; Merli, M.; Roger, P. Overconfidence, risk perception and the risk-taking behavior of finance professionals. *Financ. Res. Lett.* **2014**, *11*, 64–73. [CrossRef]
49. Sun, Y.; Li, S. The effect of risk on intertemporal choice. *J. Risk Res.* **2010**, *13*, 805–820. [CrossRef]
50. Toloie-Eshlaghy, A.; Homayonfar, M. MCDM methodologies and applications: A literature review from 1999 to 2009. *Res. J. Int. Stud.* **2011**, *21*, 86–137.

51. Saaty, T.L. Decision making—The analytic hierarchy and network processes (AHP/ANP). *J. Syst. Sci. Syst. Eng.* **2004**, *13*, 1–35. [CrossRef]
52. Gal, D. A psychological law of inertia and the illusion of loss aversion. *Judgm. Decis. Mak.* **2006**, *1*, 23–32.

 mathematics

Article

Some Examples of BL-Algebras Using Commutative Rings

Cristina Flaut [1,*] and Dana Piciu [2]

[1] Faculty of Mathematics and Computer Science, Ovidius University, Bd. Mamaia 124, 900527 Constanța, Romania
[2] Faculty of Science, University of Craiova, A.I. Cuza Street, 13, 200585 Craiova, Romania
* Correspondence: cflaut@univ-ovidius.ro or cristina_flaut@yahoo.com

Abstract: BL-algebras are algebraic structures corresponding to Hajek's basic fuzzy logic. The aim of this paper is to analyze the structure of BL-algebras using commutative rings. Due to computational considerations, we are interested in the finite case. We present new ways to generate finite BL-algebras using commutative rings and provide summarizing statistics. Furthermore, we investigated BL-rings, i.e., commutative rings whose the lattice of ideals can be equipped with a structure of BL-algebra. A new characterization for these rings and their connections to other classes of rings is established. Furthermore, we give examples of finite BL-rings for which the lattice of ideals is not an MV-algebra and, using these rings, we construct BL-algebras with $2^r + 1$ elements, $r \geq 2$, and BL-chains with k elements, $k \geq 4$. In addition, we provide an explicit construction of isomorphism classes of BL-algebras of small n size $(2 \leq n \leq 5)$.

Keywords: commutative ring; BL-ring; ideal; residuated lattice; MV-algebra; BL-algebra

MSC: 03G10; 03G25; 06A06; 06D05; 08C05; 06F35

Citation: Flaut, C.; Piciu, D. Some Examples of BL-Algebras Using Commutative Rings. *Mathematics* 2022, 10, 4739. https://doi.org/10.3390/math10244739

Academic Editors: Irina Cristea, Yuriy Rogovchenko, Justo Puerto, Gintautas Dzemyda and Patrick Siarry

Received: 11 November 2022
Accepted: 3 December 2022
Published: 13 December 2022

Publisher's Note: MDPI stays neutral with regard to jurisdictional claims in published maps and institutional affiliations.

Copyright: © 2022 by the authors. Licensee MDPI, Basel, Switzerland. This article is an open access article distributed under the terms and conditions of the Creative Commons Attribution (CC BY) license (https://creativecommons.org/licenses/by/4.0/).

1. Introduction

The origin of residuated lattices is in mathematical logic. They were introduced by Dilworth and Ward, through the papers [1,2]. The study of residuated lattices originated in 1930 in the context of the theory of rings, with the study of ring ideals. It is known that the lattice of ideals of a commutative ring is a residuated lattice; see [3]. Several researchers ([3–6], etc.) have been interested in this construction.

Two important subvarieties of residuated lattices are BL-algebras (corresponding to Hajek's logic; see [7]) and MV-algebras (corresponding to Łukasiewicz's many-valued logic; see [8,9]). For instance, rings for which the lattice of ideals is a BL-algebra are called BL-rings and were introduced in [5].

In this paper, we obtain a description for BL-rings using a new characterization of BL-algebras, given in Theorem 1, i.e., residuated lattices L in which $[x \odot (x \to y)] \to z = (x \to z) \vee (y \to z)$ for every $x, y, z \in L$. Then, BL-rings are unitary and commutative rings A with the property that $K : [I \otimes (J : I)] = (K : I) + (K : J)$, for every $I, J, K \in Id(A)$; see Corollary 1.

Additionally, we show that the class of BL-rings contains other known classes of commutative rings: rings that are principal ideal domains and some types of finite unitary commutative rings; see Theorem 2, Corollaries 2 and 3.

One recent application of BCK algebras is in coding theory. In fact, MV-algebras are commutative BCK-algebras, see [10].

Due to computational considerations, in this paper, we are interested in finding ways to generate finite BL-algebras using finite commutative rings, since a solution that is computationally tractable is to consider algebras with a small number of elements. First, we give examples of finite BL-rings whose lattice of ideals is not an MV-algebra. Using these rings, we construct BL-algebras with $2^r + 1$ elements, $r \geq 2$ (see Theorem 3) and BL-chains with $k \geq 4$ elements (see Theorem 4).

In [11], isomorphism classes of BL-algebras of size $n \leq 12$ were only counted, not constructed, using computer algorithms. Up to an isomorphism, there is 1 BL-algebra of size 2, 2 BL-algebras of size 3, 5 BL-algebras of size 4, 9 BL-algebras of size 5, 20 BL-algebras of size 6, 38 BL-algebras of size 7, 81 BL-algebras of size 8, 160 BL-algebras of size 9, 326 BL-algebras of size 10, 643 BL-algebra of size 11 and 1314 BL-algebras of size 12. In Theorem 6, we present a way to generate (up to an isomorphism) finite BL-algebras with $2 \leq n \leq 5$ elements by using the ordinal product of residuated lattices, and we present summarizing statistics. The described method can be used to construct finite BL-algebras of larger size, the inconvenience being the large number of BL-algebras that must be generated.

2. Preliminaries

Definition 1 ([1,2]). *A (commutative) residuated lattice is an algebra $(L, \wedge, \vee, \odot, \rightarrow, 0, 1)$ such that:*

(LR1) $(L, \wedge, \vee, 0, 1)$ *is a bounded lattice;*
(LR2) $(L, \odot, 1)$ *is a commutative ordered monoid;*
(LR3) $z \leq x \rightarrow y$ *iff* $x \odot z \leq y$*, for all* $x, y, z \in L$.

The property (LR3) is called *residuation*, where $\leq$ is the partial order of the lattice $(L, \wedge, \vee, 0, 1)$.

In a residuated lattice, an additional operation is defined; for $x \in L$, we denote $x^* = x \rightarrow 0$.

Example 1 ([12]). *Let $(\mathcal{B}, \wedge, \vee, ', 0, 1)$ be a Boolean algebra. If we define for every $x, y \in \mathcal{B}$, $x \odot y = x \wedge y$ and $x \rightarrow y = x' \vee y$, then $(\mathcal{B}, \wedge, \vee, \odot, \rightarrow, 0, 1)$ becomes a residuated lattice.*

Example 2. *It is known that, for a commutative unitary ring A, if we denote by $Id(A)$ the set of all ideals, then for $I, J \in Id(A)$, the following sets*

$$I + J = <I \cup J> = \{i + j, i \in I, j \in J\},$$

$$I \otimes J = \{\sum_{k=1}^{n} i_k j_k,\ i_k \in I, j_k \in J\},$$

$$(I:J) = \{x \in A, x \cdot J \subseteq I\},$$

$$Ann(I) = (0:I), \text{ where } \mathbf{0} = <0>,$$

are also ideals of A, called sum, product, quotient and annihilator; see [13]. If we preserve these notations, $(Id(A), \cap, +, \otimes \rightarrow, 0 = \{0\}, 1 = A)$ is a residuated lattice in which the order relation is $\subseteq$ and $I \rightarrow J = (J:I)$, for every $I, J \in Id(A)$; see [6].

In a residuated lattice $(L, \wedge, \vee, \odot, \rightarrow, 0, 1)$, we consider the following identities:

$$(prel) \quad (x \rightarrow y) \vee (y \rightarrow x) = 1 \quad (prelinearity);$$
$$(div) \quad x \odot (x \rightarrow y) = x \wedge y \quad (divisibility).$$

Definition 2 ([10,12,14]). *A residuated lattice L is called a BL-algebra if L verifies $(prel) + (div)$ conditions.*

A *BL-chain* is a totally ordered BL-algebra, i.e., a BL-algebra such that its lattice order is total.

Definition 3 ([8,9]). *An MV-algebra is an algebra $(L, \oplus, ^*, 0)$ satisfying the following axioms:*
(MV1) $(L, \oplus, 0)$ *is an abelian monoid;*

(MV2) $(x^*)^* = x$;
(MV3) $x \oplus 0^* = 0^*$;
(MV4) $(x^* \oplus y)^* \oplus y = (y^* \oplus x)^* \oplus x$, for all $x, y \in L$.

In fact, a residuated lattice L is an MV-algebra iff it satisfies the additional condition:

$$(x \to y) \to y = (y \to x) \to x,$$

for every $x, y \in L$; see [12].

Remark 1 ([12]). *If, in a BL- algebra L, $x^{**} = x$, for every $x \in L$, and for $x, y \in L$ we denote*

$$x \oplus y = (x^* \odot y^*)^*,$$

then we obtain an MV-algebra $(L, \oplus, ^*, 0)$. Conversely, if $(L, \oplus, ^*, 0)$ is an MV-algebra, then $(L, \wedge, \vee, \odot, \to, 0, 1)$ becomes a BL-algebra, in which for $x, y \in L$:

$$x \odot y = (x^* \oplus y^*)^*,$$

$$x \to y = x^* \oplus y, 1 = 0^*,$$

$$x \vee y = (x \to y) \to y = (y \to x) \to x \text{ and } x \wedge y = (x^* \vee y^*)^*.$$

In fact, MV-algebras are exactly involutive BL-algebras.

Example 3 ([10]). *We give an example of a finite BL-algebra which is not an MV-algebra. Let $L = \{0, a, b, c, 1\}$; we define the following operations on L:*

$\to$	0	c	a	b	1
0	1	1	1	1	1
c	0	1	1	1	1
a	0	b	1	b	1
b	0	a	a	1	1
1	0	c	a	b	1

$\odot$	0	c	a	b	1
0	0	0	0	0	0
c	0	c	c	c	c
a	0	c	a	c	a
b	0	c	c	b	b
1	0	c	a	b	1

We have, $0 \leq c \leq a, b \leq 1$, but a, b are incomparable; hence, L is a BL-algebra that is not a chain. We remark that $x^{**} = 1$ for every $x \in L, x \neq 0$.

3. BL-Rings

Definition 4 ([5]). *A commutative ring whose lattice of ideals is a BL-algebra is called a BL-ring.*

In particular, we can call a commutative ring whose lattice of ideals is an MV-algebra an MV-ring.

We recall that, in [15], we showed that a commutative unitary ring A is an MV-ring iff it has the Chang property, i.e.,

$$I + J = (J : (J : I)),$$

for every $I, J \in Id(A)$. Obviously, every MV-ring is also a BL-ring.

BL-rings are closed under finite direct products, arbitrary direct sums and homomorphic images; see [5].

In the following, using the connections between BL-algebras and BL-rings, we give new characterizations for commutative and unitary rings for which the lattice of ideals is a BL-algebra.

Proposition 1 ([10]). *Let $(L, \vee, \wedge, \odot, \to, 0, 1)$ be a residuated lattice. Then, we have the equivalences:*

(i) L satisfies $(prel)$ condition;

(ii) $(x \wedge y) \to z = (x \to z) \vee (y \to z)$, for every $x, y, z \in L$.

Lemma 1. *Let $(L, \vee, \wedge, \odot, \to, 0, 1)$ be a residuated lattice. The following assertions are equivalent:*
(i) L satisfies (prel) condition;
(ii) For every $x, y, z \in L$, if $x \wedge y \leq z$, then $(x \to z) \vee (y \to z) = 1$.

Proof. $(i) \Rightarrow (ii)$. Following Proposition 1.
$(ii) \Rightarrow (i)$. Using (ii), for $z = x \wedge y$ we deduce that $1 = (x \to (x \wedge y)) \vee (y \to (x \wedge y)) = [(x \to x) \wedge (x \to y)] \vee [(y \to x) \wedge (y \to y)] = (x \to y) \vee (y \to x)$, so L satisfies $(prel)$ condition. □

Lemma 2. *Let $(L, \vee, \wedge, \odot, \to, 0, 1)$ be a residuated lattice. The following assertions are equivalent:*
(i) L satisfies (div) condition;
(ii) For every $x, y, z \in L$, if $x \odot (x \to y) \leq z$, then $x \wedge y \leq z$.

Proof. $(i) \Rightarrow (ii)$, evidently.
$(ii) \Rightarrow (i)$. Using (ii), for $z = x \odot (x \to y)$ we can deduce that $x \wedge y \leq x \odot (x \to y)$. Since in a residuated lattice, $x \odot (x \to y) \leq x \wedge y$, we deduce that L satisfies (div) condition. □

Using Lemmas 1 and 2 we deduce Proposition 2.

Proposition 2. *Let $(L, \vee, \wedge, \odot, \to, 0, 1)$ be a residuated lattice. The following assertions are equivalent:*
(i) L is a BL-algebra;
(ii) For every $x, y, z \in L$, if $x \odot (x \to y) \leq z$, then $(x \to z) \vee (y \to z) = 1$;
(iii) $[x \odot (x \to y)] \to z = (x \to z) \vee (y \to z)$, for every $x, y, z \in L$.

Proof. $(i) \Rightarrow (ii)$. Let $x, y, z \in L$ such that $x \odot (x \to y) \leq z$. Since every BL-algebra satisfies (div) condition, by Lemma 2, we can deduce that $x \wedge y \leq z$. Since every BL-algebra satisfies $(prel)$ condition, following Lemma 1, we can deduce that $1 = (x \to z) \vee (y \to z)$.
$(ii) \Rightarrow (i)$. First, we prove that L satisfies condition (ii) from Lemma 1. Therefore, let $x, y, z \in L$ such that $x \wedge y \leq z$. Thus, $(x \wedge y) \to z = 1$. Since $x \odot (x \to y) \leq x \wedge y$, we deduce that $1 = (x \wedge y) \to z \leq (x \odot (x \to y)) \to z$. Then, $x \odot (x \to y) \leq z$. By hypothesis, $(x \to z) \vee (y \to z) = 1$.
To prove that L verifies condition (ii) from Lemma 2, let $x, y, z \in L$ such that $x \odot (x \to y) \leq z$. By hypothesis, we deduce that, $(x \to z) \vee (y \to z) = 1$. Since $(x \to z) \vee (y \to z) \leq (x \wedge y) \to z$, we obtain $(x \wedge y) \to z = 1$, that is, $x \wedge y \leq z$.
$(iii) \Rightarrow (ii)$, evidently.
$(ii) \Rightarrow (iii)$. If we denote $t = [x \odot (x \to y)] \to z$, we have $1 = t \to t = t \to [(x \odot (x \to y)) \to z] = [x \odot (x \to y)] \to (t \to z)$; hence, $x \odot (x \to y) \leq t \to z$.
By hypothesis, we deduce that, $(x \to (t \to z)) \vee (y \to (t \to z)) = 1$.
Then, $1 = (t \to (x \to z)) \vee (t \to (y \to z)) \leq t \to [(x \to z) \vee (y \to z)]$. Thus, $t \leq (x \to z) \vee (y \to z)$.
However, $(x \to z) \vee (y \to z) \leq (x \wedge y) \to z \leq [x \odot (x \to y)] \to z = t$.
We conclude that $t = (x \to z) \vee (y \to z)$, that is, $[x \odot (x \to y)] \to z = (x \to z) \vee (y \to z)$, for every $x, y, z \in L$. □

Using Proposition 2 we obtain a new characterization for BL-algebras:

Theorem 1. *A residuated lattice L is a BL-algebra if and only if for every $x, y, z \in L$,*

$$[x \odot (x \to y)] \to z = (x \to z) \vee (y \to z).$$

Using this result, we can give a new description for BL-rings:

Corollary 1. *Let A be a commutative and unitary ring. The following assertions are equivalent:*
 (i) *A is a BL-ring;*
 (ii) $K : [I \otimes (J : I)] = (K : I) + (K : J)$, *for every* $I, J, K \in Id(A)$.

Theorem 2. *Let A be a commutative ring that is a principal ideal domain. Then, A is a BL-ring.*

Proof. Since A is a principal ideal domain, let $I = <a>$, $J = <b>$ be the principal non-zero ideals generated by $a, b \in A \setminus \{0\}$.
 If $d = gcd\{a,b\}$, then $d = a \cdot \alpha + b \cdot \beta$, $\alpha, \beta \in A$, $a = a_1 d$ and $b = b_1 d$, with $1 = gcd\{a_1, b_1\}$. Thus, $I + J = <d>$, $I \cap J = <ab/d>$, $I \otimes J = <ab>$ and $(I : J) = <a_1>$.
 The conditions (*prel*) are satisfied, $(I : J) + (J : I) = <a_1> + <b_1> = <1> = A$ and (*div*) is also satisfied: $J \otimes (I : J) = <b> \otimes <a_1> = <ab/d> = I \cap J$.
 If $I = \{0\}$, since A is an integral domain, we have that $(0 : J) + (J : 0) = Ann(J) + A = A$ and $J \otimes (0 : J) = J \otimes Ann(J) = 0 = 0 \cap J = 0 \otimes (J : 0)$ for every $J \in Id(A) \setminus \{0\}$.
 Moreover, we remark that $(I : (I : J)) = (J : (J : I)) = I + J$ for every non-zero ideal $I, J \in Id(A)$. Additionally, since A is an integral domain, we obtain $Ann(Ann(I)) = A$, for every $I \in Id(A) \setminus \{0\}$. We conclude that $Id(A)$ is a BL-algebra that is not an MV-algebra. □

Corollary 2. *A ring factor of a principal ideal domain is a BL-ring.*

Proof. We use Theorem 2 since BL-rings are closed under homomorphic images; see [5]. Moreover, we remark that *a ring factor of a principal ideal domain* is, in particular, an MV-ring, see [15]. □

Corollary 3. *A finite commutative unitary ring of the form $A = \mathbb{Z}_{k_1} \times \mathbb{Z}_{k_2} \times ... \times \mathbb{Z}_{k_r}$ (direct product of rings, equipped with componentwise operations) where $k_i = p_i^{\alpha_i}$, with p_i a prime number, is a BL-ring.*

Proof. We apply Corollary 2 using the fact that BL-rings are closed under finite direct products; see [5].
 Moreover, we remark that if A is a finite commutative unitary ring of the above form, then $Id(A) = Id(\mathbb{Z}_{k_1}) \times Id(\mathbb{Z}_{k_2}) \times ... \times Id(\mathbb{Z}_{k_r})$ is an MV-algebra $(Id(A), \oplus, ^*, 0 = \{0\})$ in which
$$I \oplus J = Ann(Ann(I) \otimes Ann(J)) \text{ and } I^* = Ann(I)$$
for every $I, J \in Id(A)$ since, $Ann(Ann(I)) = I$; see [15]. □

Example 4. (1) *Following Theorem 2, the ring of integers $(\mathbb{Z}, +, \cdot)$ is a BL-ring in which $(Id(\mathbb{Z}), \cap, +, \otimes \to, 0 = \{0\}, 1 = A)$ is not an MV-algebra. Indeed, since $\mathbb{Z}$ is the principal ideal domain, we have $Ann(Ann(I)) = \mathbb{Z}$, for every $I \in Id(\mathbb{Z}) \setminus \{0\}$.*
 (2) *Let K be a field and $K[X]$ be the polynomial ring. For $f \in K[X]$, the quotient ring $A = K[X]/(f)$ is a BL-ring. Indeed, the lattice of ideals of this ring is an MV-algebra; see [15].*

4. Examples of BL-Algebras Using Commutative Rings

In this section, we present ways to generate finite BL-algebras using finite commutative rings.

First, we give examples of finite BL-rings whose lattice of ideals is not an MV-algebra. Using these rings we construct BL-algebras with $2^r + 1$ elements, $r \geq 2$ (see Theorem 3) and BL-chains with $k \geq 4$ elements (see Theorem 4).

We recall that, in [15], we proved the following proposition.

Proposition 3 ([15]). *If A is a finite commutative unitary ring of the form $\mathbb{Z}_{k_1} \times \mathbb{Z}_{k_2} \times ... \times \mathbb{Z}_{k_r}$ (direct product of rings, equipped with componentwise operations), where $k_i = p_i^{\alpha_i}$, with p_i a prime number, for all $i \in \{1, 2..., r\}$ and $Id(A)$ denotes the set of all ideals of the ring A, then $(Id(A), \vee, \wedge, \odot, \to, 0, 1)$ is an MV-algebra, where the order relation is $\subseteq$, $I \odot J = I \otimes J$,*

$I^* = Ann(I)$, $I \to J = (J : I)$, $I \vee J = I + J$, $I \wedge J = I \cap J$, $0 = \{0\}$ and $1 = A$. The set $Id(A)$ has $\mathcal{N}_A = \prod_{i=1}^{r}(\alpha_i + 1)$ elements.

In the following, we give examples of finite BL-rings whose lattice of ideals is not an MV-algebra.

Definition 5 ([13]). *Let R be a commutative unitary ring. The ideal M of the ring R is maximal if it is maximal with respect of the set inclusion, amongst all proper ideals of the ring R. That means there are no other ideals different from R contained in M. The ideal J of the ring R is a minimal ideal if it is a nonzero ideal that contains no other nonzero ideals. A commutative local ring R is a ring with a unique maximal ideal.*

Example 5. *(i) A field F is a local ring, with $\{0\}$ being the maximal ideal in this ring.*
(ii) In $(\mathbb{Z}_8, +, \cdot)$, the ideal $J = \{\widehat{0}, \widehat{4}\}$ is a minimal ideal and the ideal $M = \{\widehat{0}, \widehat{2}, \widehat{4}, \widehat{6}\}$ is the maximal ideal.

Remark 2. *Let R be a local ring with M its maximal ideal. Then, the quotient ring $R[X]/(X^n)$ with n being a positive integer is local. Indeed, the unique maximal ideal of the ring $R[X]/(X^n)$ is $\overrightarrow{M} = \{\widehat{f} \in R[X]/(X^n) / f \in R[X], f = a_0 + a_1 X + ... + a_{n-1} X^{n-1}, \text{ with } a_0 \in M\}$. For other details, the reader is referred to [16].*

In the following, we consider the ring $(\mathbb{Z}_n, +, \cdot)$ with $n = p_1 p_2 ... p_r$, $p_1, p_2, ..., p_r$ being distinct prime numbers, $r \geq 2$ and the factor ring $R = \mathbb{Z}_n[X]/(X^2)$.

Remark 3. *(i) With the above notations, in the ring $(\mathbb{Z}_n, +, \cdot)$, the ideals generated by $\widehat{p}_i$, $M_{p_i} = (\widehat{p}_i)$, are maximals. The ideals of $\mathbb{Z}_n$ are of the form $I_d = (\widehat{d})$, where d is a divisor of n.*
(ii) Each element from $\mathbb{Z}_n - \{M_{p_1} \cup M_{p_2} \cup ... \cup M_{p_r}\}$ is an invertible element. Indeed, if $\widehat{x} \in \mathbb{Z}_n - \{M_{p_1} \cup M_{p_2} \cup ... \cup M_{p_r}\}$, we have $\gcd\{x, n\} = 1$; therefore, x is an invertible element.

Proposition 4. *(i) With the above notations, the factor ring $R = \mathbb{Z}_n[X]/(X^2)$ has $2^r + 1$ ideals including $\{0\}$ and R.*
(ii) For $\widehat{\gamma} \in \mathbb{Z}_n - \{M_{p_1} \cup M_{p_2} \cup ... \cup M_{p_r}\}$, the element $X + \widehat{\gamma}$ is an invertible element in R.

Proof. (i) Indeed, the ideals are: $J_{p_i} = (\widehat{\alpha} X + \widehat{\alpha}_i), \widehat{\alpha}_i \in M_{p_i}, i \in \{1, 2, ..., r\}$, which are maximal, $J_d = (\widehat{\beta} X + \widehat{\beta}_d), \widehat{\beta}_d \in I_d$, I_d is not maximal, $\widehat{\alpha}, \widehat{\beta} \in R, d \neq n$, where d is a proper divisor of n, the ideals (X), for $d = n$ and (0). Therefore, we have C_n^0 ideals for ideal (X), C_n^1 ideals for ideals J_{p_i}, C_n^2 ideals for ideals $J_{p_i p_j}$, $p_i \neq p_j$,...,C_n^n ideals for ideal R, for $d = 1$, resulting in a total of $2^r + 1$, if we add ideal (0). Here, $C_n^k = \begin{pmatrix} k \\ n \end{pmatrix}$ are combinations.

(ii) Since $\widehat{\gamma} \in \mathbb{Z}_n - \{M_{p_1} \cup M_{p_2} \cup ... \cup M_{p_r}\}$, we have that $\widehat{\gamma}$ is invertible, with $\widehat{\delta}$ being its inverse. Therefore, $(X + \widehat{\gamma})[-\widehat{\delta}^{-2}(X - \widehat{\gamma})] = 1$. As a result, $X + \widehat{\gamma}$ is invertible; therefore, $(X + \widehat{\gamma}) = R$. □

Since, for any commutative unitary ring, the lattice of ideals is a residuated lattice (see [6]), in particular, for the unitary and commutative ring $A = \mathbb{Z}_n[X]/(X^2)$, we have that $(Id(\mathbb{Z}_n/(X^2)), \cap, +, \otimes \to, 0 = \{0\}, 1 = A)$ is a residuated lattice with $2^r + 1$ elements.

Remark 4. *As we remarked above, the ideals in the ring $R = \mathbb{Z}_n[X]/(X^2)$ are:*
(i) (0);
(ii) of the form $J_d = (\widehat{\alpha} X + \widehat{\beta}_d), \widehat{\alpha} \in R, \widehat{\beta}_d \in I_d$, where d is a proper divisor of $n = p_1 p_2 ... p_r$, $p_1, p_2, ..., p_r$ being distinct prime numbers, $r \geq 2$, by using the notations from Remark 3. If $I_d = (\widehat{p}_i)$, then J_d is denoted J_{p_i} and is a maximal ideal in $R = \mathbb{Z}_n[X]/(X^2)$;

(iii) The ring R, if $d = 1$;
(iv) (X), if $d = n$.

Remark 5. *We remark that for all nonzero ideals I of the above ring R, we have $(X) \subseteq I$ and the ideal (X) is the only minimal ideal of $\mathbb{Z}_n[X]/(X^2)$.*

Remark 6. *Let $D_d = \{p \mid p \in \{p_1, p_2, ..., p_r\}$ such that $d = \prod p\}, d \neq 1$.*
(1) We have $J_{d_1} \cap J_{d_2} = J_{d_1} \otimes J_{d_2} = J_{d_3}$, where $D_{d_3} = \{p \in D_{d_1} \cup D_{d_2}, d_3 = \prod p\}$ for d_1, d_2 proper divisors.

If $d_1 = 1$, we have $R \otimes J_{d_2} = J_{d_2} = R \cap J_{d_2}$.
If $d_1 = n, d_2 \neq n$, we have $(X) \otimes J_{d_2} = (X) \cap J_{d_2} = (X)$. If $d_2 = n$, we have $(X) \otimes (X) = (0)$.

(2) We have $(J_{d_1} : J_{d_2}) = J_{d_3}$, with $D_{d_3} = D_{d_1} - D_{d_2}$. Indeed, $(J_{d_1} : J_{d_2}) = \{y \in R, y \cdot J_{d_2} \subseteq J_{d_1}\} = J_{d_3}$, for d_1, d_2 proper divisors.

If $J_{d_1} = (0)$, we have $(0 : J_{d_2}) = (0)$. Indeed, if $(0 : J_{d_2}) = J \neq (0), J \otimes J_{d_2} = (0)$. However, from the above, $J \otimes J_{d_2} = J \cap J_{d_2} \neq (0)$, which is false.
If $J_{d_2} = (0)$, we have $(J_{d_1} : 0) = R$.
If $d_1 = 1$, we have $(R : J_{d_2}) = R$ and $(J_{d_2} : R) = J_{d_2}$.
If $d_1 = n, d_2 \neq n$, we have $J_{d_1} = (X)$; therefore, $(J_{d_1} : J_{d_2}) = J_{d_1} = (X)$. If $d_1 \neq n, d_2 = n$, we have $J_{d_2} = (X)$; therefore, $(J_{d_1} : J_{d_2}) = R$. If $d_1 = d_2 = n$, we have $J_{d_1} = J_{d_2} = (X)$ and $(J_{d_1} : J_{d_2}) = R$.

Theorem 3. *(i) For $n \geq 2$, with the above notations, the residuated lattice $(Id(\mathbb{Z}_n[X]/(X^2)), \cap, +, \otimes \to, 0 = \{0\}, 1 = R), R = \mathbb{Z}_n[X]/(X^2)$ is a BL-algebra with $2^r + 1$ elements.*
(ii) By using notations from Remark 4, we have that $(Id_{p_i}(\mathbb{Z}_n[X]/(X^2)), \cap, +, \otimes \to, 0 = \{0\}, 1 = R)$, where $Id_{p_i}(\mathbb{Z}_n[X]/(X^2)) = \{(0), J_{p_i}, R\}$ is a BL-sublattice of the lattice $Id(\mathbb{Z}_n[X]/(X^2))$ with 3 elements.

Proof. (i) First, we will prove the $(prel)$ condition:

$$(I \to J) \vee (J \to I) = (J : I) \vee (I : J) = \mathbb{Z}_n[X]/(X^2),$$

for every $I, J \in Id(\mathbb{Z}_n[X]/(X^2))$.

Case 1. If d_1 and d_2 are proper divisors of n, we have $(J_{d_1} \to J_{d_2}) \vee (J_{d_2} \to J_{d_1}) = (J_{d_2} : J_{d_1}) \vee (J_{d_1} : J_{d_2}) = J_{d_4} \vee J_{d_5}$, where $D_{d_5} = D_{d_1} - D_{d_2}$ and $D_{d_4} = D_{d_2} - D_{d_1}$. We remark that $D_{d_4} \cap D_{d_5} = \emptyset$; then, $gcd\{d_4, d_5\} = 1$. From here, there are the integers a and b such that $ad_4 + bd_5 = 1$. We obtain that $J_{d_4} \vee J_{d_5} = < J_{d_4} \cup J_{d_5} > = R$ from Proposition 4, (ii).

Case 2. If d_1 is a proper divisor of n and $d_2 = n$, we have $J_{d_2} = (X)$. Therefore, $(J_{d_1} \to J_{d_2}) \vee (J_{d_2} \to J_{d_1}) = (J_{d_2} : J_{d_1}) \vee (J_{d_1} : J_{d_2}) = J_{d_2} \vee R = R$ using Remark 6.

Case 3. If d_1 is a proper divisor of n and $J_{d_2} = (0)$, we have $(J_{d_1} \to J_{d_2}) \vee (J_{d_2} \to J_{d_1}) = (0 : J_{d_1}) \vee (J_{d_1} : 0) = 0 \vee R = R$ using Remark 6.

Case 4. If d_1 is a proper divisor of n and $J_{d_2} = R$, it is clear. From here, the condition $(prel)$ is satisfied.

Now, we prove condition (div):

$$I \otimes (I \to J) = I \otimes (J : I) = I \cap J,$$

for every $I, J \in Id(\mathbb{Z}_n[X]/(X^2))$.

Case 1. If d_1 and d_2 are proper divisors of n, we have $J_{d_1} \otimes (J_{d_2} : J_{d_1}) = J_{d_1} \otimes J_{d_3} = J_{d_4} = J_{d_1} \cap J_{d_2}$, since $D_{d_3} = D_{d_2} - D_{d_1}$ and $D_{d_4} = \{p \in D_{d_1} \cup D_{d_3}, d_4 = \prod p\} = \{p \in D_{d_1} \cup D_{d_2}, d_4 = \prod p\}$.

Case 2. If d_1 is a proper divisor of n and $d_2 = n$, we have $J_{d_2} = (X)$. We obtain $J_{d_1} \otimes (J_{d_2} : J_{d_1}) = J_{d_1} \otimes ((X) : J_{d_1}) = J_{d_1} \otimes (X) = J_{d_1} \cap (X)$ since $(X) \subset J_{d_1}$.

Case 3. If $d_1 = n$ and d_2 is a proper divisor of n, we have $J_{d_1} = (X)$. We obtain $J_{d_1} \otimes (J_{d_2} : J_{d_1}) = (X) \otimes (J_{d_2} : (X)) = (X) \otimes R = (X) = J_{d_2} \cap (X)$ since $(X) \subset J_{d_2}$.

Case 4. If d_1 is a proper divisor of n and $J_{d_2} = (0)$, we have $J_{d_1} \otimes (J_{d_2} : J_{d_1}) = J_{d_1} \otimes (0 : J_{d_1}) = J_{d_1} \otimes (0) = (0) = J_{d_1} \cap (0)$ from Remark 6.

Case 5. If $J_{d_1} = (0)$ and d_2 is a proper divisor of n, we have $J_{d_1} \otimes (J_{d_2} : J_{d_1}) = 0 \otimes (J_{d_2} : 0) = 0$.

Case 6. If d_1 is a proper divisor of n and $J_{d_2} = R$, we have $J_{d_1} \otimes (J_{d_2} : J_{d_1}) = J_{d_1} \otimes (R : J_{d_1}) = J_{d_1} \otimes R = J_{d_1}$. If $J_{d_1} = R$ and d_2 is a proper divisor of n, we have $J_{d_1} \otimes (J_{d_2} : J_{d_1}) = R \otimes (J_{d_2} : R) = R \otimes J_{d_2} = J_{d_2}$. From here, the condition (div) is satisfied and the proposition is proven.

(ii) It is clear that $J_{p_i} \odot J_{p_i} = J_{p_i} \otimes J_{p_i} = J_{p_i}$; we obtain the following tables:

$\to$	O	J_{p_i}	R
O	R	R	R
J_{p_i}	O	R	R
R	O	J_{p_i}	R

$\odot$	O	J_{p_i}	R
O	O	O	O
J_{p_i}	O	J_{p_i}	J_{p_i}
R	O	J_{p_i}	R

therefore showing a BL-algebra of order 3. □

Theorem 4. *Let $n = p^r$ with p a prime number, $p \geq 2$, r a positive integer, $r \geq 2$. We consider the ring $R = \mathbb{Z}_n[X]/(X^2)$. The set $(Id(\mathbb{Z}_n[X]/(X^2)), \cap, +, \otimes \to, 0 = \{0\}, 1 = R)$ is a BL-chain with $r+2$ elements. In this way, for a given positive integer $k \geq 4$, we can construct BL-chains with k elements.*

Proof. The ideals in $\mathbb{Z}_n$ are of the form: $(0) \subseteq (p^{r-1}) \subseteq (p^{r-2}) \subseteq ... \subseteq (p) \subseteq \mathbb{Z}_n$. The ideal (p^{r-1}) and the ideal (p) are the only maximal ideals of $\mathbb{Z}_n$. The ideals in the ring R are $(0) \subseteq (X) \subseteq (\alpha_{r-1}X + \beta_{r-1}) \subseteq (\alpha_{r-2}X + \beta_{r-2}) \subseteq ... \subseteq (\alpha_1 X + \beta_1) \subseteq R$, where $\alpha_i \in \mathbb{Z}_n, i \in \{1,...,r-1\}, \beta_{r-1} \in (p^{r-1}), \beta_{r-2} \in (p^{r-2}), ..., \beta_1 \in (p)$, meaning $r+2$ ideals. We denote these ideals with $(0), (X), I_{p^{r-1}}, I_{p^{r-2}}, ... I_p, R$, with I_p being the only maximal ideal in R.

First, we prove the $(prel)$ condition:

$$(I \to J) \vee (J \to I) = (J : I) \vee (I : J) = \mathbb{Z}_n[X]/(X^2),$$

for every $I, J \in Id(\mathbb{Z}_n[X]/(X^2))$.

Case 1. We suppose that I and J are proper ideals and $I \subseteq J$. We have $(I \to J) \vee (J \to I) = (J : I) \vee (I : J) = R \vee (I : J) = R$.

Case 2. $I = (0)$ and J are a proper ideal, we have $(I \to J) \vee (J \to I) = (J : (0)) \vee ((0) : J) = R$. Therefore, the condition $(prel)$ is satisfied.

Now, we prove the (div) condition:

$$I \otimes (I \to J) = I \otimes (J : I) = I \cap J,$$

for every $I, J \in Id(\mathbb{Z}_n[X]/(X^2))$.

Case 1. We suppose that I and J are proper ideals and $I \subseteq J$. We have $I \otimes (I \to J) = I \otimes (J : I) = I \otimes R = I = I \cap J$. If $J \subseteq I$, we have $I \otimes (I \to J) = I \otimes (J : I) = J = I \cap J$.

Case 2. $I = (0)$ and J is a proper ideal. We have $(0) \otimes ((0) \to J) = (0) \otimes (J : (0)) = (0) = I \cap J$. If $I \neq (X)$ is a proper ideal and $J = (0)$, we have $I \otimes (I \to J) = I \otimes ((0) : I) = I \otimes (0) = (0)$. If $I = (X)$ and $J = (0)$, we have $I \otimes (I \to J) = (X) \otimes ((0) : (X)) = (X) \otimes (X) = (0)$ and $(0) \cap (X) = (0)$.

From here, the condition (div) is satisfied and the theorem is proven. □

Example 6. *In Theorem 3, we take $n = 2 \cdot 3$; therefore, the ideals of $\mathbb{Z}_6$ are $(0), (2), (3), \mathbb{Z}_6$, with (2) and (3) maximal ideals. The ring $\mathbb{Z}_6[X]/(X^2)$ has five ideals: $O = (0) \subset A = (X), B = (\alpha X + \beta), C = (\gamma X + \delta), E = \mathbb{Z}_6[X]/(X^2)$, with $\alpha, \gamma \in \mathbb{Z}_4, \beta \in (2)$ and $\delta \in (3)$. From the following tables, we have a BL-structure on $Id(\mathbb{Z}_6[X]/(X^2))$:*

$\to$	O	A	B	C	E
O	E	E	E	E	E
A	A	E	E	E	E
B	O	C	E	C	E
C	O	B	B	E	E
E	O	A	B	C	E

$\odot$	O	A	B	C	E
O	O	O	O	O	O
A	O	O	A	A	A
B	O	A	B	A	B
C	O	A	A	C	C
E	O	A	B	C	E

From Theorem 3, if we consider $J_{p_i} = B$, we have the following BL-algebra of order 3:

$\to$	O	B	E
O	E	E	E
B	O	E	E
E	O	B	E

$\odot$	O	B	E
O	O	O	O
B	O	B	B
E	O	B	E

Example 7. In Theorem 3, we take $n = 2 \cdot 3 \cdot 5$; therefore, the ideals of the ring $\mathbb{Z}_{30}$ are $(0), (2), (3), (5), (6), (10), (15), \mathbb{Z}_{30}$, with $(2), (3)$ and (5) being maximal ideals. The ring $\mathbb{Z}_{30}[X]/(X^2)$ has nine ideals: $O = (0) \subset A = (X), B = (\alpha_1 X + \beta_1), C = (\alpha_2 X + \beta_2), D = (\alpha_3 X + \beta_3), E = (\alpha_4 X + \beta_4), F = (\alpha_5 X + \beta_5), G = (\alpha_6 X + \beta_6), R = \mathbb{Z}_{30}[X]/(X^2)$, with $\alpha_i \in \mathbb{Z}_{30}, i \in \{1,2,3,4,5,6\}, \beta_1 \in (6), \beta_2 \in (10), \beta_3 \in (15), \beta_4 \in (2), \beta_5 \in (3)$ and $\beta_6 \in (5)$. The ideals E, F and G are maximal. From the following tables, we have a BL-structure on $Id(\mathbb{Z}_{30}[X]/(X^2))$:

$\to$	O	A	B	C	D	E	F	G	R
O	R	R	R	R	R	R	R	R	R
A	A	R	R	R	R	R	R	R	R
B	O	G	R	G	G	R	R	G	R
C	O	F	F	R	F	R	F	R	R
D	O	E	E	E	R	E	R	R	R
E	O	D	F	G	D	R	F	G	R
F	O	C	E	C	G	E	R	G	R
G	O	B	B	E	F	E	F	R	R
R	O	A	B	C	D	E	F	G	R

$\odot$	O	A	B	C	D	E	F	G	R
O	O	O	O	O	O	O	O	O	O
A	O	O	A	A	A	A	A	A	A
B	O	A	B	A	A	B	B	A	B
C	O	A	A	C	A	C	C	A	C
D	O	A	A	A	D	A	D	D	D
E	O	A	B	C	A	E	A	A	E
F	O	A	B	A	D	A	F	A	F
G	O	A	A	C	D	A	A	G	G
R	O	A	B	C	D	E	F	G	R

Example 8. In Theorem 4, we consider $p = 2, r = 2$. The ideals in $(\mathbb{Z}_4, +, \cdot)$ are $(0) \subset (2) \subset \mathbb{Z}_4$ and $\mathbb{Z}_4$ is a local ring. The ring $\mathbb{Z}_4[X]/(X^2)$ has four ideals: $O = (0) \subset A = (X) \subset B = (\alpha X + \beta) \subset E = \mathbb{Z}_4[X]/(X^2)$, with $\alpha \in \mathbb{Z}_4, \beta \in (2)$. From the following tables, we have a BL-structure for $Id(\mathbb{Z}_4[X]/(X^2))$:

$\to$	O	A	B	E
O	E	E	E	E
A	A	E	E	E
B	O	B	E	E
E	O	A	B	E

$\odot$	O	A	B	E
O	O	O	O	O
A	O	O	A	A
B	O	A	A	B
E	O	A	B	E

Example 9. In Theorem 4, we consider $p = 2, r = 3$. The ideals in $(\mathbb{Z}_8, +, \cdot)$ are $(0) \subset (4) \subset (2) \subset \mathbb{Z}_8$. The ring $\mathbb{Z}_8[X]/(X^2)$ has five ideals: $O = (0) \subset A = (X) \subset B = (\alpha X + \beta) \subset C = (\gamma X + \delta) \subset E = \mathbb{Z}_8[X]/(X^2)$, with $\alpha, \gamma \in \mathbb{Z}_8, \beta \in (4)$ and $\delta \in (2)$. From the following tables, we have a BL-structure for $Id(\mathbb{Z}_8[X]/(X^2))$:

$\to$	O	A	B	C	E
O	E	E	E	E	E
A	A	E	E	E	E
B	O	B	E	E	E
C	O	B	B	E	E
E	O	A	B	C	E

$\odot$	O	A	B	C	E
O	O	O	O	O	O
A	O	O	A	A	A
B	O	A	A	A	B
C	O	A	A	B	C
E	O	A	B	C	E

In the following, we present a way to generate finite BL-algebras using the ordinal product of residuated lattices.

We recall that, in [10], Iorgulescu studied the influence of the conditions ($prel$) and (div) on the ordinal product of two residuated lattices.

It is known that if $\mathcal{L}_1 = (L_1, \wedge_1, \vee_1, \odot_1, \to_1, 0_1, 1_1)$ and $\mathcal{L}_2 = (L_2, \wedge_2, \vee_2, \odot_2, \to_2, 0_2, 1_2)$ are two residuated lattices such that $1_1 = 0_2$ and $(L_1\backslash\{1_1\}) \cap (L_2\backslash\{0_2\}) = \varnothing$, then the ordinal product of $\mathcal{L}_1$ and $\mathcal{L}_2$ is the residuated lattice $\mathcal{L}_1 \boxtimes \mathcal{L}_2 = (L_1 \cup L_2, \wedge, \vee, \odot, \to, 0, 1)$ where

$$0 = 0_1 \text{ and } 1 = 1_2,$$

$x \leq y$ if $(x, y \in L_1$ and $x \leq_1 y)$ or $(x, y \in L_2$ and $x \leq_2 y)$ or $(x \in L_1$ and $y \in L_2)$,

$$x \to y = \begin{cases} 1, & \text{if } x \leq y, \\ x \to_i y, & \text{if } x \not\leq y, \ x, y \in L_i, \ i = 1, 2, \\ y, & \text{if } x \not\leq y, \ x \in L_2, \ y \in L_1\backslash\{1_1\}. \end{cases}$$

$$x \odot y = \begin{cases} x \odot_1 y, & \text{if } x, y \in L_1, \\ x \odot_2 y, & \text{if } x, y \in L_2, \\ x, & \text{if } x \in L_1\backslash\{1_1\} \text{ and } y \in L_2. \end{cases}$$

The ordinal product is associative, but is not commutative; see [10].

Proposition 5 ([10] (Corollary 3.5.10)). *Let $\mathcal{L}_1$ and $\mathcal{L}_2$ be BL-algebras.*
(i) If $\mathcal{L}_1$ is a chain, then the ordinal product $\mathcal{L}_1 \boxtimes \mathcal{L}_2$ is a BL-algebra;
(ii) If $\mathcal{L}_1$ is not a chain, then the ordinal product $\mathcal{L}_1 \boxtimes \mathcal{L}_2$ is only a residuated lattice satisfying (div) condition.

Remark 7. *(i) An ordinal product of two BL-chains is a BL-chain. Indeed, using the definition of implication in an ordinal product for every x, y we have $x \to y = 1$ or $y \to x = 1$;*
(ii) An ordinal product of two BL-algebras is a BL-algebra that is not an MV-algebra. Indeed, if $\mathcal{L}_1$ and $\mathcal{L}_2$ are two BL-algebras (the first being a chain), using Proposition 5, the residuated lattice $\mathcal{L}_1 \boxtimes \mathcal{L}_2$ is a BL-algebra in which we have $(1_1)^{**} = (1_1 \to 0_1)^* = (0_1)^* = 0_1 \to 0_1 = 1 = 1_2 \neq 1_1$. Thus, $\mathcal{L}_1 \boxtimes \mathcal{L}_2$ is not an MV-algebra.

For a natural number $n \geq 2$, we consider the decomposition (which is not unique) of n in factors greater than 1. We only count the decompositions one time with the same terms, but with other orders of terms in the product. We denote by $\pi(n)$ the number of all such decompositions. Obviously, if n is prime, then $\pi(n) = 0$.

We recall that an MV-algebra is finite iff it is isomorphic to a finite product of MV-chains; see [17]. Furthermore, for two MV-algebras L_1 and L_2, the algebras $L_1 \times L_2$ and $L_2 \times L_1$ are isomorphic; see [18]. Using these results, in [15], we showed that for every natural number $n \geq 2$, there are $\pi(n) + 1$ non-isomorphic MV-algebras with n elements of which only one is a chain.

Example 10. *For $n = 6$, we have $6 = 2 \cdot 3 = 3 \cdot 2$; thus, $\pi(6) = 1$. Therefore, there are $\pi(6) + 1 = 2$ types (up to an isomorphism) of MV-algebras with six elements.*

In Table 1, we briefly describe a way of generating finite MV-algebras M with $2 \leq n \leq 8$ elements using commutative rings; see [15].

Table 1. Rings that Generate MV-algebras of order n, $2 \leq n \leq 8$.

$|M| = n$	No. of MVs	Rings that Generate MV
$n = 2$	1	$Id(\mathbb{Z}_2)$ (chain)
$n = 3$	1	$Id(\mathbb{Z}_4)$ (chain)
$n = 4$	2	$Id(\mathbb{Z}_8)$ (chain) and $Id(\mathbb{Z}_2 \times \mathbb{Z}_2)$
$n = 5$	1	$Id(\mathbb{Z}_{16})$ (chain)
$n = 6$	2	$Id(\mathbb{Z}_{32})$ (chain) and $Id(\mathbb{Z}_2 \times \mathbb{Z}_4)$
$n = 7$	1	$Id(\mathbb{Z}_{64})$ (chain)
$n = 8$	3	$Id(\mathbb{Z}_{128})$ (chain) and $Id(\mathbb{Z}_2 \times \mathbb{Z}_8)$ and $Id(\mathbb{Z}_2 \times \mathbb{Z}_2 \times \mathbb{Z}_2)$

Using the construction of the ordinal product, Proposition 5 and Remark 7, we can generate BL-algebras (which are not MV-algebras) using commutative rings.

Example 11. *In [15] we show that there is one MV-algebra with three elements (up to an isomorphism); see Table 1. This MV-algebra is isomorphic to $Id(\mathbb{Z}_4)$ and is a chain. To generate a BL-chain with three elements (which is not an MV-algebra) using the ordinal product, we must consider only the MV-algebra with two elements (which is, in fact, a Boolean algebra). In the commutative ring $(\mathbb{Z}_2, +, \cdot)$, the ideals are $Id(\mathbb{Z}_2) = \{\{\hat{0}\}, \mathbb{Z}_2\}$. Obviously, $(Id(\mathbb{Z}_2), \cap, +, \otimes \to, 0 = \{0\}, 1 = \mathbb{Z}_2)$ is an MV-chain. Now we consider two MV-algebras isomorphic with $Id(\mathbb{Z}_2)$ denoted $\mathcal{L}_1 = (L_1 = \{0, a\}, \wedge, \vee, \odot, \to, 0, a)$ and $\mathcal{L}_2 = (L_2 = \{a, 1\}, \wedge, \vee, \odot, \to, a, 1)$. Using Proposition 5, we can construct the BL-algebra $\mathcal{L}_1 \boxtimes \mathcal{L}_2 = (L_1 \cup L_2 = \{0, a, 1\}, \wedge, \vee, \odot, \to, 0, 1)$ with $0 \leq a \leq 1$ and the following operations:*

$\to$	0	a	1
0	1	1	1
a	0	1	1
1	0	a	1

and

$\odot$	0	a	1
0	0	0	0
a	0	a	a
1	0	a	1

obtaining the same BL-algebra of order 3 as in Example 6.

Obviously, $\mathcal{L}_1 \boxtimes \mathcal{L}_2$ is a BL-chain that is not an MV-chain, since, for example, $a^{**} = 1 \neq a$.

Example 12. *To generate the non-linearly ordered BL-algebra with five elements from Example 3, we consider the commutative rings $(\mathbb{Z}_2, +, \cdot)$ and $(\mathbb{Z}_2 \times \mathbb{Z}_2, +, \cdot)$. For $\mathbb{Z}_2 \times \mathbb{Z}_2 = \{(\hat{0}, \hat{0}), (\hat{0}, \hat{1}), (\hat{1}, \hat{0}), (\hat{1}, \hat{1})\}$, we obtain the lattice $Id(\mathbb{Z}_2 \times \mathbb{Z}_2) = \{(\hat{0}, \hat{0})\}, \{(\hat{0}, \hat{0}), (\hat{0}, \hat{1})\}, \{(\hat{0}, \hat{0}), (\hat{1}, \hat{0})\}, \mathbb{Z}_2 \times \mathbb{Z}_2\} = \{O, R, B, E\}$, which is an MV-algebra $(Id(\mathbb{Z}_2 \times \mathbb{Z}_2), \cap, +, \otimes \to, 0 = \{(\hat{0}, \hat{0})\}, 1 = \mathbb{Z}_2 \times \mathbb{Z}_2)$. In $Id(\mathbb{Z}_2 \times \mathbb{Z}_2)$, we have the following operations:*

$\to$	O	R	B	E
O	E	E	E	E
R	B	E	B	E
B	R	R	E	E
E	O	R	B	E

,

$\otimes = \cap$	O	R	B	E
O	O	O	O	O
R	O	R	O	R
B	O	O	B	B
E	O	R	B	E

and

$+$	O	R	B	E
O	O	R	B	E
R	R	R	E	E
B	B	E	B	E
E	E	E	E	E

.

If we consider two MV-algebras isomorphic with $(Id(\mathbb{Z}_2), \cap, +, \otimes \to, 0 = \{0\}, 1 = \mathbb{Z}_2)$ and $(Id(\mathbb{Z}_2 \times \mathbb{Z}_2), \cap, +, \otimes \to, 0 = \{(\hat{0}, \hat{0})\}, 1 = \mathbb{Z}_2 \times \mathbb{Z}_2)$, denoted by $\mathcal{L}_1 = (L_1 = \{0, c\}, \wedge_1, \vee_1, \odot_1, \to_1, 0, c)$ and $\mathcal{L}_2 = (L_2 = \{c, a, b, 1\}, \wedge_2, \vee_2, \odot_2, \to_2, c, 1)$, then, using Proposition 5, we generate the BL-algebra $\mathcal{L}_1 \boxtimes \mathcal{L}_2 = (L_1 \cup L_2 = \{0, c, a, b, 1\}, \wedge, \vee, \odot, \to, 0, 1)$ from Example 3.

Remark 8. *Using the model from Examples 11 and 12 for two BL-algebras $\mathcal{L}_1$ and $\mathcal{L}_2$ we can use these algebras to obtain two BL-algebras $\mathcal{L}'_1$ and $\mathcal{L}'_2$, isomorphic with $\mathcal{L}_1$ and $\mathcal{L}_2$, respectively, that satisfy the conditions imposed by the ordinal product.*

We denote by $\mathcal{L}_1 \boxdot \mathcal{L}_2$ the ordinal product $\mathcal{L}'_1 \boxtimes \mathcal{L}'_2$.

From Proposition 5 and Remark 7, we deduce the following.

Theorem 5. *(i) To generate a BL-algebra with $n \geq 3$ elements as an ordinal product $\mathcal{L}_1 \boxtimes \mathcal{L}_2$ of two BL-algebras $\mathcal{L}_1$ and $\mathcal{L}_2$ we have the following possibilities:*

$\mathcal{L}_1$ *is a BL-chain with i elements and $\mathcal{L}_2$ is a BL-algebra with j elements*

and

$\mathcal{L}_1$ *is a BL-chain with j elements and $\mathcal{L}_2$ is a BL-algebra with i elements*

or

$\mathcal{L}_1$ *is a BL-chain with k elements and $\mathcal{L}_2$ is a BL-algebra with k elements*

for $i, j \geq 2, i + j = n + 1, i < j$ and $k \geq 2, k = \frac{n+1}{2} \in \mathbb{N}$,

(ii) To generate a BL-chain with $n \geq 3$ elements as the ordinal product $\mathcal{L}_1 \boxtimes \mathcal{L}_2$ of two BL-algebras $\mathcal{L}_1$ and $\mathcal{L}_2$, we have the following possibilities:

$\mathcal{L}_1$ *is a BL-chain with i elements and $\mathcal{L}_2$ is a BL-chain with j elements*

and

$\mathcal{L}_1$ *is a BL-chain with j elements and $\mathcal{L}_2$ is a BL-chain with i elements*

or

$\mathcal{L}_1$ *is a BL-chain with k elements and $\mathcal{L}_2$ is a BL-chain with k elements*

for $i, j \geq 2, i + j = n + 1, i < j$ and $k \geq 2, k = \frac{n+1}{2} \in \mathbb{N}$.

We make the following notations:

$$\mathcal{BL}_n = \text{the set of BL-algebras with } n \text{ elements;}$$

$$\mathcal{BL}_n(c) = \text{the set of BL-chains with } n \text{ elements;}$$

$$\mathcal{MV}_n = \text{the set of MV-algebras with } n \text{ elements;}$$

$$\mathcal{MV}_n(c) = \text{the set of MV-chains with } n \text{ elements.}$$

Theorem 6. *(i) Finite BL-algebras (up to an isomorphism) that are not MV-algebras with $3 \leq n \leq 5$ elements can be generated using the ordinal product of BL-algebras.*

(ii) The number of non-isomorphic BL-algebras with n elements (with $2 \leq n \leq 5$) is

$$|\mathcal{BL}_2| = |\mathcal{MV}_2| = \pi(2) + 1,$$

$$|\mathcal{BL}_3| = |\mathcal{MV}_3| + |\mathcal{BL}_2| = \pi(3) + \pi(2) + 2,$$

$$|\mathcal{BL}_4| = |\mathcal{MV}_4| + |\mathcal{BL}_3| + |\mathcal{BL}_2| = \pi(4) + \pi(3) + 3 \cdot \pi(2) + 4,$$

$$|\mathcal{BL}_5| = |\mathcal{MV}_5| + |\mathcal{BL}_4| + |\mathcal{BL}_3| + |\mathcal{BL}_2| =$$

$$= \pi(5) + \pi(4) + 2 \cdot \pi(3) + 5 \cdot \pi(2) + 8.$$

Proof. From Proposition 5 and Remark 7, we remark that using the ordinal product of two BL-algebras, we can generate only BL-algebras that are not MV-algebras.

We generate all BL-algebras with n elements ($2 \leq n \leq 5$) that are not MV-algebras.

Case $n = 2$.

We obviously only have a BL-algebra (up to an isomorphism) isomorphic with

$$(Id(\mathbb{Z}_2), \cap, +, \otimes \to, 0 = \{0\}, 1 = \mathbb{Z}_2).$$

In fact, this residuated lattice is a BL-chain and is the only MV-algebra with 2 elements. We deduce that
$$|\mathcal{MV}_2| = |\mathcal{BL}_2| = \pi(2) + 1 = 1$$
$$|\mathcal{MV}_2(c)| = |\mathcal{BL}_2(c)| = 1.$$

Case $n = 3$.

Using Theorem 5, to generate a BL-algebra with 3 elements as an ordinal product $\mathcal{L}_1 \boxtimes \mathcal{L}_2$ of two BL-algebras $\mathcal{L}_1$ and $\mathcal{L}_2$, we must consider:

$\mathcal{L}_1$ is a BL-chain with two elements and $\mathcal{L}_2$ is a BL-algebra with two elements.

Since there is only one BL-algebra (up to an isomorphism) with two elements and it is a chain, we obtain the BL-algebra
$$Id(\mathbb{Z}_2) \boxdot Id(\mathbb{Z}_2),$$

which is a chain.

We deduce that

$$|\mathcal{MV}_3| = \pi(3) + 1 \text{ and } |\mathcal{BL}_3| = |\mathcal{MV}_3| + 1 \cdot |\mathcal{BL}_2| = \pi(3) + \pi(2) + 2 = 2$$

$$|\mathcal{MV}_3(c)| = 1 \text{ and } |\mathcal{BL}_3(c)| = |\mathcal{MV}_3(c)| + 1 = 1 + 1 = 2.$$

We remark that $|\mathcal{BL}_3| = |\mathcal{MV}_3| + |\mathcal{BL}_2|$.

Case $n = 4$.

Using Theorem 5, to generate a BL-algebra with four elements as the ordinal product $\mathcal{L}_1 \boxtimes \mathcal{L}_2$ of two BL-algebras $\mathcal{L}_1$ and $\mathcal{L}_2$, we must consider:

$\mathcal{L}_1$ is a BL-chain with two elements and $\mathcal{L}_2$ is a BL-algebra with three elements;

$\mathcal{L}_1$ is a BL-chain with three elements and $\mathcal{L}_2$ is a BL-algebra with two elements.

We obtain the following BL-algebras:

$$Id(\mathbb{Z}_2) \boxdot Id(\mathbb{Z}_4) \text{ and } Id(\mathbb{Z}_2) \boxdot (Id(\mathbb{Z}_2) \boxdot Id(\mathbb{Z}_2))$$

and
$$Id(\mathbb{Z}_4) \boxdot Id(\mathbb{Z}_2) \text{ and } (Id(\mathbb{Z}_2) \boxdot (Id(\mathbb{Z}_2)) \boxdot Id(\mathbb{Z}_2).$$

Since $\boxtimes$ is associative, we obtain three BL-algebras (up to an isomorphism) that are chains with Remark 7.

We deduce that
$$|\mathcal{MV}_4| = \pi(4) + 1$$

$$|\mathcal{BL}_4| = |\mathcal{MV}_4| + 1 \cdot |\mathcal{BL}_3| + 2 \cdot |\mathcal{BL}_2| - 1 = \pi(4) + \pi(3) + 3 \cdot \pi(2) + 4 = 5$$

$$|\mathcal{MV}_4(c)| = 1 \text{ and } |\mathcal{BL}_4(c)| = |\mathcal{MV}_3(c)| + 3 = 1 + 3 = 4.$$

We remark that $|\mathcal{BL}_4| = |\mathcal{MV}_4| + |\mathcal{BL}_3| + |\mathcal{BL}_2|$.

Case $n = 5$.

To generate a BL-algebra with five elements as the ordinal product $\mathcal{L}_1 \boxtimes \mathcal{L}_2$ of two BL-algebras $\mathcal{L}_1$ and $\mathcal{L}_2$, we must consider:

$\mathcal{L}_1$ is a BL-chain with two elements and $\mathcal{L}_2$ is a BL-algebra with four elements;

$\mathcal{L}_1$ is a BL-chain with four elements and $\mathcal{L}_2$ is a BL-algebra with two elements;

$\mathcal{L}_1$ is a BL-chain with three elements and $\mathcal{L}_2$ is a BL-algebra with three elements. We obtain the following BL-algebras:

$$Id(\mathbb{Z}_2) \boxdot Id(\mathbb{Z}_8),\ Id(\mathbb{Z}_2) \boxdot Id(\mathbb{Z}_2 \times \mathbb{Z}_2),\ Id(\mathbb{Z}_2) \boxdot [Id(\mathbb{Z}_2) \boxdot Id(\mathbb{Z}_4)],$$
$$Id(\mathbb{Z}_2) \boxdot [Id(\mathbb{Z}_4) \boxdot Id(\mathbb{Z}_2)]\ \text{and}\ Id(\mathbb{Z}_2) \boxdot [Id(\mathbb{Z}_2) \boxdot (Id(\mathbb{Z}_2) \boxdot Id(\mathbb{Z}_2))]$$

and

$$Id(\mathbb{Z}_8) \boxdot Id(\mathbb{Z}_2),\ [Id(\mathbb{Z}_2) \boxdot Id(\mathbb{Z}_4)] \boxdot Id(\mathbb{Z}_2),$$
$$[Id(\mathbb{Z}_4) \boxdot Id(\mathbb{Z}_2)] \boxdot Id(\mathbb{Z}_2)\ \text{and}\ [Id(\mathbb{Z}_2) \boxdot (Id(\mathbb{Z}_2) \boxdot Id(\mathbb{Z}_2))] \boxdot Id(\mathbb{Z}_2)$$

and

$$Id(\mathbb{Z}_4) \boxdot Id(\mathbb{Z}_4),\ [Id(\mathbb{Z}_2) \boxdot Id(\mathbb{Z}_2)] \boxdot [Id(\mathbb{Z}_2)) \boxdot Id(\mathbb{Z}_2)]$$
$$Id(\mathbb{Z}_4) \boxdot [Id(\mathbb{Z}_2) \boxdot Id(\mathbb{Z}_2)]\ \text{and}\ [Id(\mathbb{Z}_2) \boxdot Id(\mathbb{Z}_2)] \boxdot Id(\mathbb{Z}_4)$$

Since $\boxtimes$ is associative, $Id(\mathbb{Z}_2) \boxdot [Id(\mathbb{Z}_4) \boxdot Id(\mathbb{Z}_2)] = [Id(\mathbb{Z}_2) \boxdot Id(\mathbb{Z}_4)] \boxdot Id(\mathbb{Z}_2)$, $Id(\mathbb{Z}_2) \boxdot [Id(\mathbb{Z}_2) \boxdot (Id(\mathbb{Z}_2) \boxdot Id(\mathbb{Z}_2))] = [Id(\mathbb{Z}_2) \boxdot (Id(\mathbb{Z}_2) \boxdot Id(\mathbb{Z}_2))] \boxdot Id(\mathbb{Z}_2)$ $= [Id(\mathbb{Z}_2) \boxdot Id(\mathbb{Z}_2)] \boxdot [Id(\mathbb{Z}_2)) \boxdot Id(\mathbb{Z}_2)]$, $[Id(\mathbb{Z}_4) \boxdot Id(\mathbb{Z}_2)] \boxdot Id(\mathbb{Z}_2) = Id(\mathbb{Z}_4) \boxdot [Id(\mathbb{Z}_2)$ $\boxdot Id(\mathbb{Z}_2)]$ and $Id(\mathbb{Z}_2) \boxdot (Id(\mathbb{Z}_2) \boxdot Id(\mathbb{Z}_4)) = [Id(\mathbb{Z}_2) \boxdot Id(\mathbb{Z}_2)] \boxdot Id(\mathbb{Z}_4)$.

We obtain eight BL-algebras of which seven are chains from Remark 7.

We deduce that

$$|\mathcal{MV}_5| = \pi(5) + 1 = 1\ \text{and}\ |\mathcal{BL}_5| = 9 = |\mathcal{MV}_5| + |\mathcal{BL}_4| + |\mathcal{BL}_3| + |\mathcal{BL}_2|$$

$$|\mathcal{MV}_5(c)| = 1\ \text{and}\ |\mathcal{BL}_5(c)| = 8.$$

□

Table 2 presents a basic summary of the structure of BL-algebras L with $2 \leq n \leq 5$ elements:

Table 2. The structure of BL-algebras of order n, $2 \leq n \leq 5$.

$|L| = n$	No. of BL-alg	Structure
$n = 2$	1	$\{Id(\mathbb{Z}_2)\}$ (chain, MV)
$n = 3$	2	$Id(\mathbb{Z}_4)$ (chain, MV) $Id(\mathbb{Z}_2) \boxdot Id(\mathbb{Z}_2)$ (chain)
$n = 4$	5	$Id(\mathbb{Z}_8)$ (chain, MV) $Id(\mathbb{Z}_2 \times \mathbb{Z}_2)$ (MV) $Id(\mathbb{Z}_2) \boxdot Id(\mathbb{Z}_4)$ (chain) $Id(\mathbb{Z}_4) \boxdot Id(\mathbb{Z}_2)$ (chain) $Id(\mathbb{Z}_2) \boxdot (Id(\mathbb{Z}_2) \boxdot Id(\mathbb{Z}_2))$ (chain)
$n = 5$	9	$Id(\mathbb{Z}_{16})$ (chain, MV) $Id(\mathbb{Z}_2) \boxdot Id(\mathbb{Z}_8)$ (chain) $Id(\mathbb{Z}_2) \boxdot Id(\mathbb{Z}_2 \times \mathbb{Z}_2)$ $Id(\mathbb{Z}_2) \boxdot (Id(\mathbb{Z}_2) \boxdot Id(\mathbb{Z}_4))$ (chain) $Id(\mathbb{Z}_2) \boxdot (Id(\mathbb{Z}_4) \boxdot Id(\mathbb{Z}_2))$ (chain) $Id(\mathbb{Z}_2) \boxdot (Id(\mathbb{Z}_2) \boxdot (Id(\mathbb{Z}_2) \boxdot Id(\mathbb{Z}_2)))$ (chain) $Id(\mathbb{Z}_8) \boxdot Id(\mathbb{Z}_2)$ (chain) $(Id(\mathbb{Z}_4) \boxdot Id(\mathbb{Z}_2)) \boxdot Id(\mathbb{Z}_2)$ (chain) $Id(\mathbb{Z}_4) \boxdot Id(\mathbb{Z}_4)$ (chain)

Finally, Table 3 present a summary of the number of MV-algebras, MV-chains, BL-algebras and BL-chains with $n \leq 5$ elements obtained used commutative rings:

Table 3. A summary of the number of the obtained BL-algebras.

	n = 2	n = 3	n = 4	n = 5
MV-algebras	1	1	2	1
MV-chains	1	1	1	1
BL-algebras	1	2	5	9
BL-chains	1	2	4	8

5. Conclusions

It is known that BL-algebras are a particular kind of residuated lattices.

In this paper, we studied rings whose ideals have a BL-algebra structure and we used some commutative rings to build certain finite BL-algebras by passing to the ideal lattice.

Using the results obtained in this paper, in further research, we will try to describe a recursive algorithm to construct all isomorphism classes of finite BL-algebras of a given size. Furthermore, we hope to obtain important results about BL-rings by studying the binary block codes associated with a BL-algebra in further research.

Author Contributions: Conceptualization, C.F. and D.P.; methodology, C.F. and D.P.; software, C.F. and D.P.; validation, C.F. and D.P.; formal analysis, C.F. and D.P.; investigation, C.F. and D.P.; resources, C.F. and D.P.; data curation, C.F. and D.P.; writing—original draft preparation, C.F. and D.P.; writing—review and editing, C.F. and D.P.; visualization, C.F. and D.P.; supervision, C.F. and D.P.; project administration, C.F. and D.P. All authors have read and agreed to the published version of the manuscript.

Funding: This research received no external funding.

Data Availability Statement: Not applicable.

Acknowledgments: The authors express their gratitude to the anonymous reviewers and editor for their careful reading of the manuscript and many valuable remarks and suggestions.

Conflicts of Interest: The authors declare no conflict of interest.

References

1. Dilworth, R.P. Abstract residuation over lattices. *Bull. Am. Math. Soc.* **1938**, *44*, 262–268. [CrossRef]
2. Ward, M.; Dilworth, R.P. Residuated lattices. *Trans. Am. Math. Soc.* **1939**, *45*, 335–354. [CrossRef]
3. Blair, R.L. Ideal lattices and the structure of rings. *Trans. Am. Math. Soc.* **1953**, *75*, 136–153. [CrossRef]
4. Belluce, L.P.; Di Nola, A. Commutative rings whose ideals form an MV-algebra. *Math. Log. Quart.* **2009**, *55*, 468–486. [CrossRef]
5. Heubo-Kwegna, O.A.; Lele, C.; Nganou, J.B. BL-rings. *Log. J. IGPL* **2016**, *26*, 290–299. [CrossRef]
6. Tchoffo Foka, S.V.; Tonga, M. Rings and residuated lattices whose fuzzy ideals form a Boolean algebra. *Soft Comput.* **2022**, *26*, 535–539. [CrossRef]
7. Hájek, P. Metamathematics of Fuzzy Logic. In *Trends in Logic-Studia Logica Library 4*; Kluwer Academic Publishers: Dordrecht, The Netherlands, 1998.
8. Cignoli, R.; D'Ottaviano, I.M.L.; Mundici, D. Algebraic Foundations of Many-Valued Reasoning. In *Trends in Logic-Studia Logica Library 7*; Kluwer Academic Publishers: Dordrecht, The Netherlands, 2000.
9. Chang, C.C. Algebraic analysis of many-valued logic. *Trans. Am. Math. Soc.* **1958**, *88*, 467–490. [CrossRef]
10. Iorgulescu, A. *Algebras of Logic as BCK Algebras*; A.S.E.: Bucharest, Romania, 2009.
11. Belohlavek, R.; Vychodil, V. Residuated lattices of size $n \leq 12$. *Order* **2010**, *27*, 147–161. [CrossRef]
12. Turunen, E. *Mathematics Behind Fuzzy Logic*; Physica-Verlag: Heidelberg, Germany, 1999.
13. Busneag, D.; Piciu, D. *Lectii de Algebra*; Ed. Universitaria: Craiova, Romania, 2002.
14. Di Nola, A.; Lettieri, A. Finite BL-algebras. *Discret. Math.* **2003**, *269*, 93–112. [CrossRef]
15. Flaut, C.; Piciu, D. Connections between commutative rings and some algebras of logic. *Iran. J. Fuzzy Syst.* **2022**, *19*, 93–110.
16. Lam, T.Y. A first course in noncommutative rings. In *Graduate Texts in Mathematics*, 2nd ed.; Springer: Berlin/Heidelberg, Germany, 2001.
17. Höhle, U.; Rodabaugh, S.E. *Mathematics of Fuzzy Sets: Logic, Topology and Measure Theory*; Springer: Berlin, Germany, 1999.
18. Flaut, C.; Vasile, R. Wajsberg algebras arising from binary block codes. *Soft Comput.* **2020**, *24*, 6047–6058. [CrossRef]

 *mathematics*

Review

Advances in Singular and Degenerate PDEs

Salvatore Fragapane

University of the Studies of Rome "La Sapienza", 00161 Rome, Italy; salvatore.fragapane@uniroma1.it

Abstract: This review was written with a dual purpose; on the one hand, to collect all the topics dealt with during the conference "Advances in Singular and Degenerate PDEs". For this reason, in the first part of this work, the abstracts of the lectures during the workshop are shown. On the other hand, as well as the workshop, this work is a way to celebrate the career of Professor Maria Agostina Vivaldi. Professor Vivaldi's long career and her work are hence highlighted in this work; moreover, some of the more recent results obtained by Professor Vivaldi about problems involving p-Laplace-type operators in fractal and pre-fractal boundary domains are here illustrated and discussed. In conclusion, some new recent outcomes and new perspectives are outlined.

Keywords: partial differential equations; singular and degenerate operators

MSC: 35J92; 35J70; 35J75

Citation: Fragapane, S. Advances in Singular and Degenerate PDEs. *Mathematics* 2022, *10*, 4760. https://doi.org/10.3390/math10244760

Academic Editor: Mirosław Lachowicz

Received: 6 November 2022
Accepted: 9 December 2022
Published: 14 December 2022

Publisher's Note: MDPI stays neutral with regard to jurisdictional claims in published maps and institutional affiliations.

Copyright: © 2022 by the author. Licensee MDPI, Basel, Switzerland. This article is an open access article distributed under the terms and conditions of the Creative Commons Attribution (CC BY) license (https://creativecommons.org/licenses/by/4.0/).

1. Introduction

The conference "Advances in Singular and Degenerate PDEs" took place on 16–17 September 2021 in the University of the Studies of Rome "La Sapienza", at the Department of Basis and Applied Science for Engineering (S.B.A.I., in the following) belonging to the Faculty of Civil and Industrial Engineering. The Scientific Committee was formed by D. Andreucci, R. Capitanelli, D. Giachetti, and M.R. Lancia, and the Organizing Committee was formed by D. Andreucci, R. Capitanelli, S. Creo, S. Fragapane, D. Giachetti, and M.R. Lancia (https://sites.google.com/uniroma1.it/advances/home, accessed on 1 November 2022).

The conference was sponsored by GNAMPA ("Gruppo Nazionale per l'Analisi Matematica, la Probabilità e le loro Applicazioni") and by the University of the Studies of Rome "La Sapienza".

During the workshop, all the participants had the opportunity to listen to very-high-level lectures of the invited speakers (see Section 2).

Participation was extensive both in person and online. The presence of so many speakers and participants gave a strong contribution to the success of the event and allowed a huge exchange of opinions and ideas among all. Moreover, this was a way to start new collaborations and research activities. In particular, many Ph.D. students and young researchers joined the workshop.

The conference was also a way to celebrate the long career of Professor Maria Agostina Vivaldi (see Section 3). In addition, some of the most recent results achieved by Professor Vivaldi, in collaboration with other authors, about problems involving p-Laplace-type operators in "bad domains", that is, domains having fractal or pre-fractal boundary, are reported and illustrated (see Section 4). In conclusion, some new perspectives and open problems have arisen thanks to these research activities, pointing out the new results reached following these new directions and their contribution and importance in the current scenario (see Section 5).

2. Lectures of the Conference

In this section, the titles and the abstracts of the lectures given by the invited speakers are listed.

ISABEAU BIRINDELLI—University of the Studies of Rome "La Sapienza"
Truncated Laplacian, a Class of Very Degenerate Operators
Abstract. I will show how the lack of ellipticity leads to surprising phenomena both in the regularity of the solutions, in particular near the boundary, and in the validity of the maximum principle.

LUCIO BOCCARDO—University of the Studies of Rome "La Sapienza"
Real Analysis Methods in Some Minimization Problems for Integral Functionals of Calculus of Variations
Abstract. Recent results. We deal with integral problems where the functional J is defined in $W_0^{1,p}(\Omega)$, $p > 1$, as

$$J(v) = \int_\Omega j(x, \nabla v) - \int_\Omega fv,$$

under usual assumptions on j, Ω and f (like $f \in L^{(*)'}(\Omega)$).

If we also assume the strict convexity of $j(x, \xi)$ with respect to ξ, then it is proved in [1] that the minimizing sequences $\{u_n\}$ of J are compact in $W_0^{1,p}(\Omega)$. The main point is the proof of the convergence in measure of $\nabla u_n(x)$.

If we consider the minimization problems

$$u_n \in C_n : J(u_n) \leq J(v), \ \forall\, v \in C_n$$

and

$$u_0 \in C_0 : J(u_0) \leq J(v), \ \forall\, v \in C_0,$$

the strong convergence in $W_0^{1,p}(\Omega)$ of the sequence $\{u_n\}$ to u_0 on the assumption that the sequence $\{C_n\}$ Mosco-converges to C_0. is proved in [2].

Let now $f \in L^1(\Omega)$. A measurable function u is a T-minimum for the functional J if

$$\begin{cases} T_i(u) \in W_0^{1,p}(\Omega), \ \forall\, i \in \mathbb{R}^+ : \\ \displaystyle\int_{\{|u-\varphi|\leq i\}} j(x, Du) - \int_\Omega f(x)\, T_i[u - \varphi] \leq \int_{\{|u-\varphi|\leq i\}} j(x, D\varphi), \quad \forall\, i \in \mathbb{R}^+, \\ \forall\, \varphi \in W_0^{1,p}(\Omega) \cap L^\infty(\Omega). \end{cases} \quad (1)$$

Existence and uniqueness of T-minima are proven in [3].

In [4] is proved that there exists a unique measurable function u such that

$$\begin{cases} u \geq \psi \text{ a.e. in } \Omega, \ T_i(u) \in W_0^{1,p}(\Omega), \ \forall i > 0, \\ \displaystyle\int_\Omega j(x, D\{\varphi + T_i[u - \varphi]\}) - \int_\Omega f(x)\, T_i[u - \varphi] \leq \int_\Omega j(x, D\varphi), \quad \forall\, i \in \mathbb{R}^+, \\ \forall\, \varphi \in W_0^{1,p}(\Omega) \cap L^\infty(\Omega), \ \varphi \geq \psi. \end{cases} \quad (2)$$

Moreover, if $\mathcal{K}(\psi_n)$ converges to $\mathcal{K}(\psi_0)$ in the sense of Mosco, then, for every $j > 0$, $T_j(u_n)$ converges to $T_j(u_0)$ weakly in $W_0^{1,p}(\Omega)$.

Work in progress: $p = 1$. Let $v \in L^1(\Omega)$,

$$I(v) = \int_\Omega \sqrt{1 + |v|^2} - \int_\Omega f(x)\, v, \quad \|f\|_{L^\infty(\Omega)} < 1.$$

Note that the minimizing sequences $\{u_n\}$ of J are bounded in $L^1(\Omega)$. Then:
- it is proved that $\{u_n\}$ is a Cauchy sequence in the distance equivalent to the convergence in measure;

- thanks to Ekeland's principle, the following inequality holds

$$I(u_n) \leq I(w) + \sqrt{\epsilon_n} \int_0^1 |u_n - w|, \quad \forall\, w \in L^1,$$

then this inequality allows us to show the equi-integrability of the sequence $\{u_n\}$;
- the proof of the last step hinges on the assumption that I does not depend on ∇v.

ITALO CAPUZZO DOLCETTA—University of the Studies of Rome "La Sapienza"
Invariant Cones for Linear Elliptic Systems with Gradient Coupling
Abstract. I will discuss first the validity of the weak Maximum Principle (**wMP**) for vector functions $u = (u_1, \ldots, u_m)$ satisfying systems of the form

$$Au + Cu \geq 0$$

in a bounded open set Ω of $\mathbb{R}^n$, where A is a diagonal matrix of linear degenerate second order elliptic operators and C is a cooperative matrix.
Next, some counterexamples to the validity of (**wMP**) are discussed when non diagonal couplings in first order partial derivatives of the u_i appear in the system. In this more general setting I will show, through a suitable reduction to a nonlinear scalar equation of Bellman type, that some algebraic condition on the structure of gradient couplings and a cooperativity condition on the matrix of zero order couplings guarantee the existence of invariant cones in the sense of Weinberger.
The presentation is mostly based on the papers [5,6].

PIERLUIGI COLLI—University of Pavia
Analysis, Estimates and Control for a Cahn-Hilliard Type System with Bio-Medical Applications
Abstract. The talk is concerned with the study of a complex PDE system related to four-species tumor growth models. The system consists of a Cahn-Hilliard equation for the tumor cell fraction coupled to a reaction-diffusion equation for a variable representing the nutrient concentration. Existence of solutions is discussed via an approximation of the system, that is done by adding two further viscosity terms with small coefficients, and then performing the asymptotic analysis as such coefficients tend to zero. Error estimates can also be proved. A distributed optimal control problem is addressed, in which the distributed control u plays in the right-hand side of the reaction-diffusion equation and can be interpreted as a nutrient supply or a medication, while the cost functional aims to keep the tumor cell fraction under control during the evolution.

GIANNI DAL MASO—SISSA Trieste
New Results on the Jerky Crack Growth in Elasto-Plastic Materials
Abstract. In the framework of a model for the quasistatic crack growth in elasto-plastic homogeneous materials in the planar case, we study the properties of the length of the crack as a function of time. We prove that, under suitable technical assumptions on the crack path, this monotone function is a pure jump function. Under stronger assumptions we prove also that the number of jumps is finite.

MARCO DEGIOVANNI—Catholic University of the Sacred Heart of Brescia
Critical Points for Functionals without Upper Growth Condition on the Principal Part
Abstract. The talk is devoted to variational methods applied to functionals of the calculus of variations. We prove the existence of multiple critical points for functionals whose principal part is not subjected to any upper growth condition. For this purpose, non-smooth variational methods are applied.

PAOLO MARCELLINI—University of Studies of Florence
Regularity for a Class of Non-Uniformly Elliptic Equations and Systems
Abstract. We give some regularity results for a class of non-uniformly elliptic equations and systems, as well as some examples and remarks about cases with possibly not regular weak solutions. Part

of the material has been published on-line in August-September 2021 and it can be found in the papers [7,8].

UMBERTO MOSCO—Worcester Polytechnic Institute
Un saluto a Maria Agostina
Abstract. I will introduce the scientific personality of Maria Agostina Vivaldi and sketch the topic of a new research which we plan to carry out together.

CARLO SBORDONE—University of Naples "Federico II"
On the Equation div u = f in the Plane and Dual Sobolev Inequalities
Abstract. Maximal integrability of the gradient $\nabla \varphi$ of the solution $\varphi \in W_0^1 L^{2,\infty}(Q_0)$, $Q_0 = [0,1]^2$ to quasilinear elliptic equation

$$L\varphi = \text{div}\, a(x, \nabla \varphi) = f \qquad f \in X \subset L^1(Q_0) \tag{3}$$

with measurable ingredients $a(\cdot, z)$, for $z \in \mathbb{R}^2$ and $a(x, \cdot)$ with linear growth at infinity for a.e. $x \in Q_0$, is studied. For $X = L^{(1,r)}(\log L)^\delta$, $Z = L^{2,r}(\log L)^\delta$ Lorentz-Zygmund spaces, $1 \leq r < \infty$, we obtain

$$\|\nabla \varphi\|_Z \leq c\|f\|_X$$

*and X is optimal among all rearrangement invariant Banach function subspaces of $L^1(Q_0)$.
In the special case $a(x,z) = z$ we compare regularity of $\nabla \varphi$ and $\nabla \psi$, where $\boldsymbol{u}$ is given in $W^1 X(Q_0; \mathbb{R}^2)$; $\psi \in W_0^1 L^{2,\infty}(Q_0)$ is the solution to*

$$\Delta \psi = \text{div}\, \boldsymbol{u},$$

with

$$\|\nabla \psi\|_Y \leq c\|\boldsymbol{u}\|_Y$$

and Y is the sharp rearrangement invariant target of X in Sobolev embedding

$$W^1 X \hookrightarrow Y.$$

The gap of regularity of $\nabla \psi$ and $\nabla \varphi$ is related to the solvability of

$$\text{div}\, \boldsymbol{u} = f,$$

with

$$\|\boldsymbol{u}\|_Y \leq C\|f\|_X$$

and the validity of dual Sobolev embedding

$$W^1(Y^\star) \hookrightarrow X^\star.$$

Work in cooperation with L. D'Onofrio, G. Manzo, R. Schiattarella.

MICHAEL STRUWE—ETH Zurich
Normalized Harmonic Map Flow
Abstract. Finding non-constant harmonic 3-spheres for a closed target manifold N is a prototype of a super-critical variational problem. In fact, the direct method fails, as the infimum of Dirichlet energy in any homotopy class of maps from the 3-sphere to any closed N is zero; moreover, the harmonic map heat flow may blow up in finite time, and even the identity map from the 3-sphere to itself is not stable under this flow. To overcome these difficulties, we propose the normalized harmonic map heat flow as a new tool, and we show that for this flow the identity map from the 3-sphere to itself now, indeed, is stable; moreover, the flow converges to a harmonic 3-sphere also when we perturb the target geometry. While our results are strongest in the perturbative setting, we also outline a possible global theory, which may open up a rich research agenda.

CRISTINA TROMBETTI—University of Naples "Federico II"
Comparison Results for Solutions to Elliptic Problems with Mixed Boundary Conditions
Abstract. Sharp estimates for solutions to Elliptic Problems with Dirichlet and Neumann boundary conditions are well established results since decades. So far not many results have been obtained in the case of Robin (or mixed) boundary conditions, and in this talk, we shall investigate some open questions related to Talenti-type estimates and Faber-Krahn inequality.

BOGDAN M. VERNESCU—Worcester Polytechnic Institute
Asymptotic Analysis of PDEs on Unbounded Domains
Abstract. The study of PDEs in long cylindrical domains can be approximated by using the solutions of the corresponding PDEs in infinite cylindrical domains and controlling the solutions' decay at infinity. For periodic heterogeneous materials in domains that become unbounded in one direction, the problems become two-parameter limit problems, as they depend both on the characteristic period size and the cylinder length. We will consider a few examples of homogenization in infinite cylindrical domain for elliptic PDEs with or without mild singularities.

VINCENZO VESPRI- University of the Studies of Florence
A Survey about Anisotropic Parabolic Operators
Abstract. We will speak about evolution anisotropic operators of the type

$$u_t = \sum_{i=1}^{N} Div(|Du|^{p_i-2}Du)$$

The first results on such class operators were found in the eighties, but still, especially for the rough regularity, the theory is incomplete and fragmented.

GIANLUCA VINTI—University of the Studies of Perugia
Some Results on Approximation and Applications
Abstract. I will present some approximation results for a family of operators and discuss some applications.

3. Professor Vivaldi's Career

Professor Maria Agostina Vivaldi graduated in Mathematics with Professor F. Scarpini in 1972 at Faculty of Mathematics, Physical and Natural Sciences at the University of the Studies of Rome "La Sapienza" with *magna cum laude*.

From 1976 to 1983, she was a Lecturer of Mathematical Analysis at Faculty of Mathematics, Physical and Natural Sciences at the University of the Studies of Rome "La Sapienza" and Assistant of Professor G. Fichera (from 1978 to 1983).

From 1983 to 1987, she was an Associate Professor at Faculty of Mathematical, Physical and Natural Sciences at the University of the Studies of Rome "La Sapienza".

From 1987 to October 1990, she became a Full Professor at Faculty of Mathematical, Physical and Natural Sciences at the University of the Studies of L'Aquila and from 1 November 1990 at Faculty of Engineering at the University of the Studies of Rome "La Sapienza".

During her long career she held several graduate courses of Mathematical Analysis I and II and Mathematical Methods for Engineering; moreover, she held various research-level courses.

She was a member of examination boards, evaluation panels, and committees for university positions and fellowships. In addition, she was an advisor of several Ph.D. students at the University of the Studies of Rome "La Sapienza" and an opponent in final Ph.D. discussions at other universities.

Furthermore, she was the coordinator of many research projects of the University of the Studies of Rome "La Sapienza", a member of several national and international research projects, and Editor of two Special Issues [9,10].

In 2016, Professor Maria Agostina Vivaldi was awarded the Medal of the National Academy of Science, "of XL", as recognition for her contributions to mathematics.

The list of her contributions ranges over various fields:

- **Convex analysis;**
- **Calculus of variations;**
- **Partial differential equations;**
- **Numerical analysis;**
- **Optimization problems;**
- **Analysis on fractal domains.**

In particular, she obtained remarkable results in the following different features concerning the fields previously listed:

- *On existence, uniqueness, asymptotics of solutions to variational, quasi-variational, and nonvariational inequalities*, see [11–22];
- *On regularity theory*, see [23–34];
- *On control theory*, see [35–39];
- *On integro-differential operators*, see [40–45];
- *On degenerate operators*, see [46,47];
- *On analysis on irregular structures*, see [48–72];
- *On asymptotic analysis of singular and degenerate problems*, see [73,74];
- *On error estimates*, see [75–77];
- *On existence, uniqueness results, and coercive estimates for systems*, see [33,78];
- *On functional inequalities*, see [79];
- *On self-organized criticality structures*, see [80,81].

The impact of her scientific work has been truly remarkable, and her contributions opened several new directions of research, some of which have been studied and developed by her students during their Ph.D. courses.

4. Professor Vivaldi's Research

As we pointed out in the previous section, during her career, Professor Vivaldi's research activity focused on many different fields and topics. Observing her long list of papers, it is immediately highlighted that "bad domains", which are fractal and pre-fractal domains and domains having fractal and pre-fractal boundary, in this case, has been widely involved; in particular, it is evident that they have been among the protagonists of her research, at least since 1999 (see [48]). In actuality, domains with angles were already considered in her previous works.

From then on, many new results were obtained by Professor Vivaldi in collaboration with other authors. Moreover, it is important to underline how these studies opened new research directions and posed new interesting questions and open problems. For example, the Ph.D. thesis of the author developed issues involving some of the topics discussed here, and where the domains considered have as boundary the Koch curve or the corresponding n-th pre-fractal approximating curve.

The following presentations deal principally with the results obtained in the framework of the topics just mentioned.

4.1. Domains and Operators

Before talking about the principal themes and results which were obtained by Professor Vivaldi's work, it is appropriate to discuss, at least briefly, the operators and the so-called "bad domains" involved.

As is well known, since their introduction due to Mandelbrot (see [82,83]), fractals have shown all their power in providing models to so many applied problems; more precisely, they are very powerful tools to describe nature in a more appropriate way, but they are useful in many other situations. Indeed, irregular structures, profiles, and shapes of natural objects can be represented in a new manner, and decidedly more accurate with respect to what the classical shapes of geometry allow. To obtain an idea of a situation in which the description allowed by fractal geometry shows all its potential, it is sufficient to think about the pulmonary alveoli. Their high branched structure can be difficult to describe, or at least surely nontrivial, with the classical shapes of geometry; on the contrary, the self-similar structure of some fractals, such as the Koch curve for instance, can allow easier modeling of such types of situations. Many other examples are provided by plants (Roman broccoli, ferns, etc.). In a physical framework, they lend themselves very well to those cases where a mathematical description of phenomena in which the surface effects are prevalent on the volume is required. All this makes it clear as to why and how they find applications in so many fields, such as physics, biology, medicine, engineering, etc.

Together with fractals, even p-Laplace-type operators occupy a prominent place in Professor Vivaldi's research. More precisely, the operators here discussed have the following general structure:

$$A_p(u) = -Div((k^2 + |\nabla u|^2)^{\frac{p-2}{2}} \nabla u), \text{ with } k \in \mathbb{R}.$$

In [84] (see also the references quoted there), the origin of operator $A_p(u)$ (in the special case of $k = 0$) is identified in the union of continuity equations and nonlinear power law.

Surely, for their interesting properties, but also for their many applications, there exists a very extensive amount of research involving p-Laplace-type operators.

In the introduction of [85], the author deals with physical motivations of the equations treated; in particular, he shows how these operators can provide mathematical models which are necessary for the study of various phenomena such as reaction–diffusion problems, non-Newtonian fluid mechanics, nonlinear filtration and diffusion (flows through porous media, plasma physics, etc.). Clearly, in each of these situations the unknown function u indicates certain physical quantities, density, and velocity, respectively. Furthermore, it is important to underline that both p and further amounts possibly involved in these equations that are in the physical models (for instance, the hydrostatic potential identifies different physical situations and properties of the media) are crucial to distinguish physical properties and situations.

In this framework, both degenerate case ($p > 2$ and $\nabla u = 0$) and singular case ($1 \leq p < 2$ and $\nabla u = 0$) could occur (see, for instance, [86,87] and the references therein). Moreover, another singular case is obtained, for example, when the source term is of the type $f(u) = \frac{1}{u^a}$, with $a > 0$, and the condition $u = 0$ on the boundary (see, for instance, ref. [85] and the references quoted there).

4.2. The Problem

The application examples just explained emphasize how the study of problems involving the domains and the operators named before are, without a doubt, useful and interesting. Nevertheless, the mathematical issues that arise when working with these problems are of equal importance and need to be examined one by one. From a theoretical point of view, these new questions were the ones which started extensive research about these topics.

The results obtained, that we will expose in the following, concern the issues of existence, regularity, uniqueness, and asymptotic behavior of the solutions of variational inequalities involving the operator $A_p(u)$, previously introduced, in domains having fractal or pre-fractal boundary. Moreover, for these problems, the numerical analysis was performed and some results about error estimates were obtained.

Now, in order to present some of the principal results obtained about the issues just listed (see [72,74,77]), let us introduce the problems.

Let $p \in (2, \infty)$ and let Ω be a bad domain of $\mathbb{R}^2$, that is, a domain having re-entrant corners. Then, let us consider the following two-obstacle problems

$$\text{find } u \in \mathcal{K}: \quad a_p(u, v-u) - \int_\Omega f(v-u) \geq 0 \quad , \forall v \in \mathcal{K}, \qquad (4)$$

with
$$a_p(u,v) = \int_\Omega (k^2 + |\nabla u|^2)^{\frac{p-2}{2}} \nabla u \nabla v, \ k \in \mathbb{R},$$
and
$$\mathcal{K} = \{v \in W_0^{1,p}(\Omega) : \varphi_1 \leq v \leq \varphi_2 \text{ in } \Omega \},$$
where f, φ_1, and φ_2 are given and belong to a suitable space.

Since, under suitable assumptions, both the operator and the convex set $\mathcal{K}$ satisfy some required conditions, for p fixed, the existence and the uniqueness of the solutions to Problem (4) can be immediately obtained (see [88]).

In the case of homogeneous Dirichlet condition, the uniqueness is guaranteed; in [89], instead, the authors do not have such type of situation, and the uniqueness is stated, making a suitable assumption on the datum f.

4.3. Regularity

Surely more delicate is the issue of the regularity.

After a careful discussion on the previous literature about the question, a new result regarding regularity, for the solution to Problem (4), is given by the authors in [72].

In order to discuss this result, let us consider Problem (4).

The model domain there considered is polygonal, with only one re-entrant corner (i.e., an angle with amplitude greater than π); however, the results hold even in the case of a domain with any fixed number of re-entrant corner; thus, also in the case in which, as Ω, it is taken a pre-fractal boundary domain. In particular, these types of domains, here considered and denoted with Ω_α^n, are polygonal and obtained starting with any regular polygon (triangle, in the cases discussed) and replacing each side with the n-th pre-fractal Koch curve K_α^n, where $n \in \mathbb{N}$ and $\alpha \in (2,4)$ is the inverse of the contraction factor.

Figure 1 shows the initial polygon and the first two following steps in the construction of the pre-fractal approximating domains Ω_α^n.

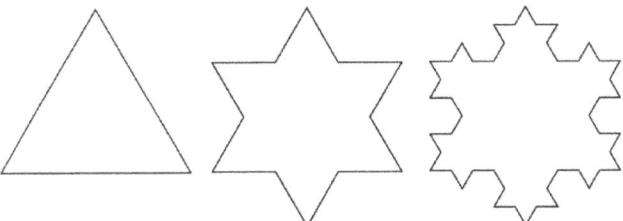

Figure 1. Ω_α^n, with $\alpha = 3$ and $n = 0$ (the initial polygon), $n = 1$, $n = 2$.

For completeness, we specify that in [77], the authors stated a regularity result in terms of Besov spaces for the solution to Problem (4), in the case where $k = 0$, directly considering the domains Ω_α^n.

Now, let us recall the following regularity result, stated in [72] (see Theorem 3.1), whose proof follows from a series of preliminary results:

Theorem 1. *Let us assume*
$$\begin{cases} f \in W^{-1,p'}(\Omega), \ \frac{1}{p} + \frac{1}{p'} = 1, \ \varphi_i \in W^{1,p}(\Omega), \ i = 1,2, \\ \varphi_1 \leq \varphi_2 \text{ in } \Omega, \ \varphi_1 \leq 0 \leq \varphi_2 \text{ in } \partial\Omega. \end{cases} \tag{5}$$

and
$$\begin{cases} k \neq 0 \\ f, A_p(\varphi_i) \in L^\infty(\Omega), \ i = 1,2, \\ A_p(\varphi_2) \wedge f \geq 0. \end{cases} \tag{6}$$

Then the solution u to double-obstacle Problem (4) belongs to the weighted Sobolev space

$$H^{2,\mu}(\Omega), \quad \mu > 1 - \gamma, \tag{7}$$

where

$$A_p(u) = -Div((k^2 + |\nabla u|^2)^{\frac{p-2}{2}} \nabla u),$$

$$H^{2,\mu}(\Omega) = \left\{ u \in H^1(\Omega) : \left(\int_\Omega \rho^{2\mu} |D^\beta u|^2 \right)^{\frac{1}{2}} < \infty \text{ for all } \beta \text{ with } |\beta| = 2 \right\}$$

and $\rho : \Omega \to \mathbb{R}$ is the distance function from the set of the vertex of the re-entrant corners. Moreover,

$$||u||_{H^{2,\mu}(\Omega)} \leq C \left\{ 1 + ||f||_{L^\infty(\Omega)} + ||A_p(\varphi_1)||_{L^\infty(\Omega)} + ||A_p(\varphi_2)||_{L^\infty(\Omega)} \right\}. \tag{8}$$

To clarify the meaning and the importance of this result, it is important to specify the structure of γ.

$$\gamma = \gamma(p, \chi) = 1 + \frac{p(1-\chi)^2 + (1-\chi)\sqrt{p^2 - \chi(2-\chi)(p-2)^2}}{2\chi(2-\chi)(p-1)}, \tag{9}$$

where $\chi \in (1,2)$ is related to the amplitude of the re-entrant corner. γ is increasing with respect to p and decreasing with respect to χ.
In practice, it describes how regularity is affected by the amplitude of the corner: as the amplitude of the angle tends to 2π, the regularity of the solution will be more "damaged". In other words, in such case, the domain becomes "very bad".
In addition to these results, even the boundedness of the gradient is investigated.

As specified by the authors, to their knowledge, for $p > 2$, there was no result about the L^2-regularity on the second derivative concerning obstacle problems. In this context, therefore, this result acquired a certain relevance.

Moreover, together with the importance in itself, this result is very useful even in the framework of numerical analysis. In fact, as we will illustrate in a following section, it allowed the authors to use a particular approach (see [90]) in order to obtain sharp estimates for the approximation error.

4.4. Error Estimates

Regarding numerical analysis, it should be specified that it is performed using the Galerkin's method. Starting from Problem (4), with $\Omega = \Omega_\alpha^n$, the authors obtained sharp error estimates exploiting the regularity stated and a suitable adapted triangulation T_h (see [91]): these are fundamental ingredients in order to follow Grisvard's approach (see [90]).

Thus, the following FEM-problem is considered:

$$\text{find } u \in \mathcal{K}_h : a_p(u, v - u) - \int_{\Omega_\alpha^n} f(v - u) \geq 0 \ \forall v \in \mathcal{K}_h \tag{10}$$

where

$$S_{h,0} = \left\{ v \in S_h : v = 0 \text{ on } \partial \Omega_\alpha^n \right\}, \text{ with } S_h = \left\{ v \in C(\bar{\Omega}_\alpha^n) : v|_\tau \text{ is affine } \forall \tau \in T_h \right\},$$

$$a_p(u, v) = \int_{\Omega_\alpha^n} (k^2 + |\nabla u|^2)^{\frac{p-2}{2}} \nabla u \nabla v$$

and

$$\mathcal{K}_h = \{ v \in S_{h,0} : \varphi_{1,h} \leq v \leq \varphi_{2,h} \text{ in } \Omega_\alpha^n \},$$

with $\varphi_{1,h} = \pi_h \varphi_1$, $\varphi_{2,h} = \pi_h \varphi_2$, and π_h is the interpolation operator.
Hence, the following result (see Theorem 5.5 in [72]) is proved.

Theorem 2. Let u_n and u_h be the solutions to Problems (4) and (10) in Ω_α^n, respectively. Let us assume that

$$\begin{cases} \varphi_i \in W^{1,p}(\Omega_\alpha^n), \ i = 1, 2 \\ \varphi_1 \leq \varphi_2 \ \text{in} \ \Omega_\alpha^n, \ \varphi_1 \leq 0 \leq \varphi_2 \ \text{in} \ \partial\Omega_\alpha^n \end{cases}, \quad (11)$$

$$\begin{cases} k \neq 0 \\ f, A_p(\varphi_i) \in L^\infty(\Omega_\alpha^n), \ i = 1, 2 \\ A_p(\varphi_2) \wedge f \geq 0 \end{cases} \quad (12)$$

and

$$\varphi_i \in H^{2,\mu}(\Omega_\alpha^n), \ i = 1, 2. \quad (13)$$

Let T_h be a triangulation adapted to the $H^{2,\mu}(\Omega_\alpha^n)$-regularity of the solution u_n. Then

$$||u_n - u_h||_{W^{1,t}(\Omega_\alpha^n)} \leq C h^{\frac{r}{t}} ||u_n||_{H^{2,\mu}(\Omega_\alpha^n)} \quad (14)$$

for any

$$r \in \left[1, \frac{2\sqrt{p^2 - \chi(2-\chi)(p-2)^2}}{\sqrt{p^2 - \chi(2-\chi)(p-2)^2} + (\chi-1)(p-2)}\right), \quad t \in [2, p]. \quad (15)$$

Note how r also depends on p and χ.

An analogous result (see Theorem 5.7 in [72]) is stated even in the case where $k = 0$, but the $H^{2,\mu}$-regularity of the solution has to be required in the assumptions.

For the sake of completeness, it should be specified that the just-cited theorems are an improvement of previous error estimates stated in [77].

Figures 2 and 3 (contained in the PhD thesis of the author, see [92]) show the difference between a classical regular and conformal triangulation and the triangulation T_h adapted to the $H^{2,\mu}$-regularity, on a polygon domain with a re-entrant corner.

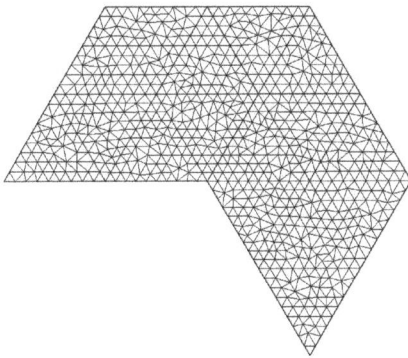

Figure 2. "Normal" triangulation.

The previous figures show that it is important to emphasize that the triangulation becomes finer only near the re-entrant corner (see [90,91]), that is, near the point in which the regularity is more affected. Moreover, the comparison between the numerical analysis performed using the two different types of meshes showed in the previous figures would highlight how the error is lower using the adapted mesh.

4.5. Asymptotic Behavior

To conclude the discussion about the principal topics analyzed, it is necessary to talk about the asymptotic behavior.

The fact is that considering problems involving p-Laplace-type operators, for $p \in (2, \infty)$, raises questions about what the limit problem as $p \to \infty$ is, about existence, uniqueness, and regularity of its solutions, and if the solution of the problem in p converges, in some way and in some space, to a solution of the limit problem.

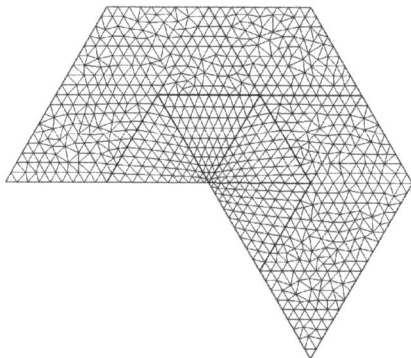

Figure 3. Adapted triangulation.

This issue in which the uniqueness can have an important role was studied by the authors in [74], and previously by many other authors for various problems (see the references quoted in [74]). In this paper, the authors state sufficient conditions which allow the possibility to obtain the convergence of the whole sequence of solutions u_p, for n both finite and infinite, to a solution of the limit problem, which is the following:

$$\int_\Omega u_\infty(x) f(x) = \max\left\{\int_\Omega w(x) f(x) : w \in \mathcal{K}^\infty\right\}, \qquad (16)$$

where

$$\mathcal{K}^\infty = \{u \in W^{1,\infty}(\Omega) : \varphi_1 \leq u \leq \varphi_2 \text{ in } \Omega_\alpha, \|\nabla u\|_{L^\infty(\Omega)} \leq 1\}.$$

This result is an improvement of results stated in [89], where the convergence is along subsequences.

Together with the asymptotic behavior with respect to p, questions concerning the behavior with respect to n also arise. Indeed, the fact is that considering a domain with pre-fractal boundary immediately raises new questions. First, it is natural to wonder if this domain converges, in some sense, to a certain domain and what this domain is; moreover, similarly to the case in which p moves, the convergence of the solution with respect to n must also be faced.

Regarding the convergence of the sets Ω_α^n, it is well known (see [93]) that they converge in the Hausdorff metric to Ω_α, which is obtained, in practice, by replacing each side of the initial polygon with the Koch curve K_α. Moreover, regarding the asymptotic behavior, in [77], under suitable assumptions, the convergence of the solution of the problem on the pre-fractal boundary domain to a solution of the problem in the corresponding fractal domains is stated, in case of p fixed and finite. According to the authors of [89], even the case of $p = \infty$ is analyzed, and the convergence is obtained again only along subsequences.

Figure 4 (compare with the one in [89]) shows, in a synthetic way, the convergence results stated by the authors in [89] and then improved in [72,94].

4.6. Other Works

In the previous sections, principally, the more recent results concerning obstacle problems involving p-Laplace-type operators on fractal and pre-fractal boundary domains were recalled.

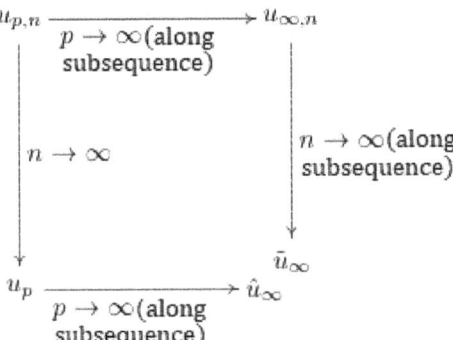

Figure 4. Summary of the convergence. The subscripts refer to p and the steps n of the pre-farctal approximating domains, respectively.

Moving further back in time, it is possible to find many other contributions that were inspired by Professor Vivaldi's work (see [19–21,37,44,46,52,53,55,56,59]) and from the collaborations of Professor Vivaldi and different remarkable authors. Among that carried out in collaboration, we recall, for instance, the following subjects and papers, again connected with the fractal framework:

- The new approach to Robin problems on fractal domains in the framework of insulating layers proposed by the author in [61] (see also the references therein).
- The vanishing viscosity approach to the construction of dynamical fractals of the so-called nested type in the plane type as collapsing thin two-dimensional manifolds, presented by the authors in [60] (see also the references therein), which is new.
- A problem consisting of two equations of the second order, which are coupled by a second-order transmission equation on the layer, firstly considered by the author in [50] (see also the references quoted there) and the proof, by the same author, in [48], that the domain of the Dirichlet form on the Koch curve K is the space $Lip_{\alpha,D}(2,\infty,K)$, where $D = \alpha$ is the Hausdorff dimension of K.

5. Perspectives and Open Problems

In the previous section, some of the principal results concerning the issues connected to prototype Problem (4) and its related problems, obtained by Professor Vivaldi together with other authors, was highlighted; moreover, anticipations of some further results developed by other authors were given.

It should be remembered that, in some case, the answers obtained were in themselves an improvement of previous results; however, in other cases, new issues arose. Indeed, we said that in [89] the authors faced the problem of the asymptotic behavior both with respect to n and p and, except in the case of p finite, they obtained a convergence along subsequences. Subsequently, this result was improved in [74], where sufficient conditions which allow to obtain the convergence of the whole sequence as $p \to \infty$ were given. Starting with the results contained in [74] (see also the references therein), it was possible to provide sufficient conditions which guaranteed the possibility to obtain even the uniqueness and the form of the solution in the case of $p = \infty$, both in the pre-fractal and in the fractal case for one obstacle problem (see [94]).

It is necessary to specify that asymptotic behavior has been the subject of study by many authors (see, for instance, [95,96] and the references quoted there). Moreover, one should not forget the connections of the limit Problem (16) with the mass transport problem (see, for instance, [97–99] and the references therein).

Furthermore, it should be emphasized how the numerical analysis also highlighted the importance of the results about asymptotic behavior. In fact, the convergence of the approximating solutions to the solution of the problem in the pre-fractal boundary domains, combined with the asymptotic behavior, which is the convergence to a solution of the problem in the corresponding fractal domains, allows, in some sense, a numerical analysis in a fractal set.

Clearly, in the framework of numerical analysis, the error estimates have a crucial role, and with them comes the study on the regularity of the solutions. The results stated in [72] permitted to obtain sharp results about the rate of vanishing of the approximation error. In any case, it would be definitely interesting to continue the study about regularity to see if and how it is possible to improve upon the results stated up to now.

Analogous studies on similar problems involving both p- and q-Laplace-type operators were carried out (see, for instance, [100] and the references quoted there). New studies on such types of problems are in progress; in particular, attention is devoted to the possibility of obtaining a definitive answer about the possibility of changing the order of the limit, with respect to p and n, obtaining the same solution of the final problem, i.e., the problem corresponding to the case of n and p both infinite; this issue, as far as we know, does not have a complete answer and remains an open problem. Hence, as it is possible to deduce if a positive answer to this question exists, an important connection among all these problems is established.

Funding: This research was funded by grant number CC120172B6D2B7E9 Sapienza Finanziamenti per convegni, seminari, workshop—Classe a—Classe a.

Acknowledgments: I want to thank Maria Agostina Vivaldi. I met her in 2015, when I started my Ph.D. studies, and she became my supervisor at the S.B.A.I. Department in the University of the Studies of Rome "La Sapienza". During those years, she was—and still is—a guide and a mentor. She has never stopped teaching and giving all her students tools to become good teachers and researchers. Her deep knowledge of mathematical analysis and her huge love for it are immediately clear talking with Maria Agostina Vivaldi. She is always ready to give both help and new ideas to allow us to continue our paths. For all that, I thank Maria Agostina Vivaldi: thanks for the patience, thanks for the help, thanks for sharing your knowledge with us, and, mostly, thanks for showing and sharing with us the love for the work and the research every day.

Conflicts of Interest: The author declares no conflict of interest.

References

1. Boccardo, L.; Gallouet, T. Compactness of minimizing sequences. *Nonlinear Anal.* **2016**, *137*, 213–221. [CrossRef]
2. Boccardo, L. Some new results about Mosco convergence. *J. Convex Anal.* **2021**, *28*, 387–394.
3. Boccardo, L. T-minima: An approach to minimization problems in L1. Contributions in honor of the memory of Ennio De Giorgi (Italian). *Ric. Mat.* **2000**, *49*, 135–154.
4. Boccardo, L.; Leone, C. T-minima on convex sets and Mosco-convergence. *Rend. Mat. Appl.* **2020**, *41*, 223–236.
5. Capuzzo Dolcetta, I.; Rossi, L.; Vitolo, A. Invariant cones for linear elliptic systems with gradient coupling. *arXiv* **2021**, arXiv:2106.05523. https://arxiv.org/abs/2106.05523v1.
6. Capuzzo Dolcetta, I.; Vitolo, A. Weak Maximum Principle for Cooperative Systems: The Degenerate Elliptic Case. *J. Convex Anal.* **2021**, *28*, 495–508.
7. Cupini, G.; Marcellini, P.; Mascolo, E.; Passarelli di Napoli, A. Lipschitz regularity for degenerate elliptic integrals with p,q-growth. In *Advances in Calculus of Variations*; De Gruyter: Berlin, Germany, 2021. [CrossRef]
8. Eleuteri, M.; Marcellini, P.; Mascolo, E.; Perrotta, S. Local Lipschitz continuity for energy integrals with slow growth. *Ann. Mat. Pura Appl.* **2022**, *201*, 1005–1032. [CrossRef]
9. Capitanelli, R.; Lancia, M.R.; Vivaldi, M.A. Preface [Issue on variational convergence and degeneracies in PDES: Fractal domains, composite media, dynamical boundary conditions]. *Discret. Contin. Dyn. Syst. Ser. S* **2019**, *12*, 35-06.
10. Andreucci, D.; Capitanelli, R.; Carillo, S.; Lancia, M.R.; Vivaldi, M.A. Foreword to special issue celebrating the Umberto Mosco's birthday. *Rend. Mat. Appl.* **2020**, *41*, 189–192.
11. Stroescu, E.; Vivaldi, M.A. Strong discrete convergence of solutions of variational inequalities. *Rend. Mat.* **1976**, *9*, 17–35.
12. Charrier, P.; Vivaldi, M.A. Existence d'une solution forte régulière d'une inéquation quasi variationnelle d'évolution. *C. R. Acad. Sci. Paris Sér. A–B* **1976**, *283*, A465–A467.
13. Capuzzo Dolcetta, I.; Vivaldi, M.A. Existence d'une solution régulière d'une inéquation quasi variationnelle elliptique sur un domaine non borné. *C. R. Acad. Sci. Paris Sér. A–B* **1977**, *284*, A1033–A1036.

14. Charrier, P.; Vivaldi, M.A. Existence d'une solution régulière d'une inéquation quasi-variationnelle d'évolution avec conditions de Dirichlet. *Boll. Un. Mat. Ital. A* **1977**, *14*, 579–589.
15. Capuzzo Dolcetta, I.; Vivaldi, M.A. Existence of a regular solution of a quasivariational inequality in an unbounded domain. *Comm. Partial Differ. Equ.* **1978**, *3*, 443–470. [CrossRef]
16. Garroni, M.G.; Vivaldi, M.A. Bilateral inequalities and implicit unilateral systems of the nonvariational type. *Manuscripta Math.* **1980**, *33*, 177–215. [CrossRef]
17. Garroni, M.G.; Vivaldi, M.A. Approximation results for bilateral nonlinear problems of nonvariational type. *Nonlinear Anal.* **1984**, *8*, 301–312. [CrossRef]
18. Garroni, M.G.; Vivaldi, M.A. Bilateral evolution problems of nonvariational type: Existence, uniqueness, Hölder-regularity and approximation of solutions. *Manuscripta Math.* **1984**, *48*, 39–69. [CrossRef]
19. Vivaldi, M.A. Existence of strong solutions for nonlinear parabolic variational inequalities. *Nonlinear Anal.* **1987**, *11*, 285–295. [CrossRef]
20. Vivaldi, M.A. Nonlinear parabolic variational inequalities: Existence of weak solutions and regularity properties. *Boll. Un. Mat. Ital. B* **1987**, *1*, 259–274.
21. Vivaldi, M.A. Nonlinear parabolic variational inequalities. *Rend. Circ. Mat. Palermo* **1987**, *2*, 181–188.
22. Garroni, M.G.; Vivaldi, M.A. Stability of free boundaries. *Nonlinear Anal.* **1988**, *12*, 1339–1347. [CrossRef]
23. Garroni, M.G.; Vivaldi, M.A. Régularité de la solution forte d'un problème non linéaire d'évolution avec contraintes dépendantes du temps. *C. R. Acad. Sci. Paris Sér. A-B* **1978**, *286*, A207–A210.
24. Garroni, M.G.; Vivaldi, M.A. Régularité de la solution forte de problèmes non linéaires d'évolution. *Czechoslov. Math. J.* **1979**, *29*, 430–450. [CrossRef]
25. Garroni, M.G.; Vivaldi, M.A. Existence, regularity and dual estimates for the solution of a quasivariational inequality relative to a quasilinear operator. *Boll. Un. Mat. Ital. B* **1979**, *16*, 154–167.
26. Struwe, M.; Vivaldi, M.A. On the Hölder continuity of bounded weak solutions of quasilinear parabolic inequalities. *Ann. Mat. Pura Appl.* **1985**, *139*, 175–189. [CrossRef]
27. Dal Maso, G.; Mosco, U.; Vivaldi, M.A. A pointwise regularity theory for the two-obstacle problem. *Acta Math.* **1989**, *163*, 57–107. [CrossRef]
28. Birindelli, I.; Vivaldi, M.A. Nonlinear two-obstacle problems: Pointwise regularity. *Rend. Mat. Appl.* **1994**, *14*, 415–455.
29. Garroni, M.G.; Solonnikov, V.A.; Vivaldi, M.A. On the oblique derivative problem in an infinite angle. *Topol. Methods Nonlinear Anal.* **1996**, *7*, 299–325. [CrossRef]
30. Garroni, M.G.; Solonnikov, V.A.; Vivaldi, M.A. Green function for the heat equation with oblique boundary conditions in an angle. Dedicated to Ennio De Giorgi. *Ann. Sc. Norm. Sup. Pisa Cl. Sci.* **1997**, *25*, 455–485.
31. Garroni, M.G.; Solonnikov, V.A.; Vivaldi, M.A. Existence and regularity results for oblique derivative problems for heat equations in an angle. *Proc. R. Soc. Edinb. Sect. A* **1998**, *128*, 47–79. [CrossRef]
32. Garroni, M.G.; Solonnikov, V.A.; Vivaldi, M.A. The exponential behaviour of the Green function in a dihedral angle. *Commun. Contemp. Math.* **2001**, *3*, 571–592. [CrossRef]
33. Garroni, M.G.; Solonnikov, V.A.; Vivaldi, M.A. Schauder estimates for a system of equations of mixed type. *Rend. Mat. Appl.* **2009**, *29*, 117–132.
34. Capitanelli, R.; Vivaldi, M.A. Uniform weighted estimates on pre-fractal domains. *Discret. Contin. Dyn. Syst. Ser. B* **2014**, *19*, 1969–1985. [CrossRef]
35. Matzeu, M.; Vivaldi, M.A. On the regular solution of a nonlinear parabolic quasivariational inequality related to a stochastic control problem. *Comm. Partial Differ. Equ.* **1979**, *4*, 1123–1147. [CrossRef]
36. Matzeu, M.; Vivaldi, M.A. A dual estimate for the Hamilton-Jacobi function of a continuous and impulsive stochastic control problem. *Boll. Un. Mat. Ital. B* **1980**, *17*, 458–477.
37. Vivaldi, M.A. A parabolic quasivariational inequality related to a stochastic impulse control problem with quadratic growth Hamiltonian. *Numer. Funct. Anal. Optim.* **1982**, *4*, 241–268. [CrossRef]
38. Matzeu, M.; Mosco, U.; Vivaldi, M.A. Sur un problème de contrôle optimal stochastique continu et impulsionnel avec hamiltonien à croissance quadratique. *C. R. Acad. Sci. Paris Sér. I Math.* **1983**, *296*, 817–820.
39. Matzeu, M.; Mosco, U.; Vivaldi, M.A. Optimal impulse and continuous control with Hamiltonian of quadratic growth. *Contrib. Oper. Res. Math. Econ.* **1984**, *51*, 59–105.
40. Garroni, M.G.; Vivaldi, M.A. Quasilinear, parabolic, integro-differential problems with nonlinear oblique boundary conditions. *Nonlinear Anal.* **1991**, *16*, 1089–1116. [CrossRef]
41. Garroni, M.G.; Solonnikov, V.A.; Vivaldi, M.A. Quasi-linear, integro-differential, parabolic problems with nonhomogeneous conditions. *Houst. J. Math.* **1992**, *18*, 481–532.
42. Garroni, M.G.; Solonnikov, V.A.; Vivaldi, M.A. Problèmes intégro-différentiels complètement non linéaires. *C. R. Acad. Sci. Paris Sér. I Math.* **1993**, *316*, 245–248.
43. Garroni, M.G.; Solonnikov, V.A.; Vivaldi, M.A. Fully nonlinear boundary conditions for quasilinear, integro-differential operators. *Pitman Res. Notes Math. Ser.* **1994**, *299*, 97.
44. Vivaldi, M.A. Existence and uniqueness results for degenerate-elliptic integro-differential problems. *Pitman Res. Notes Math. Ser.* **1995**, *325*, 213–223.
45. De Cicco, V.; Vivaldi, M.A. Harnack inequalities for Fuchsian type weighted elliptic equations. *Comm. Partial Differ. Equ.* **1996**, *21*, 1321–1347. [CrossRef]

46. Vivaldi, M.A. Oscillation and energy decay of solutions to obstacle problems involving quasi-linear, degenerate-elliptic operators. *Pitman Res. Notes Math. Ser.* **1992**, *266*, 259–273.
47. De Cicco, V.; Vivaldi, M.A. A Liouville type theorem for weighted elliptic equations. *Adv. Math. Sci. Appl.* **1999**, *9*, 183–207.
48. Lancia, M.R.; Vivaldi, M.A. Lipschitz spaces and Besov traces on self-similar fractals. *Rend. Accad. Naz. Sci. XL Mem. Mat. Appl.* **1999**, *23*, 101–116.
49. Lancia, M.R.; Vivaldi, M.A. On the regularity of the solutions for transmission problems. *Adv. Math. Sci. Appl.* **2002**, *12*, 455–466.
50. Lancia, M.R.; Vivaldi, M.A. Asymptotic convergence of transmission energy forms. *Adv. Math. Sci. Appl.* **2003**, *13*, 315–341.
51. Mosco, U.; Vivaldi, M.A. Variational problems with fractal layers. *Rend. Accad. Naz. Sci. XL Mem. Mat. Appl.* **2003**, *27*, 237–251.
52. Vivaldi, M.A. Transmission problems with highly conductive fractal layers. *Far East J. Appl. Math.* **2004**, *15*, 151–170.
53. Vivaldi, M.A. Variational principles and transmission conditions for fractal layers. *Fractal Geom. Stochastics III* **2004**, *57*, 205–217.
54. Mosco, U.; Vivaldi, M.A. An example of fractal singular homogenization. *Georgian Math. J.* **2007**, *14*, 169–193. [CrossRef]
55. Vivaldi, M.A. Fractal and Euclidean interaction in some transmission problems. *Matematiche* **2007**, *62*, 327–343.
56. Vivaldi, M.A. Variational principles and transmission problems with fractal layers. In *Mathematical Modelling of Bodies with Complicated Bulk and Boundary Behavior*; Birkhäuser: Basel, Switzerland, 2007; pp. 239–259.
57. Lancia, M.R.; Mosco, U.; Vivaldi, M.A. Homogenization for conductive thin layers of pre-fractal type. *J. Math. Anal. Appl.* **2008**, *347*, 354–369. [CrossRef]
58. Mosco, U.; Vivaldi, M.A. Fractal reinforcement of elastic membranes. *Arch. Ration. Mech. Anal.* **2009**, *194*, 49–74. [CrossRef]
59. Vivaldi, M.A. Irregular conductive layers. *Oper. Theory Adv. Appl.* **2009**, *193*, 303–318.
60. Mosco, U.; Vivaldi, M.A. Vanishing viscosity for fractal sets. *Discret. Contin. Dyn. Syst.* **2010**, *28*, 1207–1235. [CrossRef]
61. Capitanelli, R.; Vivaldi, M.A. Insulating layers and Robin problems on Koch mixtures. *J. Differ. Equ.* **2011**, *251*, 1332–1353. [CrossRef]
62. Capitanelli, R.; Vivaldi, M.A. Trace Theorems on Scale Irregular Fractals. In *Classification and Application of Fractals*; Nova Publishers: New York, NY, USA, 2011; pp.363–382.
63. Capitanelli, R.; Vivaldi, M.A. On the Laplacean transfer across fractal mixtures. *Asymptot. Anal.* **2013**, *83*, 1–33. [CrossRef]
64. Capitanelli, R.; Lancia, M.R.; Vivaldi, M.A. Insulating layers of fractal type. *Differ. Integral Equ.* **2013**, *26*, 1055–1076.
65. Mosco, U.; Vivaldi, M.A. Thin fractal fibers. *Math. Methods Appl. Sci.* **2013**, *36*, 2048–2068. [CrossRef]
66. Mosco, U.; Vivaldi, M.A. Layered fractal fibers and potentials. *J. Math. Pures Appl.* **2015**, *103*, 1198–1227. [CrossRef]
67. Capitanelli, R.; Vivaldi, M.A. Weighted estimates on fractal domains. *Mathematika* **2015**, *61*, 370–384. [CrossRef]
68. Capitanelli, R.; Vivaldi, M.A. Reinforcement problems for variational inequalities on fractal sets. *Calc. Var. Partial Differ. Equ.* **2015**, *54*, 2751–2783. [CrossRef]
69. Capitanelli, R.; Vivaldi, M.A. Quasi-filling fractal layers. *Atti Accad. Naz. Lincei Rend. Lincei Mat. Appl.* **2015**, *26*, 465–473. [CrossRef]
70. Capitanelli, R.; Vivaldi, M.A. Dynamical quasi-filling fractal layers. *SIAM J. Math. Anal.* **2016**, *48*, 3931–3961. [CrossRef]
71. Camilli, F.; Capitanelli, R.; Vivaldi, M.A. Absolutely minimizing Lipschitz extensions and infinity harmonic functions on the Sierpinski gasket. *Nonlinear Anal.* **2017**, *163*, 71–85. [CrossRef]
72. Capitanelli, R.; Fragapane, S.; Vivaldi, M.A. Regularity results for p-Laplacians in pre-fractal domains. *Adv. Nonlinear Anal.* **2019**, *8*, 1043–1056. [CrossRef]
73. Giachetti, D.; Vernescu, B.; Vivaldi, M.A. Asymptotic analysis of singular problems in perforated cylinders. *Differ. Integral Equ.* **2016**, *29*, 531–562.
74. Capitanelli, R.; Vivaldi, M.A. Limit of p-Laplacian obstacle problems. *Adv. Calc. Var.* **2022**, *15*, 265–286. [CrossRef]
75. Scarpini, F.; Vivaldi, M.A. Évaluation de l'erreur d'approximation pour une inéquation parabolique relative aux convexes dépendant du temps. *Appl. Math. Optim.* **1977**, *4*, 121–138. [CrossRef]
76. Scarpini, F.; Vivaldi, M.A. Error estimates for the approximation of some unilateral problems. *RAIRO Anal. Numér.*, **1977**, *11*, 197–208. [CrossRef]
77. Capitanelli, R.; Vivaldi, M.A. FEM for quasilinear obstacle problems in bad domains. *ESAIM Math. Model. Numer. Anal.* **2017**, *51*, 2465–2485. [CrossRef]
78. Solonnikov, V.A.; Vivaldi, M.A. Mixed type, nonlinear systems in polygonal domains. *Atti Accad. Naz. Lincei Rend. Lincei Mat.* **2013**, *24*, 39–81. [CrossRef]
79. Capitanelli, R.; Vivaldi, M.A.; Sharp Trudinger type inequalities for measure-valued Lagrangeans. *J. Convex Anal.* **2021**, *28*, 471–494.
80. Mosco, U.; Vivaldi, M.A. On a discrete self-organized-criticality finite time result.*Discret. Contin. Dyn. Syst.* **2020**, *40*, 5079–5103. [CrossRef]
81. Mosco, U.; Vivaldi, M.A. On the external approximation of Sobolev spaces by M-convergence. In *Fractals in Engineering: Theoretical Aspects and Numerical Approximations*; Springer: Cham, Switzerland, 2021; pp. 125–154.
82. Mandelbrot, B.B. *The Fractal Geometry of Nature*; W. H. Freeman & Co: New York, NY, USA, 1982.
83. Mandelbrot, B.B. *Fractals and Scaling in Finance*; Springer: Berlin/Heidelberg, Germany, 1997.
84. Benedikt, J.; Girg, P.; Kotrla, L.; Takáč P. Origin of the p-Laplacian and A. Missbach. *Math. Comp.* **1993**, *61*, 523–537.
85. Diaz, J.I. *Nonlinear Partial Differential Equations and Free Boundaries*; Vol. I. Elliptic Equations. Research Notes in Mathematics; Pitman: Boston, MA, USA, 1985; Volume 106.
86. Lindqvist, P. Notes of p-Laplace Equation. Available online: https://folk.ntnu.no/lqvist/p-laplace.pdf (accessed on 1 November 2022).
87. Heinonen, J.; Kilpeläinen T.; Martio, O. *Nonlineal Potential Theory of Degenerate Elliptic Equations*; Oxford University Press: Oxford, UK, 1993.
88. Troianiello, G.M. *Elliptic Differential Equations and Obstacle Problems*; The University Series in Mathematics; Plenum Press: New York, NY, USA, 1987.

89. Capitanelli, R.; Fragapane, S. Asymptotics for quasilinear obstacle problems in bad domains. *Discret. Contin. Dyn. Syst. Ser. S* **2019**, *12*, 43–56. [CrossRef]
90. Grisvard, P. Elliptic problems in nonsmooth domains. In *Monographs and Studies in Mathematics*; Pitman: Boston, MA, USA, 1985.
91. Raugel, G.; Résolution numérique par une méthode d'éléments finis du problème de Dirichlet pour le laplacien dans un polygone. *C. R. Acad. Sci. Paris Sér. A–B* **1978**, *286*, A791–A794.
92. Fragapane, S. Regularity and asymptotics for p-Laplace type operators in fractal and pre-fractal domains. PhD thesis, "Sapienza" University of Rome, Roma, Italy, 2019.
93. Hutchinson, J.E. Fractals and selfsimilarity. *Indiana Univ. Math. J.* **1981**, *30*, 713–747. [CrossRef]
94. Fragapane, S. ∞-Laplacian obstacle problems in fractal domains. In *Fractals in Engineering: Theoretical Aspects and Numerical Approximations*; Springer: Cham, Switzerland, 2021; pp. 55–77.
95. Bhattacharya, T.; DiBenedetto, E.; Manfredi, J. Limits as $p \to +\infty$ of $\Delta_p u_p = f$ and related extremal problems. *Rend. Sem. Mat. Univ. Politec. Torino* **1989**, *47*, 15–68.
96. Ishii, H.; Loreti, P.; Limits of solutions of p-Laplace equations as p goes to infinity and related variational problems. *SIAM J. Math. Anal.* **2005**, *37*, 411–437. [CrossRef]
97. Mazón J. M.; Rossi, J.D.; Toledo, J. Mass transport problems for the Euclidean distance obtained as limits of p-Laplacian type problems with obstacles. *J. Differ. Equ.* **2014**, *256*, 3208–3244. [CrossRef]
98. Evans, L.C.; W. Gangbo, W. Differential equations methods for the Monge-Kantorovich mass transfer problem. *Mem. Am. Math. Soc.* **1999**, *137*. [CrossRef]
99. Villani, C. Optimal transport. Old and new. In *Grundlehren der Mathematischen Wissenschaften [Fundamental Principles of Mathematical Sciences]*; Springer: Berlin/Heidelberg, Germany, 2009; Volume 338.
100. Bonheure, D.; Rossi, J.D. The behavior of solutions to an elliptic equation involving a p-Laplacian and q-Laplacian for large p. *Nonlinear Anal.* **2017**, *150*, 104–113. [CrossRef]

Article

Two Families of Continuous Probability Distributions Generated by the Discrete Lindley Distribution

Srdjan Kadić [1,*,†], Božidar V. Popović [1,†] and Ali İ. Genç [2,†]

[1] Faculty of Science and Mathematics, University of Montenegro, 81000 Podgorica, Montenegro
[2] Department of Statistics, Cukurova University, 01290 Adana, Turkey
* Correspondence: skadic@ucg.ac.me
† These authors contributed equally to this work.

Abstract: In this paper, we construct two new families of distributions generated by the discrete Lindley distribution. Some mathematical properties of the new families are derived. Some special distributions from these families can be constructed by choosing some baseline distributions, such as exponential, Pareto and standard logistic distributions. We study in detail the properties of the two models resulting from the exponential baseline, among others. These two models have different shape characteristics. The model parameters are estimated by maximum likelihood, and related algorithms are proposed for the computation of the estimates. The existence of the maximum-likelihood estimators is discussed. Two applications prove its usefulness in real data fitting.

Keywords: discrete lindley distribution; EM algorithm; existence of the maximum likelihood estimate; moments

MSC: 62E15; 62F10 ; 60E05

Citation: Kadić, S.; Popović, B.V.; Genç, A.İ. Two Families of Continuous Probability Distributions Generated by the Discrete Lindley Distribution. *Mathematics* 2023, 11, 290. https://doi.org/10.3390/math11020290

Academic Editors: Irina Cristea, Yuriy Rogovchenko, Justo Puerto, Gintautas Dzemyda and Patrick Siarry

Received: 21 November 2022
Revised: 17 December 2022
Accepted: 26 December 2022
Published: 5 January 2023

Copyright: © 2023 by the authors. Licensee MDPI, Basel, Switzerland. This article is an open access article distributed under the terms and conditions of the Creative Commons Attribution (CC BY) license (https://creativecommons.org/licenses/by/4.0/).

1. Introduction

Compound discrete distributions serve as probabilistic models in various areas of applications, for instance, in ecology, genetics and physics. See, for example, [1]. Distributions obtained by compounding a parent distribution with a discrete distribution are very common in statistics and in many applied areas. Suppose we have a system consisting of N components, the lifetime of each of which is a random variable. Let X be the maximum lifetime of the components. Clearly, X has a compound distribution arising out of a random number N of components; i.e., $X = \max\{Z_1, \ldots, Z_N\}$. On the other hand, in case of a system consisting of N components whose energy consumption is a random variable, and assuming that Z is the component whose energy consumption is minimal, we obtain the compound distribution of $Y = \min\{Z_1, \ldots, Z_N\}$. The compounding principle is applied in the many different areas: insurance [2], ruin problems [3], compound risk models and their actuarial applications [4,5]. The development of the theory of compounding distribution is skipped here, because it has been covered in detail in [6].

The random variable N is often determined by economy, customer demand, etc. There is a practical reason why N might be considered as a random variable. A failure can occur due to initial defects being present in the system. A discrete version of this distribution has been studied in [7], having its applications in count data related to insurance.

We will say that random variable X possesses the discrete Lindley distribution introduced by [7] if its probability mass function is given by

$$P(X = x) = \frac{\lambda^x}{1 - \log \lambda}[\lambda \log \lambda + (1 - \lambda)(1 - \log \lambda^{x+1})],$$

where $x = 0, 1, \ldots$ and $0 < \lambda < 1$. The probability generating function (PGF) (see Equation (4) in [7]) is given by the typo error. The corrected version is defined by

$$\Phi(s) = \frac{(\lambda - 1)(\lambda s - 1) - (1 - 2\lambda + \lambda^2 s)\log(\lambda)}{(1 - \lambda s)^2 (1 - \log(\lambda))}, \ s < 1/\lambda, \ 0 < \lambda < 1. \tag{1}$$

In this manuscript, we consider the previously discrete Lindley distribution for the random variable N. Why do we assume a discrete Lindley distribution? For example, using a Poisson distribution has an important assumption: equidispersion of data. The assumption of equidispersion is not valid in real cases. Some alternative distributions to the model of overdispersed data are available—binomial negative, generalized Poisson or zero inflated Poisson. However, judging by the number of parameters used, these alternatives are more complex than the Poisson distribution. That is why we are introducing a continuous Lindley distribution with one parameter, which is similar to the Poisson distribution. The application of the Lindley distribution in modeling the number of claim data is less suitable because the number of claims data is a discrete number, as opposed to the Lindley distribution's continuous nature. That is why we are introducing a new discrete Lindley distribution, created through discretisation of a continuous Lindley distribution with one parameter.

Assuming that M is the zero truncated version of N with PGF (1), we will construct two new families of distributions: the discrete Lindley-generated families of distributions of the first and second kinds.

The paper is organized as follows. In Section 1, we construct two discrete Lindley generated families. Section 2 is devoted to shape characteristics. In Section 3 we derive some mathematical properties of the families. Estimation issues are investigated in Sections 4 and 5. The simulation study is presented in Section 6. Two applications to real data are addressed in Section 7. The paper is finalized with concluding remarks.

2. Construction of the Families of Distributions

There are various methods for getting the discrete Lindley distribution. For example, in [8], the authors considered a method of infinite series for constructing the discrete Lindley distribution. On the other hand, in [9], the discrete Lindley distribution was built using the survival function method. In this manuscript, we employ the so-called max-min procedure. This construction is widely used in practice. For a comprehensive literature review, we refer the reader to [10] and references therein.

In this section, we introduce two new families of distributions as follows. Let $\{Z_i\}_{i \geq 1}$ be a sequence of independent and identically distributed (iid) random variables with baseline cumulative distribution function (CDF) $F(x) = F(x; \psi)$, where $x \in \mathbb{R}$ and ψ is the parameter vector. Suppose that N is a discrete random variable with the PGF $\Phi(s)$ and let M have the zero-truncated distribution of the random variable N obtained by removing zero from N. Then, the probability mass function (pmf) of M is given by

$$P(M = m) = \frac{P(N = m)}{1 - \Phi(0)}, \ m \in \{1, 2, \ldots\}. \tag{2}$$

In order to prove that $\sum_{m=1}^{+\infty} P(M = m) = 1$, let us recall that $P(N = m) = \frac{\Phi^m(0)}{m!}$. After some algebra, we find

$$P(N = m) = \lambda^m \frac{\lambda - 1 + \log \lambda - 2\lambda \log \lambda}{\log \lambda - 1} + \frac{m \lambda^m (1 - \lambda) \log \lambda}{\log \lambda - 1}.$$

Using serial representations $\sum_{m=1}^{+\infty} \lambda^m = \frac{\lambda}{1-\lambda}$ and $\sum_{m=1}^{+\infty} m\lambda^m = \frac{\lambda}{(1-\lambda)^2}$, one can calculate

$$\sum_{m=1}^{+\infty} P(N=m) = \frac{\lambda(1-2\log\lambda)}{1-\log\lambda}. \tag{3}$$

Equation (3) coincides with $1 - \Phi(0)$. This completes the proof that $\sum_{m=1}^{+\infty} P(M=m) = 1$.

First, we introduce the family of distributions based on the maximum of random variables. We define the random variable $X = \max\{Z_i\}_{i=1}^M$. Then, the CDF and probability density function (PDF) of X are given by

$$G_X(x) = \frac{\Phi[F(x)]}{1-\Phi(0)}, \quad x \in \mathbb{R}$$

and

$$g_X(x) = \frac{f(x)\Phi'[F(x)]}{1-\Phi(0)}, \quad x \in \mathbb{R},$$

respectively.

Further, if we suppose that the random variable N has the PGF given by (1), the CDF and PDF of X for $x \in \mathbb{R}, \lambda \in (0,1)$ are given by

$$G_1(x) = G_1(x;\theta,\lambda) = \frac{F(x)[1-\lambda+(3\lambda-2)\log(\lambda)-\lambda(1-\lambda+(2\lambda-1)\log(\lambda))F(x)]}{(1-2\log(\lambda))[1-\lambda F(x)]^2}, \tag{4}$$

and

$$g_1(x) = \frac{f(x)[1-\lambda+(3\lambda-2)\log(\lambda)-\lambda(1-\lambda+\lambda\log(\lambda))F(x)]}{(1-2\log(\lambda))[1-\lambda F(x)]^3}, \tag{5}$$

respectively. We say that the family of distributions defined by (4) and (5) is the *discrete Lindley generated family of the first kind* ("LiG1" for short). A random variable X having PDF (5) is denoted by $X \sim \text{LiF1}(\lambda, \psi)$.

The hazard rate function (HRF) of X can be expressed as

$$\tau_1(x) = \frac{h_F(x)[1-\lambda+(3\lambda-2)\log(\lambda)-\lambda(1-\lambda+\lambda\log(\lambda))F(x)]}{[1-\lambda F(x)][1-2\log(\lambda)-\lambda(1-\log(\lambda))F(x)]}, x \in \mathbb{R}, \lambda \in (0,1). \tag{6}$$

Let us study the identifiable property of the distribution given by (4) under the exponential baseline distribution $F(x;\theta) = 1 - e^{-\theta x}$. We will get the discrete Lindley exponential distribution of the first kind. We will designate this distribution LiE1.

Theorem 1. *The LiE1 distribution is identifiable with respect to the parameters λ and θ.*

Proof. Let us suppose that

$$G_1(x;\theta_1,\lambda_1) = G_1(x;\theta_2,\lambda_2) \tag{7}$$

for all $x > 0$ and when $F(x)$ is the CDF of exponential distribution. If we let $x \to \infty$ into both sides of (7) and after some algebra, it can be concluded that $\lambda_1 = \lambda_2$. Now it is not hard to verify that $\theta_1 = \theta_2$. Hence the proof of the theorem. □

Second, in [6], it was demonstrated that the random variable $Y = \min\{Z_i\}_{i=1}^M$ has CDF and PDF given by

$$G_Y(y) = \frac{1-\Phi[1-F(y)]}{1-\Phi(0)}, \quad y \in \mathbb{R}, \tag{8}$$

and

$$g_Y(y) = \frac{f(y)\Phi'[1-F(y)]}{1-\Phi(0)}, \quad y \in \mathbb{R}, \tag{9}$$

respectively.

Now, inserting (1) in Equation (8), the CDF of the random variable Y becomes

$$G_2(x) = G_2(x;\theta,\lambda) = \frac{F(x)[1 - 2\log(\lambda) - \lambda(1 - \log(\lambda))\overline{F}(x)]}{(1 - 2\log(\lambda))[1 - \lambda\overline{F}(x)]^2}, \quad x \in \mathbb{R}, \lambda \in (0,1), \quad (10)$$

where $\overline{F}(x) = 1 - F(x)$ is the survival function of the random variable Z_1.

In a similar manner, by replacing (1) in the Equation (9), the PDF of Y reduces to

$$g_2(x) = \frac{f(x)[1 - \lambda + (3\lambda - 2)\log(\lambda) - \lambda(1 - \lambda + \lambda\log(\lambda))\overline{F}(x)]}{(1 - 2\log(\lambda))[1 - \lambda\overline{F}(x)]^3}, \quad x \in \mathbb{R}, \lambda \in (0,1). \quad (11)$$

The random variable Y having the PDF (11) is called the discrete Lindley generated family of the second kind, $Y \sim \text{LiF2}(\lambda, \psi)$.

From Equations (10) and (11), the HRF of Y follows as

$$\tau_2(x) = \frac{h_F(x)[1 - \lambda + (3\lambda - 2)\log(\lambda) - \lambda(1 - \lambda + \lambda\log(\lambda))\overline{F}(x)]}{[1 - \lambda\overline{F}(x)][1 - \lambda + (3\lambda - 2)\log(\lambda) - \lambda(1 - \lambda + (2\lambda - 1)\log(\lambda))\overline{F}(x)]}, \quad x \in \mathbb{R}, \lambda \in (0,1), \quad (12)$$

where $\tau_F(x) = f(x)/\overline{F}(x)$ is the HRF of the random variable Z_i.

There are at least four motivations for having two families of distributions: Reliability: From the stochastic representations X and Y, we note that the two families can arise in parallel and series systems with identical components, which appear in many industrial applications and biological organisms. The first-activation scheme: If we assume that an individual is susceptible to a cancer type, then we can call the number of carcinogenic cells that survived the initial treatment M, and Z_i is the time needed for the i−th carcinogenic cell to metastasise into a detectable tumour, for $i \geq 1$. If we assume that $\{Z_i\}_{i \geq 1}$ is a sequence of a total of iid random variables, all independent of M, where M is given by (2), we can conclude that the time to relapse of cancer of a susceptible individual is defined by the random variable Y. Last-activation scheme: Let us assume that M equals the number of latent factors that have to be active by failure, and Z_i is the time of disease resistance due to the latent factor i. According to the last-activation scheme, the failure occurs once all N factors are active. If the Z_is are iid random variables that are independent of N having the baseline distribution F, where N follows (2), the random variable X can model time to the failure according to the last-activation scheme. The times to the last and first failures: Let us assume that the device failure happens due to initial defects numbering M, and that these can be identified only after causing the failure, and that they are being repaired perfectly. We will define Z_i as the time to the device failure due to the defect number i, where $i \geq 1$. Under the assumptions that the Z_is are iid random variables independent of M given by (2), the random variables X and Y are appropriate for modeling the times to the last and first failures.

3. Shape Characteristics of the Proposed Models under the Exponential Baseline Distribution

Let us examine the shapes of the PDF and HRF for the case of the exponential baseline distribution. Let the random variables Z_1 have the exponential distribution with scale parameter $\theta > 0$. If we set $F(x) = 1 - e^{-\theta x}$ and replace it in (5), we will get the LiE1 distribution. Its PDF is for $x > 0, \theta > 0, \lambda \in (0,1)$

$$g_1(x;\theta,\lambda) = \frac{\theta e^{-\theta x}[1 - \lambda + (3\lambda - 2)\log(\lambda) - \lambda(1 - \lambda + \lambda\log(\lambda))(1 - e^{-\theta x})]}{(1 - 2\log(\lambda))[1 - \lambda(1 - e^{-\theta x})]^3}.$$

The exponential distribution is widely used due to its simplicity and applicability. For its usage in the theory of the compounding distribution, we recommend [10], where it is possible to find a long list of the corresponding references.

In order to study the shape of the last PDF, firstly we will give the following example. The next example will serve us to prove Theorem 2. It will play a crucial role in the study of the inequality that is important for drawing the conclusion about the PDF's shape.

Example 1. *Suppose* $\lambda \in (0,1)$. *Find* λ *such that* $(8\lambda^2 - 9\lambda + 2)\log(\lambda) > 2\lambda^2 - 3\lambda + 1$.

Solution: An analytical solution of the above inequality is not possible, so we will use numerical algorithms. Let us consider the corresponding equation $(8\lambda^2 - 9\lambda + 2)\log(\lambda) = 2\lambda^2 - 3\lambda + 1$. Using function Solve in Mathematica software ([11]), we get that $\lambda \approx 0.3536$. Furthermore, using the function Reduce we see that for $\lambda \in (0.3536, 1)$ the inequality holds. The graphical solution is given in Figure 1.

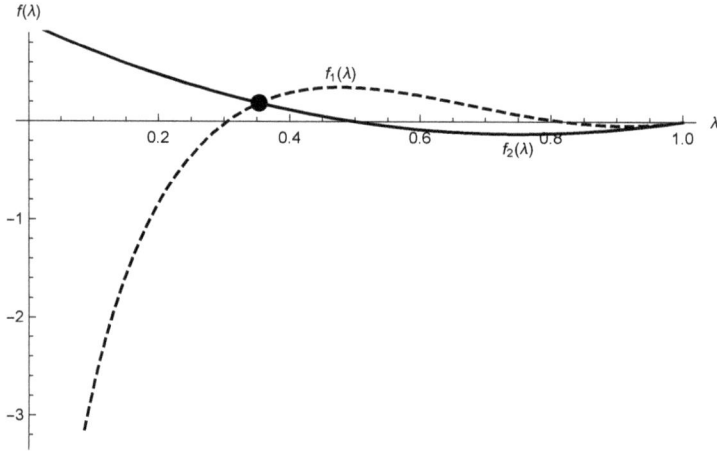

Figure 1. Graphical solution of the inequality $f_1(\lambda) > f_2(\lambda)$, where $f_1(\lambda) = (8\lambda^2 - 9\lambda + 2)\log(\lambda)$ and $f_2(\lambda) = 2\lambda^2 - 3\lambda + 1$.

Theorem 2. *The PDF of LiE1 with parameters* $\theta > 0$ *and* $\lambda \in (0,1)$ *is unimodal if* $\lambda \in (0.3536, 1)$. *Otherwise, it is decreasing.*

Proof. The first derivative of the logarithm of the PDF $g_1(x)$ can be represented in the form

$$[\log g_1(x)]' = \frac{-\theta s(x)}{(1 - \lambda(1 - e^{-\theta x}))(a + b(1 - e^{-\theta x}))},$$

where $s(x) = (a+b)(1-\lambda) - 2(a\lambda + b)e^{-\theta x} + \lambda b e^{-2\theta x}$, $a = 1 - \lambda + (3\lambda - 2)\log(\lambda)$ and $b = -\lambda(1 - \lambda + \lambda \log(\lambda))$. We transform the function $s(x)$ to a quadratic function $s(y) = \lambda b y^2 - 2(b + a\lambda)y + (a+b)(1-\lambda)$, $y \in [0,1]$. Let y_1 and y_2 represent the roots of the equation $s(y) = 0$. Some calculations indicate that $a > 0$, $b < 0$, $b + a\lambda > 0$ and $a + b > 0$. Thus,

$$y_1 + y_2 = \frac{2(a\lambda + b)}{\lambda b} < 0,$$

$$y_1 y_2 = \frac{(a+b)(1-\lambda)}{\lambda b} < 0,$$

so we have $y_1 < 0 < y_2$ and $|y_1| > y_2$. After some calculations, it can be shown that discriminant $D = 4(a\lambda + b)^2 - 4\lambda b(1 - \lambda)$ is positive and that $s(y)$ is concave. We need to find when solution $y_2 \in (0,1)$. If we set $u = -b$, one gets

$$y_2 = \frac{\sqrt{(a\lambda - u)^2 + \lambda u(a - u)(1 - \lambda)} - (a\lambda - u)}{\lambda u}.$$

If $y_2 < 1$, then
$$\sqrt{(a\lambda - u)^2 + \lambda u(a-u)(1-\lambda)} < \lambda u + a\lambda - u. \tag{13}$$

It is not difficult to verify that the right-hand side of the last inequality is positive and we can quadrate (13). Then, the inequality (13) reduces to

$$\lambda u(3\lambda a - u - a) > 0.$$

Now, the assertion of the first part of Theorem follows from Example 1.

In case $\lambda < 0.3536$, $s(y)$ is always positive on the interval $(0,1)$, and hence the PDF is decreasing. □

Different shapes of the PDF in cases of LiE1 model are given in Figure 2.

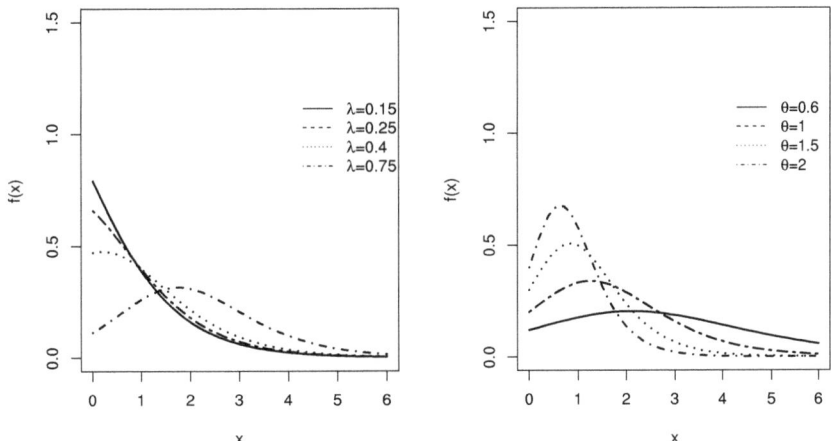

Figure 2. The plots of the density function of the LiE1 distribution for various choices of parameters with $\theta = 1$ (**left**) and $\lambda = 0.65$ (**right**).

The HRF of the LiE1 distribution is

$$h_1(x) = \frac{\theta[1 - \lambda + (3\lambda - 2)\log(\lambda) - \lambda(1 - \lambda + \lambda\log(\lambda))(1 - e^{-\theta x})]}{[1 - \lambda(1 - e^{-\theta x})][1 - 2\log(\lambda) - \lambda(1 - \log(\lambda))(1 - e^{-\theta x})]}, x > 0, \theta > 0, \lambda \in (0,1).$$

Determining the shape of a HRF of a distribution is an important issue in statistical reliability and survival analysis. We give it for the LiE1 model in the following theorem.

Theorem 3. *The HRF of the LiE1 with parameters $\theta > 0$ and $\lambda \in (0,1)$ is an increasing function.*

Proof. The first derivative of the $\log h_1(x)$ can be represented as

$$[\log h_1(x)]' = \frac{-\theta e^{-\theta x} s(x)}{(a + b(1 - e^{-\theta x}))(1 - \lambda(1 - e^{-\theta x}))(d - c(1 - e^{-\theta x}))},$$

where a and b were defined in Theorem 2, $c = \lambda(1 - \log(\lambda))$, $d = 1 - 2\log(\lambda)$ and $s(x) = \lambda bce^{-2\theta x} - 2\lambda c(a+b)e^{-\theta x} + 2\lambda ac - \lambda ad - bd + \lambda cb - ca$. After extensive calculations, it can be shown that $2\lambda ac - \lambda ad - bd + \lambda cb - ca < 0$.

Again, using the transformation $y = e^{-\theta x}$, where $y \in [0,1]$, we get quadratic equation $s(y) = 0$ with

$$y_1 + y_2 = \frac{2\lambda c(a+b)}{\lambda b} < 0,$$

$$y_1 y_2 = \frac{2\lambda ac - \lambda ad - bd + \lambda cb - ca}{\lambda b} > 0.$$

Thus, we have $y_1 < y_2 < 0$. The function $s(y)$ is concave, and it holds that $s(y) < 0$ for all $y \in [0,1]$. Finally, the HRF is increasing. Hence, we proved Theorem. □

Different shapes of the HRF in the case of the LiE1 model are outlined in Figure 3.

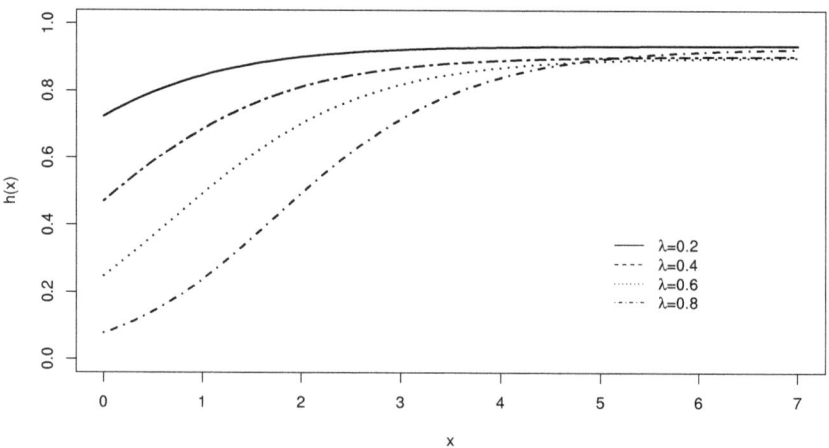

Figure 3. The plots of the HRF of the LiE1 distribution for various choices of parameter λ with $\theta = 1$.

Now, we will study the shapes of the discrete Lindley exponential distribution of the second kind (LiE2) of distribution. By replacing $\overline{F}(x) = e^{-\theta x}$ in Equation (11), we obtain the PDF of the LiE2 distribution as

$$g_2(x;\theta,\lambda) = \frac{\theta e^{-\theta x}[1 - \lambda + (3\lambda - 2)\log(\lambda) - \lambda(1 - \lambda + \lambda \log(\lambda))e^{-\theta x}]}{(1 - 2\log(\lambda))(1 - \lambda e^{-\theta x})^3}, \quad x > 0, \theta > 0, \lambda \in (0,1).$$

The shapes of the LiE2 distribution are given by the following theorem.

Theorem 4. *The PDF of the LiE2 with parameters $\theta > 0$ and $\lambda \in (0,1)$ is a decreasing function with $\lim_{x \to 0} g_2(x) = \frac{\theta(1 - \lambda + (\lambda - 2)\log(\lambda))}{(1-\lambda)^2(1 - 2\log(\lambda))}$ and $\lim_{x \to \infty} g(x) = 0$.*

Proof. Similarly to in Theorem 2, we have

$$[\log g_2(x)]' = \frac{-\theta s(x)}{(1 - \lambda e^{-\theta x})(a + be^{-\theta x})},$$

where $s(x) = a - 4\lambda a e^{-\theta x} - 3\lambda b \lambda e^{-2\theta x}$, $a = 1 - \lambda + (3\lambda - 2)\log(\lambda)$ and $b = -\lambda(1 - \lambda + \lambda \log(\lambda))$. We can prove that $s(x)$ is positive for all $x > 0$. Letting $y = e^{-\theta x}$, we transform the function $s(x)$ to a quadratic function $s(y) = b\lambda y^2 + 2(b + a\lambda)y + a$; $y \in [0,1]$. Let

$y_1 < y_2$ represent the roots of the equation $s(y) = 0$. Since we have $a > 0, b < 0$ and $b + a\lambda > 0$,

$$y_1 + y_2 = \frac{4a}{3b} < 0,$$
$$y_1 y_2 = -\frac{a}{3b\lambda} > 0,$$

which implies $y_1 < y_2 < 0$. Since $b\lambda < 0$ and the discriminant $D = 4(b + a\lambda)^2 - 4ab\lambda$ is positive, it follows that $s(y)$ is concave and positive on $[y_1, y_2]$, which means that $s(y)$ is positive for $y \in [0, 1]$. Finally, $s(x)$ is positive for all $x > 0$ and $g_2'(x) < 0$. □

The HRF of the LiE2 distribution for $x > 0, \theta > 0, \lambda \in (0, 1)$ is given by

$$h_2(x) = h_2(x; \theta, \lambda) = \frac{\theta[1 - \lambda + (3\lambda - 2)\log(\lambda) - \lambda(1 - \lambda + \lambda \log(\lambda))e^{-\theta x}]}{[1 - \lambda e^{-\theta x}][1 - \lambda + (3\lambda - 2)\log(\lambda) - \lambda(1 - \lambda + (2\lambda - 1)\log(\lambda))e^{-\theta x}]}.$$

The shape of the HRF of the LiE2 distribution is given in the following theorem.

Theorem 5. *The HRF of the LiE2 distribution with parameters $\theta > 0$ and $\lambda \in (0, 1)$ is an increasing function with $\lim_{x \to 0} h_2(x) = \frac{\theta(1 - \lambda + (\lambda - 2)\log(\lambda))}{(1 - \lambda)^2(1 - 2\log(\lambda))}$ and $\lim_{x \to \infty} h_2(x) = \theta$.*

Proof. We consider the logarithm of the HRF $h_2(x)$. Its first derivative can be expressed as

$$[\log h_2(x)]' = \frac{-\theta e^{-\theta x} t(x)}{(a + be^{-\theta x})(1 - \lambda e^{-\theta x})(a + ce^{-\theta x})},$$

where a and b are defined as in the proof of the previous theorem, $c = -\lambda[1 - \lambda + (2\lambda - 1)\log(\lambda)]$ and $t(x) = bc\lambda e^{-2\theta x} + 2ac\lambda e^{-\theta x} + a(b + a\lambda - c)$. By letting $y = e^{-\theta x}$, we transform the function $t(x)$ to the quadratic function $t(y) = bc\lambda y^2 + 2ac\lambda y + a(b + a\lambda - c)$; $y \in (0, 1)$. As before, let $y_1 < y_2$ be the roots of the equation $t(y) = 0$. Some calculations indicate that $a > 0, b < 0, c < 0$ and $b + a\lambda - c > 0$, which implies that

$$y_1 + y_2 = -\frac{2a}{b} > 0,$$
$$y_1 y_2 = \frac{a(b + a\lambda - c)}{bc\lambda} > 0,$$
$$(1 - y_1)(1 - y_2) = 1 + \frac{a}{bc\lambda}(b + a\lambda + 2c\lambda - c) = 1 + \frac{a}{bc}[1 - 3\lambda + 2\lambda^2 - (3 - 6\lambda + 4\lambda^2)\log(\lambda)] > 0.$$

Thus, two cases can be considered, $0 < y_1 < y_2 < 1$ and $1 < y_1 < y_2$. The first case is not possible, since

$$y_1 y_2 - 1 = \frac{a(b + a\lambda) - c(a + b\lambda)}{bc\lambda} > 0,$$

which follows from the fact that $a + b\lambda = (1 - \lambda)^2(1 + \lambda - (\lambda + 2)\log(\lambda)) > 0$. Thus, $1 < y_1 < y_2$. Since $bc\lambda > 0$ and the discriminant $D = -8ac\lambda^3(1 - \lambda)^2 \log^2(\lambda)$ is positive, it follows that $t(y)$ is a convex function and positive on $(0, 1)$. This implies that $t(x)$ is positive for all $x > 0$. Finally, $h_2'(x) < 0$, which means that the HRF is an increasing function. □

Using similar calculations, we can derive the shapes of the PDF and HRF of X and Y given by (5), (6), (11) and (12), respectively, under various baseline distributions.

Figure 4 represents plots of the LiE2 density function, while on Figure 5 we have plots of the LiE2 hazard rate functions for various parameter values.

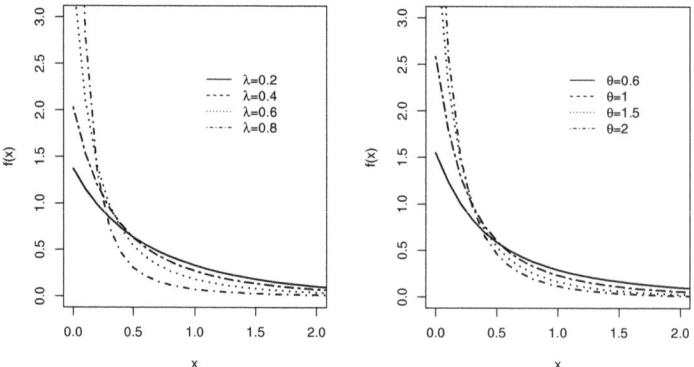

Figure 4. The plots of the density function of the LiE2 distribution for various choices of parameters with $\theta = 1$ (**left**) and $\lambda = 0.5$ (**right**).

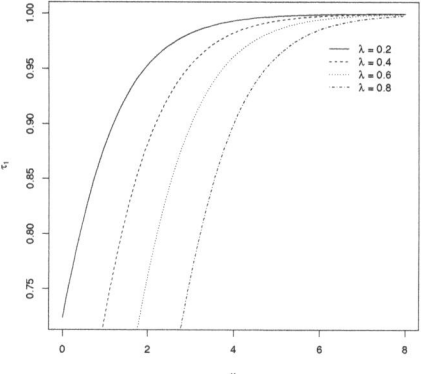

Figure 5. The hazard plots of the LiE2 distribution for various choices of parameter λ with $\theta = 1$.

Theorem 6. *The LiE2 distribution function is identifiable with respect to the parameters θ and λ.*

Proof. As was the case in the proof of Theorem 1, we will assume that $G_2(x; \theta_1, \lambda_2) = G_2(x; \theta_2, \lambda_2)$ for all $x > 0$ and $F(x)$ is the CDF of an exponential distribution. As a consequence, we have $h_2(x; \theta_1, \lambda_2) = h_2(x; \theta_2, \lambda_2)$. Then, from Theorem 5, we have that $\theta_1 = \theta_2$ when $x \to \infty$. Now, since $\theta_1 = \theta_2$ after some algebra, it can be shown that from $h_2(0; \theta_1, \lambda_2) = h_2(0; \theta_2, \lambda_2)$ follows $\lambda_1 = \lambda_2$. □

4. Some Mathematical Properties

4.1. Mixture Representations

In this section, we obtain a very useful representation for the LiG1 density function. For $|z| < 1$ and $\rho > 0$, we can write

$$(1-z)^{-\rho} = \sum_{j=0}^{\infty} w_j \, z^j, \tag{14}$$

where $w_j = \Gamma(\rho + j) / [\Gamma(\rho) j!]$ and $\Gamma(\rho) = \int_0^{\infty} t^{\rho-1} e^{-t} dt$ is the gamma function. For $\alpha \in (0,1)$, we can apply (14) in Equation (5) to obtain

$$g_1(x) = f(x) \left[a(\lambda) + b(\lambda) F(x) \right] \sum_{j=0}^{\infty} v_j \, F(x)^j, \tag{15}$$

where $a(\lambda) = 1 - \lambda + (3\lambda - 2)\log(\lambda)$, $b(\lambda) = -\lambda[1 - \lambda + \lambda\log(\lambda)]$ and

$$v_j = v_j(\lambda) = \frac{\Gamma(j+3)\,\lambda^j}{2(1 - 2\log(\lambda))\,j!}.$$

Henceforth, T_a as a random variable will be said to have the exponentiated-F ("exp-F") distribution, its power parameter being $a > 0$, say, $T_a \sim exp - F(a)$, if its PDF and CDF are given by

$$h_a(x) = a\,f(x)\,F^{a-1}(x) \quad \text{and} \quad H_a(x) = F^a(x),$$

respectively.

Then, using the exp-F distribution, we can write Equation (15) as

$$g_1(x) = \sum_{j=0}^{\infty} [t_j\,h_{j+1}(x) + s_j\,h_{j+2}(x)] = \sum_{j=0}^{\infty} p_j\,h_{j+1}(x), \tag{16}$$

where $t_j = a(\lambda)\,v_j/(j+1)$, $s_j = b(\lambda)\,v_j/(j+2)$, $p_j = t_j + s_{j-1}$ (for $j \geq 0$) and $s_{-1} = 0$.

Equation (16) is this section's main result. It shows that the LiF1 family density function is a mixture of $exp - F$ ditributions. Therefore, there are structural properties (for instance incomplete and ordinary moments, generating functions, mean deviations) of the LiF1 family that can be obtained from the corresponding properties of the exp-G distribution. The exp-F mathematical properties have been studied by many authors in recent years, such as Nadarajah and Kotz (2006). In the following sections, we provide some mathematical properties of the LiG1 family distribution.

4.2. Moments

Henceforth, let T_{j+1} have the the exp-F density $h_{j+1}(x)$ with power parameter $j + 1$, say, $T_{j+1} \sim$exp-$F(j+1)$. A first formula for the nth moment of the LiF1 family can be obtained from (16) as

$$\mu'_n = E(X^n) = \sum_{j=0}^{\infty} p_j\,E(T^n_{j+1}). \tag{17}$$

Nadarajah and Kotz [12] provide explicit expressions for moments of some exponentiated distributions. They can be used to produce μ'_n.

A second formula for μ'_n can be obtained from (17) in terms of the baseline quantile function (qf) $Q_F(u)$. We obtain

$$\mu'_n = \sum_{j=0}^{\infty}(j+1)\,p_j\,\tau(n,j), \tag{18}$$

where the integral can be expressed as a function of the F quantile function (qf), say, $Q_F(u) = F^{-1}(u)$, as $\tau(n,j) = \int_0^1 Q_F(u)^n\,u^j du$.

Even though there is an infinite sum in the moments' equation, it is not difficult to calculate its values. For example, if we set an error to 10^{-6}, then four iterations would be enough for moments' calculation.

Equations (17) and (18) can be used to directly determine the ordinary moments of some LiF1 distributions. Three examples will be provided here. Here, we consider three examples. LiE1 distribution moments (with scale parameter $\theta > 0$ from the exponential baseline distribution) are given by

$$\mu'_n = \frac{n!}{\theta^n}\sum_{j=0}^{\infty}\sum_{i=0}^{\infty}\binom{j}{i}(-1)^i p_j(j+1)\frac{1}{(i+1)^{n+1}}.$$

Particularly, we have

$$E(X) = \sum_{j=0}^{\infty} p_j [\psi(j+2) - \psi(1)],$$

where $\psi(\cdot)$ is the digamma function defined by $\psi(\cdot) = \Gamma'(\cdot)/\Gamma(\cdot)$.

For the discrete Lindley Pareto of the first kind (LiPa1) of distribution, the baseline distribution is $F(x) = 1 - (1+x)^{-\nu}$, $x > 0$ and we have

$$\mu'_n = \sum_{j=0}^{\infty} \sum_{i=0}^{n} \binom{n}{i} (-1)^i p_j (j+1) B\left(j+1, 1 - \frac{i}{\nu}\right), \quad \nu > n,$$

where $B(a,b) = \int_0^1 t^{a-1}(1-t)^{b-1} dt$ is the standard beta function.

For the discrete Lindley standard logistic of the first kind (LiSL1) of distribution, the baseline distribution is $F(x) = (1 + e^{-x})^{-1}$ and $-\infty < x < \infty$. Using an integral result from [13], we have

$$\mu'_n = \sum_{j=0}^{\infty} \sum_{i=0}^{n} \binom{n}{i} (-1)^{2n-i} \frac{j+1}{\Gamma(j+2)} p_j \Gamma_{(1)}^{(i)} \Gamma_{(j+1)}^{(n-i)},$$

where

$$\Gamma_{(a)}^{(m)} = \int_0^{\infty} (\ln x)^m x^{a-1} e^{-x} dx.$$

Further, central moments, that is, moments around the mean, can also be computed. The relation between the central moments (μ_r) and the moments about the origin are given by

$$\mu_r = \sum_{k=0}^{r} (-1)^k \binom{r}{k} (\mu'_1)^k \mu'_{r-k}.$$

The cumulants of the distribution can also be computed together with the skewness and kurtosis measures. For this approach, we refer the reader to [14]. The skewness and kurtosis plots for these distributions are sketched in Figures 6–9. We observe that various skewness and kurtosis values can be obtained from these models.

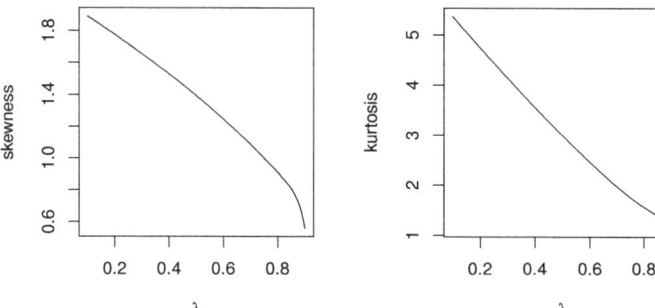

Figure 6. Skewness and kurtosis plots of the LiE1 distribution as a function of parameter λ.

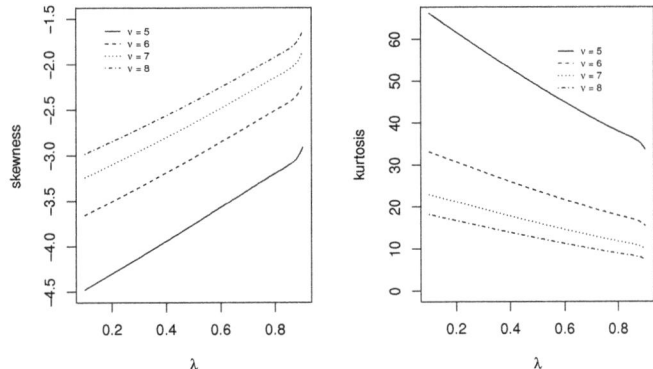

Figure 7. Skewness and kurtosis plots of the LiPa1 distribution as a function of parameter λ.

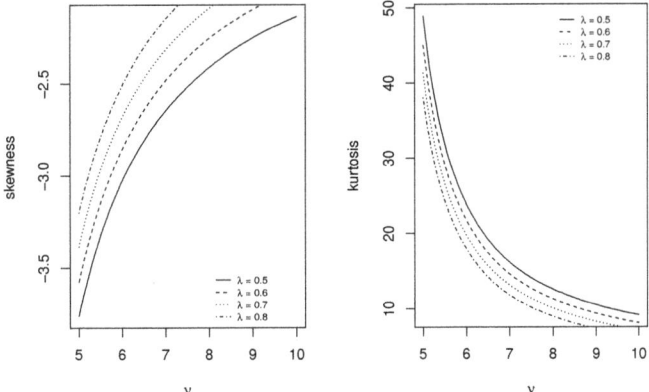

Figure 8. Skewness and kurtosis plots of the LiPa1 distribution as a function of parameter ν.

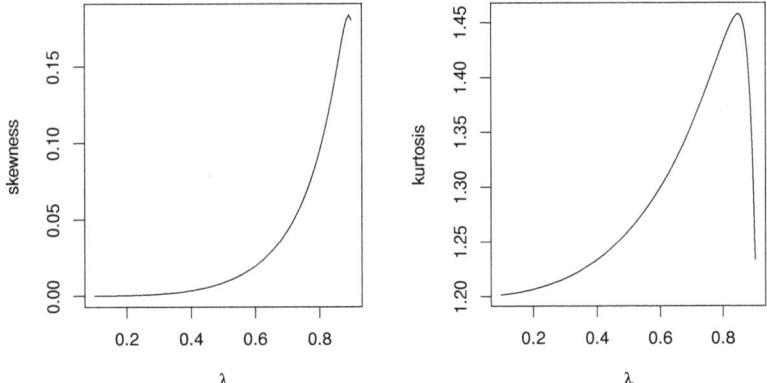

Figure 9. Skewness and kurtosis plots of the LiSL1 distribution as a function of parameter λ.

4.3. Generating Function

As far as the moment generating function (mgf) $M(t) = E(e^{tX})$ of X is concerned, we will provide two formulae. The first $M(t)$ formula comes from (16) as

$$M(t) = \sum_{j=0}^{\infty} p_j \, M_{j+1}(t), \tag{19}$$

where $M_{j+1}(t)$ is the mgf of T_{j+1}. Therefore, $M(t)$ is determined by the generating function of the $exp - F(j+1)$ distribution. The second $M(t)$ formula is derived from (16)

$$M(t) = \sum_{j=0}^{\infty} (j+1) \, p_j \, \rho(t,j), \tag{20}$$

where $\rho(t,j)$ can be calculated from $Q_F(x)$ as

$$\rho(t,j) = \int_0^1 \exp\{t \, Q_G(u)\} \, u^j du. \tag{21}$$

It is possible to get several mgf of some LiG1 distributions using Equations (20) and (21), which can be used to directly obtain the mgf of several LiG1 distributions. For example, we have the mgfs of the LiE1 (with parameter λ) and and LiSL1 as

$$M(t) = \sum_{j=0}^{\infty} (j+1) \, B(j+1, 1 - \lambda t) \, p_j, \quad t > \lambda,$$

and

$$M(t) = \sum_{j=0}^{\infty} (j+1) \, B(t+j+1, 1 - t) \, p_j, \quad t < 1,$$

respectively.

4.4. Incomplete Moments and Mean Deviations

The shapes of many of the distributions can, for empirical reasons, be conveniently described as incomplete moments. Such moments are important in measuring inequality, such as income quantiles and Lorenz and Bonferroni curves, which depend on the distribution incomplete moments. The $n-$th incomplete moment of the random variable X is defined as

$$m_n(y) = \int_0^y g_1(x) dx = \sum_{j=0}^{\infty} (j+1) \int_0^{F(y)} Q_F(u)^n \, u^j du. \tag{22}$$

The integral in (22) can be computed in the closed-form for several baseline F distributions.

The mean deviations about the mean ($\delta_1 = E(|X - \mu_1'|)$) and about the median ($\delta_2 = E(|X - M|)$) of X can be expressed as $\delta_1 = 2\mu_1' \, G_1(\mu_1') - 2m_1(\mu_1')$ and $\delta_2 = \mu_1' - 2m_1(M)$, respectively, where $\mu_1' = E(X)$, $M = Median(X)$ is the median of X computed from

$$G_1(M) = \frac{F(M)\{1 - \lambda + (3\lambda - 2)\log(\lambda) - \lambda[1 - \lambda + (2\lambda - 1)\log(\lambda)]F(x)\}}{[1 - 2\log(\lambda)][1 - \lambda F(M)]^2} = 0.5,$$

$G_1(\mu_1')$ is easily calculated from (4) and $m_1(z) = \int_{-\infty}^{z} x f(x) dx$ is the first exp-F incomplete moment.

We will provide two ways to compute $delta_1$ and $delta_2$. In the first instance, we can derive a general equation for $m_1(z)$ from (16) by setting $u = F(x)$ as

$$m_1(z) = \sum_{j=0}^{\infty} (j+1) A_j(z), \tag{23}$$

where

$$A_j(z) = \int_{-\infty}^{z} x\, h_{j+1}(x) dx = \int_{0}^{F(z)} Q_F(u)\, u^j du. \tag{24}$$

Equation (24) provides the basic quantity for computing the mean deviations of the exp-F distributions. Hence, the mean deviations δ_1 and δ_2 depend only on the exp-F mean deviations. Thus, alternative representations for δ_1 and δ_2 are given by $\delta_1 = 2\mu'_1 G_1(\mu'_1) - 2\sum_{j=0}^{\infty}(j+1) A_j(\mu'_1)$ and $\delta_2 = \mu'_1 - 2\sum_{j=0}^{\infty}(j+1) A_j(M)$.

In a similar way, the mean deviations of any LiF1 distribution can be computed from Equations (23) and (24). For example, the mean deviations of the LiE1 (with parameter λ), LiPa1 (with parameter $0 < \nu < 1$) and LiSL1 are determined immediately (by using the generalized binomial expansion) from the functions

$$A_j(z) = \lambda^{-1} \Gamma(j) \sum_{m=0}^{\infty} \frac{(-1)^m \{1 - \exp(-m\lambda z)\}}{\Gamma(j-m)(m+1)!},$$

and

$$A_j(z) = \sum_{m=0}^{\infty} \sum_{r=0}^{m} \frac{(-1)^m}{(1-r\nu)} \binom{j+1}{m} \binom{m}{r} z^{1-r\nu},$$

and

$$A_j(z) = \frac{1}{\Gamma(j)} \sum_{m=0}^{\infty} \frac{(-1)^m \Gamma(j+m+1) \{1 - \exp(-mz)\}}{(m+1)!},$$

respectively.

Bonferroni and Lorenz curves defined can be given to obtain for a given probability π by $B(\pi) = T(q)/(\pi \mu'_1)$ and $L(\pi) = T(q)/\mu'_1$, respectively, where $\mu'_1 = E(X)$ and $q = Q(\pi)$ is the LiG1-F qf at π.

5. On the Maximum-Likelihood Estimation of Parameters

We propose to use the maximum likelihood (ML) estimation method for the parameter estimation of the introduced distributions. The log-likelihood function for the general case (5) is given by

$$\mathcal{L}(\lambda, \psi) = -n \log(1 - 2\log(\lambda)) - 3 \sum_{i=1}^{n} \log(1 - \lambda F(x_i; \psi)) + \sum_{i=1}^{n} \log f(x_i; \psi)$$

$$+ \sum_{i=1}^{n} \log[1 - \lambda + (3\lambda - 2)\log(\lambda) - \lambda(1 - \lambda + \lambda \log(\lambda)) F(x_i; \psi)].$$

In this special case, we consider the exponential baseline distribution. Thus, for the LiE1 model, the estimating equations are given by

$$\frac{\partial \mathcal{L}(\lambda,\theta)}{\partial \theta} = 3\lambda\theta \sum_{i=1}^{n} \frac{e^{-\theta x_i}}{1 - \lambda(1 - e^{-\theta x_i})} + b\theta \sum_{i=1}^{n} \frac{e^{-\theta x_i}}{a + b(1 - e^{\theta x_i})} + \frac{n}{\theta} - \sum_{i=1}^{n} x_i = 0 \qquad (25)$$

$$\frac{\partial \mathcal{L}(\lambda,\theta)}{\partial \lambda} = 3 \sum_{i=1}^{n} \frac{1 - e^{-x_i\theta}}{1 - \lambda(1 - e^{-x_i\theta})} + \frac{2n}{\lambda(1 - 2\log(\lambda))}$$
$$+ \sum_{i=1}^{n} \frac{2 - \frac{2}{\lambda} + 3\log(\lambda) - (1 - e^{-x_i\theta})\lambda\log(\lambda) - (1 - e^{-x_i\theta})(1 - \lambda + \lambda\log(\lambda))}{1 - \lambda + (-2 + 3\lambda)\log(\lambda) - (1 - e^{-x_i\theta})(1 - \lambda + \lambda\log(\lambda))} = 0. \qquad (26)$$

Now, we will study the existence of the ML estimators when the other parameter is known in advance (or given).

Theorem 7. *If the parameter λ is known, then the Equation (25) has at least one root in the interval $(0, +\infty)$.*

Proof. One can readily verify that $\lim\limits_{\theta \to +\infty} \frac{\mathcal{L}(\lambda,\theta)}{\partial \theta} = -\sum_{i=1}^{n} x_i$ and $\lim\limits_{\theta \to 0+0} \frac{\mathcal{L}(\lambda,\theta)}{\partial \theta} = +\infty$. Thus, there exists at least one root of the Equation (25). □

Theorem 8. *Assuming that*

$$\sum_{i=1}^{n} e^{-x_i\theta} < \frac{n}{2}$$

and if the parameter θ is known, then (26) has at least one root on the interval $(0, 1)$.

Proof. Applying L'Hôpital's rule, we get $\lim\limits_{\lambda \to 1-0} \frac{\mathcal{L}(\lambda,\theta)}{\partial \lambda} = -\infty$ and $\lim\limits_{\lambda \to 0+0} \frac{\mathcal{L}(\lambda,\theta)}{\partial \lambda} = 3 \sum_{i=1}^{n}(1 - e^{-x_i\theta}) - \frac{3n}{2}$.

In order to have at least one solution, it is necessary to have $3 \sum_{i=1}^{n}(1 - e^{-x_i\theta}) - \frac{3n}{2} > 0$. Hence the theorem. □

On the other hand, the estimating equations for the LiE2 model are given by

$$\frac{\partial \mathcal{L}(\lambda,\theta)}{\partial \theta} = -3\lambda\theta \sum_{i=1}^{n} \frac{e^{-\theta x_i}}{1 - \lambda e^{-\theta x_i}} - b\theta \sum_{i=1}^{n} \frac{e^{-\theta x_i}}{a + be^{\theta x_i}} + \frac{n}{\theta} - \sum_{i=1}^{n} x_i = 0 \qquad (27)$$

$$\frac{\partial \mathcal{L}(\lambda,\theta)}{\partial \lambda} = 3 \sum_{i=1}^{n} \frac{e^{-x_i\theta}}{1 - \lambda e^{-x_i\theta}} + \frac{2n}{\lambda(1 - 2\log(\lambda))}$$
$$+ \sum_{i=1}^{n} \frac{2 - \frac{2}{\lambda} + 3\log(\lambda) - e^{-x_i\theta}\lambda\log(\lambda) - e^{-x_i\theta}(1 - \lambda + \lambda\log(\lambda))}{1 - \lambda + (-2 + 3\lambda)\log(\lambda) - e^{-x_i\theta}(1 - \lambda + \lambda\log(\lambda))} = 0. \qquad (28)$$

The next two theorems examine the existence problem of the ML estimates via (27) and (28). Their proofs are very similar to those cases of Theorems 7 and 8, so we here omit them.

Theorem 9. *If the parameter λ is known, then the Equation (27) has at least one root on the interval $(0, +\infty)$.*

Theorem 10. *If the parameter θ is known and if it is assumed that*

$$\sum_{i=1}^{n} e^{-x_i\theta} > \frac{n}{2},$$

then the Equation (28) has at least one root on the interval $(0, 1)$.

Clearly, the log-likelihood estimating equations for the parameters are nonlinear in the sense that the estimators cannot be obtained in closed forms. Thus, a numerical iterative method such as the Newton–Raphson one should be used in the estimation.

6. Estimation of Parameters via the EM Algorithm

We propose to use the method of maximum likelihood in estimating the parameters of the introduced models. The construction method of the models suggests using an EM (expectation maximization) algorithm. In this section, we provide EM algorithms for the estimation of the unknown parameters θ and λ for both exponential-discrete Lindley distributions.

6.1. EM Algorithm for the LiE1 Model

The missing data random variable will be the random variable M with the zero-truncated discrete Lindley distribution. Let us derive its probability mass function as

$$P(M=m) = \frac{P(N=m)}{1-P(N=0)}$$
$$= \frac{\lambda^{m-1}[\lambda \log(\lambda) + (1-\lambda)(1-(m+1)\log(\lambda))]}{1-2\log(\lambda)}, \, m=1,2,\ldots,$$

where N is a random variable with the discrete Lindley distribution with the parameter $\lambda \in (0,1)$. Next, the random variable $X = \max(Z_1, \ldots, Z_M)$ for a given $M = m$ has the CDF $(1-e^{-\theta x})^m$. Then, the PDF of the complete-data distribution is given by

$$f(x,m) = \frac{\theta m \lambda^{m-1}\{\lambda \log(\lambda) + (1-\lambda)[1-(m+1)\log(\lambda)]\}e^{-\theta x}(1-e^{-\theta x})^{m-1}}{1-2\log(\lambda)}.$$

The marginal PDF of X is given by

$$f_X(x) = \frac{\theta e^{-\theta x}\{1-\lambda+(3\lambda-2)\log(\lambda)-(1-e^{-\theta x})\lambda[\lambda(\log(\lambda)-1)+1]\}}{(1-2\log(\lambda))[1-(1-e^{-\theta x})\lambda]^3}.$$

Then, the conditional PDF of M for given $X = x$ is given by

$$f_{M|X}(m|x) = \frac{m(1-e^{-\theta x})^{m-1}\lambda^{m-1}[1-(1-e^{-\theta x})\lambda]^3\{\lambda \log(\lambda) + (1-\lambda)[1-(m+1)\log(\lambda)]\}}{1-\lambda+(3\lambda-2)\log(\lambda)-(1-e^{-\theta x})\lambda[\lambda(\log(\lambda)-1)+1]},$$

where $m = 1, 2, 3, \ldots$.

The E-step of the EM algorithm requires the computation of the conditional expectation of the random variable M for a given $X = x$. Now, we have

$$E(M|X) =$$
$$= \frac{\lambda \log(\lambda)(3-\xi^2(x;\lambda,\theta) + 4\xi(x;\lambda,\theta)) - (4\xi(x;\lambda,\theta)+2)\log(\lambda) + (1-\lambda)(1-\xi^2(x;\lambda,\theta))}{(1-\xi(x;\lambda,\theta))\{1-\lambda+(3\lambda-2)\log(\lambda)-\xi(x;\lambda,\theta)[\lambda(\log(\lambda)-1)+1]\}},$$

where $\xi(x;\lambda,\theta) = \lambda(1-e^{-\theta x})$.

In the M-step, we consider the complete data log-likelihood function, which is given by

$$l_c(\theta,\lambda) = n\log(\theta) + \sum_{i=1}^n \log(m_i) - \theta \sum_{i=1}^n x_i + \sum_{i=1}^n (m_i-1)\log(1-e^{-\theta x_i}) + \left(\sum_{i=1}^n m_i - n\right)\log(\lambda)$$
$$+ \sum_{i=1}^n \log\{\lambda \log(\lambda) + (1-\lambda)[1-(m_i+1)\log(\lambda)]\} - n\log(1-2\log(\lambda)).$$

Maximizing the log-likelihood function $l_c(\theta, \lambda)$, the obtained estimates in the $k+1$ iteration are given by

$$\theta^{(k+1)} = n \left\{ n\bar{x} - \sum_{i=1}^{n} \frac{x_i(m_i^{(k+1)} - 1)e^{-\theta^{(k+1)}x_i}}{1 - e^{-\theta^{(k+1)}x_i}} \right\}^{-1}$$

$$\lambda^{(k+1)} = \left[\frac{n(1 + 2\log(\lambda^{(k+1)}))}{2\log(\lambda^{(k+1)}) - 1} - \sum_{i=1}^{n} m_i^{(k+1)} \right]$$

$$\times \left\{ \sum_{i=1}^{n} \frac{(m_i + 2)\log(\lambda^{(k+1)}) - ((1 - \lambda^{(k+1)})/\lambda^{(k+1)})(m_i^{(k+1)} + 1)}{\lambda^{(k+1)} \log(\lambda^{(k+1)}) + (1 - \lambda^{(k+1)}) \left[1 - (m_i^{(k+1)} + 1)\log(\lambda^{(k+1)})\right]} \right\}^{-1},$$

where $\bar{x}$ is the sample mean and

$$m_i^{(k+1)} = \left\{ \lambda^{(k)} \log(\lambda^{(k)})(3 - \xi^2(x_i; \lambda^{(k)}, \theta^{(k)}) + 4\xi(x_i; \lambda^{(k)}, \theta^{(k)})) - (4\xi(x_i; \lambda^{(k)}, \theta^{(k)}) + 2)\log(\lambda^{(k)}) \right.$$
$$+ (1 - \lambda^{(k)})(1 - \xi^2(x_i; \lambda^{(k)}, \theta^{(k)})) \right\} / \left\{ (1 - \xi(x_i; \lambda^{(k)}, \theta^{(k)})) \left[1 - \lambda^{(k)} + (3\lambda^{(k)} - 2)\log(\lambda^{(k)}) \right. \right.$$
$$\left. \left. - \xi(x_i; \lambda^{(k)}, \theta^{(k)}) \left(\lambda^{(k)}(\log(\lambda^{(k)}) - 1) + 1 \right) \right] \right\}.$$

The solutions for these equations can be found using an iterative numerical process. For example, one can use the `uniroot` function in R (R Core Team, 2020).

6.2. EM Algorithm for the LiE2 Model

In this case, the random variable $Y = \min(Z_1, \ldots, Z_M)$ for a given $M = m$ has the exponential distribution with the scale parameter θm. Thus, the PDF of the hypothetical complete-data distribution is

$$f(y, m) = \frac{\lambda^{m-1}[\lambda \log(\lambda) + (1 - \lambda)(1 - (m+1)\log(\lambda))]\theta m e^{-\theta m y}}{1 - 2\log(\lambda)}, \quad y > 0, m = 1, 2, \ldots$$

Following some calculations, we can deduce that the marginal PDF of the random variable Y is given by

$$f(y) = \frac{\theta e^{-\theta y}[1 - \lambda + (3\lambda - 2)\log(\lambda) - \lambda(1 - \lambda + \lambda \log(\lambda))e^{-\theta y}]}{(1 - 2\log(\lambda))(1 - \lambda e^{-\theta y})^3}, \quad y > 0,$$

which implies that the conditional PDF of M for given $Y = y$ has the form

$$f_{M|Y}(m|y) = \frac{m\lambda^{m-1}e^{-\theta(m-1)y}(1 - \lambda e^{-\theta y})^3[\lambda \log(\lambda) + (1 - \lambda)(1 - (m+1)\log(\lambda))]}{1 - \lambda + (3\lambda - 2)\log(\lambda) - \lambda(1 - \lambda + \lambda \log(\lambda))e^{-\theta y}}, \quad m = 1, 2, \ldots$$

The E-step of the EM algorithm requires the computation of the conditional expectation of the random variable M for a given $Y = y$. We have that

$$E(M|Y = y) = \frac{1 - \lambda + (3\lambda - 2)\log(\lambda) - 4(1 - \lambda)\lambda e^{-\theta y}\log(\lambda) - \lambda^2(1 - \lambda + \lambda \log(\lambda))e^{-2\theta y}}{(1 - \lambda e^{-\theta y})(1 - \lambda + (3\lambda - 2)\log(\lambda) - \lambda(1 - \lambda + \lambda \log(\lambda))e^{-\theta y})}.$$

In the M-step, we need the complete data log-likelihood function, which is given by

$$l_c(\theta, \lambda) = n\log(\theta) + \sum_{i=1}^{n} \log(m_i) - \theta \sum_{i=1}^{n} m_i y_i + \left(\sum_{i=1}^{n} m_i - n \right) \log(\lambda)$$
$$+ \sum_{i=1}^{n} \log[\lambda \log \lambda + (1 - \lambda)(1 - (m_i + 1)\log(\lambda))] - n\log(1 - 2\log(\lambda)).$$

By maximizing the log-likelihood function $l_c(\theta, \lambda)$, we obtain the estimates in the $k + 1$ iteration as follows:

$$\theta^{(k+1)} = \frac{n}{\sum_{i=1}^{n} y_i m_i^{(k+1)}},$$

$$\sum_{i=1}^{n} \frac{\lambda^{(k+1)}(m_i^{(k+1)} + 2)\log(\lambda^{(k+1)}) - (1 - \lambda^{(k+1)})(1 + m_i^{(k+1)})}{\lambda^{(k+1)}\log(\lambda^{(k+1)}) + (1 - \lambda^{(k+1)})(1 - (m_i^{(k+1)} + 1)\log(\lambda^{(k+1)}))} + \frac{2n}{1 - 2\log(\lambda^{(k+1)})} =$$

$$= n - \sum_{i=1}^{n} m_i^{(k+1)},$$

where

$$m_i^{(k+1)} = \left\{ 1 - \lambda^{(k)} + (3\lambda^{(k)} - 2)\log(\lambda^{(k)}) - 4(1 - \lambda^{(k)})\lambda^{(k)}\log(\lambda^{(k)})e^{-\theta^{(k)}y_i} - \lambda^{2(k)}(1 - \lambda^{(k)}) \right.$$
$$\left. + \lambda^{(k)}\log(\lambda^{(k)}))e^{-2\theta^{(k)}y_i} \right\} / \left\{ (1 - \lambda^{(k)}e^{-\theta^{(k)}y_i})(1 - \lambda^{(k)} + (3\lambda^{(k)} - 2)\log(\lambda^{(k)})) \right.$$
$$\left. - \lambda^{(k)}(1 - \lambda^{(k)} + \lambda^{(k)}\log(\lambda^{(k)}))e^{-\theta^{(k)}y_i} \right\}.$$

7. Simulation Study

In this section, we consider LiE1 and LiE2 models and present a simulation study testing the performances of the estimators using the EM algorithm. We generated 10,000 random samples in batches of 50, 100 and 200 from both models.

We can generate random numbers from the *LiE*1 distribution by using the inverse transform method. Let u be a random number from the uniform distribution on $[0,1]$. Employing some algebra, we have $x = -\log(1-y)/\theta$, a number from the *LiE*1 distribution. Here,

$$y = \frac{2\lambda au + c - \sqrt{\Delta_1}}{2(b + \lambda^2 au)},$$

where $a = 1 - 2\log(\lambda)$, $b = \lambda[1 - \lambda + (2\lambda - 1)\log(\lambda)]$, $c = 1 - \lambda + (3\lambda - 2)\log(\lambda)$ and $\Delta_1 = (2\lambda au + c)^2 - 4(\lambda^2 au + b)au$.

Similarly, we can generate random numbers from the *LiE*2 distribution by using the inverse transform method. Let u be a random number from the uniform distribution on $[0,1]$. Following some calculations, we have $y = -\log(x)/\theta$, a number from the *LiE*2 distribution. Here,

$$x = \frac{d + a(1 - 2u\lambda) - \sqrt{\Delta_2}}{2(d - \lambda^2 au)},$$

where $d = \lambda[1 - \log(\lambda)]$ and $\Delta_2 = [(2u\lambda - 1)a - d]^2 - 4a(d - ua\lambda^2)(1 - u)$.

We used R (R Core Team, 2020) with `uniroot` to run the EM algorithms. We took the parameter values as the starting points for the iterations in the algorithms. The algorithms stopped when $|\lambda^{(k+1)} - \lambda^{(k)}| < 10^{-5}$. The simulation results of the empirical means and mean square errors (MSEs) are reported in Tables 1 and 2. We observe that the estimates are close to the parameter values and the MSEs decrease with increasing sample size. This makes the use of the EM algorithm plausible for estimation.

Table 1. Empirical means and MSEs of the maximum-likelihood estimates of the LiE1 for different values of the parameters.

n	λ	θ	$\hat{\lambda}$	$\hat{\theta}$	λ	θ	$\hat{\lambda}$	$\hat{\theta}$	λ	θ	$\hat{\lambda}$	$\hat{\theta}$
50	0.6	0.5	0.5954	0.5159	0.6	1	0.5963	1.0350	0.6	2	0.5965	2.0675
			(0.0163)	(0.0089)			(0.0161)	(0.0369)			(0.0159)	(0.1448)
100			0.5952	0.5068			0.5957	1.0143			0.5952	2.0264
			(0.0081)	(0.0041)			(0.0080)	(0.0164)			(0.0082)	(0.0685)
200			0.5954	0.5020			0.5970	1.0067			0.5949	2.0058
			(0.0040)	(0.0020)			(0.0041)	(0.0083)			(0.0040)	(0.0334)

Table 2. Empirical means and the MSEs of the maximum-likelihood estimates of the LiE2 for different values of the parameters.

n	λ	θ	λ̂	θ̂	λ	θ	λ̂	θ̂	λ	θ	λ̂	θ̂
50	0.6	0.2	0.5335	0.2379	0.6	1	0.5344	1.1898	0.8	1	0.6883	1.7007
			(0.0368)	(0.0119)			(0.0375)	(0.2993)			(0.0434)	(1.7356)
100			0.5526	0.2252			0.5455	1.1424			0.7331	1.4154
			(0.0240)	(0.0068)			(0.0248)	(0.1737)			(0.0213)	(0.7965)
200			0.5668	0.2176			0.5669	1.0838			0.7616	1.2371
			(0.0127)	(0.0036)			(0.0128)	(0.0884)			(0.0093)	(0.3335)

8. Real Data Fitting

In this section, we investigate the performance of the introduced distributions in data fitting. We also compare them with their natural competitor, that is, the generalized exponential (GE) distribution studied in [15]. The GE distribution was proposed as an alternative to exponential, gamma and Weibull distributions. A lot of work in the literature has shown that it is a flexible model with reverse J-shaped and positively skewed unimodal data fitting. The PDF of the GE distribution is given by

$$f(x;\alpha,\theta) = \alpha\theta e^{-\theta x}(1-e^{-\theta x})^{\alpha-1}, \quad x,\alpha,\beta > 0.$$

We consider the maximum likelihood method in the estimation. Since we compare the models, we used the direct maximization of the respective log-likelihood functions.

8.1. Carbon Data Set

Let us consider a data set (uncensored) from [16], which includes 100 observations regarding breaking stress of carbon fibers in Gba. The data are given in Table 3.

Table 3. Data on the breaking stress of carbon fibers.

0.39	0.81	0.85	0.98	1.08	1.12	1.17	1.18	1.22	1.25
1.36	1.41	1.47	1.57	1.57	1.59	1.59	1.61	1.61	1.69
1.69	1.71	1.73	1.80	1.84	1.84	1.87	1.89	1.92	2.00
2.03	2.03	2.05	2.12	2.17	2.17	2.17	2.35	2.38	2.41
2.43	2.48	2.48	2.50	2.53	2.55	2.55	2.56	2.59	2.67
2.73	2.74	2.76	2.77	2.79	2.81	2.82	2.83	2.85	2.87
2.88	2.93	2.95	2.96	2.97	2.97	3.09	3.11	3.11	3.15
3.15	3.19	3.19	3.22	3.22	3.27	3.28	3.31	3.31	3.33
3.39	3.39	3.51	3.56	3.60	3.65	3.68	3.70	3.75	4.20
4.38	4.42	4.70	4.90	4.91	5.08	5.56			

The data were also used in [17].

We used the LiE1 distribution in fitting instead of LiE2, since the data exhibits a unimodal shape (see Figure 10). One can also use the total time test (TTT) plot procedure to determine an appropriate model shape.

The TTT plots were introduced by [18] for model identification purposes, that is, for choosing a suitable lifetime distribution. These plots were studied in detail by [19]. Let $x_{(1)} \leq \cdots \leq x_{(n)}$ denote the ordered observations from the random sample of size n. The TTT plot is obtained in the following way:

- Let $s_0 = 0$.
- Calculate the TTT values $s_j = s_{j-1} + (n-j+1)(x_{(j)} - x_{(j-1)})$ for $j = 1,2,\ldots,n$.
- Obtain the normalized TTT values by $u_j = s_j/s_n$ for $j = 0,1,2,\ldots,n$.
- Plot the points $(j/n, u_j)$ for $j = 0,1,2,\ldots,n$, and then join them by line segments.

A TTT plot is a diagnostic tool in the sense that it gives an insight about the aging properties of the underlying distribution. Then, one can choose an appropriate lifetime distribution for modeling the data. For example, when the TTT plot is concave, a life distribution with an increasing failure rate should be used. The TTT plot for the Carbon data set is sketched in the lhs of Figure 10. It can be seen that it is concave. Thus, a model with increasing failure rate like LiE1 should be used.

Further, the HRF can not only be increasing, but also be constant, decreasing or even a U-shaped. These futures may also be inferred from the TTT plot. The HRF is constant when the TTT plot is straight diagonal, decreases when the TTT plot is convex and is U-shaped if the TTT plot is S-shaped—that is, first convex and then changed to a concave shape. When the ordering is reversed in the S-shaped case, a HRF with a unimodal characteristic is obtained.

Alternatively, we also fit LiSL1 and GE distributions to this data set and computed the parameter estimates using the optim function in R [20]. The results are reported in Table 4. We observe that the Lie1 distribution is better than the others according to the Akaike information criterion (AIC). The Kolmogorov–Simirnov test statistic was 0.074605 with p-value 0.6338. Figure 10 also supports this good fit. On the other hand, the EM algorithm gave $\hat{\lambda} = 0.9415187$ and $\hat{\theta} = 1.432148$, which are similar values to those obtained from direct maximization.

Table 4. Maximum-likelihood estimates with standard errors in parentheses, log-likelihood and AIC values for Carbon data.

Model	$\hat{\lambda}$	$\hat{\theta}$	$\hat{\alpha}$	log-lik	AIC
LiE1	0.9419	1.4344		−142.1633	288.3266
	(0.0169)	(0.1187)			
LiSL1	0.9528	1.5067		−142.9535	289.9069
	(0.0127)	(0.1109)			
GE		1.0132	7.7883	−146.1823	296.3646
		(0.0875)	(1.4962)		

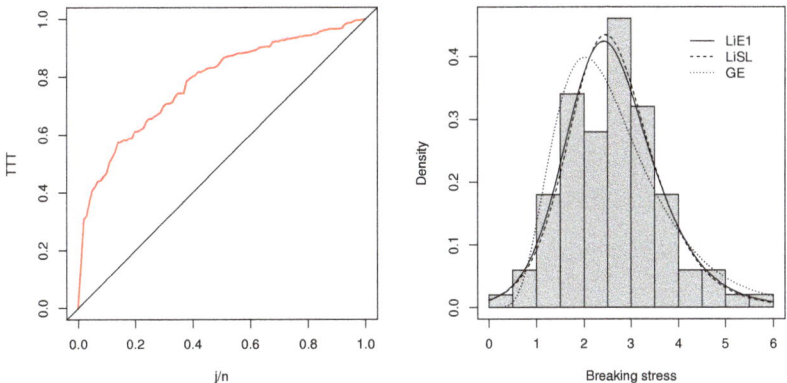

Figure 10. TTT plot of the data set (on the **left**) and several fits for the Carbon data (on the **right**).

8.2. Failure Data Set

The data set is based on the number of successive failures of air conditioning systems on 13 Boeing 720 air planes. The data set is from [21] and was recently analyzed in [22]. Since the data exhibit a reversed J-shape (see Figure 11), we used the LiE2 distribution in fitting. TTT plot sketched in the lhs of Figure 11 also supports this conjecture, since it produces a convex shape.

For convenience, the data are given Table 5.

Table 5. Data on the successive failures for the air conditioning system of each member in a fleet of 13 Boeing 720 jet air planes.

194	413	90	74	55	23	97	50	359	50	130	487	57	102	15
14	10	57	320	261	51	44	9	254	493	33	18	209	41	58
60	48	56	87	11	102	12	5	14	14	29	37	186	29	104
35	98	54	100	11	181	65	49	12	239	14	18	39	3	12
5	36	79	59	33	246	1	79	3	27	201	84	27	156	21
16	88	130	14	118	44	15	42	106	46	230	26	59	153	104
20	206	5	66	34	29	26	35	5	82	31	118	326	12	54
36	34	18	25	120	31	22	18	216	139	67	310	3	46	210
57	76	14	111	97	62	39	30	7	44	11	63	23	22	23
14	18	13	34	16	18	130	90	163	208	1	24	70	16	101
52	208	95	62	11	191	14	7							

The fitting results are given in Table 6. According to the AIC, the LiE2 fit is better than the GE fit. The Kolmogorov–Simirnov test statistic is 0.050017 with a p-value of 0.7347. In addition, the EM algorithm gave $\hat{\lambda} = 0.3837683$ and $\hat{\theta} = 0.007553028$, which are close to those obtained from direct maximization.

Table 6. Maximum-likelihood estimates with standard errors in parentheses, log-likelihood and AIC values for failure data.

Model	$\hat{\lambda}$	$\hat{\theta}$	$\hat{\alpha}$	log-lik	AIC
LiE2	0.3800	0.0076		−1033.644	2071.288
	(0.1180)	(0.0014)			
GE		0.0102	0.9005	−1036.907	2077.814
		(0.0010)	(0.0852)		

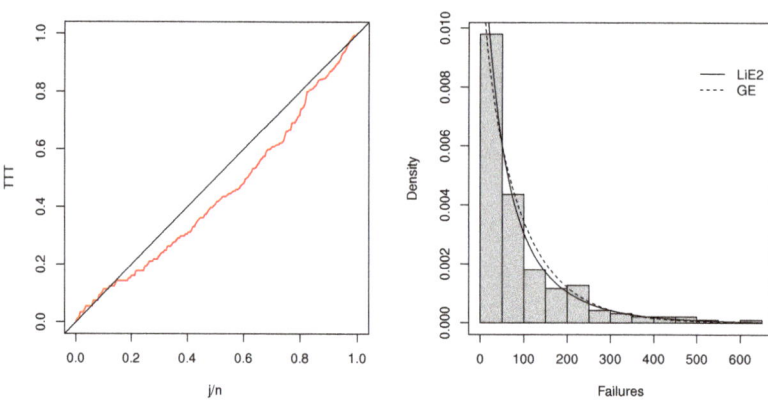

Figure 11. TTT plot of the data set (on the **left**) and two competing fits for the Failure data (on the **right**).

9. Conclusions

In this manuscript, we constructed two general probability distribution families using the discrete Lindley distribution. The families contain a baseline distribution which can be manipulated by the user to obtain probability distributions of different shapes. The resulting distributions are not so complex in the sense that the number of parameters of the baseline distribution is increased by one only. As an alternative to the direct maximization of the log-likelihood, we constructed an EM algorithm to compute the ML estimates of the parameters. We mainly focused on the exponential baseline distribution and used the newly defined distributions in real data fitting.

As a part of further research, the introduced distributions may be studied in detail using other simple baseline distributions like Pareto. Also, the Marshall-Olkin approach of construction of bivariate distributions can be used to define the bivariate extensions of the models introduced.

Author Contributions: Conceptualization, S.K. and B.V.P.; methodology, S.K., B.V.P. and A.İ.G.; software, A.İ.G.; validation, S.K., B.V.P. and A.İ.G.; investigation, B.V.P. All authors have read and agreed to the published version of the manuscript.

Funding: This research received no external funding.

Institutional Review Board Statement: Not applicable.

Informed Consent Statement: Not applicable.

Data Availability Statement: Data sets are given in the manuscript.

Conflicts of Interest: The authors declare no conflict of interest.

References

1. Johnson, N.L.; Kemp, A.W.; Kotz, S. *Univariate Discrete Distributions*; John Wiley & Sons, Inc.: Hoboken, NJ, USA, 2005
2. Hu, X.; Zhang, L.; Sun, W. Risk model based on the first-order integer-valued moving average process with compound Poisson distributed innovations. *Scand. Actuar. J.* **2018**, *5*, 412–425. [CrossRef]
3. Asmussen, S. *Ruin Probabilities*; World Scientific Publishing: Singapore, 2000.
4. Klugman, S.; Panjer, H.H.; Willmot, G.E. *Loss Models: From Data to Decisions*; Wiley: New York, NY, USA, 1998.
5. Panjer, H.H.; Willmot, G.E. *Insurance Risk Models*; Society of Actuaries: Schaumburg, IL, USA, 1992.
6. Nadarajah, S.; Popović, B.V.; Ristić, M.M. Compounding: An R package for computing continuous distributions obtained by compounding a continuous and a discrete distribution. *Comput. Stat.* **2013**, *28*, 977–992. [CrossRef]
7. Gómez-Déniz, E.; Calderín-Ojeda, E. The discrete Lindley distribution: Properties and applications. *J. Stat. Comput. Simul.* **2011**, *81*, 1405–1416. [CrossRef]
8. Abebe, B.; Shanker, R.A. A discrete lindley distribution with applications in biological sciences. *Biom. Biostat. Int. J.* **2018**, *7*, 48–52. [CrossRef]
9. Oliveira, R.P.; Mazucheli, J.; Achcar, J.A. A comparative study between two discrete Lindley distributions. *Cienc. Nat.* **2017**, *39*, 539–552. [CrossRef]
10. Tahir, M.H.; Cordeiro, G.M. Compounding of distributions: A survey and new generalized classes. *J. Stat. Distrib. Appl.* **2016**, *3*, 13. [CrossRef]
11. Wolfram Research, Inc. *Mathematica, Version 9.0.*; Wolfram Research, Inc.: Champaign, IL, USA, 2012.
12. Nadarajah, S.; Kotz, S. The Exponentiated Type Distributions. *Acta Appl. Math.* **2006**, *92*, 97–111. [CrossRef]
13. Brazauskas, V. Information matrix for Pareto (IV), Burr, and related distributions. *Commun. Stat.-Theory Methods* **2003**, *32*, 315–325. [CrossRef]
14. Cordeiro, G.M.; Brito, R.S. The Beta Power distribution. *Braz. J. Probab. Stat.* **2012**, *26*, 88–112.
15. Gupta, R.D.; Kundu, D. Generalized exponential distributions. *Aust. N. Z. J. Stat.* **1999**, *41*, 173–188. [CrossRef]
16. Nichols, M.D.; Padgett, W.J. A Bootstrap control chart for Weibull percentiles. *Qual. Reliab. Eng. Int.* **2006**, *22*, 141–151. [CrossRef]
17. Lemonte, A.J.; Cordeiro, G.M. The exponentiated generalized inverse Gaussian distribution. *Stat. Probab. Lett.* **2011**, *81*, 506–517. [CrossRef]
18. Barlow, R.E.; Campo, R. Total time on test processes and applications to failure data analysis. In *Reliability and Fault Tree Analysis*; Barlow, R.E., Fussell, J., Singpurwalla, N.D., Eds.; SIAM: Philadelphia, PA, USA, 1975; pp. 451–481.
19. Klefsjö, B. TTT-plotting—A tool for both theoretical and practical problems. *J. Stat. Plan. Inference* **1991**, *29*, 99–110. [CrossRef]
20. R Core Team. *R: A Language and Environment for Statistical Computing*; R Foundation for Statistical Computing: Vienna, Austria, 2020. Available online: https://www.R-project.org/ (accessed on 12 November 2022).
21. Proschan, F. Theoretical explanation of observed decreasing failure rate. *Technometrics* **1963**, *5*, 375–383. [CrossRef]
22. Al-Saiary, Z.A.; Bakoban, R.A. The Topp-Leone generalized inverted exponential distribution with real data applications. *Entropy* **2020**, *22*, 1144. [CrossRef] [PubMed]

Disclaimer/Publisher's Note: The statements, opinions and data contained in all publications are solely those of the individual author(s) and contributor(s) and not of MDPI and/or the editor(s). MDPI and/or the editor(s) disclaim responsibility for any injury to people or property resulting from any ideas, methods, instructions or products referred to in the content.

Article

On the Existence and Stability of Solutions for a Class of Fractional Riemann–Liouville Initial Value Problems

Luís P. Castro *,† and Anabela S. Silva †

CIDMA—Center for Research and Development in Mathematics and Applications, University of Aveiro, 3810-193 Aveiro, Portugal; anabela.silva@ua.pt
* Correspondence: castro@ua.pt
† These authors contributed equally to this work.

Abstract: This article deals with a class of nonlinear fractional differential equations, with initial conditions, involving the Riemann–Liouville fractional derivative of order $\alpha \in (1,2)$. The main objectives are to obtain conditions for the existence and uniqueness of solutions (within appropriate spaces), and to analyze the stabilities of Ulam–Hyers and Ulam–Hyers–Rassias types. In fact, different conditions for the existence and uniqueness of solutions are obtained based on the analysis of an associated class of fractional integral equations and distinct fixed-point arguments. Additionally, using a Bielecki-type metric and some additional contractive arguments, conditions are also obtained to guarantee Ulam–Hyers and Ulam–Hyers–Rassias stabilities for the problems under analysis. Examples are also included to illustrate the theory.

Keywords: fractional differential equations; Riemann–Liouville derivative; fixed point theory; Ulam–Hyers stability; Ulam–Hyers–Rassias stability

MSC: 34A08; 26A33; 34A12; 34B15; 34D20; 45M10; 47H10

Citation: Castro, L.P.; Silva, A.S. On the Existence and Stability of Solutions for a Class of Fractional Riemann–Liouville Initial Value Problems. *Mathematics* **2023**, *11*, 297. https://doi.org/10.3390/math11020297

Academic Editors: Irina Cristea, Yuriy Rogovchenko, Gintautas Dzemyda and Patrick Siarry

Received: 15 December 2022
Revised: 3 January 2023
Accepted: 4 January 2023
Published: 6 January 2023

Copyright: © 2023 by the authors. Licensee MDPI, Basel, Switzerland. This article is an open access article distributed under the terms and conditions of the Creative Commons Attribution (CC BY) license (https://creativecommons.org/licenses/by/4.0/).

1. Introduction

Given the importance that fractional derivatives and integrals [1–7] have shown to have in the optimization and improvement of mathematical models of real events or even of those associated with other areas of knowledge (namely through making these models more accurate when compared to what they effectively model), we have recently witnessed a large development in the mathematical analysis of classes of fractional order differential and integral equations.

In this context, it is essential to know about the possible existence of several solutions to the problems in question, possible sufficient conditions to obtain a unique solution and even conditions that eventually guarantee distinct forms of stability of the solutions (this being a crucial aspect, in particular, for the study of approximate solutions to the problems in analysis). The most used techniques in these problems involve the consideration and identification of operators that (in a sense) represent the problem (in some "equivalent" way) and usually involve different principles of contraction, as well as different estimates, usually framed, or dependent, on norms (or metrics), within the spaces framework most suited to the problems under study.

For this type of problem, the analysis of their eventual stability is also a study of significant importance. Namely, through the Ulam–Hyers and Ulam–Hyers–Rassias stabilities [1,8–17] which, with their specific characteristics, make it possible to identify forms of a slight disturbance in the system (that defines the problem) does not have a too disturbing effect on that system.

Having this general framework in mind, we would like to start by emphasizing that in [18], Chai studied the existence of solutions to the boundary value problem

$$\begin{cases} {}^C\mathcal{D}_{0+}^\alpha x(t) + r {}^C\mathcal{D}_{0+}^{\alpha-1} x(t) = f(t, x(t)), & t \in (0,1), \\ x(0) = x(1), \ x(\xi) = \eta, \ \xi \in (0,1), \end{cases}$$

where ${}^C\mathcal{D}_{a+}^\alpha$ and ${}^C\mathcal{D}_{a+}^{\alpha-1}$ denote the standard Caputo derivatives of order α and $\alpha - 1$, respectively, in this case with $1 < \alpha \leq 2$, and $r \neq 0$. Additionally, more recently, Xu et al. [19] considered the existence of solutions and the Ulam–Hyers stability for the fractional boundary value problem

$$\begin{cases} \lambda \mathcal{D}_{0+}^\alpha x(t) + \mathcal{D}_{0+}^\beta x(t) = f(t, x(t)), & t \in (0, T), \\ x(0) = 0, \ \mu \mathcal{D}_{0+}^{\gamma_1} x(T) + I_{0+}^{\gamma_2} x(\eta) = \gamma_3, \end{cases}$$

where $\mathcal{D}_{0+}^\vartheta$ denotes the Riemann–Liouville fractional derivative operator of order ϑ, $1 < \alpha \leq 2$, $1 \leq \beta < \alpha$, $0 < \lambda \leq 1$, $0 < \mu \leq 1$, $0 \leq \gamma_1 \leq \alpha - \beta$, $\gamma_2 \geq 0$, $I_{0+}^{\gamma_2}$ denotes the Riemann–Liouville fractional integral operator of order γ_2, and $0 < \eta < T$. Moreover, in [20], Ahmad et al. investigated the existence of solutions and the Ulam–Hyers stability for a fractional initial value problem given by

$$\begin{cases} ({}^C\mathcal{D}_{a+}^\alpha x(t) + \lambda_1 {}^C\mathcal{D}_{a+}^{\alpha-1} x(t) + \lambda_2 {}^C\mathcal{D}_{a+}^{\alpha-2} x(t) = f(t, x(t)), & t \in [a, T], \\ x^{(k)}(a) = b_k, \ k = 0, 1, 2, \end{cases}$$

where ${}^C\mathcal{D}_{a+}^\alpha$ is again the Caputo fractional derivative of order $\alpha \in (2,3)$, and λ_1 and λ_2 are nonzero constants. In [21], Alvan et al. investigated the existence of solutions for the fractional boundary value problem

$$\begin{cases} {}^C\mathcal{D}_{0+}^\alpha x(t) + 2r {}^C\mathcal{D}_{0+}^{\alpha-1} x(t) + r^2 {}^C\mathcal{D}_{0+}^{\alpha-2} x(t) = f(t, x(t), \mathcal{D}_{0+}^{\sigma-1}), & r > 0, \ t \in (0,1), \\ x(0) = x(1), \ x'(0) = x'(1), \ x'(\xi) + r x(\xi) = \eta, \ \xi \in (0,1), \end{cases}$$

where $2 \leq \alpha < 3$ and η is a positive real number. Bilgici and Şan [22] considered the existence and uniqueness of solutions to the problem

$$\begin{cases} \lambda \mathcal{D}_{0+}^\alpha x(t) = f(t, x(t), \mathcal{D}_{0+}^{\alpha-1} x(t)), & t > 0, \\ x(0) = 0, \ \mathcal{D}_{0+}^{\alpha-1} x(t)|_{t=0} = b, \end{cases}$$

where $\alpha \in (1, 2)$ and $b \neq 0$.

Motivated by the analysis and the results already achieved for the above-mentioned problems (included in the works [18–22]), we investigate in this paper the stabilities of Ulam–Hyers and Ulam–Hyers–Rassias types [1,8–11,14,16], and the existence and uniqueness of solutions to the following initial value problem of fractional order (IVPFO)

$$\begin{cases} \mathcal{D}_{a+}^\alpha x(t) + \lambda (\mathcal{D}_{a+}^{\alpha-1} x)(t) = f(t, x(t)), & t \in [a, b], \\ x(a) = x'(a) = 0, \end{cases} \quad (1)$$

where $1 < \alpha < 2$, λ is a nonzero constant, $a, b \in \mathbb{R}$ (with $a < b$) and $f : [a, b] \times \mathbb{R} \to \mathbb{R}$ is a continuous function. Thus, this problem can also be viewed as a class of problems depending on the parameter λ, and with the form of a single-point boundary problem "a" of a two-term fractional differential equation.

The remaining part of the work is organized as follows: Section 2 contains the necessary definitions and the fundamental tools that are used in the sections that follow; in Section 3, we derive different conditions for the existence and uniqueness of solutions for the IVPFO (1); in Section 4, we discuss the Ulam–Hyers and the Ulam–Hyers–Rassias stabilities and obtain conditions for their existence. Finally, some examples are included to describe the obtained results in a more concrete way.

2. Preliminaries and Background Material

We start this section by presenting the known basic definitions of the main objects that we will use.

Definition 1. *The Riemann–Liouville fractional integral of order $\alpha \in \mathbb{R}^+$ of a function x (on $[a,b]$) is defined by*

$$I_{a+}^\alpha x(t) = \frac{1}{\Gamma(\alpha)} \int_a^t (t-s)^{\alpha-1} x(s) ds \quad (a \le t \le b)$$

provided the right-hand side is pointwise defined and where Γ denotes the Euler Gamma function (given by $\Gamma(\alpha) = \int_0^\infty t^{\alpha-1} e^{-t} dt$, $\alpha > 0$).

Definition 2. *The Riemann–Liouville fractional derivative of order $\alpha > 0$ of a function x (on $[a,b]$) is defined by*

$$\mathcal{D}_{a+}^\alpha x(t) = \frac{1}{\Gamma(n-\alpha)} \frac{d^n}{dt^n} \int_a^t (t-s)^{n-\alpha-1} x(s) ds,$$

with $n = [\alpha] + 1$.

In what follows, we denote by $L^1([a,b])$ the Banach space of Lebesgue integrable functions from $[a,b]$ into $\mathbb{R}$ with the norm $\|x\|_{L^1} = \int_a^b |x(t)| dt$ and by $C([a,b])$ the Banach space of all continuous functions $g : [a,b] \to \mathbb{R}$ endowed with the norm $\|g\| = \sup_{t \in [a,b]} |g(t)|$.

Lemma 1 ([3])**.** *Assume that $x \in C([a,b]) \cap L^1([a,b])$ with a fractional derivative of order $\alpha > 0$. Then*

$$\mathcal{D}_{a+}^\alpha I_{a+}^\alpha x(t) = x(t)$$

and

$$I_{a+}^\alpha \mathcal{D}_{a+}^\alpha x(t) = x(t) + c_1(t-a)^{\alpha-1} + c_2(t-a)^{\alpha-2} + \cdots + c_n(t-a)^{\alpha-n},$$

for some $c_i \in \mathbb{R}$, $i = 1, 2, \ldots, n$, where n is the smallest integer greater than or equal to α.

For the reader's convenience, let us recall some classic principles of contraction and inequalities that we will use later.

Theorem 1 (Banach contraction principle)**.** *Let (X,d) be a generalized complete metric space, and consider a mapping $T : X \to X$ which is a strictly contractive operator, that is*

$$d(Tx, Ty) \le L d(x,y), \quad \forall x, y \in X,$$

for some constant $0 \le L < 1$. Then:
- *(a) the mapping T has a unique fixed point $x^* = Tx^*$;*
- *(b) the fixed point x^* is globally attractive, namely, for any starting point $x \in X$, the following identity holds:*

$$\lim_{n \to \infty} T^n x = x^*;$$

- *(c) we have the following inequalities:*

$$d(T^n x, x^*) \le L^n d(x, x^*), \quad n \ge 0, \ x \in X;$$

$$d(T^n x, x^*) \le \frac{1}{1-L} d(T^n x, T^{n+1} x), \quad n \ge 0, \ x \in X;$$

$$d(x, x^*) \le \frac{1}{1-L} d(x, Tx), \quad x \in X.$$

Theorem 2 (Schauder's fixed point theorem). *If Ω is a closed, bounded, convex subset of a Banach space X and the mapping $T : \Omega \to \Omega$ is completely continuous, then T has a fixed point in Ω.*

Keeping in mind some parts of the proofs of the next results, let us recall an important integral inequality that we will actually use later.

Theorem 3 ([23], [Theorem 11.2]). *Let $u(t)$, $b(t)$, $\sigma(t)$ and $k(t,s)$ be nonnegative continuous functions for $a \leq s \leq t \leq b$ and suppose that*

$$u(t) \leq c_1 + \sigma(t)\left(c_2 + \int_a^t b(s)u(s)ds + \int_a^t \int_a^s k(s,\tau)u(\tau)d\tau ds\right),$$

for $t \in [a,b]$, where $c_1, c_2 \geq 0$ are constants. Then,

$$u(t) \leq c_2 e^{\int_a^t B(s)\sigma(s)ds} + \int_a^t c_1 B(s) e^{\int_s^t B(\tau)\sigma(\tau)d\tau} ds,$$

where $B(s) = b(s) + \int_a^s k(s,\tau)d\tau$.

We denote by $C^2([a,b])$ the space of functions x which are 2-times continuously differentiable on $[a,b]$ endowed with the norm

$$\|x\|_{C^2} = \sum_{k=0}^{2} \sup_{t \in [a,b]} |x^{(k)}(t)|.$$

It is well-known that $(C^2([a,b]), \|\cdot\|_{C^2})$ is a Banach space.

In our next analysis of the existence and uniqueness of solutions for the IVPFO (1), we will make use of the following auxiliary property (which may be considered as a very natural and expectable property; cf., e.g., [24]).

Lemma 2 (See also [24]). *Let $\alpha \in (1,2)$ and $x \in C^2([a,b])$ with $x(a) = x'(a) = 0$. Then $\mathcal{D}_{a+}^\alpha x \in C([a,b])$ and*

$$(\mathcal{D}_{a+}^\alpha x)(t) = \frac{1}{\Gamma(2-\alpha)} \int_a^t (t-s)^{1-\alpha} x''(s) ds.$$

Moreover,

$$(\mathcal{D}_{a+}^\alpha x)(t) = (\mathcal{D}_{a+}^{\alpha-1} x')(t). \quad (2)$$

Proof. For the reader's convenience, we have chosen to include here a proof of this lemma. Within the stated conditions, we simply have to use integration by parts to obtain

$$\int_a^t (t-s)^{1-\alpha} x(s) ds = \frac{1}{2-\alpha} \int_a^t (t-s)^{2-\alpha} x'(s) ds,$$

$$\int_a^t (t-s)^{2-\alpha} x'(s) ds = \frac{1}{3-\alpha} \int_a^t (t-s)^{3-\alpha} x''(s) ds.$$

And so, it follows

$$(\mathcal{D}_{a+}^{\alpha}x)(t) = \frac{1}{\Gamma(2-\alpha)}\left(\frac{d}{dt}\right)^2 \int_a^t (t-s)^{1-\alpha} x(s)\,ds$$

$$= \frac{1}{\Gamma(3-\alpha)}\left(\frac{d}{dt}\right)^2 \int_a^t (t-s)^{2-\alpha} x'(s)\,ds$$

$$= \frac{1}{\Gamma(4-\alpha)}\left(\frac{d}{dt}\right)^2 \int_a^t (t-s)^{3-\alpha} x''(s)\,ds$$

$$= \frac{1}{\Gamma(2-\alpha)} \int_a^t (t-s)^{1-\alpha} x''(s)\,ds.$$

Since under the present conditions $\int_a^t (t-s)^{1-\alpha} x''(s)\,ds$ is continuous on $[a,b]$, we conclude that $\mathcal{D}_{a+}^{\alpha} x$ is continuous on $[a,b]$.

Moreover,

$$(\mathcal{D}_{a+}^{\alpha}x)(t) = \frac{1}{\Gamma(2-\alpha)}\left(\frac{d}{dt}\right)^2 \int_a^t (t-s)^{1-\alpha} x(s)\,ds$$

$$= \frac{1-\alpha}{\Gamma(2-\alpha)} \frac{d}{dt}\int_a^t (t-s)^{-\alpha} x(s)\,ds.$$

Integrating by parts, and using the circumstance that $x(a) = 0$, we obtain

$$(\mathcal{D}_{a+}^{\alpha}x)(t) = \frac{1}{\Gamma(2-\alpha)} \frac{d}{dt}\int_a^t (t-s)^{1-\alpha} x'(s)\,ds = (\mathcal{D}_{a+}^{\alpha-1}x')(t),$$

which concludes the proof. □

Remark 1. *Proceeding in a similar way as in the previous lemma, for $\alpha \in (1,2)$, $x \in C^2([a,b])$ and $x(a) = x'(a) = 0$, it follows that $\mathcal{D}_{a+}^{\alpha-1} x \in C([a,b])$ and*

$$(\mathcal{D}_{a+}^{\alpha-1}x)(t) = \frac{1}{\Gamma(3-\alpha)} \int_a^t (t-s)^{2-\alpha} x''(s)\,ds.$$

3. Different Conditions for the Existence and Uniqueness of Solutions

In the present section, we will analyse conditions to ensure the existence of solutions to the IVPFO (1) and also conditions to guarantee the uniqueness of the solution. In view of this, let us first start to "translate" the IVPFO (1) through a fractional integral equation.

Proposition 1. *As before, let $\alpha \in (1,2)$, $f : [a,b] \times \mathbb{R} \to \mathbb{R}$ be a continuous function and $\lambda \neq 0$. A function $x \in C^2([a,b])$ is a solution of the IVPFO (1) if and only if x satisfies the integral equation*

$$x(t) = \frac{e^{-\lambda t}}{\Gamma(\alpha-1)} \int_a^t \int_a^u (u-s)^{\alpha-2} e^{\lambda u} f(s, x(s))\,ds\,du. \tag{3}$$

Proof. Let $x \in C^2([a,b])$ be the solution of IVPFO (1). By Lemma 2, we have that $\mathcal{D}_{a+}^{\alpha}x, \mathcal{D}_{a+}^{\alpha-1}x \in C([a,b])$ and $\mathcal{D}_{a+}^{\alpha}x = \mathcal{D}_{a+}^{\alpha-1}x'$. Thus, we can rewrite our main equation in (1),

$$(\mathcal{D}_{a+}^{\alpha}x)(t) + \lambda(\mathcal{D}_{a+}^{\alpha-1}x)(t) = f(t,x(t)),$$

in the form

$$(\mathcal{D}_{a+}^{\alpha-1}x')(t) + \lambda(\mathcal{D}_{a+}^{\alpha-1}x)(t) = f(t,x(t)). \tag{4}$$

In view of Lemma 1, one has

$$(I_{a+}^{\alpha-1}\mathcal{D}_{a+}^{\alpha-1}x)(t) = x(t) + c_1(t-a)^{\alpha-2},$$
$$(I_{a+}^{\alpha-1}\mathcal{D}_{a+}^{\alpha-1}x')(t) = x'(t) + d_1(t-a)^{\alpha-2},\ t \in [a,b].$$

Thus, applying $I_{a+}^{\alpha-1}$ to both members of Equation (4), we obtain

$$x'(t) + \lambda x(t) + (\lambda c_1 + d_1)(t-a)^{\alpha-2} = [I_{a+}^{\alpha-1} f(\cdot, x(\cdot))](t). \tag{5}$$

Since $x(a) = x'(a) = 0$, we conclude that

$$\lambda c_1 + d_1 = 0,$$

and so it follows

$$x'(t) + \lambda x(t) = [I_{a+}^{\alpha-1} f(\cdot, x(\cdot))](t). \tag{6}$$

Let $y(t) = e^{\lambda t} x(t)$. One has that

$$x'(t) = -\lambda e^{-\lambda t} y(t) + e^{-\lambda t} y'(t).$$

Substituting the last two identities in (6), we obtain

$$y'(t) = e^{\lambda t} [I_{a+}^{\alpha-1} f(\cdot, e^{-\lambda \cdot} y(\cdot))](t). \tag{7}$$

Since $x \in C^2([a,b])$, we have that $y' \in C^1([a,b])$. Moreover, $I_{a+}^{\alpha-1} f$ is a continuously differentiable function. Thus, integrating Equation (7) from a to t, we obtain

$$y(t) = y(a) + \frac{1}{\Gamma(\alpha-1)} \int_a^t \int_a^u (u-s)^{\alpha-2} e^{\lambda u} f(s, e^{-\lambda s} y(s)) ds du.$$

Taking into account that $y(t) = e^{\lambda t} x(t)$, it follows that

$$x(t) = e^{-\lambda(t-a)} x(a) + \frac{e^{-\lambda t}}{\Gamma(\alpha-1)} \int_a^t \int_a^u (u-s)^{\alpha-2} e^{\lambda u} f(s, x(s)) ds du,$$

and using the initial conditions, we conclude that

$$x(t) = \frac{e^{-\lambda t}}{\Gamma(\alpha-1)} \int_a^t \int_a^u (u-s)^{\alpha-2} e^{\lambda u} f(s, x(s)) ds du.$$

Conversely, assume that x is given by (3), and thus

$$e^{\lambda t} x(t) = \frac{1}{\Gamma(\alpha-1)} \int_a^t \int_a^u (u-s)^{\alpha-2} e^{\lambda u} f(s, x(s)) ds du. \tag{8}$$

It is clear that $x(a) = 0$ and since x is continuously differentiable on $[a,b]$, differentiating both sides of (8), we get

$$e^{\lambda t} x'(t) + \lambda e^{\lambda t} x(t) = \frac{e^{\lambda t}}{\Gamma(\alpha-1)} \int_a^t (t-s)^{\alpha-2} f(s, x(s)) ds,$$

which is equivalent to

$$x'(t) + \lambda x(t) = \frac{1}{\Gamma(\alpha-1)} \int_a^t (t-s)^{\alpha-2} f(s, x(s)) ds. \tag{9}$$

Thus $x'(a) = 0$ and since $x \in C^2([a,b])$, accordingly to Lemma 2, we have that $\mathcal{D}_{a+}^{\alpha} x$ and $\mathcal{D}_{a+}^{\alpha-1} x$ exist. Applying $\mathcal{D}_{a+}^{\alpha-1}$ to both sides of Equation (9), using Lemma 1 and (2), we also obtain

$$(\mathcal{D}_{a+}^{\alpha} x)(t) + \lambda (\mathcal{D}_{a+}^{\alpha-1} x)(t) = f(t, x(t)),$$

which completes the proof. □

Having in mind Proposition 1, we realize that studying the solutions of IVPFO (1) is the same as studying the solutions of

$$x = Tx,$$

where T is the fractional integral operator given by

$$(Tx)(t) = \frac{e^{-\lambda t}}{\Gamma(\alpha-1)} \int_a^t \int_a^u (u-s)^{\alpha-2} e^{\lambda u} f(s, x(s)) ds du, \qquad (10)$$

for $x \in C^2([a,b])$ and $\lambda \in \mathbb{R} \setminus \{0\}$.

Remark 2. *Another way to discover an integral form of $x(t)$ is to consider the integral equation*

$$x(t) = -\lambda \int_a^t x(s) ds + \frac{1}{\Gamma(\alpha)} \int_a^t (t-s)^{\alpha-1} f(s, x(s)) ds. \qquad (11)$$

In fact, applying I_{a+}^α to both members of equation $(\mathcal{D}_{a+}^\alpha x)(t) + \lambda (\mathcal{D}_{a+}^{\alpha-1} x)(t) = f(t, x(t))$, and using Lemma 1, we obtain

$$x(t) + a_1(t-a)^{\alpha-1} + a_2(t-a)^{\alpha-2} + \lambda \int_a^t \left(x(s) + b_1(s-a)^{\alpha-2} \right) ds = [I_{a+}^\alpha f(\cdot, x(\cdot))](t)$$

$(a_1, a_2, b_1 \in \mathbb{R})$, which is equivalent to

$$x(t) = -\left(a_1 + \lambda \frac{b_1}{\alpha-1} \right)(t-a)^{\alpha-1} - a_2(t-a)^{\alpha-2} - \lambda \int_a^t x(s) ds + [I_{a+}^\alpha f(\cdot, x(\cdot))](t).$$

Since $x(a) = 0$, it follows that $a_2 = 0$. Observing that

$$x'(t) = -((\alpha-1)a_1 + \lambda b_1)(t-a)^{\alpha-2} - \lambda x(t) + [I_{a+}^{\alpha-1} f(\cdot, x(\cdot))](t),$$

and using the initial condition $x'(a) = 0$, we also conclude that $a_1 + \lambda \frac{b_1}{\alpha-1} = 0$, and thus, Equation (11) is obtained.

Let us fix the following notation

$$k_- = \frac{(b-a)^{\alpha-1}}{\lambda \Gamma(\alpha)} \left[1 - (1 - \lambda + \lambda^2) e^{-\lambda(b-a)} \right],$$

$$k_+ = \frac{(b-a)^{\alpha-1}}{\lambda \Gamma(\alpha)} \left[1 + 2\lambda + 2\lambda^2 - (1 + \lambda + \lambda^2) e^{-\lambda(b-a)} \right],$$

and

$$K = K(\lambda) := \begin{cases} k_-, & \lambda < 0 \\ k_+, & \lambda > 0 \end{cases}. \qquad (12)$$

Theorem 4. *If $f : [a,b] \times \mathbb{R} \to \mathbb{R}$ is continuously differentiable, then the IVPFO (1) has at least one solution in $C^2([a,b])$.*

Proof. We will use the Schauder fixed point theorem for the fractional integral operator T, defined in (10). The continuity of Tx follows from the continuity of f. Moreover, we have that

$$\begin{aligned}(Tx)'(t) &= \frac{-\lambda e^{-\lambda t}}{\Gamma(\alpha-1)}\int_a^t\int_a^u e^{\lambda u}(u-s)^{\alpha-2}f(s,x(s))dsdu \\ &\quad + \frac{1}{\Gamma(\alpha-1)}\int_a^t(t-s)^{\alpha-2}f(s,x(s))ds \\ &= \frac{-\lambda e^{-\lambda t}}{\Gamma(\alpha-1)}\int_a^t\int_a^u e^{\lambda u}(u-s)^{\alpha-2}f(s,x(s))dsdu \\ &\quad + \frac{1}{\Gamma(\alpha)}\left((t-a)^{\alpha-1}f(a,0)+\int_a^t(t-s)^{\alpha-1}f'(s,x(s))ds\right),\end{aligned}$$

and

$$\begin{aligned}(Tx)''(t) &= \frac{\lambda^2 e^{-\lambda t}}{\Gamma(\alpha-1)}\int_a^t\int_a^u e^{\lambda u}(u-s)^{\alpha-2}f(s,x(s))dsdu \\ &\quad - \frac{\lambda}{\Gamma(\alpha-1)}\int_a^t(t-s)^{\alpha-2}f(s,x(s))ds \\ &\quad + \frac{1}{\Gamma(\alpha-1)}\left((t-a)^{\alpha-2}f(a,0)+\int_a^t(t-s)^{\alpha-2}f'(s,x(s))ds\right).\end{aligned}$$

Since f is continuously differentiable, there exist positive constants A and B such that $|f(t,x(t))|\leq A$ and $|f'(t,x(t))|\leq B$, $t\in[a,b]$. Define $\Omega=\{x\in C^2([a,b]):\|x\|_{C^2}\leq R\}$ with R being a positive real number satisfying

$$R\geq KA+\frac{(b-a)^{\alpha-2}}{\Gamma(\alpha-1)}f(a,0)+\frac{(b-a)^{\alpha-1}}{\Gamma(\alpha)}B.$$

It is clear that Ω is a closed, bounded and convex subset of $C^2([a,b])$. Moreover, we have that

$$\begin{aligned}|(Tx)(t)| &= \left|\frac{e^{-\lambda t}}{\Gamma(\alpha-1)}\int_a^t\int_a^u(u-s)^{\alpha-2}e^{\lambda u}f(s,x(s))dsdu\right| \\ &\leq \frac{e^{-\lambda t}}{\Gamma(\alpha-1)}\int_a^t e^{\lambda u}\int_a^u(u-s)^{\alpha-2}|f(s,x(s))|dsdu \\ &\leq \frac{e^{-\lambda t}A}{\Gamma(\alpha-1)}\int_a^t e^{\lambda u}\int_a^u(u-s)^{\alpha-2}dsdu \\ &\leq \frac{e^{-\lambda t}}{\Gamma(\alpha)}A(b-a)^{\alpha-1}\int_a^t e^{\lambda u}du \\ &= \frac{(b-a)^{\alpha-1}}{\lambda\Gamma(\alpha)}(1-e^{-\lambda(t-a)})A,\end{aligned}$$

$$\begin{aligned}|(Tx)'(t)| &\leq \left|\frac{-\lambda e^{-\lambda t}}{\Gamma(\alpha-1)}\int_a^t\int_a^u(u-s)^{\alpha-2}e^{\lambda u}f(s,x(s))dsdu\right| \\ &\quad + \left|\frac{1}{\Gamma(\alpha-1)}\int_a^t(t-s)^{\alpha-2}f(s,x(s))ds\right| \\ &\leq \frac{(b-a)^{\alpha-1}}{\lambda\Gamma(\alpha)}\left(|\lambda|(1-e^{-\lambda(t-a)})+\lambda\right)A,\end{aligned}$$

and

$$|(Tx)''(t)| \leq \left|\frac{\lambda^2 e^{-\lambda t}}{\Gamma(\alpha-1)}\int_a^t\int_a^u e^{\lambda u}(u-s)^{\alpha-2}f(s,x(s))dsdu\right|$$
$$+\left|\frac{\lambda}{\Gamma(\alpha-1)}\int_a^t (t-s)^{\alpha-2}f(s,x(s))ds\right|$$
$$+\left|\frac{1}{\Gamma(\alpha-1)}\left((t-a)^{\alpha-2}f(a,0)+\int_a^t(t-s)^{\alpha-2}f'(s,x(s))ds\right)\right|$$
$$\leq \frac{(b-a)^{\alpha-1}}{\lambda\Gamma(\alpha)}\left(\lambda^2(1-e^{-\lambda(t-a)})\lambda|\lambda|\right)A+\frac{(b-a)^{\alpha-2}}{\Gamma(\alpha-1)}f(a,0)+\frac{(b-a)^{\alpha-1}}{\Gamma(\alpha)}B.$$

Thus, we have that

$$\|Tx\|_{C^2} \leq \sup_{t\in[a,b]}\left\{\frac{(b-a)^{\alpha-1}}{\lambda\Gamma(\alpha)}(1-e^{-\lambda(t-a)})A\right\}$$
$$+\sup_{t\in[a,b]}\left\{\frac{(b-a)^{\alpha-1}}{\lambda\Gamma(\alpha)}\left(|\lambda|(1-e^{-\lambda(t-a)})+\lambda\right)A\right\}$$
$$+\sup_{t\in[a,b]}\left\{\frac{(b-a)^{\alpha-1}}{\lambda\Gamma(\alpha)}\left(\lambda^2(1-e^{-\lambda(t-a)})+\lambda|\lambda|\right)A\right.$$
$$\left.+\frac{(b-a)^{\alpha-2}f(a,0)}{\Gamma(\alpha-1)}+\frac{(b-a)^{\alpha-1}}{\Gamma(\alpha)}B\right\}.$$

Thus, if $\lambda < 0$, we have that

$$\|Tx\|_{C^2} \leq \frac{(b-a)^{\alpha-1}}{\lambda\Gamma(\alpha)}\left[1-\lambda+\lambda^2-(1-\lambda+\lambda^2)e^{-\lambda(b-a)}+\lambda-\lambda^2\right]A$$
$$+\frac{(b-a)^{\alpha-2}}{\Gamma(\alpha-1)}f(a,0)+\frac{(b-a)^{\alpha-1}}{\Gamma(\alpha)}B$$
$$= k_- A+\frac{(b-a)^{\alpha-2}}{\Gamma(\alpha-1)}f(a,0)+\frac{(b-a)^{\alpha-1}}{\Gamma(\alpha)}B \leq R,$$

and if $\lambda > 0$, we have

$$\|Tx\|_{C^2} \leq \frac{(b-a)^{\alpha-1}}{\lambda\Gamma(\alpha)}\left[1+\lambda+\lambda^2-(1+\lambda+\lambda^2)e^{-\lambda(b-a)}+\lambda+\lambda^2\right]A$$
$$+\frac{(b-a)^{\alpha-2}}{\Gamma(\alpha-1)}f(a,0)+\frac{(b-a)^{\alpha-1}}{\Gamma(\alpha)}B$$
$$= k_+ A+\frac{(b-a)^{\alpha-2}}{\Gamma(\alpha-1)}f(a,0)+\frac{(b-a)^{\alpha-1}}{\Gamma(\alpha)}B \leq R.$$

Consequently, we conclude that T is a bounded operator on $\Omega \subset C^2([a,b])$.

Let us prove that operator $T : \Omega \to \Omega$ is completely continuous. For $t_1, t_2 \in [a,b]$, $t_1 < t_2$, one has

$$\begin{aligned}
|(Tx)(t_2) - (Tx)(t_1)| &= \left| \frac{e^{-\lambda t_2}}{\Gamma(\alpha-1)} \int_a^{t_2} \int_a^u (u-s)^{\alpha-2} e^{\lambda u} f(s, x(s)) ds du \right. \\
&\quad \left. - \frac{e^{-\lambda t_1}}{\Gamma(\alpha-1)} \int_a^{t_1} \int_a^u (u-s)^{\alpha-2} e^{\lambda u} f(s, x(s)) ds du \right| \\
&\leq \frac{e^{-\lambda t_2}}{\Gamma(\alpha-1)} \int_{t_1}^{t_2} \int_a^u |(u-s)^{\alpha-2} e^{\lambda u} f(s, x(s))| ds du \\
&\quad + \frac{|e^{-\lambda t_2} - e^{-\lambda t_1}|}{\Gamma(\alpha-1)} \int_a^{t_1} \int_a^u |(u-s)^{\alpha-2} e^{\lambda u} f(s, x(s))| ds du,
\end{aligned}$$

which tends to zero as $t_2 \to t_1$ (independently of x and λ). In the same way, we get

$$\begin{aligned}
&|(Tx)'(t_2) - (Tx)'(t_1)| \\
&= |\lambda||(Tx)(t_2) - (Tx)(t_1)| + \frac{1}{\Gamma(\alpha-1)} \int_{t_1}^{t_2} (t_2-s)^{\alpha-2} |f(s, x(s))| ds + \\
&\quad + \frac{1}{\Gamma(\alpha-1)} \int_a^{t_1} [(t_2-s)^{\alpha-2} - (t_1-s)^{\alpha-2}] |f(s, x(s))| ds,
\end{aligned}$$

which tends to zero as $t_2 \to t_1$. Finally, we observe that

$$\begin{aligned}
&|(Tx)''(t_2) - (Tx)''(t_1)| \\
&= |\lambda||(Tx)'(t_2) - (Tx)'(t_1)| + \frac{1}{\Gamma(\alpha-1)} \int_{t_1}^{t_2} (t_2-s)^{\alpha-2} |f'(s, x(s))| ds + \\
&\quad + \frac{1}{\Gamma(\alpha-1)} \int_a^{t_1} [(t_2-s)^{\alpha-2} - (t_1-s)^{\alpha-2}] |f'(s, x(s))| ds \\
&\quad + \frac{(t_2-a)^{\alpha-2} - (t_1-a)^{\alpha-2}}{\Gamma(\alpha-1)} f(a, 0)
\end{aligned}$$

tends to zero as $t_2 \to t_1$. Thus, we conclude that $T\Omega$ is equicontinuous. Following Arzelà-Ascoli Theorem, we obtain that T is completely continuous. Applying Schauder's fixed point theorem (cf. Theorem 2), we conclude that the operator T has at least one fixed point, which means that the IVPFO (1) has at least one solution and the proof is completed. □

We will now exhibit other conditions under which, besides the existence of solutions, we will also guarantee the uniqueness of the solution to the IVPFO (1).

Theorem 5. *Let $f : [a, b] \times \mathbb{R} \to \mathbb{R}$ be a continuously differentiable function and suppose that there are L_1 and $L_2 \geq 0$ such that, for $t \in [a, b]$,*

$$|f(t, x(t)) - f(t, y(t))| \leq L_1 |x(t) - y(t)|, \tag{13}$$
$$|f'(t, x(t)) - f'(t, y(t))| \leq L_2 (|x(t) - y(t)| + |x'(t) - y'(t)|). \tag{14}$$

If

$$KL_1 + L_2 \frac{(b-a)^{\alpha-1}}{\Gamma(\alpha)} < 1,$$

then the problem (1) has a unique solution on $C^2([a, b])$.

Proof. Since f is a continuously differentiable function, according to Theorem 4, the IVPFO (1) admits at least one solution. Let us assume that conditions (13)–(14) hold. Thus, we can obtain that, for $x, y \in C^2([a,b])$,

$$
\begin{aligned}
|(Tx)(t) - (Ty)(t)| &\leq \frac{e^{-\lambda t}}{\Gamma(\alpha-1)} \int_a^t e^{\lambda u} \int_a^u (u-s)^{\alpha-2} |f(s,x(s)) - f(s,y(s))| ds du \\
&\leq \frac{L_1 e^{-\lambda t}}{\Gamma(\alpha-1)} \int_a^t e^{\lambda u} \int_a^u (u-s)^{\alpha-2} |x(s) - y(s)| ds du \\
&\leq L_1 \|x-y\|_{C^2} \frac{(b-a)^{\alpha-1}(1 - e^{-\lambda(t-a)})}{\lambda \Gamma(\alpha)},
\end{aligned}
$$

$$
\begin{aligned}
|(Tx)'(t) - (Ty)'(t)| &\leq \frac{1}{\Gamma(\alpha-1)} \int_a^t (t-s)^{\alpha-2} |f(s,x(s)) - f(s,y(s))| ds \\
&\quad + \frac{|\lambda| e^{-\lambda t}}{\Gamma(\alpha-1)} \int_a^t e^{\lambda u} \int_a^u (u-s)^{\alpha-2} |f(s,x(s)) - f(s,y(s))| ds du \\
&\leq \frac{L_1}{\Gamma(\alpha-1)} \int_a^t (t-s)^{\alpha-2} |x(s) - y(s)| ds \\
&\quad + \frac{L_1 |\lambda| e^{-\lambda t}}{\Gamma(\alpha-1)} \int_a^t e^{\lambda u} \int_a^u (u-s)^{\alpha-2} |x(s) - y(s)| ds du \\
&\leq L_1 \|x-y\|_{C^2} \frac{(b-a)^{\alpha-1}\left(\lambda + |\lambda|(1 - e^{-\lambda(t-a)})\right)}{\lambda \Gamma(\alpha)},
\end{aligned}
$$

and

$$
\begin{aligned}
|(Tx)''(t) - (Ty)''(t)| &\leq \frac{\lambda^2 e^{-\lambda t}}{\Gamma(\alpha-1)} \int_a^t \int_a^u e^{\lambda u} (u-s)^{\alpha-2} |f(s,x(s)) - f(s,y(s))| ds du \\
&\quad + \frac{|\lambda|}{\Gamma(\alpha-1)} \int_a^t (t-s)^{\alpha-2} |f(s,x(s)) - f(s,y(s))| ds \\
&\quad + \frac{1}{\Gamma(\alpha-1)} \int_a^t (t-s)^{\alpha-2} |f'(s,x(s)) - f'(s,y(s))| ds \\
&\leq \frac{L_1 \lambda^2 e^{-\lambda t}}{\Gamma(\alpha-1)} \int_a^t \int_a^u e^{\lambda u} (u-s)^{\alpha-2} |x(s) - y(s)| ds du \\
&\quad + \frac{|\lambda| L_1}{\Gamma(\alpha-1)} \int_a^t (t-s)^{\alpha-2} |x(s) - y(s)| ds \\
&\quad + \frac{L_2}{\Gamma(\alpha-1)} \int_a^t (t-s)^{\alpha-2} (|x(s) - y(s)| + |x'(s) - y'(s)|) ds \\
&\leq L_1 \|x-y\|_{C^2} \frac{(b-a)^{\alpha-1}\left(\lambda^2(1 - e^{-\lambda(t-a)}) + \lambda|\lambda|\right)}{\lambda \Gamma(\alpha)} \\
&\quad + L_2 \|x-y\|_{C^2} \frac{(b-a)^{\alpha-1}}{\Gamma(\alpha)}.
\end{aligned}
$$

Thus, we conclude that, for $\lambda > 0$

$$
\begin{aligned}
\|Tx - Ty\|_{C^2} &= \sup_{t \in [a,b]} |(Tx)(t) - (Ty)(t)| + \sup_{t \in [a,b]} |(Tx)'(t) - (Ty)'(t)| + \sup_{t \in [a,b]} |(Tx)''(t) - (Ty)''(t)| \\
&\leq \|x - y\|_{C^2} \left[L_1 \frac{(b-a)^{\alpha-1}[1 + 2\lambda + 2\lambda^2 - (1 + \lambda + \lambda^2) e^{-\lambda(b-a)}]}{\lambda \Gamma(\alpha)} + L_2 \frac{(b-a)^{\alpha-1}}{\Gamma(\alpha)} \right] \\
&= \left(k_+ L_1 + L_2 \frac{(b-a)^{\alpha-1}}{\Gamma(\alpha)} \right) \|x - y\|_{C^2},
\end{aligned}
$$

and for $\lambda < 0$,

$$\begin{aligned}\|Tx - Ty\|_{C^2} &\leq \|x-y\|_{C^2}\left[L_1\frac{(b-a)^{\alpha-1}[1-e^{-\lambda(b-a)}+\lambda e^{-\lambda(b-a)}-\lambda^2 e^{-\lambda(b-a)}]}{\lambda\Gamma(\alpha)}+L_2\frac{(b-a)^{\alpha-1}}{\Gamma(\alpha)}\right]\\ &= \left(k_-L_1+L_2\frac{(b-a)^{\alpha-1}}{\Gamma(\alpha)}\right)\|x-y\|_{C^2}.\end{aligned}$$

Since $KL_1 + L_2\frac{(b-a)^{\alpha-1}}{\Gamma(\alpha)} < 1$, we have that T is a contractive operator. Thus, by Banach contraction principle (cf. Theorem 1), we conclude that T has a unique fixed point, which from Proposition 1 means that the IVPFO (1) has a unique solution on $C^2([a,b])$. □

4. Ulam–Hyers and Ulam–Hyers–Rassias Stabilities

In this section, we analyse the Ulam–Hyers and the Ulam–Hyers–Rassias stabilities of the above class of problems. In fact, since from Proposition 1 we have a new Equation (3) to describe the IVPFO (1) equivalently, we may choose to discuss the stabilities of (1) or (3). Thus, in here, we choose to exhibit, in detail, conditions for the Ulam–Hyers stability of (1) and the Ulam–Hyers–Rassias stability of (3). To this purpose, let us first point out what are the definitions of such stabilities in each of those cases.

Definition 3. *The IVPFO (1) is Ulam–Hyers stable if there exists a real constant $k > 0$ such that, for each $\epsilon > 0$ and for each solution $y \in C^2([a,b])$ of the inequality problem*

$$\begin{cases} \left|\mathcal{D}_{a+}^{\alpha}y(t) + \lambda(\mathcal{D}_{a+}^{\alpha-1}y)(t) - f(t,y(t))\right| \leq \epsilon, & t \in [a,b],\\ y(a) = y'(a) = 0, \end{cases} \tag{15}$$

there exists a solution $x \in C^2([a,b])$ of the problem (1) (or, equivalently, of (3)) such that

$$|y(t) - x(t)| \leq k\epsilon, \quad t \in [a,b].$$

Remark 3. *If we look at what is inside the modulus function in (15) as a single "new" function h, it directly follows that a function $y \in C^2([a,b])$ is a solution of the inequality in (15) if and only if there exists a function $h \in C([a,b])$ (which depends on y) such that*
(i) $|h(t)| \leq \epsilon, t \in [a,b]$,
(ii) $y(a) = y'(a) = 0$,
(iii) $\mathcal{D}_{a+}^{\alpha}y(t) + \lambda(\mathcal{D}_{a+}^{\alpha-1}y)(t) - f(t,y(t)) = h(t), t \in [a,b]$.

Definition 4. *The fractional integral Equation (3) is Ulam–Hyers–Rassias stable with respect to $\varphi : [a,b] \to \mathbb{R}^+$ if there exists a real constant $k_\varphi > 0$ such that, for each $\epsilon > 0$ and for each solution y of*

$$\left|y(t) - \frac{e^{-\lambda t}}{\Gamma(\alpha-1)}\int_a^t\int_a^u(u-s)^{\alpha-2}e^{\lambda u}f(s,y(s))\,ds du\right| \leq \epsilon\varphi(t), \quad t \in [a,b], \tag{16}$$

there exists a solution x of the problem (3) with

$$|y(t) - x(t)| \leq k_\varphi \epsilon \varphi(t), \quad t \in [a,b].$$

4.1. Ulam–Hyers Stability

As indicated above, we will start by identifying conditions that guarantee the Ulam–Hyers of the IVPFO (1).

Theorem 6. *Let the continuously differentiable function f satisfy the Lipschitz conditions (13)–(14), for all $t \in [a,b]$, and assume that*

$$KL_1 + L_2 \frac{(b-a)^{\alpha-1}}{\Gamma(\alpha)} < 1. \qquad (17)$$

If $y \in C^2([a,b])$ satisfies the inequality and initial conditions (15) (with $\epsilon > 0$), for all $t \in [a,b]$, then there exists a unique solution $x \in C^2([a,b])$ of the IVPFO (1) such that

$$|y(t) - x(t)| \leq k\epsilon, \quad t \in [a,b],$$

for

$$k = \frac{(b-a)^{\alpha-1}}{\alpha-1} e^{L_1 \frac{\left(1-e^{-\lambda(b-a)}\right)(b-a)^{\alpha-1}}{\lambda \Gamma(\alpha)}} \qquad (18)$$

which, in particular, means that the IVPFO (1) is Ulam–Hyers stable.

Proof. According to the hypothesis, there exists a unique solution of the IVPFO (1).

Let $y \in C^2([a,b])$ be any solution of the inequality of (15). By Remark 3, following the procedure of Proposition 1, one has that

$$\begin{aligned} y(t) &= \frac{e^{-\lambda t}}{\Gamma(\alpha-1)} \int_a^t \int_a^u (u-s)^{\alpha-2} e^{\lambda u} f(s,y(s)) ds du \\ &+ \frac{e^{-\lambda t}}{\Gamma(\alpha-1)} \int_a^t \int_a^u (u-s)^{\alpha-2} e^{\lambda u} h(s) ds du, \end{aligned}$$

with $|h(t)| < \epsilon$. Thus, we have that

$$\begin{aligned} |x(t) - y(t)| &= \left| \frac{e^{-\lambda t}}{\Gamma(\alpha-1)} \int_a^t \int_a^u (u-s)^{\alpha-2} e^{\lambda u} (f(s,x(s)) - f(s,y(s))) ds du \right. \\ &\quad \left. - \frac{e^{-\lambda t}}{\Gamma(\alpha-1)} \int_a^t \int_a^u (u-s)^{\alpha-2} e^{\lambda u} h(s) ds du \right| \\ &\leq \frac{e^{-\lambda t}}{\Gamma(\alpha-1)} \int_a^t \int_a^u (u-s)^{\alpha-2} e^{\lambda u} |f(s,x(s)) - f(s,y(s))| ds du \\ &\quad + \frac{e^{-\lambda t}}{\Gamma(\alpha-1)} \int_a^t \int_a^u (u-s)^{\alpha-2} e^{\lambda u} |h(s)| ds du \\ &\leq L_1 \frac{e^{-\lambda t}}{\Gamma(\alpha-1)} \int_a^t e^{\lambda u} \int_a^u (u-s)^{\alpha-2} |x(s) - y(s)| ds du \\ &\quad + \epsilon \frac{e^{-\lambda t}}{\Gamma(\alpha-1)} \int_a^t e^{\lambda u} \int_a^u (u-s)^{\alpha-2} ds du \\ &\leq L_1 \frac{1 - e^{-\lambda(t-a)}}{\lambda \Gamma(\alpha-1)} \int_a^t \int_a^u (u-s)^{\alpha-2} |x(s) - y(s)| ds du \\ &\quad + \epsilon \frac{(1 - e^{-\lambda(t-a)})(b-a)^{\alpha-1}}{\lambda \Gamma(\alpha)} \\ &\leq \frac{1 - e^{-\lambda(t-a)}}{\lambda \Gamma(\alpha-1)} \left(\epsilon \frac{(b-a)^{\alpha-1}}{\alpha-1} + \int_a^t \int_a^u L_1 (u-s)^{\alpha-2} |x(s) - y(s)| ds du \right) \\ &\leq \frac{1 - e^{-\lambda(b-a)}}{\lambda \Gamma(\alpha-1)} \left(\epsilon \frac{(b-a)^{\alpha-1}}{\alpha-1} + \int_a^t \int_a^u L_1 (u-s)^{\alpha-2} |x(s) - y(s)| ds du \right). \end{aligned}$$

Thus, according to Theorem 3, we have that

$$|x(t) - y(t)| \leq \epsilon \frac{(b-a)^{\alpha-1}}{\alpha-1} e^{\frac{1-e^{-\lambda(b-a)}}{\lambda\Gamma(\alpha-1)}L_1 \frac{(t-a)^{\alpha-1}}{\alpha-1}}$$

$$\leq \epsilon \frac{(b-a)^{\alpha-1}}{\alpha-1} e^{L_1 \frac{\left(1-e^{-\lambda(b-a)}\right)(b-a)^{\alpha-1}}{\lambda\Gamma(\alpha)}},$$

and we conclude the above claimed inequality and that the IVPFO (1) is Ulam–Hyers stable. □

4.2. *Ulam–Hyers–Rassias Stability*

We will now consider the Ulam–Hyers–Rassias stability. For that purpose, we consider the space $C([a,b])$ equipped with the Bielecki type metric

$$d(x,y) = \sup_{t \in [a,b]} \frac{|x(t) - y(t)|}{\sigma(t)},$$

where σ is a non-decreasing continuous function $\sigma : [a,b] \to \mathbb{R}^+$. It is known that $(C([a,b]), d)$ is a complete metric space (cf. [25]).

Theorem 7. *Let $f : [a,b] \times \mathbb{R} \to \mathbb{R}$ be a continuous function satisfying the Lipschitz condition*

$$|f(t, \rho_1) - f(t, \rho_2)| \leq L|\rho_1 - \rho_2|, \ \rho_1, \rho_2 \in \mathbb{R}, \ t \in [a,b],$$

with $L > 0$. Additionally, let $\sigma : [a,b] \to \mathbb{R}^+$ be a nondecreasing function and suppose that exist a constant $\xi \in [0,1)$ such that

$$\frac{e^{-\lambda t}}{\Gamma(\alpha-1)} \int_a^t \int_a^u (u-s)^{\alpha-2} e^{\lambda u} \sigma(s) ds du \leq \xi \sigma(t), \ t \in [a,b].$$

If y satisfies

$$\left| y(t) - \frac{e^{-\lambda t}}{\Gamma(\alpha-1)} \int_a^t \int_a^u (u-s)^{\alpha-2} e^{\lambda u} f(s, y(s)) ds du \right| \leq \epsilon \sigma(t), \ t \in [a,b],$$

and $L\xi < 1$, then there exist a solution x of the fractional integral Equation (3) such that

$$|x(t) - y(t)| \leq \frac{\epsilon \sigma(t)}{1 - L\xi}, \ t \in [a,b],$$

i.e., under the present conditions, the fractional integral Equation (3) has the Ulam–Hyers–Rassias stability.

Proof. Having in mind the fractional integral Equation (3), we will consider (in the framework of the above presented Bielecki type metric) the operator $T : C([a,b], d) \to C([a,b], d)$ defined by

$$(Ty)(t) = \frac{e^{-\lambda t}}{\Gamma(\alpha-1)} \int_a^t \int_a^u (u-s)^{\alpha-2} e^{\lambda u} f(s, y(s)) ds du.$$

Let us first prove that T is strictly contractive in $C([a,b],d)$. For any $v,w \in C([a,b],d)$, we have

$$
\begin{aligned}
d(Tv, Tw) &= \sup_{t \in [a,b]} \frac{\left| \frac{e^{-\lambda t}}{\Gamma(\alpha-1)} \int_a^t \int_a^u (u-s)^{\alpha-2} e^{\lambda u} (f(s,v(s)) - f(s,w(s))) ds du \right|}{\sigma(t)} \\
&\leq L \sup_{t \in [a,b]} \frac{\left| \frac{e^{-\lambda t}}{\Gamma(\alpha-1)} \int_a^t \int_a^u (u-s)^{\alpha-2} e^{\lambda u} \sigma(s) \frac{|v(s)-w(s)|}{\sigma(s)} ds du \right|}{\sigma(t)} \\
&\leq L\xi d(v,w).
\end{aligned}
$$

Consequently, for $L\xi < 1$, we have that T is strictly contractive in the present framework, and we have a unique solution x to the equation $Ty = y$.

Let us now identify ϵ as an upper bound for $d(Ty, y)$, and use this knowledge. Indeed, from the hypothesis, we have

$$
|y(t) - Ty(t)| = \left| y(t) - \frac{e^{-\lambda t}}{\Gamma(\alpha-1)} \int_a^t \int_a^u (u-s)^{\alpha-2} e^{\lambda u} f(s,y(s)) ds du \right| < \epsilon \sigma(t),
$$

which allows us to conclude that

$$
d(x,y) \leq \frac{1}{1-L\xi} d(y, Ty) \leq \frac{\epsilon}{1-L\xi},
$$

and so

$$
|x(t) - y(t)| \leq \frac{\epsilon}{1-L\xi} \sigma(t), \ t \in [a,b].
$$

□

The Ulam–Hyers stability is a particular case of the Ulam–Hyers–Rassias stability in the sense that instead of having a function φ controlling the differences in the last stability, we simply have a constant k in the first one. Thus, attending that

$$
\frac{e^{-\lambda t}}{\Gamma(\alpha-1)} \int_a^t \int_a^u (u-s)^{\alpha-2} e^{\lambda u} ds du \leq \frac{(b-a)^{\alpha-1}}{\lambda \Gamma(\alpha)} (1 - e^{-\lambda(b-a)}), \ t \in [a,b],
$$

and proceeding in an identical way to the proof of Theorem 7, we would pass from an upper bound that depends on a function (of the variable t) to an upper bound in the form of a constant, which is here directly concluded (following the proof of Theorem 7) in the next result:

Corollary 1. *Let $f : [a,b] \times \mathbb{R} \to \mathbb{R}$ be a continuous function satisfying the Lipschitz condition*

$$
|f(t, \rho_1) - f(t, \rho_2)| \leq L|\rho_1 - \rho_2|, \ \rho_1, \rho_2 \in \mathbb{R}, \ t \in [a,b],
$$

with $L > 0$. Let

$$
\eta = \frac{(b-a)^{\alpha-1}}{\lambda \Gamma(\alpha)} (1 - e^{-\lambda(b-a)}). \tag{19}
$$

If $L\eta < 1$ and y satisfies

$$
\left| y(t) - \frac{e^{-\lambda t}}{\Gamma(\alpha-1)} \int_a^t \int_a^u (u-s)^{\alpha-2} e^{\lambda u} f(s,y(s)) ds du \right| \leq \epsilon, \ t \in [a,b],
$$

then there exist a solution x of the fractional integral Equation (3) such that

$$
|x(t) - y(t)| \leq \frac{\epsilon}{1-L\eta}, \ t \in [a,b], \tag{20}
$$

i.e., under the above conditions, the fractional integral Equation (3) has the Ulam–Hyers stability.

Remark 4. *Please, note that the constants k in (18) and $\frac{1}{1-L\eta}$ in (20) cannot be compared for all the values of the parameters. Consider, for example, the following cases. Admit that $L = L_1 = L_2 = \frac{1}{20}$, $\alpha = \frac{7}{4}$ and consider two intervals, one of amplitude equal 1 and another one with amplitude 0.8. With these values, we have that, for $\lambda \in]-2,0[\cup]0,5[$ condition (17) is verified and also, $L\eta < 1$ for η as defined in (19). For the case $b - a = 1$, it is possible to observe that $k > \frac{1}{1-L\eta}$ (cf. Figure 1, where $p(\lambda) > q(\lambda)$). For the case $b - a = 0.8$, we verify that $k < \frac{1}{1-L\eta}$ (cf. Figure 2, where $p(\lambda) < q(\lambda)$).*

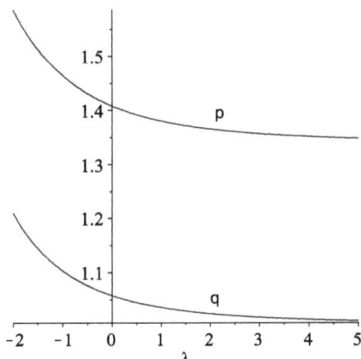

Figure 1. The graphs of $p(\lambda) = k(\lambda)$ and $q(\lambda) = \frac{1}{1-L\eta(\lambda)}$ for $\lambda \in [-2,0]\cup[0,5]$: case $b - a = 1$.

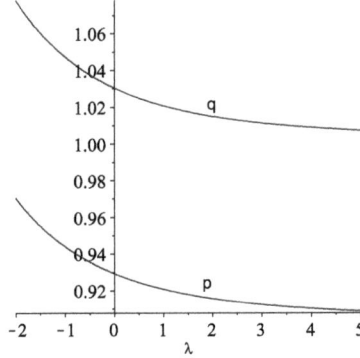

Figure 2. The graphs of $p(\lambda) = k(\lambda)$ and $q(\lambda) = \frac{1}{1-L\eta(\lambda)}$ for $\lambda \in [-2,0]\cup[0,5]$: case $b - a = 0.8$.

4.3. Concrete Examples

Let us now consider some concrete examples to illustrate the above theory.
We start by considering the following IVPFO

$$\begin{cases} (\mathcal{D}^{\frac{3}{2}}x)(t) + \lambda(\mathcal{D}^{\frac{1}{2}}x)(t) = \frac{t}{75}(x(t) + \sin(t)), \\ x(2) = x'(2) = 0, \end{cases} \quad (21)$$

for $t \in [2,3]$. Thus, in the previous notation, we have in here $\alpha = \frac{3}{2}$, $a = 2$, $b = 3$ and

$$f(t,\rho) = \frac{t}{75}(\rho + \sin(t)),$$

being clear that f is a continuously differentiable function.

According to Theorem 4, there exists, at least, one solution of the IVPFO (21). In addition, having in mind that $f'(t, x(t)) = \frac{1}{75}(x(t) + t x'(t) + \sin(t) + t \cos(t))$, for $t \in [2, 3]$, one has that

$$|f(t, x(t)) - f(t, y(t))| \leq \frac{1}{25}|x(t) - y(t)|,$$

$$|f'(t, x(t)) - f'(t, y(t))| \leq \frac{1}{25}(|x'(t) - y'(t)| + |x(t) - y(t)|).$$

Following Theorem 5 and its notation, we have in here $L_1 = L_2 = \frac{1}{25}$. Thus, for $a = 2$ and $b = 3$, we obtain that

$$KL_1 + L_2 \frac{(b-a)^{\alpha-1}}{\Gamma(\alpha)} < 1,$$

for $\lambda \in [-1, 0] \cup [0, 9]$ (cf. (12) and Figure 3). Thus, for these cases of λ, the IVPFO (21) admits a unique solution in $C^2([2, 3])$. Moreover, from Theorem 6, we also know that for those λ the IVPFO (21) is Ulam–Hyers stable.

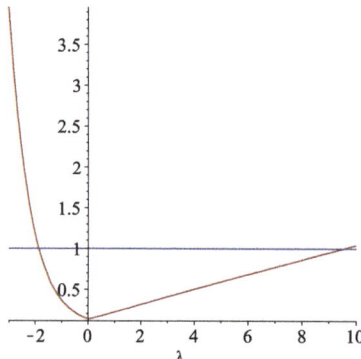

Figure 3. The graphs of $z_1(\lambda) = K(\lambda)L_1 + \frac{L_2}{\Gamma(\frac{3}{2})}$ and $z_2 = 1$.

The example we have just analyzed allows us to see that there really are classes of problems, dependent on λ, in which the conditions required in Theorem 5 are met, and there are still other cases (for different parameters λ) in which this is not the case. In view of this, and keeping in mind that the conditions of Theorem 5 are just sufficient conditions, an open analysis eventually involves obtaining other weaker conditions according to which the uniqueness of solution for those classes of problems can still be guaranteed. The same can be envisaged for Theorem 6 and its sufficient conditions to guarantee the stability of the Ulam–Hyers type.

Let us now investigate the Ulam–Hyers–Rassias stability of

$$x(t) = \frac{e^{-\lambda t}}{\Gamma(\frac{3}{2} - 1)} \int_2^t \int_2^u (u-s)^{\frac{3}{2}-2} e^{\lambda u} \frac{t}{75}(y(s) + \sin(s)) \, ds du, \qquad (22)$$

for $t \in [2, 3]$ and $\lambda = 3$.

Letting $\sigma(t) = e^t$, we have that σ is a non-decreasing function and

$$\frac{e^{-3t}}{\Gamma(\frac{1}{2})} \int_2^t \int_2^u (u-s)^{\frac{3}{2}-2} e^{3u} \sigma(s) ds du \leq \frac{1}{5}\sigma(t), \ t \in [2, 3]$$

(cf. Figure 4). Thus, for the notation of Theorem 7, we have $L = \frac{1}{25}$, $\xi = \frac{1}{5}$ and so $L\xi = \frac{1}{125} < 1$.

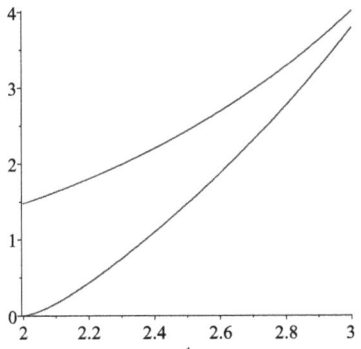

Figure 4. The graphs of $p_1(t) = \frac{1}{5}\sigma(t) = \frac{1}{5}e^t$ (the upper one), and $p_2(t) = \frac{e^{-3t}}{\Gamma(\frac{3}{2})} \int_2^t \int_2^u (u-s)^{\frac{3}{2}-2} e^{3u} \sigma(s) ds du$, $t \in [2,3]$.

Take $y(t) = \frac{1}{10}(t-2)^2$. We have that $y \in C^2([2,3])$ and $y(2) = y'(2) = 0$. We have that (cf. Figure. 5)

$$\left| y(t) - \frac{e^{-3t}}{\Gamma(\frac{3}{2})} \int_2^t \int_2^u (u-s)^{-\frac{1}{2}} e^{3u} \frac{s}{75}(y(s) + \sin(s)) ds du \right| \leq \frac{1}{200}\sigma(t), \quad t \in [2,3].$$

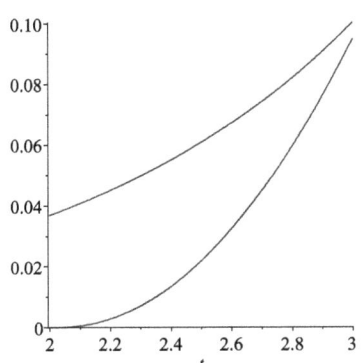

Figure 5. The graphs of $q_1(t) = \frac{1}{200}\sigma(t)$ (the upper one) and $q_2(t) = \left| y(t) - \frac{e^{-3t}}{\Gamma(\frac{3}{2})} \int_2^t \int_2^u (u-s)^{-\frac{1}{2}} e^{3u} \frac{s}{75}(y(s) + \sin(s)) ds du \right|$, $t \in [2,3]$.

Thus, according to Theorem 7, the problem (22) is Ulam–Hyers–Rassias stable with respect to $\sigma(t) = e^t$ and

$$|y(t) - x(t)| \leq \frac{5e^t}{992}, \quad t \in [2,3].$$

Moreover, we can also observe that

$$\left| y(t) - \frac{e^{-3t}}{\Gamma(\frac{3}{2})} \int_2^t \int_2^u (u-s)^{-\frac{1}{2}} e^{3u} \frac{s}{75}(y(s) + \sin(s)) ds du \right| \leq \frac{1}{10}, \quad t \in [2,3].$$

Thus, applying Corollary 1 and the respective notation, we have that $\epsilon = \frac{1}{10}$. Additionally, $\eta = \frac{1 - e^{-3}}{3\Gamma(\frac{3}{2})} \approx 0.36$ and we conclude that

$$|x(t) - y(t)| \leq 0.1.$$

In this last example, it is relevant to emphasize the importance of the function σ in the whole process, with special predominance, from the outset, in the determination of the exhibited upper bounds. In this case, we chose to work with the exponential function, and this had expected consequences given the growth that the function presents. Incidentally, the importance of the choice and the impact that the σ function has is well evidenced by the fact that the same problem can be Ulam–Hyers–Rassias stable for a given σ_1 function and not Ulam–Hyers–Rassias stable for another σ_2 function. Thus, it is precisely for this reason that the Ulam–Hyers–Rassias stability is determined depending on the chosen σ function (and it is also for this reason that this is explicitly mentioned in the name of this type of stability).

Let us now consider the following different IVPFO

$$\begin{cases} (\mathcal{D}^{\frac{6}{5}}x)(t) + \lambda(\mathcal{D}^{\frac{1}{5}}x)(t) = \frac{t}{10}x(t) - e^{-t}, \ t \in [0,1], \\ x(0) = x'(0) = 0. \end{cases} \quad (23)$$

Accordingly to the previous notations, we have now $\alpha = \frac{6}{5}$, $a = 0$, $b = 1$ and $f(t,x(t)) = \frac{t}{10}x(t) - e^{-t}$. It is clear that f is a continuously differentiable function in $[0,1] \times \mathbb{R}$. Thus there exists, at least, one solution of the IVPFO (23) (cf. Theorem 4). Moreover, one has that

$$|f(t,x(t)) - f(t,y(t))| \leq \frac{1}{10}|x(t) - y(t)|,$$

$$|f'(t,x(t)) - f'(t,y(t))| \leq \frac{1}{10}(|x'(t) - y'(t)| + |x(t) - y(t)|).$$

Following Theorem 5, we have $L_1 = L_2 = \frac{1}{10}$. Since $a = 0$ and $b = 1$, we obtain that for $\lambda \in]-1, 0[\cup]0, \frac{5}{2}[$, the condition

$$KL_1 + L_2 \frac{(b-a)^{\alpha-1}}{\Gamma(\alpha)} < 1$$

is verified (cf. Figure 6), which means that the IVPFO (23) admits a unique solution in $C^2([0,1])$ when considering those values of λ (cf. Theorem 5).

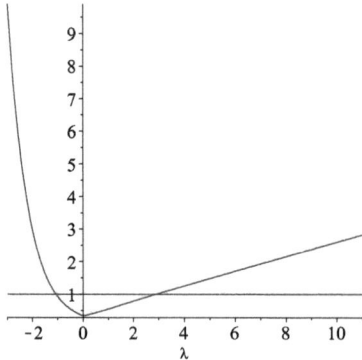

Figure 6. The graphs of $h_1(\lambda) = K(\lambda)L_1 + \frac{L_2}{\Gamma(\frac{6}{5})}$ and $h_2 = 1$.

Thus, for these cases of λ, the IVPFO (23) admits a unique solution in $C^2([0,1])$. Moreover, from Theorem 6, we also know that for those λ the IVPFO (23) is Ulam–Hyers stable.

Let us now analyse the Ulam–Hyers–Rassias stability of

$$x(t) = \frac{e^{-\lambda t}}{\Gamma(\frac{6}{5}-1)} \int_0^t \int_0^u (u-s)^{\frac{6}{5}-2} e^{\lambda u}\left(\frac{s}{10}x(s) - e^{-s}\right) ds du, \tag{24}$$

for $t \in [0,1]$, $\lambda = 2$, and with respect to $\sigma(t) = t$. Let $x \in C^2([0,1])$ be the exact solution of the IVPFO (23), and let us consider $y(t) = \sin(t) - t$. It follows that $y \in C^2([0,1])$ and $y(0) = y'(0) = 0$. We have that σ is a nondecreasing function and

$$\frac{e^{-2t}}{\Gamma(\frac{1}{5})} \int_0^t \int_0^u (u-s)^{-\frac{4}{5}} e^{2u} \sigma(s) ds du \leq \frac{1}{4}\sigma(t), \, t \in [0,1]$$

(cf. Figure 7).

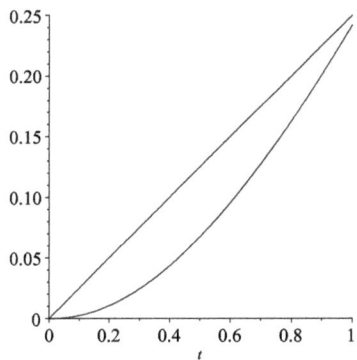

Figure 7. The graphs of $m_1(t) = \frac{e^{-2t}}{\Gamma(\frac{1}{5})} \int_0^t \int_0^u (u-s)^{-\frac{4}{5}} e^{2u} \sigma(s) ds du$ and $m_2(t) = \frac{1}{4}\sigma(t) = \frac{t}{4}$, $t \in [0,1]$.

For the notation of Theorem 7, we have $L = \frac{1}{25}$ and $\zeta = \frac{1}{4}$, and so $L\zeta = \frac{1}{100} < 1$. Thus,

$$\left| y(t) - \frac{e^{-2t}}{\Gamma(\frac{1}{5})} \int_0^t \int_0^u (u-s)^{-\frac{4}{5}} e^{2u} \left(\frac{s}{10}y(s) - e^{-s}\right) ds du \right| \leq \frac{7}{50}\sigma(t), \quad t \in [0,1]$$

(cf. Figure 8).

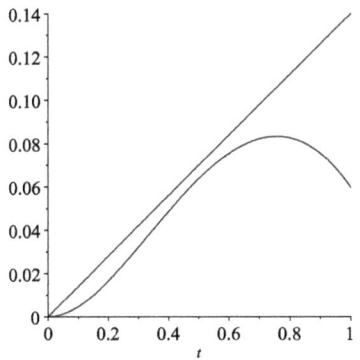

Figure 8. The graphs of $w_1(t) = \left| y(t) - \frac{e^{-2t}}{\Gamma(\frac{1}{5})} \int_0^t \int_0^u (u-s)^{-\frac{4}{5}} e^{2u}\left(\frac{s}{10}y(s) - e^{-s}\right) ds du \right|$ (the lower one) and $w_2(t) = \frac{7}{50}\sigma(t)$, $t \in [0,1]$.

Therefore, according to Theorem 7, the problem (24) is Ulam–Hyers–Rassias stable with respect to $\sigma(t) = t$ and

$$|y(t) - x(t)| \leq \frac{14}{99}\sigma(t), \; t \in [0,1].$$

In this last example, we deliberately chose $\sigma(t) = t$ to work with $y(t) = \sin(t) - t$, which can be considered not the most ideal choice (which, by the way, can be easily noticed when we look at Figure 8 and see, on the right, the "greatest" distance between the two functions represented there). Anyway, we consider this example important because it emphasizes that the theoretical conditions obtained earlier are robust enough to guarantee stability in less favorable or obvious choices.

Moreover, according to Corollary 1, we can also conclude the Ulam–Hyers stability. Using the respective notation of the Corollary, we have that $\epsilon = \frac{7}{50}$, $\eta = \frac{1-e^{-2}}{2\Gamma\left(\frac{6}{5}\right)} \approx 0.47$ and $L = \frac{1}{25}$. Thus, we conclude that $|x(t) - y(t)| \leq \frac{7}{50}$.

5. Conclusions

We conclude this article by summarizing the results obtained. We analyze a class of nonlinear fractional differential equations, with initial conditions, characterized by having the Riemann–Liouville fractional derivative of order $\alpha \in (1,2)$. Having made use of distinct fixed-point arguments, we were able to deduce conditions that guarantee the existence and uniqueness of solutions in a frame of adequate spaces, and we also obtained sufficient conditions to have the Ulam–Hyers and Ulam–Hyers–Rassias stabilities of the problems in the analysis (where the use of a Bielecki-type metric and some additional contractive arguments were of crucial importance). In the last section, some examples were included mainly to illustrate that the conditions obtained in the theoretical part really exist and can be considered in particular cases.

Author Contributions: Conceptualization, L.P.C. and A.S.S.; methodology, L.P.C. and A.S.S.; formal analysis, L.P.C. and A.S.S.; investigation, L.P.C. and A.S.S.; writing—original draft preparation, L.P.C. and A.S.S.; writing—review and editing, L.P.C. and A.S.S. All authors have read and agreed to the published version of the manuscript.

Funding: This work is supported by the Center for Research and Development in Mathematics and Applications (CIDMA) through the Portuguese Foundation for Science and Technology (FCT—Fundação para a Ciência e a Tecnologia), reference UIDB/04106/2020. Additionally, A. Silva is also funded by national funds (OE), through FCT, I.P., in the scope of the framework contract foreseen in the numbers 4, 5, and 6 of article 23, of the Decree-Law 57/2016, of 29 August, changed by Law 57/2017, of 19 July.

Data Availability Statement: Not applicable.

Acknowledgments: The authors would like to thank the Referees for their work in reviewing the present investigation and for providing their observations and suggestions.

Conflicts of Interest: The authors declare no conflict of interest. The funders had no role in the design of the study; in the collection, analyses, or interpretation of data; in the writing of the manuscript, or in the decision to publish the results.

References

1. Castro, L.P.; Silva, A.S. On the solution and Ulam–Hyers-Rassias stability of a Caputo fractional boundary value problem. *Math. Biosci. Eng.* **2022**, *19*, 10809–10825. [CrossRef] [PubMed]
2. Fahad, H.M.; Fernandez, A.; Ur, R.M.; Siddiqi, M. Tempered and Hadamard-type fractional calculus with respect to functions. *Mediterr. J. Math.* **2021**, *18*, 143. [CrossRef]
3. Kilbas, A.A.; Srivastava, H.M.; Trujillo, J.J. *Theory and Applications of Fractional Differential Equations*; Elsevier: Amsterdam, The Netherlands, 2016.
4. Mali, A.D.; Kucche, K.D.; Fernandez, A.; Fahad, H.M. On tempered fractional calculus with respect to functions and the associated fractional differential equations. *Math. Methods Appl. Sci.* **2022**, *45*, 11134–11157. [CrossRef]

5. Miller, K.; Ross, B. *An Introduction to the Fractional Calculus and Fractional Differential Equations*; Wiley: New York, NY, USA, 1993.
6. Podlubny, I. *Fractional Differential Equations*; Academic Press: San Diego, CA, USA, 1999.
7. Samko, S.G.; Kilbas, A.A.; Marichev, O.I. *Fractional Integrals and Derivatives. Theory and Applications*; Translated from the 1987 Russian Original; Gordon and Breach Science Publishers: Yverdon, Switzerland, 1993.
8. Aoki, T. On the stability of the linear transformation in Banach spaces. *J. Math. Soc. Jpn.* **1950**, *2*, 64–66. [CrossRef]
9. Castro, L.P.; Simões, A.M. Hyers-Ulam-Rassias stability of nonlinear integral equations through the Bielecki metric. *Math. Methods Appl. Sci.* **2018**, *41*, 7367–7383. [CrossRef]
10. Castro, L.P.; Simões, A.M. Different types of Hyers-Ulam-Rassias stabilities for a class of integro-differential equations. *Filomat* **2017**, *31*, 5379–5390. [CrossRef]
11. Hyers, D.H. On the stability of the linear functional equation. *Proc. Natl. Acad. Sci. USA* **1941**, *27*, 222–224. [CrossRef] [PubMed]
12. Marian, D. Semi-Hyers–Ulam–Rassias stability of the convection partial differential equation via Laplace transform. *Mathematics* **2021**, *9*, 2980. [CrossRef]
13. Marian, D.; Ciplea, S.A.; Lungu, N. Hyers–Ulam stability of a system of hyperbolic partial differential equations. *Mathematics* **2022**, *10*, 2183. [CrossRef]
14. Rassias, T.M. On the stability of the linear mapping in Banach spaces. *Proc. Am. Math. Soc.* **1978**, *72*, 297–300. [CrossRef]
15. Sousa, J.V.d.C.; Oliveira, D.S.; Capelas de Oliveira, E. A note on the mild solutions of Hilfer impulsive fractional differential equations. *Chaos Solitons Fractals* **2021**, *147*, 110944. [CrossRef]
16. Ulam, S.M. *Problems in Modern Mathematics*; John Wiley & Sons: New York, NY, USA, 1940.
17. Vanterler da Costa Sousa, J.; Kucche, K.D.; de Oliveira, E.C. Stability of mild solutions of the fractional nonlinear abstract Cauchy problem. *Electron Res. Arch.* **2022**, *30*, 272–288.
18. Chai, G. Existence results for boundary value problems of nonlinear fractional differential equations. *Comp. Math. Appl.* **2011**, *62*, 2374–2382. [CrossRef]
19. Xu, L.; Dong, Q.; Li, G. Existence and Hyers–Ulam stability for three-point boundary value problems with Riemann–Liouville fractional derivatives and integrals. *Adv. Differ. Equations* **2018**, *2018*, 458. [CrossRef]
20. Ahmad, B.; Matar, M.M.; El-Salmy, O.M. Existence of Solutions and Ulam Stability for Caputo Type Sequential Fractional Differential Equations of Order $\alpha \in (2,3)$. *Int. J. Anal. Appl.* **2017**, *15*, 86–101.
21. Alvan, M.; Darzi, R.; Mahmoodi, A. Existence results for a new class of boundary value problems of nonlinear fractional differential equations. *Mathematics* **2016**, *4*, 13. [CrossRef]
22. Bilgici, S.S.; Şan, M. Existence and uniqueness results for a nonlinear singular fractional differential equation of order $\sigma \in (1,2)$. *AIMS Math.* **2021**, *6*, 13041–13056. [CrossRef]
23. Bainov, D.; Simeonov, P. *Integral Inequalities and Applications*; Kluwer Academic Publishers: Dordrecht, The Netherlands, 1992.
24. Bai, Z.; Sun, W. Existence and multiplicity of positive solutions for singular fractional boundary value problems. *Comput. Math. Appl.* **2012**, *63*, 1369–1381. [CrossRef]
25. Rolewicz, S. *Functional Analysis and Control Theory: Linear Systems*; Mathematics and its Applications (East European Series), 29. D. Reidel Publishing Co.: Dordrecht, The Netherlands; PWN–Polish Scientific Publishers: Warsaw, Poland, 1987.

Disclaimer/Publisher's Note: The statements, opinions and data contained in all publications are solely those of the individual author(s) and contributor(s) and not of MDPI and/or the editor(s). MDPI and/or the editor(s) disclaim responsibility for any injury to people or property resulting from any ideas, methods, instructions or products referred to in the content.

MDPI AG
Grosspeteranlage 5
4052 Basel
Switzerland
Tel.: +41 61 683 77 34

Mathematics Editorial Office
E-mail: mathematics@mdpi.com
www.mdpi.com/journal/mathematics

Disclaimer/Publisher's Note: The statements, opinions and data contained in all publications are solely those of the individual author(s) and contributor(s) and not of MDPI and/or the editor(s). MDPI and/or the editor(s) disclaim responsibility for any injury to people or property resulting from any ideas, methods, instructions or products referred to in the content.

www.ingramcontent.com/pod-product-compliance
Lightning Source LLC
LaVergne TN
LVHW070429100526
838202LV00014B/1553